'A Great Educational Tradition'

'A Great Educational Tradition'

A HISTORY OF HUTCHESONS' GRAMMAR SCHOOL

Brian R. W. Lockhart

First published in Great Britain in 2015 by
John Donald, an imprint of Birlinn Ltd

West Newington House
10 Newington Road
Edinburgh
EH9 1QS

www.birlinn.co.uk

ISBN: 978 1 906566 88 3

The publishers gratefully acknowledge the support of (??)
towards the publication of this book

British Library Cataloguing-in-Publication Data
A catalogue record for this book is available on request from the British Library

Typeset by Tom Johnstone Editorial Services

Printed and bound in Malta by Gutenberg Press

For more of my grandchildren – Makena Camille, Eloïse Anna, Matilda Iris, Barclay James and Cecelia Joy

CONTENTS

ILLUSTRATIONS

1. Stained glass window in the grand restaurant of Hutchesons' Bar and Brasserie; after a painting by Scougall: George Hutcheson was the founder of Hutchesons' Hospital (then meaning a home for the old and destitute).

2. Stained glass window in the grand restaurant of Hutchesons' Bar and Brasserie; after a painting supposed to be by Vandyck: Thomas Hutcheson was the founder of Hutchesons' Hospital School.

3. George Hutcheson's Kist, or chest, which contained all George's financial dealings and was kept in the Trongate immediately adjacent to the Tolbooth, centre of the city's administration.

4. 'Partick Castle' as a late-eighteenth-century ruin, built for George Hutcheson in 1611 as the country-house of a landed laird.

5. The Monument of Thomas Hutcheson and Marion Stewart at Glasgow Cathedral.

6. The Trongate Frontage of the first Hutchesons' Hospital in 1794. It is the only surviving image of the Hospital.

7. The earliest image of the Glasgow skyline from the south-east by John Slezer in 1693.

8. Drawing of the Hospital (back view) reputed to have been completed at the time of its demolition in 1795.

9. The new Hospital, built between 1802 and 1805 on Hospital lands to the rear of the Trongate. It was designed by David Hamilton.

10. Thomas Menzies, the nineteenth Headteacher of Hutchesons' Hospital School, between 1861 and 1875, and the first Rector of Hutchesons' Grammar School from 1876 until 1902.

11. The first Programme of Annual Examination (14 May 1877) of the Grammar School.

12. 'Magnificent Pavilions' (*Glasgow Herald*) – the rebuilding of Crown Street, 1876, to make it Hutchesons' Grammar School, a full secondary as well as elementary school.

13. The first Hutchesons' Girls' Grammar School in Elgin Street, formerly the Gorbals' Youth School.

14. James Lochhead, the first Head of the Girls' School, 1876 to 1885, who took office when the School opened in Elgin Street.

15. (Dr) William Thomson, appointed Head of the Girls' School in 1885, who proved an innovative leader until retirement in 1914.

16. Head Thomson and the staff of the Girls' School c.1907.

17. William Joseph McVicar, who joined the staff of Elgin Street in 1882 and, as right-hand man to Dr Thomson, succeeded him in Headship between 1914 and 1927.

18. Characters from the Boys' staff – Muirhead, the Drill Sergeant at School for forty-three years.

19. Characters from the Boys' staff – Robson, Singing Master until the age of ninety-six.

20. Characters from the Boys' staff – Hanbridge, the Drawing Master.

21. Menzies and an early staff photo c.1900.

22. Robert Philp, Principal Teacher (Mathematics) at the Grammar School from 1876 until 1902 and Head of the Boys' School between 1903 and 1913.

23. Philp and his staff at the beginning of his Headship.

24. The new Girls' Grammar School in Kingarth Street, opened in 1912

25. William 'Pa' McVicar (with staff), Headmaster of the Girls' School from 1914 to 1927.

26. The new Gymnasium in Kingarth Street in 1912, located on the top floor of a separate building especially designed for Physical Education, 'Housewifery' and Domestic Science.

27. W. King Gillies, Rector of the Boys' School for the comparatively short period of six years, between 1913 and 1919.

28. The Soccer First Eleven, 1915–16.

29. Girls' Hockey, 1920s.

ACKNOWLEDGEMENTS

Following my retirement in 2004 I have spent a considerable amount of time researching and writing histories of a number of significant Scottish Schools. My own education as pupil, teacher and Principal Teacher of History at George Heriot's School in Edinburgh; my time as Deputy Rector at The High School of Glasgow; and my tenure as Headmaster of Robert Gordon's College in Aberdeen, gave me the basis for three books. My Honours degree in History and Politics gained at the University of Aberdeen and networking while serving on the University Court made a book on Aberdeen Grammar School possible and with the help of Arthur McCombie it was published in 2012.

Most recently my interest has focused on Hutchesons' Grammar School. This was partly a result of its connections with Heriot's and partly from my own contacts with the School. I had been short-leeted and interviewed for the post of Rector in May 1986 when David Ward was appointed; I had served as a Trustee on the Glasgow and Marshall Trust from 1989 until 1996 (which was operated from the School); I was involved as educational adviser to the Governing Board when Dr Greig was appointed in 2005 and I served on the Governing Body of the Hutchesons' Educational Trust (HET) from 2006 until 2012. I was Convener of the Joint Consultative Committee and was also the Convener of the Board's Education Committee. When my time on the Board ended, my offer to the Governors to research and write a fifth book was accepted.

As always when writing a history one relies a great deal on those who went before and this work is no exception. William H. Hill produced the only full scale book on Hutchesons' Hospital in 1881, and this is the starting point for any serious research on the antecedents of the School. Hill hoped that 'from the narrative of the actings and experiences of their predecessors, the present and future Patrons (Governors) of Hutchesons' Hospital may derive interesting information, and some useful precedents for the wise and successful administration of this, the oldest and the noblest Institution of its kind in the West of Scotland'.

We had to wait until 1992 for the next major study on the history of the School from A.D. Dunlop and this has also been invaluable to me. He described the 'changes which have made a tiny charity school into the second largest independent in the country, with a reputation for academic excellence second to none'. Dunlop also explored the relationship between the School and the city of Glasgow.

I am indebted to these men for their pioneering work. I hope I have added to our knowledge. In particular, as well as introducing more material on the leadership of both the Hospital School and the modern Schools I have also included a chapter on prominent staff, for which I relied heavily on the Hutchesons' Educational Trust Minutes, and another chapter devoted to short biographical notes of the School's most famous Former Pupils. For the latter I used the 'objective' criterion of entries in the *Oxford Dictionary of National Biography*; *Who's Who*; *Who's Who in Scotland*; *Who Was Who* and the *Memoirs and Portraits of a Hundred Glasgow Men*. Those mentioned in these volumes who attended the Boys' or Girls' School have been included in this work. And what a galaxy of talent there has been. There are few schools which can claim a contribution from so many successful Former Pupils. Even former Prime Minister, Gordon Brown, in his biography of James Maxton, describes how at Hutchesons' Maxton 'joined a great educational tradition, famous in Glasgow and the West of Scotland for its academic standards and its record of solid achievement, and there he received a grounding in the basic educational disciplines upon which his later achievements rested'.

Unfortunately, a considerable number of individuals who attended the School have not published details of their schooling. Others who perhaps merit inclusion may have been inadvertently missed. I apologise for such omissions.

With regard to archival material, I am grateful for the assistance and courtesy shown me by the staff of the Mitchell Library in Glasgow, Michelle Gait of the Special Libraries at the University of Aberdeen and John McKenzie, Librarian of the Royal Faculty of Procurators in Glasgow.

During the last two years I came to rely on a team of people. The Rector, Ken Greig, was unfailingly welcoming to me and always found time to support the enterprise. The Bursar and Clerk, Iain Keter, proved an important source of advice on a number of occasions, while a significant group of former staff – teaching and non-teaching – and former pupils helped me to understand better the special ethos of the School. In this regard Graham MacAllister was full of insights while offering a balanced view at all times, and Gordon Casely put at my disposal his expertise in heraldry and tartan which shines through the two appendices he kindly researched and produced for me.

But I owe the biggest debt to Kate Keter, whose work in the School's Archives resulted in a much improved chapter on Former Pupils and the inclusion of a significant number of interesting photographs. I hope she is pleased with the book, for she can take much credit for its final contents.

I would also like to acknowledge the work of all those at Birlinn who have been involved in the production of this book, especially Mairi Sutherland. I appreciate too the technical help from Mark Simmet and the proof-reading of Elizabeth W. McCombie. I take responsibility for any remaining mistakes.

Brian R. W. Lockhart

NOTE ON STYLE
AND ABBREVIATIONS

Spelling and punctuation are as in the original, where this is quoted in the text and in the endnotes. Reference to 'the School' always refers to Hutchesons' Grammar School; reference to the Boys' School refers to Hutchesons' Boys' Grammar School and reference to the Girls' School refers to Hutchesons' Girls' Grammar School. Normally, other than when indicated otherwise, figures for money are given in sterling. The conversion rate of pounds sterling to Scots pounds was 1:12, while that of pounds sterling to Scots merks was 1:18.

The following abbreviations have also been used in the book:

AHT	Assistant Head Teacher
APT	Assistant Principal Teacher
ATS	Auxiliary Territorial Service
BA	Bachelor of Arts
BBC	British Broadcasting Corporation
BD	Bachelor of Divinity
BL	Bachelor of Law
BMA	British Medical Association
BMus	Bachelor of Music
BSc	Bachelor of Science
CA	Chartered Accountant
CBE	Commander of the British Empire
CBI	Confederation of British Industries
CEO	Chief Executive Officer
CMG	Companion, Order of St Michael and St George
DA	Diploma in Art
DD	Doctor of Divinity
DSC	Distinguished Service Cross
Debr.	Debrett's *People of Today*

EA	Education Authority
EIS	Educational Institute of Scotland
FBA	Fellow, British Academy
FCH	First Class Honours
FICM	Faculty of Intensive Care Medicine
FP	Former Pupil
FRCA	Fellow, Royal College of Art
FRCOG	Fellow, Royal College of Obstetricians and Gynaecologists
FRCP	Fellow of the Royal College of Physicians London
FRFPS	Fellow, Royal Faculty of Physicians and Surgeons (Glasgow)
FRIAS	Fellow, Royal Incorporation of Architects of Scotland
FRIBA	Fellow, Royal Institute of British Architects
FRS	Fellow, Royal Society
FRSA	Fellow, Royal Society of Arts
FRSAMD	Fellow, Royal Scottish Academy of Music and Drama
FRSE	Fellow of the Royal Society Edinburgh
GA	General Assembly of the Church of Scotland
G and THA	George and Thomas Hutchesons' Award
GCM	Glasgow Corporation Minutes
GP	General Practitioner
GS	Grammar School
HET	Hutchesons' Educational Trust
HBGS	Hutchesons' Boys' Grammar School
HGGS	Hutchesons' Girls' Grammar School
HGS	Hutchesons' Grammar School
HMI	Her (His) Majesty's Inspector
HS	High School
IFA	Independent Financial Advisor
ILP	Independent Labour Party
IT	Information Technology
KBE	Knight Commander, Order of the British Empire
KC	King's Counsel
KCB	Knight Commander, Order of the British Empire
KCVO	Knight Commander, Royal Victorian Order
LLB	Bachelor of Laws
LLP	Limited Liability Partnership
LRAM	Licenciate, Royal Academy of Music
MA	Master of Arts
MBE	Member, Order of the British Empire

MC	Military Cross
MD	Doctor of Medicine
MEd	Master of Education
MLitt	Master of Letters
MO	Medical Officer
MSB	Minutes of School Board
MSc	Master of Science
MVO	Member, Royal Victorian Order
NAS	National Archives of Scotland
NHS	National Health Service
NUT	National Union of Teachers
OBE	Officer, Order of the British Empire
ODNB	*Oxford Dictionary of National Biography*
OStJ	Officer, Venerable Order of the Hospital of St John of Jerusalem
PE	Physical Education
PhD	Doctor of Philosophy
PGA	Professional Golfers' Association
PT	Principal Teacher (or Head of Department)
QC	Queen's Counsel
QS	Quantity Surveyor
QSM	Queen's Service Medal (New Zealand)
RA	Royal Artillery
RAF	Royal Air Force
RAMC	Royal Army Medical Corps
RAFVR	Royal Air Force Voluntary Reserve
RE	Religious Education
RGN	Registered General Nurse
RI	Religious Instruction
RN	Royal Navy
RSA	Royal Scottish Academician
RSAMD	Royal Scottish Academy of Music and Drama
RSPB	Royal Society for the Protection of Birds
SCEEB	Scottish Certificate of Education Examination Board
SED	Scottish (Scotch) Education Department
SU	Scripture Union
TC	Town Council
TD	Territorial (Efficiency) Decoration
TUC	Trades Union Congress

UN	United Nations
UNESCO	United Nations Educational, Scientific and Cultural Organisation
UNICEF	United Nations International Children's (Emergency) Fund
UNRWA	United Nations Relief and Works Agency
UWS	University of the West of Scotland
WEA	Workers' Educational Association
WW	*Who's Who*
WW1	World War 1
WW2	World War 2
WWS	*Who's Who in Scotland*
WWW	*Who Was Who*

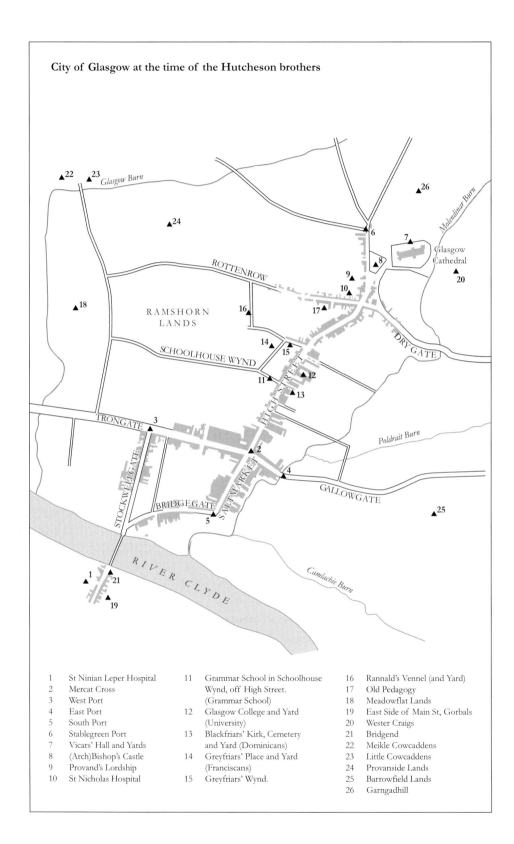

City of Glasgow at the time of the Hutcheson brothers

1	St Ninian Leper Hospital	11	Grammar School in Schoolhouse Wynd, off High Street. (Grammar School)	16	Rannald's Vennel (and Yard)
2	Mercat Cross			17	Old Pedagogy
3	West Port			18	Meadowflat Lands
4	East Port	12	Glasgow College and Yard (University)	19	East Side of Main St, Gorbals
5	South Port			20	Wester Craigs
6	Stablegreen Port	13	Blackfriars' Kirk, Cemetery and Yard (Dominicans)	21	Bridgend
7	Vicars' Hall and Yards			22	Meikle Cowcaddens
8	(Arch)Bishop's Castle	14	Greyfriars' Place and Yard (Franciscans)	23	Little Cowcaddens
9	Provand's Lordship			24	Provanside Lands
10	St Nicholas Hospital	15	Greyfriars' Wynd.	25	Barrowfield Lands
				26	Garngadhill

ONE   Glasgow and the Hutchesons

Although early records on schools are sparse, most standard histories regard the advent of Christianity as the starting point of Scottish education.[1] The first missionaries founded settlements which were not only places of Christian community and devotion but also schools for training their successors. The instruction centred on Latin, the language of the Church, thereby enabling future ecclesiastics to read and copy the books of Scripture.

Whithorn, in the Solway region of south-west Scotland, has been regarded as 'the cradle of Scottish Christianity', as a consequence of St Ninian founding his church there and his tomb becoming the focus of a healing cult. According to tradition, Ninian dedicated a small cemetery on the bank of the Molendinar Burn in the area which became known as Glasgow, within which St Kentigern (also known as Mungo) is said to have built a cathedral for his own diocese in the later sixth century. Despite the tenuous written evidence connecting Kentigern with Glasgow, he is nonetheless thought to have become bishop of an area roughly corresponding to the British kingdom of Strathclyde, and on his death around 614 he was buried in Ninian's cemetery. Although, for the next few centuries, there is little information on ecclesiastical use of the Glasgow site, by the early twelfth century its traditions and legends were widely accepted as fact.

By then medieval Glasgow consisted of two centres, the ecclesiastical upper town on its hill and the commercial lower town near the Molendinar Burn, which was an essential water source for the development of early craft and market activity, including fulling,[2] tanning, skinning and fishing.

The upper town was dominated by Glasgow Cathedral, substantially complete by 1300, with the Bishop's Castle nearby. The residence of the bishop gave a security and importance to Glasgow out of proportion to its modest size and activity. Southwards from the Cathedral ran the track that became the High Street, which was crossed by Glasgow's two oldest thoroughfares – the Drygate from the east and Rottenrow from the west. The mercantile centre was where the north-south line of the High Street and its continuation, the Saltmarket, was crossed by the Trongate on the west and the Gallowgate on the east.

Although the two towns gradually grew to meet each other, the pace of economic development in Glasgow was slow, and in 1367 the city was ranked as only twenty-first out of the thirty-four burghs represented in the Scottish league table of monies paid as taxes to the Crown.

Glasgow was given the right to trade overseas, but practical obstacles hindered development. Northern France, the Low Countries, the Baltic and England were Scotland's favoured trading partners. For the most part, these markets were more readily accessible to the east coast burghs and Glasgow had to resort to transporting goods for export overland to Linlithgow's port of Blackness and also to Leith. Rivalries with Rutherglen, Renfrew and Dumbarton existed, with the last controlling the mouth of the Clyde. This led Glasgow into making an agreement with Irvine, which, in effect, acted as Glasgow's seaport.[3]

The northern nucleus of the burgh, Townhead, was augmented in 1451 when a university was established by Pope Nicholas V. This helped to put Glasgow on the European map. Moreover, Glasgow's role as a judicial and administrative centre was considerably heightened when Pope Innocent VIII raised the see to an archbishopric in 1492.

By the middle of the sixteenth century, the economic business of the city had moved from the upper town to around Glasgow Cross, which was sited at the intersection of Gallowgate and Trongate and the High Street, which was by now filled with buildings. Moreover, as a result of the decay of the medieval ecclesiastical city, congestion in this whole area increased significantly following the Reformation in 1560.

The occupational structure of Glasgow at the end of the sixteenth century indicated a broad manufacturing base, especially in clothing, textiles and food-processing. Glasgow had the only soap-boiling factory in the country at Candleriggs (opened in 1573–4), three sugar refineries, glass-making and a candle industry, and while it had more maltmen, leather tanners and weavers than Edinburgh, it had fewer than half the number of merchants. Significantly, however, in 1581, Glasgow paid 66% of the share of the upper Clyde customs tax: increasingly the city was the reception area for the region's exports as well as imports.

Incorporated trades emerged – Skinners and Furriers (1516); Websters[4] (1528); Tailors (1546) and Dyers – although their numbers were still inconsiderable. No artisan was allowed to practise his craft unless he belonged to the appropriate body. By the end of the sixteenth century, craftsmen and related brethren, chiefly manufacturers, totalled 363.[5] The latter included maltmen (55), leather-workers (50), websters (30) and baxters[6] (27). They were supplemented in 1582 by an incorporation of merchants – a measure viewed with justifiable suspicion by the small tradesmen. It took till 1605, when the Letter of Guildry introduced arbitration to regulate differences, for matters to be resolved for the next two centuries. During this time the Trades' and Merchants' Houses shared burgh government and ended their internal struggles.[7]

At the same time the population grew from around 4,500 in 1560 to approximately 7,500 in the early seventeenth century. It increased again in the next century and had reached 13,000 by 1707. This enabled Glasgow to consolidate its position as the primary commercial centre in western Scotland. She took an increasing share in overseas trade and built up her commercial fleet.

The credit for the beginnings of transatlantic trade – from Ayr in 1642 and Glasgow in 1672 – lay largely with a relatively small group of merchant families. They not only dominated civic offices, overseas trade and commercial ventures, but were also the major landowners in and around Glasgow. From their total, at most only between 80 and 125 traded overseas. From this small group, a central core with close links of kinship operated merchant partnerships and joint-stock organisations that brought wealth to their own families and to the City as a whole.

Glasgow's growing prosperity was reflected in its urban setting. While the greater part of the increasing population was crammed into the hinterlands, town houses with elegant facades were built in the Saltmarket, Bridgegate and Trongate. New and imposing public buildings also appeared. A new Town House or Tolbooth[8] was begun in 1626. Although it hinted at a new architectural style it was three other buildings which displaced Gothic as the natural style for architecture: Hutchesons' Hospital[9] in the Trongate[10] was begun in 1649; the Merchants' House in Bridgegate was constructed a decade later; while meantime in 1656 Glasgow University was given its new home in splendid buildings to the east of the High Street.[11]

Although the burgess class was relatively small in number, its members shared the commercial and legal privileges which were customary to all burgesses. They held land directly, in their own names, and the ownership of a plot of burgage[12] was the token of burgess status. The portions were originally laid out in narrow 'rigs'.[13] Hutcheson Street had four rigs, side by side, and was originally purchased by the Patrons of Hutchesons' Hospital as a site for their almshouse in 1643.

Not all shared in the prosperity, however, and as Glasgow grew, caring for the poor and less fortunate became more significant and several charitable institutions were founded. Generally, these institutions were located peripherally, in what were then the outskirts of the city, partly as a deliberate intention to isolate their inmates.

Its first hospital dated from 1180 and was situated at Levern Water, Crookston (East Renfrewshire); the earliest poor-house dated from 1285 – the St John and St Mary Magdalene at Polmadie (near the Gorbals) – and the first leper hospital for the City's plague victims was dedicated to St Ninian and was opened south of the Clyde at the south end of Stockwell Bridge, on the east side of Main Street, Gorbals, in 1359, by Lady Lochow, mother of Colin, first Earl of Argyll, and daughter of Robert, Duke of Albany. It had only six persons receiving treatment at the end of the sixteenth century, as leprosy and pestilence gradually abated.

In 1471, St Nicholas Hospital was founded and endowed by Bishop Andrew Muirhead near his own palace at the Townhead to house twelve poor old men and a priest. It was further endowed by Bishop Leighton and remained in use until late in the eighteenth century. The Chapel of Little St Mungo was endowed in 1500 east of the burgh. The town acquired it in May 1593 to be 'ane hospital for the puir'.

Roland Blackadder, nephew of Robert Blackadder, first Archbishop of Glasgow, founded a hospital in 1524 'for the support of the poor and indigent coming into the country'. It had six beds and few comforts, and was acquired by the crafts of Glasgow for its members. When this project fell through, in its place the Trades' Almshouse was set up in 1605 by the Trades' House, which consisted of the fourteen Incorporations of Glasgow's trades-people. It was housed in the Morebattle Manse just south of St Nicholas Hospital and took in thirteen poor Freemen of Trades' rank, whose uniform was an ample coat, waistcoat and knee-breeks of blue serge.

Following the Reformation, the Friaries of the Blackfriars (Dominican) Order were closed and Mary, Queen of Scots, issued a Charter in March 1566 transferring their properties to the Town Council for the erection and endowment of a hospital for the poor and infirm in the burgh. The Franciscans (Greyfriars) also lost their foothold during the Reformation.

The religious upheaval at this time had led to almost all the property of the Roman Catholic Church being seized by nobles and others, while education lost nearly all the endowments it had formally enjoyed. John Knox and the other Reformers proposed that the money necessary for carrying into effect the scheme of education outlined in the *First Book of Discipline* should be obtained from the funds the old Church had devoted to education. But these funds were no longer available, so the Scottish Parliament in 1594 passed an Act for the recovery of the revenues of the schools, so they might regain 'their former state and integrity'. However, the Act failed to remedy the evil, and education never recovered its lost endowments.

Meantime, the city took forward philanthropy and it would appear that the cycle of crisis and recovery which Glasgow had previously experienced was broken in the early 1600s. By this time it had acquired a much greater economic stability and was able to respond more effectively in the Wars of the Covenant, as well as to the setbacks of plague in 1645–46, to the destruction of congested and wooden hovels in the fire of 1652, which affected around a thousand families and to the disruptions after the Restoration of 1660 (with Glasgow constantly billeted with troops).

The century after the Reformation in Glasgow was also a time of an unusual concentration of episcopal[14] landed wealth, which was then available for disposal. This provided the prosperous middle-class with an inducement to seek civic office as well as significant opportunities for securing title to urban properties and to large common or church lands on the fringes of the old city. The greatest prize, Wester Craigs, became the property of Sir Matthew Stewart of Minto, twice Provost in the 1580s. George Elphinstone also obtained lands – in Gorbals, Bridgend, Blythswood, Woodside, Cowcaddens and Nether Newton. He was knighted in 1594 and appointed Provost in 1600. This close association between landholding and civic office continued throughout the seventeenth century and the Bells, Andersons, Walkinschaws, and Campbells repeated Elphinstone's story. Indeed, these four families almost monopolised the offices of Provost and Bailie from 1635–1700.

The Gorbals and Bridgend lands which had belonged to Elphinstone were bought by the Trades' House, Hutchesons' Hospital, and the Provost and Burgesses of Glasgow, and subsequently rendered a handsome profit when they were developed in the late eighteenth century. But most of the other lands, which were ready for development in the early and mid-eighteenth century, were not retained by public bodies. The Royal Commission of 1835 asserted that if the town's land had not been sold off at such a low price then burgh taxes would not be nearly as hefty as they were.

It was in this climate that Glasgow developed a modest 'professional' class. Its rising population resulted in a growing body of notaries necessary to meet the demands of an expanding economy. The Hutcheson brothers – George and Thomas – were among the most successful of that group. At a time when it was still expected that the Corporation would play an important part in the planning and building of any extensions to the City, together with Hutchesons' Hospital and School they still controlled the lands of Ramshorn and Meadowflats, which stood directly in the path of any westerly extension of Glasgow.

THE HUTCHESON FAMILY

It was towards the end of the fifteenth century that separate branches of the Huchesone and Hutchison families came to prominence in Glasgow and a number of their members were mentioned in the documents of the period and beyond.

In September 1471, about a century before the Reformation, George Huchesone, merchant and burgess of Glasgow, gave twenty shillings Scots[15] to the Vicars of the Choir of Glasgow Cathedral to ensure that a Mass would be said for his soul and those of his family in all time coming.[16] Around the same time, John Hutchison, the likely progenitor of the Scotstoun branch of the family, on the other hand, took a particular interest in the newly established University of Glasgow and spent significant money in building a new kitchen and repairing the New Hall of Pedagogy. As a result, in 1494 John Hutchison was appointed Dean of the Faculty of Arts.

The Huchesones had become tenants of the lands of Gairbraid in Maryhill, a mile to the west of the City, and after the Reformation of 1560, when the old annual rents were converted into feu-duties, they became the owners of that property.

Thomas Huchesone (c.1520–1594), younger son of John Huchesone of Gairbraid, was active in the land market especially in his final years. From the Archbishop he acquired Lambhill (in Govan) in 1579 and within a decade had added to his portfolio, from Walter Stewart of Blantyre, Hutchesontoune, which was up the Clyde at Carmyle. He also owned smaller properties in Provanside, the Gallowgate and the Drygate. Furthermore, he had a house on the north side of the Trongate adjoining the Tolbooth, which later became the home and also the place of business of his son, George.

By the time of the reigns of James V of Scotland and his daughter, Mary, Queen of Scots, the sons of the branches of the Hutcheson families were attending the University. They were therefore educated men particularly knowledgeable about land.[17]

Thomas's reputation grew in his community, no doubt enhanced by his University education. In 1574, he was chosen by his neighbours to witness and attest the division of lands in Dumbreck previously held in common, while in 1587 in his notary work he represented Walter Stewart, the lay possessor of the barony[18] of Glasgow.

Thomas had two sons who were to become the founders of Hutchesons' Hospital and Hospital School in 1641: George, the eldest of his family, born around 1560, and founder of the Hospital, and Thomas, the youngest of his family, born about 1590, and founder of the Hospital School. There were also three daughters – Janet, Bessie (Elizabeth) and Helen. The gap of at least thirty years between the brothers has led some historians[19] to doubt whether they were born of the same woman and to suggest that Thomas was illegitimate. There is no firm evidence on this.

Historically there were two different ways of spelling 'Hutcheson'. This probably resulted from the circumstance that Francis Hutchison of Scotstoun was Town-Clerk of Glasgow when the Hospital of the Lambhill Hutchesones was founded and he was the first Secretary to its Patrons. His clerk, when writing up the Minute Book, naturally spelt the names of its founders in the way to which he was accustomed, like his employer. Thus at a time when spelling was still far from standardised, although the Founders themselves invariably spelt their name, 'Huchesone', they soon gained the surname with which history is familiar – Hutcheson.[20]

Janet, the eldest of the three sisters, married David Duncan, but had only one child, George, who was mentioned in his uncle George's will in 1639 and succeeded to the estate of Barrowfield.[21] George was thanked by Glasgow Town Council in August 1643 for his gift of six hundred merks (£33 6s 8d sterling) for a bell for Blackfriars' Kirk. He died without issue in 1657.

Bessie (Elizabeth), the middle sister, married James Pollok, a cooper[22] and burgess of Glasgow, and their six children all received legacies of a hundred merks in the settlement of George's will in 1639. The eldest, John, married Margaret Allan of Dalmarnock, and succeeded to part of the lands of Yoker and Blawarthill in Govan parish. They had three children – Thomas who died unmarried, Marion, who married John Anderson, a baker, and Janet who died without issue.

Bessie's second son, Robert Pollok, on succeeding to the lands of Auchengray and Caldercruix in the Monklands, which were left to him by his uncle Thomas, assumed the name Hutcheson. He also shared in the Yoker and Blawarthill property[23] and married Grizel Maxwell of Auldhouse. Their son, John, succeeded to both Auchengray and Auldhouse in 1667 but fell on hard times, and according to the Hospital Records, in May 1681 he was admitted as a pensioner to the Institution, which paid his funeral expenses on 13 May 1684. Meantime, Robert's only daughter, Margaret, married Alexander Porterfield and had family of one son and five daughters.

Bessie's third son, George Pollok, married Helen Orr, the daughter of a merchant seaman in Glasgow, with whom he had four children. The eldest, George, graduated from Glasgow University in 1664, married Elizabeth Douglas and left issue, one of whom, Thomas, was admitted as one of the poor boys in the School from 1692 until 1697 when the family moved to Virginia. Pollok's other three children all had families: second son John married Margaret Blair and their son, John, became minister at Roxburgh; third son David married Margaret Kilpatrick and had issue Charles and Helen; and daughter Bessie married Hugh Miller, maltman in Glasgow, and their son, Charles, attended the Hospital School in 1678[24] and was apprenticed to trade.[25] He was later to become Lord Provost of Glasgow, 1723–25.

Margaret Pollok, Bessie Hutcheson's eldest daughter, was admitted as a Pensioner to the Hospital in September 1659. This unprecedented move owed much to a letter of support from Marion Stewart, widow of Thomas Hutchesone. Stressing the close family connection – Margaret was his niece – the Patrons were quick to accede to her wishes. Margaret had married James Pollok, a cordiner[26] and burgess of Glasgow, and on his death their surviving son, George, was placed in the School where he remained for five years, before in October 1665 being apprenticed to his father's trade as a tanner.

The other daughters of Bessie Hutcheson, Janet and Christian, received legacies in their Uncle George's will. It is usually inferred from the placing of their elder sister in the Hospital that they died unmarried, and probably before her admission in 1659.

Helen Hutcheson, the third and youngest sister of the Hutcheson family, in 1609 married Ninian Hill of Garioch, a merchant and burgess in Glasgow, born in 1583. Although she lived until the early 1650s, he died in 1623 but not before they produced Ninian, Margaret, Elizabeth (Elspeth), Helen and Marion.[27]

Ninian, her surviving son, was born in 1623 and succeeded to the lands of Lambhill and Gairbraid. He married firstly Margaret Crawford of Cloberhill in 1654, and secondly Jean Caldwell, who produced a son and four daughters. He was a strong Covenanter and was fined a thousand merks and imprisoned in Edinburgh in July 1676 for attendance at Conventicles. He died in 1682 and his only son, also Ninian, perhaps because of the heavy fine paid by his father, sold the Ramshorn and Meadowflat part of his land to the Hospital. In July 1685 Ninian Hill married Margaret Crawfurd of Jordanhill and they had three sons and four daughters.

The third son, Laurence, was minister of Kilmarnock in 1724 and of the Barony parish of Glasgow from 1750 until 1774. His only surviving son, James Hill of Cartside, a lawyer in Glasgow, was elected Factor on their Gorbals' lands by the Patrons of the Hospital in September 1758. In November 1789 they then elected him Clerk and Factor – offices which were subsequently held by his descendants.

Margaret Hill, Helen Hutcheson's daughter, married firstly John Bryson, a merchant in Glasgow, which resulted in three sons: John, Walter and Thomas. The oldest, John, became a successful Glasgow merchant and was a Bailie of the City in 1685. In order to repay his great-uncle Thomas for many 'kindnesses', in August 1706 he mortified[28] to the Patrons of the Hospital three acres of land in Garngadhill. He died in 1708 and the sum of fifteen shillings Scots was paid from the Hospital funds on 17 October of that year to ring the Hutchesons' Bell at his funeral.

Of the children of Helen Hutcheson's daughter, Margaret, by her second husband, Bailie James Pollock, two, Janet and George, died unmarried. The third, Elizabeth Pollock, married Robert Chapman, a merchant in Glasgow. Elizabeth (Elspeth) Hill, Helen Hutcheson's second daughter, married Thomas Pollock of Balgray, a merchant and burgess of Glasgow. Nothing is known of their sons, James and George, but Thomas migrated to New England and Helen married David Robb, minister at Erskine. The third daughter of Helen Hutcheson, Helen, married John Maxwell of Auldhouse and produced Ninian, Bessie and Janet Maxwell. The youngest daughter of Helen Hutcheson, Marion, married William Gray of Carntyne and produced one son, John Gray.

Such were the main kinship strands of the Hutcheson brothers and their family around the time of its increasing prominence. Some eighteen of their number benefited from financial legacies left by George Huchesone in his will and a significant number of the family married well, consolidating their property in the Glasgow area.[29]

GEORGE AND THOMAS HUTCHESON[30]

George Hutcheson (c.1560–1639), known as 'Maister George', was the eldest child of Thomas Huchesone and Helen Herbertsone. By the time his father died in 1594 and he had succeeded to his considerable estates, George already held a significant position as a writer (the traditional Scots word for solicitor) and notary public in Glasgow. He lived and carried on his business on the ground floor of a large 'heich'[31] tenement, which was on the north side of the Trongate immediately adjacent to the Tolbooth, the centre of the city's administration. He kept his financial papers in a Dutch-built, spring-locked 'kist'[32] in his bedroom on the first floor.

He also possessed another house on the south side of the Trongate – opposite the property which he later mortified for the erection of a hospital – and an adjacent tenement which his brother occupied at times. In 1611, however, he built for his residence a country house in the style of a landed laird at Partick on an elevated site on the Kelvin River near its junction with the Clyde. During the building he interfered constantly with the Kilwinning mason, William Wilson, who had been charged with its construction. Nonetheless, the final mansion, which cost 530 merks to build, reflected his status. It seems probable that it was situated on the very spot where the Bishops of Glasgow had a residence in much earlier times.[33]

The other landed properties he owned included Barrowfield to the east of the city, on which Bridgeton was built; Gartsherrie, Auchengray and Caldercruix in Monklands; Yoker and Blawarthill to the west in Renfrew; Deanfield (acquired in 1607) also in Renfrew; Grainges in Ayrshire; Over and Nether Gairbraid and part of Garioch in what became Maryhill; Ramshorn and Meadowflat, which included what became George Square and the site of the City Chambers in the city itself, and the paternal estate of Lambhill to the north. An Inventory on his death confirmed that, as well as these lands, he had some 87 tenants paying rent to him in kind. All of this indicated the extensive nature of his rural as well as his urban possessions.

The Inventory also detailed the annual money interest due to him and the persons by whom they were payable. Among these were clientele of an aristocratic background including the Bishop of Glasgow, Walter Stewart, Lord Blantyre, Lord Montgomerie, the Earl of Wigtown, the Earl of Abercorn and the Marquis of Argyll as well as numerous others of local significance, such as Sir Robert Montgomerie, Sir William Hamilton, Sir

James Hamilton of Fingalton, Cunninghame of Carlung, and the lairds of Gadgirth and Achinemes. The amounts taken on loan varied from 100 merks to 5,000 merks.[34]

The magistrates and Town Council of Glasgow also turned to Hutcheson for financial help. However, on occasion it appears that interest was paid on the loan by crediting him with a portion of the stent or rates payable by him.[35] Such a cosy arrangement resulted in the intermingling of Council and Hutcheson monies from an early stage and one can only speculate how much the former benefited at the expense of the latter.

It seems that as there were, as yet, no banks, George found it profitable to make loans to those who needed them, which would appear to have been almost the entire upper and middle-class of the west of Scotland. After the Union of the Crowns in 1603, particular reasons for increased borrowing were both the lure to Scotsmen of winning appointments and titles at the London Court and also the colonising scheme in Nova Scotia in 1621 of Sir William Alexander, Earl of Stirling.

George restricted his clerk to charging no more than three halfpence sterling for his legal services, but lent money at the Scottish rate of 8%, which was higher than south of the border and led to the criticism of usury against him. He used a new way of money-lending. Instead of the complex wadset, or mortgage on estates, which was not available to a merchant whose possessions were likely to be cargoes at sea and widely scattered book debts, he lent against bills of exchange or personal bonds secured by two or more persons of substance. By being in the vanguard of these changes in banking practice, he was soon hailed as the first and most important banker in Glasgow.[36]

Although business life for George Hutcheson was proving successful, his personal life seems to have been less smooth. At a Glasgow Kirk session meeting on 28 August 1588, he announced his willingness to marry Elspeth (Elizabeth) Craig, probably a relative of John Craig, also a writer and notary public. She had given birth to a female child (who died young) and he was ordered to marry her within a month. For due compliance with these injunctions, his father became his security to the amount of forty pounds Scots.

Outside of this marriage, which lasted until Elspeth's death in October 1632, George had another daughter, Janet, who lived and died in Holland. She clearly fell on hard times, for in January 1679 the Town Council of Glasgow began paying her an annual pension as she was a 'naturall daughter' of George Hutcheson.[37] The same accounts in September 1683 detailed the payment of sixty pounds Scots as her yearly pension, and in July 1684 the Council paid thirty pounds Scots for her funeral expenses.

George acquired a high reputation for honesty, and, as an illustration of the moderation in his charges, it has been held that he would never take more than sixteen pennies Scots for writing an ordinary bond, whatever its length. His work commitments were time-consuming and, as he explained to one of his clients, Mrs Marion Luke of Claythorn, in February 1589, this necessitated farming out some of his routine administrative work to others.

Part of his work was the feuing of the lands of the Barony and Regality of Glasgow on behalf of the Commendator of Blantyre[38] to the annual tenants of the archbishops. According to Sir Robert Douglas of Glenbervie, this 'he performed to good purpose'. Hutcheson also acted as the Glasgow law agent both for Ludovic, Duke of Lennox, and for the archbishops. A Charter of the Duke endowing a University bursary in 1604 was written and witnessed by him and his name was included in a Charter from the Archbishop granting the University additional measures of meal from the mill at Partick. He was also employed in the action taken by Glasgow and Dumbarton against John Lubbart, master and owner of an Amsterdam ship, for disposing of his timber cargo privately in Glasgow before offering it to the burgh authorities.

George was also employed as an agent for Glasgow University. In 1606 he was paid for pursuing John Stewart to Edinburgh for debt, and again in 1608 he ensured the same man appeared before the Commissary Court[39] in Hamilton. A decade later he carried out the sasine[40] of the Kirks of Kilbride and Renfrew, and in 1628 and 1629 he acted for both parties in drawing up various charters granted by Archbishop Law to the University. Hutcheson also supported the University more directly, contributing a hundred merks in 1632 toward its building extension.

In June 1630 he was appointed Judge-Depute in the Commissary Courts of Glasgow and Hamilton. The main business of these local courts was the confirmation of testaments, the registration of inventories and settlements and other executory matters. They also had jurisdiction in actions of slander, actions for aliment[41] and actions for debt up to forty pounds Scots.

Archbishop Law had appointed John Boyle of Kelburne as the Commissary Judge but he was too busy with the king's business and his own work to perform duties in the Commissary Court. He, therefore, appointed Hutcheson (with the Archbishop's consent) as his depute. Hutcheson paid Kelburne nine hundred pounds Scots per annum, and as a result Hutcheson could pronounce sentences, issue decrees and examine witnesses without any interference.

George Hutcheson was a man with a temper and of a somewhat truculent nature. In November 1601 he was cited for chasing Archibald Eglinton, who was slow to pay a debt, round the High Kirk brandishing his dagger[42] and later refused to give an account of himself before the Church Session. Again, in September 1633, his hot-headedness got him into trouble and after having threatened John Ross of Stobcross and his family, George was bound over to keep the peace. Brother Thomas and others gave guarantees of George's future conduct.[43]

George Hutcheson's Last Will and Testament, dated 18 April 1639, a mere eight months before his death, was written in his own hand and found him 'somquhat seik in bodie, bot of perfyte mind and memorie'. He nominated his brother as his executor. In addition to legacies to his sisters and their children he gave others to his servants and left the remainder of his estate to Thomas. He concluded his Testament by repeating the offer he had made as early as 1614 to support a parish school in Govan.

It was probably this latter scheme that led George to contemplate further the founding of a school in Glasgow instead of a Hospital, in the tenement he was to mortify subsequently for the Hospital. There is extant the draft Contract for a School written in 1639 in his own handwriting as the basis of an agreement between himself and the Town Council led by Provost Patrick Bell. In it he paid tribute to the many clerks and scholars who had risen from humble beginnings and had contributed to Church and State. He therefore planned to provide a tenement on the north side of the High Street for 'the dwelling and residence of ane honest man, skillit in learning, for instructing the youth' so that they have 'ane perfyte entrance in their gramer'. It was hoped to include as many young orphans, fatherless and motherless bairns, or otherwise poor and destitute of male support, of eight years of age, who could be maintained in 'meitt, drink, clothing, and bedding'. Those with the surname Hutcheson or Herbertson were to be given priority.

The curriculum was to be restricted: the boys would be taught, instructed and entertained 'in the principals of the treue (Protestant) religioun' and would learn to worship God. The Master would also give insight into (Latin) grammar. The boys would remain until the age of fifteen and then leave to be scholars, tradesmen or craftsmen. It seems that George wanted them to go to University, for he makes no provision for, or thinks about, apprenticeships or how the boys will be able to forge a career without skills. In this, his ideas were conventional for Reformation Scotland, seeing education as a means of salvation and the teaching of Latin as necessary for eight-year-old boys.

As one would expect, George went into detail about the finance he intended to donate to the project and about the cautioners whom he expected to guarantee its success. Nonetheless, the emphasis of the document is on giving care and nurture to those boys who have been deprived of family life, and hints of his desire to have a family of his own.

But time was running out for George, for he had already had a 'long lyffe' and was approaching eighty years of age. Moreover, the Town Council was unimpressed with his idea for a school and did not want competition for its long-established Grammar School in Grammar School Wynd. So with his health deteriorating, probably he and Thomas decided to leave the endowment of the School to Thomas, who had a network of connections to University professors. Instead he substituted a plan to mortify a hospital (which would include a refuge for destitute old men, so augmenting the provisions of the Merchants' Hospital and the Trades' House) instead of founding a school, and he finalised these arrangements on 16 December 1639, just ten days before his death. His Hospital was the first personally funded charitable institution in Glasgow.

He made available a parcel of land on the west side of the Old West Port of Glasgow consisting of yard and tenement for the building of 'one perfyte hospital for entertainment of the poor, aiged decrippit men to be placed thair into', for whose maintenance, after the Hospital was in operation, he also mortified certain bonds amounting to the principal sum of twenty thousand merks. He determined that the old men should number eleven and be above fifty years of age, and should have been of 'honest life and conversation'. The inmates would be provided with four shillings Scots daily and every year given a gown to wear.

The only instruction George gave for regulating the Hospital was to ensure that one of the old men would need to be able to read, as he was expected to read prayers, morning and evening.

George Hutcheson died on 26 December 1639 a widower, without lawful issue, and was buried in the family sepulchre on the right of the south entrance of Glasgow Cathedral, where his brother Thomas was also subsequently interred.

Thomas Hutcheson (c.1590–1641) was the youngest child of Thomas Hutcheson and Helen Herbertsone. His much older brother looked after his education. Thomas entered Glasgow University in 1607 and graduated in 1610 qualifying for the professions of either Law or Divinity. While Thomas was still a student George gave him land and property, appreciating that this was a way to attract patronage and a possible career as a minister. However, competition was fierce for placements in the Church, and so he followed his elder brother into the law, taking up the profession of writer and notary public.

About 1627 he became the first keeper of the register of sasines of Glasgow and district. Again like his brother, he acted as an agent for the University, and in August 1640 he was named a Commissioner for the visiting of the University. He also supported the University financially: he gave 1,000 pounds Scots to enlarge its library and 1,000 merks for a Librarian. On 24 April 1640 he was created a burgess of Glasgow for his work in setting up the Hospital.

The Council wanted to ensure that Thomas, as executor of George's will, acted swiftly to ratify his brother's Mortification. In this he obliged them.

On 27 June 1640 Thomas drew up the contract to be entered into between himself and the Patrons of the Hospital to begin building. He also assigned to the Hospital a considerable amount of past interest, and to ensure that it 'should be built large and in a comely form', he conveyed to the Patrons[44] another tenement of land in the Trongate, adjoining and to the west of that gifted by his brother.

Besides ratifying the Mortification deeds of his brother on 9 March 1641, he paid tribute to his deceased brother who 'under God, was the fountane from quhome my means and estaitt did flow'. At this stage Thomas added a third tenement of land in the Trongate, adjoining those on which the Hospital buildings were then in the course of being erected. He went on to mortify certain bonds amounting to 20,200 merks for the erection for the Hospital, a 'commodious and distinct house by itself for educating and harbouring twelve male children, indigent orphans, or others of the like condition and quality, sons of burgesses'.

Thomas was clearer than his brother on the details of the proposed School. In this he showed more vision as an educational thinker, and he followed John Knox. The boys were to be seven or even younger if they were 'found capable of instruction'. They were to be schooled for about four years before being bound to crafts and trades and, in a modern view of education, 'according to their several dispositions'. To set them on their way they were to leave the School with a full year's maintenance. Thomas expected most boys to be apprenticed to a trade, seeing the importance of educated artisans to the City's future. However, he made provision for boys with an aptitude for learning: they would attend the Grammar School for up to five years with their fees paid – and they would continue to be 'entertained' in the House during their student days. This raised the entry age to University from 12 to 16.

Progress was to be by attainment (not attendance) and open to the talents, not dependent on means. He made no mention of either Latin or religion in his proposed curriculum, which was highly unusual for the times. He wanted the boys to be able to read and to write, and saw this as the proper scope of an elementary education.

His Deed was also more specific about the patronage of the Mortification. Each year the Town Council was expected to elect, from among themselves, a 'Master of the Hospital' and four others, who, with the ministers of the city, were appointed to meet twice a year in the Hospital to deal with all the affairs of the Institution. So the brothers gave management of their bequest to the City. They wanted Glasgow to flourish.

Thomas supplemented this on 3 July 1641 with an Eik[45] of bonds amounting to another 10,000 merks and on 14 July 1641 with a further additional sum of 10,500 merks to assist in building the Hospital. He himself laid its foundation on 19 March of the same year, extending the scope of the establishment beyond the upkeep of twelve old men to include a 'publick School, where the twelve boys that are on the foundation are taught gratis'.

The two brothers were thus joint founders of the Hospital or Endowment for Pensioners; but the School, which was to co-exist with the Hospital under the name of Hutchesons' Hospital School, owed its origin to the benevolence of Thomas Hutcheson. And yet it seems unlikely that a school would have emerged if Thomas had not seen the founding of a school as unfinished business on the death of his brother.

Thomas died on 1 September 1641 in his 52nd year. Two weeks before his death he appointed Colin Campbell, former bailie of the city and merchant, to be the Master and Collector[46] of the Hospital. In conjunction with the Dean of Guild and another member of the Council Hutcheson personally superintended the construction of the Hospital. After Thomas's death Campbell continued with this task until May 1647, when he was replaced by William Hume. It was not until 12 February 1664 that the head of the institution was styled 'Preceptor'.

Thomas was buried beside his brother George who had a Latin inscription in his memory. This was paid for by Thomas's widow, Marion, daughter of James Stewart of Blackhall, who proved a strong-minded, extravagant-living lady. She fell out first with the Hutchesons' three sisters over the will, then with the mediating judge, who shut her out of both the Trongate tenement and Partick House.

The memorial to Thomas is judged to date from shortly before her death in 1670, and it perhaps was something of a status-symbol, matching the monuments which had begun to appear in the Necropolis opened in 1651.[47] As an ironic gesture Glasgow people called Marion 'Lady Hutcheson', a title which she did not discourage. Certainly the monument commemorates Thomas and their marriage, making no mention of George.

Until recent years historiography has dealt unkindly with Thomas. Usually a comparison of the brothers would describe the strong, tough and aggressive George and the weaker, anxious to please and easy-going Thomas. But the main charge against Thomas results mainly from the poor opinion of his capacity voiced by George in the latter's will. In this document he instructed Thomas to 'follow sage advice of counsel of friends in his adoes, because it hes not pleased God to give him sic knowledge as his place and affers now requires'. And yet such comments did not stop him giving Thomas power of executor. Presumably it was not intelligence but experience that Thomas lacked.

A more sympathetic study of the brothers would give more credit to Thomas. Despite an Episcopalian background, both of them, but especially Thomas, were able to disassociate themselves from what was increasingly likely to be the losing side in the religious strife of the 1630s in Scotland. They (particularly Thomas) proved shrewd and sure-footed men of business who, in violent times, eased tensions between the Covenanting city and the Episcopalian College authorities. Both were rewarded by being made burgesses of their city but even here Thomas had the edge, for he was made a Guild brother, the highest rank of burgess, and entered that body gratis, while George had to pay the usual fee.

George may have been moved by a guilt-complex or the desire to make up for the misdeeds of a sinful life or a fear of God. Certainly as a result of his part in the upbringing of his younger brother, George developed a strong desire to help other fatherless bairns whose situation was less happy than his own. In order to work out details of how to bring this about, the brothers were fortunate in having an extraordinary example for them to follow.

THE INFLUENCE OF GEORGE HERIOT

George Heriot (the founder of Heriot's Hospital) was born into an established family in Edinburgh in June 1563, contemporaneous with George

Hutcheson. By a real stroke of luck he came to the attention of Queen Anne (of Denmark), the Consort, since 1589, of James VI. She was a compulsive spendthrift whose extravagance became renowned. Heriot became one of her jewellers in 1597, and was soon acting as one of her principal money-lenders and bankers.

George Heriot followed his sovereigns to London in 1603 at the Union of the Crowns, and, having no surviving children of his own, he determined to leave the bulk of his fortune to found and erect a Hospital School in Edinburgh. It was to be in imitation of Christ's Hospital which had been founded by Edward VI of England in 1552. He left some £23,626 sterling[48] – about half of his estate – in order to do so. He gave administration of the School to the Edinburgh Town Council and hoped to encourage others to follow his example. The Hutcheson brothers were among the first to do so.

Heriot died with no legal heir in February 1624 and his instructions, giving Rev. Dr Walter Balcanquall a pivotal role in his legacy arrangements, were followed. It was Balcanquall who determined the general lines of the ground plan and crucially in July 1627 presented the Town Council of Edinburgh with the detailed Statutes – the rules and regulations of the Hospital School – for approval. They were twenty three in number. They were comprehensive in their content and were to be the yardstick for the workings of Heriot's Hospital for over two and a half centuries.

It can be assumed that the example of George Heriot as a prototype encouraged the Hutcheson brothers in their venture in Glasgow. George Hutcheson's 'Draft Contract' for 'Founding a School' and Thomas Hutcheson's 'Mortification' 'for the Foundation and endowment of the School' both indicated a wish to found a Hospital for the fatherless and motherless poor[49] and to bind it to Glasgow.

The Town Council of Glasgow were impressed by the 'pauper palace' which gradually took shape in Edinburgh following the laying of the Hospital's foundation stone in July 1628. However, the work was seriously interrupted from 1639, and the 'Wark', as the populace affectionately called it, remained incomplete until the later 1650s. Much of the problem was the determination of the Governors to buy land at every opportunity which led to a shortage of money;[50] precisely the problem that Hutchesons' Hospital had, especially in its earliest years. It was in April 1659 that Heriot's Hospital School finally opened, with thirty boys under its schoolmaster.

In Glasgow the close link between its Hospital and the city was also to lead to the buying of the land, this time in the Gorbals, and the resulting bankruptcy of the former by the latter in 1654. However, the Council was also responsible for preserving the Hospital's existence, ensuring that it began to take in boys again in 1661.

Was the long awaited opening of Heriot's Hospital for schooling in 1659 the important stimulus to the revival of the Hutchesons' School in the west? Certainly Glasgow did not wish to be left behind Edinburgh in this respect as the new notion of civic pride developed. An important demonstration of this was the ruling by Glasgow Town Council in 1667 that the Master at Hutchesons' be paid more than his equivalent at Heriot's – in this case £20 sterling per annum as opposed to the £17 sterling being paid in Edinburgh.

As in the Heriot case, there were times at Hutchesons' when the duties of the municipal dignitaries controlling the bequest conflicted with their duties as trustees, and the interests of the Hospital and School were seemingly of secondary importance. Nonetheless, in both cases, in the longer term, the funds of the Hospitals greatly increased. Between 1641 – when the Hutchesons' brothers left some £4,000 sterling for their legacy – and 1880, the original capital had grown to £373,000 with annual revenue of £18,000.

The Hutcheson brothers knew at first hand of the significance of Heriot's large legacy to Edinburgh and learned some of their business skills from him. According to the official historian,[51] Heriot was one of the very first to receive money on deposit, allowing interest thereon, and to honour cheques, on short notice, for customers. George Hutcheson carried on the business as a money-lender and he may be regarded as the first or earliest banker in Glasgow.

it is somewhat of a surprise that Glasgow has never claimed that Hutchesons' Hospital and School, rather than Heriot's Hospital, was the first of its type in Scotland. Certainly the foundation stone of Heriot's Hospital was laid on 1 July 1628 and its building was more or less complete by late 1631, a considerable time before Hutchesons' had even begun its building. However, the ravages of the Civil War and then the occupation of Heriot's as a military hospital by Oliver Cromwell ensured that Heriot's did not begin to operate as a boarding school until 1659, while Hutchesons', although opened in the Trongate in 1648, was soon closed. When it did begin operating again in 1661, it did so as a day school.

TWO   Mortification Deeds and Heritable Properties

HUTCHESONS' HOSPITAL AND SCHOOL

The total amount of money, mortified by the brothers Hutcheson for the endowment of the Hospital and School, amounted to 72,320 merks Scots, or £4,017 15s 7d sterling. The proportions in which these Mortifications were destined for the respective purposes of the Hospital and School were as follows (in sterling):

For the Boys:	£1,122 4s 5d
For the Old Men:	£1,694 8s 11d
For both jointly:	£1,201 2s 3d

From these amounts, destined respectively for the erection of the Hospital buildings and the School, it may be inferred that approximately two-thirds of the mortified property was intended for the old men, or the Hospital, and the remaining one-third for the boys, or the School. This conclusion is further borne out by the actions of the Patrons during the earliest days of the Institution, when, it may be presumed, that they were to some extent personally acquainted with the views and wishes of the Founders themselves.

Numerous donations and bequests have from time to time been made by charitable persons in aid of the general funds of the Institution. The following separate Mortifications prescribed specific instructions for their administration by the Patrons

Blair's Mortification (1713)

James Blair, merchant, had married Christian Gemmill, the daughter of a Glasgow merchant and bailie who had founded a Sugar House, but their children had all died in infancy. Besides legacies to his brothers' and sisters' children, Blair mortified a considerable sum to the poor of

Irvine, and £100 Scots to the poor of the Merchants' House of Glasgow. On 21 June 1710 he further assigned 10,000 merks (£555 11s 1d sterling) to Hutchesons' Hospital. The interest from this sum, which he estimated at 500 merks, was to be distributed annually by the Provost, three bailies, the Dean of Guild, the Deacon Convener, and the ministers of the burgh of Glasgow, as pensions of £5 11s 1d sterling to each of 'three old, indigent men who have formerly been of credit'; and the balance of £11 2s 3d sterling for the education of 'four boys, at or above six years of age, fit to be schooled, who are to continue at school till they come to be twelve years old'. Those with the surnames of Blair and Gemmill, in that order, were to be preferred.

Blair's mortification was the first of significance received by the Hospital and School since the Hutchesons' foundation had begun.[1] It closely followed the model set down by the Founders. It would appear that Glasgow was not far behind Edinburgh, where the Statutes of Heriot's Hospital were copied first by Mary Erskine, who opened the Trades' Maiden Hospital in 1704, and then by Watson's Hospital, which accepted its first foundationers in 1741.

Baxter's Mortification

Daniel Baxter was a well-known stationer and bookseller in Glasgow in the later eighteenth century and indeed was Preceptor of the Town's Hospital from 1759 until 1769. His Mortification, dated 14 October 1776, had two codicils dated the day of his Mortification and 24 February 1779. He was married to Mary Cameron, who survived him, but without leaving issue. By his Deed, Baxter, amongst other provisions, gave six children of burgesses £100 Scots each yearly, for the space of four years. Their ages were to be between eight years of age and ten years, and during this time they were to receive an education. With the help of this contribution, which amounted to £3,000 in total, the number on the School roll reached thirty-six.

Scotstarvet Mortification

During the years 1797–1811 the Hospital received the feu and rents of lands of Peckie and Peckie's Mill in Fife, amounting to £40 10s per annum, in respect of twelve boys being educated in the School on the Scotstarvet Foundation. In its first days the interest covered the expenditure on the boys, but as the number of boys increased there came a time when it was considered that the continued education of the Scotstarvet boys necessitated an additional member of staff or an increase of expenditure more than proportionate to the amount of rents received. The Scotstarvet boys were accordingly transferred to George Wilson's Charity School, to make up a sufficient number of children fully to engage an efficient Master, whom the Governors of that institution were enabled to employ, through their income being augmented by the rents of the Scotstarvet property.

Scott's Mortification

Under the Trust settlement of William Scott, tobacconist in Glasgow, dated 14 October 1818, the Hospital received payment of a sum of £12,500 – the remainder of his estate, after payment of legacies bequeathed to his four nephews. The income of this fund was for 'the support of old men, old women, and the maintenance, clothing, and education of boys according to the existing rules of the Hospital, as to qualification of applicants or otherwise, in the proportion of one-fourth of the income to men, one-fourth to women, and one-half to the boys'. Scott added that he wanted the annual pensions to be not less than £20 to old men and £15 to old women, and that the sums given in maintenance to boys should not be less than £4 (all sterling) besides the usual allowances for clothing and education, and those with the names of Scott and Anderson to have preference.

Generally the interest of the mortified fund was divided as prescribed by Scott. In 1880, £123 10s was expended in pensions for ten men; £181 in pensions for twelve women, and £270 was contributed towards the general expense of the Hospital School.

Hood's Mortification

Miss Mary Hood resided in the Drygate and was the daughter of James Hood, a deceased excise officer, and sister of her deceased brother, Alexander Hood of Mountserrat. She left her whole estate in 1817 to certain Trustees, with a direction that the residue should go to Glasgow charities. Accordingly, in March 1827, Hutchesons' Hospital was paid £6,000, the interest on which was to be paid over in pensions. Applicants with the name Hood were to be preferred and female relatives also, provided they were of good character, in indigent circumstances, unmarried and had lived in Glasgow for at least five years. The pensions were to range from £5 to £20 per annum.

In summary, the principal additions to the funds of the Hospital and Hospital School were:

James Blair's:	£555 7s 1d
Daniel Baxter's:	£3,000
William Scott's:	£12,500
Mary Hood's Trustees:	£6,000
In total:	£22,055. 7. 1

By the end of the Hospital School in 1875, by careful administration and management and with wise counsel of the Founders, the Preceptor and the Patrons had been able to buy arable land in the neighbourhood of Glasgow. The resulting capital of the Hospital amounted, by a moderate computation, to £376,543.[2]

At this time (1875), 99 men and 811 women received pensions and 286 children attended the Hospital School. By 1880, there were 146 men and 1,017 women receiving pensions and 1,083 boys and 719 girls attended Hutchesons' Schools.

Like many similar charitable institutions, their funds declined in the first half of the twentieth century. However, the impulse for giving was not completely lost, and in recent years Hutchesons' Grammar School has been the recipient of significant philanthropist support.

THE ORIGINAL HOSPITAL BUILDINGS AND THE SCHOOL IN THE TRONGATE

Thomas Hutcheson had died only months after the laying of the foundation stone of his Glasgow Hospital in 1641. The main fabric of the building would appear to have been completed by 1643, for the slating was finished in that year at a cost of £119 10s sterling, but, although the building was occupied to some degree from then on, much remained to be done. The walls were lime-cast in 1650 but were not plastered until 1660.

Progress on the Hospital was interrupted by various events. The Burgh Records for 18 March 1648, by which time it would appear the wainscoting had been fitted or was ready for fitting, related how 'sax wainscott' were borrowed from the building for constructing the pulpit in 'The Hie Kirk' (the Cathedral). Six, however, were not enough, as on 29 April the Town Council instructed 'ane uthir wainscot and ane half to be tane out of Hutchesones Hospitall for making of the pulpit in the Hie Kirk, and to be repayit by the toune'.

Although building work continued throughout the 1640s, the intended design was never completed. It was modelled on the much grander plan of Heriot's Hospital in Edinburgh, which dated from June 1627[3] and which was in an Italian style, new to Scotland, of a courtyard enclosed on four sides. However, only two wings of the Hutcheson Hospital were built. With its frontage to the Trongate of 73 feet, and a depth of 30 feet and a steeple of about 100 feet[4] it was not unlike the old Merchants' House in the Bridgegate. The edifice cost £2,182 10s 9d sterling.

In 1649, a clock and a bell were placed in the steeple, costing £34 1s 2d sterling[5] and £49 6s 2d sterling[6] respectively. The Patrons were, from an early date, anxious to take special care to protect it by using lead at the top of the steeple.[7] Despite such efforts the clock had to be replaced on 7 December 1683, when £300 Scots was paid to James Colquhoun, a mason and builder and the Town's Master of Works, 'for putting up and gilding the horologue in the steeple of Hutchesons' Hospital'. The original bell was ordered on 4 August 1649. It came from Holland. It was seven feet nine inches in circumference, with the following inscription: 'Cornelius Ouderogge, Fecit, Rotterdam, 1649'. The price of the latter included the cost of bringing it from Bo'ness where it was unshipped.

THE STATUES OF THE HUTCHESON BROTHERS

The Accounts of November 1643 contained an entry referring to two blocks of fine freestone being brought at a cost of £99 Scots from Loudon in Ayrshire. On 14 April 1649, there was also recorded a fee of £66 13s 4d Scots being paid 'in part payment of cutting George and Mr. Thomas Hutcheson's yair portraitors'. The Town Council Minutes and the Hospital Records mentioned further authorisation of payments to James Colquhoun, mason and builder in Glasgow (also a bailie of the City)[8] at that time the Town's Master of Works, 'for the hewing, forming, and putting up of Mr Thomas Hutchesons (sic) portraiture in the Hospital'[9] and 'for perfyting and upsetting of umqll[10] Mr. Thomas Hutcheson his picture'.[11]

Whether this extended timescale reflected a delay in the making of the works or in the settlement of the sculptor's fee cannot be determined. The probability is that the former statue or 'portraiture' was that of George, while the latter was of Thomas Hutcheson.

The 'portraitures' were not portraits but sculptures, as is made clear from subsequent accounts. In April 1673 £13 15s Scots is entered 'for wages to twa measons for seven days and a halfe, with a ladie, dressing the portraits and mullars';[12] also £7 6s 8d Scots 'to twa pynters for grinding and laying on ye collor on ye portrates'. This strongly suggests that the statues were originally painted.[13]

It is presumed that in sculpting the statues Colquhoun had the benefit of contemporary portraits. Tradition has it that a portrait of Thomas was painted by Van Dyck, who visited Scotland in the early seventeenth century, but that seems unlikely. There is, however, extant a painting of Thomas said to be by George Jamesone, and also a painting of George after George Scougall which is referred to in the Hospital Records of 12 September 1717.

In his statue George is dressed in a doublet, knee-breeches, shoes and stockings, a falling ruff, an indoor cap trimmed with lace and long gown of the type worn at this time by professionals and officials. He holds a money-bag in his right hand, and an engraving published in 1838 suggests that he originally held a scroll in his left hand. In his statue Thomas is shown wearing a doublet, pantaloons trimmed with ribbons, boots, a cap and a demi-gown. He holds a book in his left hand.

It should be noted that the date of George Hutcheson's death is wrongly given on the pedestal as 1693. The misalignment of the last two digits suggests that they may have been replaced after becoming detached at some point, the restorer inadvertently reversing the numbers.

Moreover, it is now believed that the inscriptions on the pedestal are incorrect. The fact that the figures were carved posthumously, and that the subjects were represented in a way that did not reflect the disparity in their ages, suggests that Colquhoun worked from existing portraits in creating their likenesses. No painted images of them have survived, but engraved copies of the Van Dyck and Scougall paintings provide a basis for comparison. In the former Thomas has a bald cranium, a full but neatly trimmed beard and a moustache brushed down over his mouth. This description is similar to the head of George in the statue. By contrast George in the engraving has a full head of hair, a long goatee beard without side whiskers and an upturned moustache, all features similar to the head on Thomas's statue.

Given that the statues were in store for nearly thirty years, and that the pedestals with their inscriptions were probably made during this period, the supposition that the brothers have been wrongly identified seems reasonable. On balance, and bearing in mind also that the inscription on the pedestal assigned to George already contains an error in the date, the conclusion can be drawn that the identities of the brothers have been reversed accidently in the inscriptions.[14]

THE HOSPITAL BUILDINGS AND THEIR USE

The Minutes of the Hospital with regard to the occupation or tenancy of the building show clearly the change in use from the original purposes of Hospital and School to mercantile uses. The last Account was paid in July 1650 and at that stage the accommodation consisted of six dormitories for the old men (pensioners), two rooms for the schoolmaster, one large sleeping apartment for the boys, the school-room, a kitchen, a hall for the Patrons, and a large sitting-room for both pensioners and boys to share.

However, the Hospital was used for all kinds of activities and storage. In his *History of Glasgow*, Wade[15] related the setting-up of a printing establishment in 1647 for the earliest Professor of Divinity in Glasgow, David Dickson, to produce an *Exposition into Matthew's Gospel*, which was printed by George Anderson in the Hospital. The Town Council Records in October 1661 mentioned that ten of the Town's twenty ladders, kept handy in case of fire, were left in the Hospital for convenience and accessibility. Subsequently, under the heading 'Water Engines'[16] it was noted that Number 9 stood at Hutchesons' with the keys to be found nearby with James Sommerville. By May 1688 'abuses' had been perpetrated by dancing and fencing masters, and in 1720 it seems that bull-baiting had been taking place in the inner yard.[17]

However, the practice of letting seemed to be getting out of hand, because the Patrons, on 18 May 1691, ordered the practice to be discontinued. Nonetheless, the practice went on, being justified on the grounds that more income could be obtained for charitable purposes than otherwise would have been the case had the buildings been kept in their original condition and used exclusively for the purposes of the Hospital and School. The Hall, in particular, was greatly in demand. It seems likely that in the eighteenth century the back wing occupied by the School, and the houses or rooms of those few pensioners who lived within the Hospital, were the only portions of the building used for their proper purposes.

Writing before 1736, John McUre[18] held the Hospital to be 'a very handsome building of ashlar[19] work. ''Tis not high but beautiful . . . besides a spacious Hall with the accommodation for twelve old men that are therein maintain'd, and a publick School, where the twelve boys that are on the foundation are taught gratis. The Hospital has a pretty steeple, one hundred foot high, bearing a proportion to the building of the house, which is covered in lead, with a clock and bell that is serviceable to the town, and from and towards the north of the hospital there are very pleasant and delectable gardens that are well kept, and much resorted to for the recreation of walking in them.'

Above the great entry to the Hospital fronting the Trongate there was an inscription (to the memory and honour of the worthy founders) upon marble in golden letters. Translated from Latin it read:

> These hospitable walls exalt the name
> Of George and Thomas Hutcheson to fame;
> Their princely bounty built this place of rest –
> For whom? You ask. For those by want oppressd.
> Twas thus they sought the sorrows to assuage
> Of orphan poverty and helpless age.
> Scorn not this house, unversed in fates decree,
> Grim want may yet oppress thy sons – or thee;
> While those whom fame shall sing – the brave or wise,
> In war or peaceful arts, may hence arise.[20]

Within the inner court fronting towards the garden of the Old Hospital there were two niches which in 1736 contained full-sized statues of the Founders in marble. They contained Latin inscriptions which were translated into English verse by a prize-winning Humanities student at Glasgow University as follows:

> Behold the brothers Hutcheson! Who came
> Heaven-sent, the wretched and the poor to bless,
> This home they built, memorial of their name –
> A resting-place of sorrow and distress;
> For when no offspring blest their lot below,
> And boundless store of golden wealth was theirs,
> Nobly they chose the sons of want and woe –
> Old men and helpless orphans – for their heirs.[21]

Prior to 1780 the Patrons were so accustomed to the complete misuse of the buildings that their disposal was looked on increasingly as a desirable measure, especially given the greatly increased value of the ground. However, the Preceptor from 1777 till 1800, John Campbell of Clathic, had grave doubts as to the legality of such a measure, and he sought the opinion of eminent counsel.

Henry, afterwards Lord Erskine; Adam Rolland; Robert Blair, afterwards Lord President of the Court of Session; William, afterwards, Lord Craig, and Ilay Campbell, afterwards Lord President of the Court of Session, produced a Memorial which recognised that for a considerable time no Hospital existed for lodging, clothing and maintaining the pensioners and schoolboys who were supported and educated from the funds of the charity. It explained the cause of this: 'As the Hospital was situated in the most public and best frequented street in Glasgow the Patrons many years ago found it expedient to abandon altogether the idea of using it as an Hospital, and to convert by far the greater portion of it into shops and warehouses, which are let at high rents, by which a considerably larger income is raised for the charitable purposes to which the funds are now appropriated than could have arisen by keeping it under its original form and management.'[22]

Despite this, they gave their opinion against the power of the Patrons to sell either the Hospital or the ground expressly mortified by the Hutchesons; although the first four were not indisposed to think that the Patrons might competently feu[23] the available or surplus ground. Lord Campbell, however, was firmly of the opinion that such 'ought neither to be sold nor feued, nor granted "in long lease"'. Nevertheless, the Patrons, anxious to augment the revenue of the Hospital, disposed of major portions of the Hospital's ground between 1788 and 1795, although not without protest.[24]

The grounds of the Hospital and School were disposed to Robert Smith jnr., Dugald Bannatyne and John Thomson and the Glasgow Building Company; the policy of out-relief by pension replaced that of residential charity, the modern Hutcheson Street was cut through the gardens of the old Hospital and School, and what was left of the building transferred in 1805 to Ingram Street, another newly-cut thoroughfare.[25]

How are we to judge such actions? Certainly the official historian, Hill, a century later, admitted that, when the practice of letting out part of the Hospital had begun, the revenues were inadequate to support either the pensioners or boys in sufficient number to fill the house. Thus it was clearly good management on the part of the Patrons to create an income by which they might more speedily achieve prosperity and ensure the Founders' instructions could be followed completely. As the revenues increased, the practice was ordered to be ended, but by then the practice of giving outdoor pensions was in full operation. The order was thus disregarded. In so acting, the Patrons' justification rested alone upon the large amount of good they thereby accomplished.[26] Later they had the sanction of a Royal Charter obtained in 1821 and of a Statute of Parliament in 1872.

THE GROWTH OF A PROPERTY PORTFOLIO

George and Thomas Hutcheson lived at a time when the ownership of land was a route to social standing rather than wealth creation, but both brothers appreciated its potential. Thomas instructed his Trustees to invest his fortune 'upon the best, cheppest and weill haldin arrabill landis they can get to buy, near this burgh'.[27]

Ramshorn and Meadowflat

The Ramshorn lands of about twenty acres and the Meadowflat lands of about fourteen acres were immediately to the west of the old town, separating Glasgow from the extensive agricultural lands of the Campbells of Blythswood. They were the centre of modern Glasgow, from West Nile Street to Portland Street and North Albion Street, and from Ingram Street to Cathedral Street. They were bought by George Hutcheson in October 1609. On his death they became the property of his brother, Thomas, to whose widow, Marion Stewart, they were later life-rented. Subject to this burden, the lands, with those of Lambhill and Gairbraid, passed to Ninian Hill, Helen Hutcheson's son, and from him they descended to his son. In 1694 he decided to sell Ramshorn and Meadowflat.

Although the lands were outwith the Royalty of the burgh, the Town Council wanted to control them and so prevent development in an area beyond its power to tax. Not having the requisite funds available, the Council proposed that the Merchants' House, Trades' House and Hutchesons' Hospital buy the land and present it to the Town. Seeing no advantage, the merchants and tradesmen declined to get involved. However, the Hospital did not have their autonomy[28] so in August 1696 the Patrons paid the full price, some 23,000 merks (Scots), for the lands which had belonged to the brothers Hutcheson.[29] The Magistrates paid no price or compensation to the Hospital for the feu-duty and rights of Superiority they obtained; indeed they were relieved of every expense in the purchase.

In the later eighteenth century the Town Council took ownership back from the Hospital and sold off the land in small lots, making a massive profit. In this important instance greater regard was clearly paid to protecting the interests of the City than to increasing the revenue or promoting the resources of the Hospital.

Gorbals

In 1648 the Town Council of Glasgow began negotiations with Sir Robert Douglas of Blakerston[30] with a view to the purchase of the Gorbals, and in early 1650 he sold the lands which were to be held one-quarter by the City, one-quarter by the Trades' Hospital and one-half by Hutchesons' Hospital. Sir Robert received in total 120,000 merks and his wife 2,000 merks. The title deeds were ratified by the Scottish Parliament on 20 May 1661, and it was declared that the lands of Gorbals and Bridgend, with the wheatmill on the River Kelvin, were united within Glasgow.

Such an arrangement was very much to the Town Council's advantage in the short term, for it was Hospital funds which made the purchase possible and Hutchesons' endowments were used as civic funds.

The Gorbals lands generated none of the hoped-for income as, owing to the Civil War, the English invasion and a sequence of bad crops, they were in a disastrous condition, and by 1654 the Hospital and School found themselves being owed 54,000 merks and in dire straits financially. Charitable allowances had to be reduced; the poor boys who were being educated and boarded in the Hospital had to be sent back to their parents' home, and the schoolmaster discharged, at least meantime.[31]

By 1659 the Town Council had written off the money 'owed' by the Hospital and the latter began collecting rents from the recovering Gorbals lands. In this way the City kept its obligation to maintain the Hospital and the municipal connection forged by the Hutchesons' brothers prevented the Hospital from extinction, the fate of many of Glasgow's privately managed endowments. It still seems a large price to pay but the interdependence between City and Hospital gradually provided more benefits for the latter in the longer term.

It was not till 1794 that the final division of the Gorbals was completed. The managers of Hutchesons' were awarded all the lands bounded on the north by the river Clyde; on the east by the lands of Little Govan; on the west by the east side of Muirhead Street, and then southwards to include St Ninian's Croft, Dockany Fauld, part of the lands of Butterbiggins and Sandy Acres. They were also awarded the lands of Kirkcroft, situated between Nicholson Street and Warrick Street on the east, and Bridge Street and Eglinton Street on the west.

With full and exclusive rights to their parcel of property, the Patrons resolved[32] that it would henceforth be called 'Hutchesontoun' and made their plans for feuing. To further this object the Patrons spent considerable sums to buy neighbouring properties, which might otherwise have inter-fered with their general plans.[33]

The value of the Hospital's property in the Gorbals increased eight-fold between 1740 and 1821 and a further twelve-fold in the next sixty years:

$$1660 - £3,388$$
$$1740 - £3,563$$
$$1785 - £9,447$$
$$1801 - £21,785$$
$$1821 - £30,592$$
$$1841 - £115,830$$
$$1861 - £190,369$$
$$1881 - £366,107^{34}$$

Increasingly the key to Glasgow's territorial expansion was held by the Patrons.

The possession of such substantial estates next to the growing commercial city was the product of a deliberate policy. By the terms of his bequest Thomas had directed the Patrons to 'invest the mortified sum in arable land in the neighbourhood of this trading and well-circumstanced city'.[35]

This policy was followed, as much as the charitable commitments of the Hospital and School allowed, until 1772. However, the only ways to realise the enhanced value of their lands were by selling them or by terminating the agricultural leases and carrying out a programme of building themselves. This they were neither equipped nor empowered to do, and so between 1772 and 1802 the large Hutcheson estates were broken up. The effect upon Glasgow's growth was immediate and spectacular.[36]

In the 1790s the break-up continued with the extensive feuing of the Gorbals. In 1792 the 27 acres of Well Croft and Stirlingfold went to James Dunlop and Andrew Houston as an investment for the Dumbarton Glass Work Company for a yearly feu of £258; in 1802 Trades Croft and Kirk Croft, another twenty acres, were sold to David Laurie, of a timber merchant family; while other lands to the east of the old village of Gorbals, in St Ninian's Croft, known as Hutchesontown, were feued out to William Dixon and Andrew McKendrick, with Dixon's, at 46 acres, the last of the large feus.

All these transactions led to protests about the alienation in large blocks of so much of the Hospital's estate.[37] But criticisms were soon overcome, given the greatly increased value of the ground, which was far beyond that originally envisaged by the Founders. The average income of the Patrons, which had stood at between five and six hundred pounds per annum in the 1770s, rose to a thousand pounds by the late 1780s and to three thousand pounds by 1810. The yearly agricultural rents of Tradescroft and Kirkcroft had been £44 8s and £78 respectively. These amounts were increased to £242 and £529 per annum when the two crofts were feued to Laurie.

The result of these feu duty sales was to bring in five or six times the land's former agricultural rents, and solved all the immediate financial difficulties of the charitable corporation, whilst temporarily satisfying the public demand for house and business accommodation. However, even the official *History* of W.H. Hill admits that the chief profit in these deals undoubtedly went to the middleman, and suggests that the Patrons were too greatly influenced by interested parties in the early stages of the feuing operations. Fortunately they reversed their policy of giving inducements to men of means to speculate in the erection of buildings on their lands. Had they continued down these paths, practically all the profits would have been swallowed up in large and subdivided feus by boldly speculative middlemen. In the event, the Patrons appreciated the extent to which they had divested themselves of their patrimony and resorted to a policy of feuing in much smaller portions by public auction, thereby retaining the profit.[38]

HOSPITAL BUILDINGS IN INGRAM STREET

When disposing of the old buildings and ground in the Trongate, the Patrons stated their intention to erect new buildings of a monumental description. Accordingly, in August 1795, a Committee was authorised to purchase ground in Ingram Street, opposite Hutcheson Street, as a suitable site for a 'new Hospital'. The first plots of land were bought in November 1795 and a sinking fund[39] was put aside in March 1799.

In March 1802, plans, prepared by David Hamilton, for a new Hospital building on the Ingram Street site, were approved by the Patrons and within four months the offer of £2,525 for the mason-work from Kenneth Mathieson was accepted. The work was completed in 1802–04 and the structure cost £5,201 5s 2d less the value of the old buildings, which were taken by the mason for £125.

There does not seem to have been any ceremonial at the laying of the foundation stone, the only notice being in the account books of a sum of £4 4s paid in August 1802 for 'drink money' for the masons. To the cost of the building should be added £168 11s paid to Messrs. Harrington, for a clock put into the steeple on its completion.

Dr Cleland in his *Annals*[40] described the building as follows: 'The basement is formed of rusticated work, on which columns of the Corinthian order are raised, supporting an entablature, over which there is an ornamented attic. Niches, designed to receive Statues of the Founders, are formed between the lateral pilasters; and the pyramidal spire, 156 feet high, rising from the back part of the buildings, gives the whole a very light and cheerful effect. The great Hall and committee rooms are fitted up in an elegant manner.'[41]

The statues of the Founders, when the old Hospital buildings in the Trongate were taken down in 1795, were removed to the Merchants' House in the Bridgegate at a cost of £2 3s 6d.[42] They probably remained there until 1817 when that building was sold, and the accounts relate that the original statues were erected in 1824 in their appropriate niches at an expense of £26.

It appears that the City Corporation, the River Trust and other public bodies, had the use of the Hospital Hall for their meetings without charge. In March 1837, given that the City now charged for the sittings of Hospital boys in the Town Churches, the Patrons recommended that the Town should pay £20 per annum and the River Trust £10 per annum for such use, and other bodies were charged proportionally.

The portion of the Hospital buildings above the Hall was designed for, and for some time used as, the Schoolroom. But it was found very inconvenient. As it had been proposed to build a house for the accommodation of the Master, on the remaining ground fronting Ingram Street, to the east of the Hospital building,[43] a more commodious Schoolroom was built there, with a shop beneath and some dwelling-house accommodation above, at a cost of £720 10s 10d. This Schoolroom also proved inadequate – ninety-two square yards of open court being the whole space available to the one hundred and twenty scholars – so the Patrons resolved to obtain entirely new premises for the School.

Accordingly, new buildings were erected for a school in Crown Street, and in 1852 the Patrons sold to Sir James Campbell (for £800), the strip of ground adjoining and to the east of the Hospital in Ingram Street, on which the old School-house, then occupied as a shoemaker's shop, was situated. An access, five feet five inches in width, on the east of the Hospital, was reserved, the purchaser being further bound not to build higher than three storeys, and an elevation to Ingram Street was introduced to harmonise with the Hospital.

Identity of interest made it necessary that the Magistrates of Glasgow Town Council, when acting as the Patrons of Hutchesons' Hospital, should keep prominently before them, that while rightly entitled to do all they could to benefit the public of Glasgow, they should not, under any circumstances, dispose of Hutcheson property below its market value.

The acquisition and disposal of the Ramshorn and Meadowflat lands, as one example, served to illustrate how easily a minor trust was ignored in the desire to benefit larger and more important interests. All involved must be single-minded in their intent to benefit and improve the property and revenue of the Hospital, for the support of the aged poor and the education of the young.

THREE

The Hospital School and
Its First Masters

The earliest mention of the School in the Hospital Minute Book was on
13 November 1643, when the Patrons elected their first pupil, Archibald
Edmiston, a burgess's son, who was both fatherless and motherless. On
the same day the first election of a Pensioner took place. John Wilson had
seemingly been previously admitted by the Preceptor to the Hospital as, in
the Accounts of 1642, a sum had been provided for a suit of clothes.[1] It made
sense, however, that both youth and pensioner shared a bedchamber, while
the former was educated at the School and furnished in provisions – meat,
drink and clothing, as well as books and other 'requisites'.

The next admission was that of James Lawson, another burgess's
child, on 22 March 1645. He was bound as an apprentice for seven years
to Cuthbert Greig, a cooper in Glasgow, but in fact did not complete his
apprenticeship and was given further financial support from the Patrons in
November 1650.

Meantime, the last payments for the building were made on 20 July
1650, suggesting a structure which had been fit for use some time previously.
Accordingly, the Patrons increased the School roll to four in 1647 and nine
in 1649. As they moved to elect the full number of boys stipulated, they
deemed it time to elect a schoolmaster. Several minutes appear on this
subject, both in the Minute Book of the Hospital and in the Records of the
Town Council. Evidently no arrangements for conducting the School in the
Hospital buildings had been made prior to this date, as the Minutes electing
both Edmiston and Lawson held that they were to be educated at one or
other of the schools in the burgh.

John McLay, First Master of Hutchesons' Hospital School (1648–52)

It must be said that it appears that there was not so much a lack of schools
in Glasgow at this time, but rather a problem with the quality of teaching
provided. The Town Council attempted to tackle this by tighter licensing of

teachers, and with regard to the election of the Hospital Schoolmaster the Town Council minute of 1 April 1648 showed how thoroughly it appreciated the importance this appointment was for the welfare and success of the School.[2] Further minutes of both Hospital and Town[3] confirm the decision to offer a trial period to John McLay, who had already a licence to teach. Significantly, he would be judged by 'raising of the psalms in Mr Patrick Gillespie's kirk'.[4] In this way it would be judged whether he was fit to teach the young ones in Hutchesons' Hospital. Apparently he gave satisfaction in this regard, for he was appointed, on 28 October 1648, as the Schoolmaster of the Hospital for a year.

Teaching methods in reading at the time followed a simple formula. The schoolmaster would read out the text and the children repeated it, line by line. They were helped by the use of song, which ensured that the message of the words was more firmly planted in the memory. So as well as leading the Psalm singing the schoolteacher used the *Shorter Catechism* which had been officially approved by the General Assembly of the Church of Scotland as the reading text in 1648.

Writing seems also to have been tackled in the very early years of the Hospital. In 1650 the Accounts include the purchase of paper, which suggests that the School was following Thomas's wish that the boys learn to write.

McLay seems to have proved successful and his reasonable salary reflected that. The Education Act of 1646 determined that a schoolmaster's salary should be between a hundred and two hundred merks. The Patrons decided to pay McLay one hundred and fifty merks, a not inconsiderable amount at a time of scarcity and upheaval in the country. Indeed, between 1648 and 1652 'the town of Glasgow was almost destroyed by misfortune'.[5]

The Minutes of the Town Council, as well as those of the Hospital, on the subject of the appointment of the Schoolmaster, relate how the boys maintained previous to this time were educated at some school unconnected with the institution, and also show the willingness of the Town Council to supplement the funds of the Hospital for the purposes of education.

The arrangements for the School being thus firmly established, the Patrons, after consideration of a report on the subject,[6] resolved that the boys should now be placed in the Hospital to make up the full number which Thomas Hutcheson had stipulated. Accordingly, the Preceptor presented to the Patrons the names of eleven young boys, all burgess's sons. They were subsequently elected and, with the one already on the Foundation, made up the full complement.

At this juncture statues of George and Thomas occupied either side of the steeple entrance, and the Hospital School was housed in a back wing of the Hospital building,[7] with two rooms being set aside for the Schoolmaster, one large sleeping apartment for the boys, a school-room 19 feet long and 15 feet broad, and a large sitting-room for the joint use of boys and pensioners. The furnishings were of the simplest. The diet of both boys and pensioners was also of plain fare – oatmeal and herring daily, kale[8] (every second day) and beef (once a month). However, the Hospital School gave up boarding in 1652, and to take the place of their keep the Patrons substituted a maintenance allowance.

Unfortunately, the terms of the various Hutcheson Deeds of Mortification, as regards the constitution of the Patronage, were never precise or altogether consistent, and their discrepancy gave rise to differences and disputes. In this regard they did not follow the Disposition of Scotland's other early seventeenth-century Hospital founder, George Heriot. Probably this explains why the position of the ministers in Glasgow as Patrons seemed in some doubt. They were not present at any meeting until 13 May 1654, when two ministers attended but decisions even at that meeting were made by 'the Magistrates and Council as Patrons'. The most important early decision made by the Patrons was in 1650 when the lands of the Gorbals were purchased. The ministers were not consulted in this decision, although their consent to such a purchase was particularly required by the Eik to the Mortification of Thomas Hutcheson, dated 3 July 1641.

From the mid-1650s some of the ministers were present at all meetings and acted in every respect as Patrons. However, at the meeting on 27 September 1659 chaired by Provost Colin Campbell, it was decided that there should be a special meeting between the Town Council and the ministers 'for clearing the Ministers' interest in the Hospital'. This meeting did not take place, but the ministers acted as Patrons at every subsequent meeting in all the affairs of the Hospital.

In 1650 the absorption of the Hospital funds, consequent on the purchase of the Gorbals lands, necessitated retrenchment.[9] Accordingly, on 3 June 1652, the Patrons resolved 'that the five poor boys that are entertained in the Hospital be put home to their parents and the Master of the House to pay them for their entertainment as he and they can best agree, and to see them trained up at School'. It was further minuted that 'John Bell undertakes to sustain John Schearilaw, because he wants, and the Master of the House is to pay him forty pounds by the year, with his clothes, and John Bell undertakes to see him trained up at School; and in like manner

John Walkinshaw undertakes to do the like for James Clydesdale, another of the poor boys, and appoints the Master of the House to furnish the poor boys' clothes.'[10]

Schoolmaster McLay was also looked after. His salary was no longer paid, but he and his family were allowed to remain in their house and had the use of the School. This, however, did not last long, and within a year they had been removed. Such retrenchment was reinforced in May 1654 when it was ordained that 'no manner of people, young or old, be placed in the Hospital until ane sure and constant rent be provided thereto'.

Accordingly, it would appear from the Accounts that no boys were regularly maintained out of the Hospital funds during the years 1653 and 1654, and although entries of payments occur leading to the inference that there were two boys in the year 1655, five in the following year, and three in the year 1657, it is not altogether clear in what position they exactly stood, whether as boys regularly elected – their presentations not being noted in the Minutes – or merely as receiving casual aid from the Preceptor, to assist in their education. Neither do any payments on account of the boys occur in the immediately subsequent years.

Nonetheless, there is evidence in the Burgh Records that between 1655 and 1657 the Hospital building was used as a school and James Clerk was allowed to teach there by the Town in August 1655 and James King was also licensed to teach there two months later.[11] By 24 January 1657, however, the Council had ended this arrangement and King was told to leave following a report being made that 'Hutchesounis Hospitall is much wrongit be the schole keepit thairin'.[12]

In 1660, the revenues of the Hospital began to improve and this led the Patrons, on 26 November, to resolve that, if possible, 'four young boys be chosen, and be brought up in the Hospital, in accordance with the foundation thereof'. Thus John Gilmour, Hugh Muir, George Pollock,[13] and David Maxwell were elected. It was arranged both with the mother of John Gilmour that she should keep her own son and Hugh Muir, and with Margaret Pollock, widow, that she should keep her own son and David Maxwell, and £50 Scots was allocated for the boarding of each individual boy.

Robert Forrest, Second Master of Hutchesons' Hospital School (1667–90)

In this way boys were again enrolled on the Hospital funds, but it does not appear that any schoolmaster was appointed to attend to their education at this time. The next Minute on this subject was after an interval of nearly fifteen years,[14] when Robert Forrest, Schoolmaster, was instructed to read and pray to the boys in the House (and the old men) for a year, 'as he has done this year bygone'. He was probably one of those who had been licensed to teach within the burgh in 1654, but of whose first election as Master of the Hospital School there is no record.

Forrest had proved his reliability by 1667, and a new contract gave him £20 sterling per annum. He stayed for twenty-three years, ensuring no interruptions to teaching and a steady roll of twelve boys. In his time it is possible that the curriculum developed and arithmetic and Latin were introduced.[15] However, such subjects made slow progress, especially when Forrest resigned in 1690 on being faced with swearing allegiance to King William of Orange,[16] who had abolished patronage in Kirk appointments, as Presbyterians had long demanded, but refused to go further and expel ministers with an Episcopalian history.

Peter Reid, Third Master of Hutchesons' Hospital School (1691–1705)

Peter Reid was elected Master in May 1691 and his fourteen years as Master coincided with Scotland experiencing a time of famine and the collapse of the Darien Scheme.[17] Fortunately, the Patrons kept the roll up and the Master's salary was protected from the worst of pay cuts. Nonetheless, poor wages, especially compared with a minister's stipend, and difficult conditions of service, ensured a sequence of short-lived appointments to the post of Master. Reid himself died in office in 1705. He had married Marion Hutcheson and their son, John, had been admitted to the School in May 1688 'in respect his mother is ane relation to the Foundators'.

The Company of Scotland had opened their subscription books for investment in a Scottish colony in 1696, and the first to sign up in Glasgow was Provost John Anderson, who pledged the maximum allowed, £3,000, for the burgh. He was followed by the Dean of Guild, John Aird, with £1,000 for the Merchants' House. The institutions which followed included one corporate investor, the East Sugar Works of Glasgow, whose partners decided to invest £3,000.[18] However, the partners of the Wester Sugar Works did not follow suit. One of them, James Blair, had other plans for his money.[19]

SCHOOLMASTERS IN THE EIGHTEENTH CENTURY

The Schoolmasters of the Hospital School in the early eighteenth century were all educated men with Latin. The Patrons wanted to introduce new 'commercial' subjects into the School curriculum which showed their dissatisfaction with what was on offer at the Grammar School and University. It helps explain why Glasgow was the first council in Scotland to introduce inspection into their schools.

George Clark, Fourth Master of Hutchesons' Hospital School (1705–06)

John McLurg, Fifth Master of Hutchesons' Hospital School (1706–08)

(Rev.) John Walker, Sixth Master of Hutchesons' Hospital School (1708–10)

George Clark, awaiting a ministry appointment, was Master for a mere nine months before an untimely death in 1706. He was followed by John McLurg who proved unsuitable and ineffective, and he was asked to leave in 1708. Things went from bad to worse. The next choice of Master, Rev. John Walker, had at least some experience in similar posts, having been Rector of Dumbarton Grammar School (from 1690 until 1695) and then an assistant teacher at Glasgow Grammar School in May 1695. However, within two years he had been dismissed from the latter post for disrespectful conduct towards its Rector. His ministerial friends protested, and in October 1698 he was reappointed to his post. But complaints against him continued and he was finally dismissed in December 1707. This led him to Hutchesons' School, where he became Schoolmaster in September 1708. It did not take long, however, for the Patrons to realise that this was a mistake, and they dismissed him within eighteen months in February 1710. Nonetheless, Walker managed to get himself elected as a pensioner in the Hospital.

William Hyndshaw, Seventh Master of Hutchesons' Hospital School (1710–16)

Another student of Divinity took Walker's place, William Hyndshaw, and he remained until April 1716, when he was sacked for refusing to carry out his duties. In particular he would not lead the old men in twice-daily prayer. This was not a new problem for the Schoolmaster, as all the Schoolmasters had difficulties trying to deal with the intransigence of the inmates. When getting rid of Wyndshaw the Patrons encouraged the pensioners to come together themselves and worship God, but in vain.

George Hutcheson in his Deed of Mortification had prescribed that the old men should 'resort to the common prayers and preaching in the Laigh Trongate Kirk', and they and the School boys appear to have attended there. In March 1703 the Dean of Guild was instructed to 'provide and prepare seats and room' in the church and it seems likely that the old men and the boys also continued to attend the Tron as long as the practice existed of boarding them in the Hospital, and the boys also until the Kirk was burned down in 1793. Divine worship continued in various churches until 1841, when arrangements were made with St Andrew's Church. Although the old men finally got out of going to church altogether, the boys attended as a body until 1876. After the Sunday morning service, they returned to School to be questioned on the sermon and to receive further catechistical examination. In the afternoon the boys went back to church for another sermon (often the same one as the morning) followed by another revision period.

Masters and Patrons attempted to maintain standards, and at an early stage a uniform coat was worn by the old men and boys on church days, although some of the former resisted this development. However, there were also difficulties over the boys' uniform from the first days of the School. Thomas wished costumes 'all of one colour and of one fashion', and until 1685 boys were supposed to be dressed in 'cloath of blew collar' with 'stockins and a black bonnet'.

Then it was decided by the Patrons that all the boys should be clothed with 'purple collared cloath'. Purple was the colour of the Hutcheson armorial bearings, but also of Glasgow's Episcopal Archbishop, which did not help gain popularity for the regulation. Little progress was made, so in August 1699 a committee, set up to examine how far the Founders' wishes were being followed, reported. It held that each of the boys should have a cloth coat 'of dark grey colour, jeated with green' which would be 'provided by the Hospital' and both old men and boys were expected to wear their distinctive uniform, despite pleas that to blazon such a distinctive badge of poverty and inferiority was humiliating. However, this uniform rule was not only rejected by the pensioners but also was viewed unfavourably by the public. Probably this explains what led McUre, writing in his *History* in 1736, to mention that while attending at the Tron Church they had no distinction or habit, except on Sundays and even then the wearing of uniform was not strictly imposed. As far as the boys were concerned the slip-coats of 1699 were the only sign of uniform worn by Hutchesonians, and probably the first such sign for several decades. This position was maintained throughout the eighteenth century.

James Brown, Eighth Master of Hutchesons' Hospital School (1716–42)

The next Master, James Brown, was in post from April 1716 until his death in 1742. He seems to have built a good reputation. Certainly, within a year of taking office he was at the receiving end of a significant pay increase, the first at the School for fifteen years. However, to put matters in perspective, he was still earning less than McLay had been getting some seventy years before, and seemingly less than the average salary in parish schools in Scotland.[20] Appreciating the situation, the Patrons increased his salary again, although not till 1729, and showed generosity to his widow by giving her a gratuity of three months of his salary in 1742.

George Park, Ninth Master of Hutchesons' Hospital School (1742–43)

James Aitken, Tenth Master of Hutchesons' Hospital School (1743–50)

After such a long period of stability, Brown's successors only remained for a short period: George Park was in post from July 1742 for sixteen months. He was followed by James Aitken who was elected Master in November 1743 and remained till death in late 1750, but he made little impact in that time.

In his Deed of Mortification Thomas made provision that if any of the boys in the School 'be likely to prove scholars, and apt for learning' then they were to be entered in the Town School, the Grammar School, to be instructed in letters freely, without payment of any fees for four or five years. During this period they were to be maintained in the Hospital and also have their books paid for. Despite such an arrangement, very few, if indeed any, boys did follow this path in the first century of the School. However, it was clear that Thomas intended a test of ability should be applied before any boy went to the Grammar School. So the Patrons decided in September 1718 that any boys doing so should first pass a proficiency examination in English administered by the Preceptor and one of the ministers.[21] Although this made no material difference to the numbers coming forward, it was significant in drawing attention to the Founders' intentions and was a corrective to those Patrons who did little to encourage boys to take up the academic challenge. Unfortunately, at this time and for another century the Grammar School and the University[22] remained loyal to a traditional curriculum, and the conviction was still held that a Classical training was a powerful, even indispensable instrument for disciplining the mind. Thus it was only in November 1861 that Thomas Hutcheson's intention was fulfilled.

Another issue pertaining to the Founders' wishes led the Patrons to decide that boys enrolling in the School would be expected in future to produce their father's burgess ticket before being allowed to do so. This followed the restriction in Thomas's Mortification that scholars 'sal be all burgessis sones of the burgh of Glasgow'. It is not mentioned elsewhere because it was not deemed necessary. No man, under the exclusive system which then and for long afterwards existed, was entitled to carry on the business of a merchant, or exercise the calling of a craftsman, within the limits of the burgh, without having first entered as a burgess. It can be presumed, therefore, that a burgess qualification was tacitly required, but no regulation was introduced on the subject until 1721, when, probably, the number of applicants was so greatly beyond the number that could be taken on the roll as to require the Patrons to produce a specific rule. Compliance with this rule was required as a preliminary to the application, and to save the time and labour which would have been uselessly spent in investigating the circumstances of persons whose status was not of the kind prescribed by the Founders. In May 1721 the Patrons therefore ordained that applicants to Hospital or School needed to produce the ticket, otherwise their petition was to be rejected. In this way concern was shown that only poor children could gain from the Foundation.

James McKenzie, Eleventh Master of Hutchesons' Hospital School (1751–85)

James McKenzie was elected the next Master in the School in January 1751. Although he too died in post, he gave over thirty years service, and his son, Daniel McKenzie of Acrehill, was to be a Preceptor of the Hospital.[23] He was followed by interim Masters: Galt held office for only two months in early 1785 and left to matriculate at Glasgow University, taking his MA in 1791, and James Mitchell held office from March 1785 until May 1786. He was fortunate to have received an increased salary from the Patrons, which ensured that the Hutchesons' Master earned about the same as burgh school teachers in the country.

By the end of the eighteenth century the Rules and Regulations of the School had been recorded and published and deemed in line with the Founders' intentions. The boys had to be the sons of burgesses, indigent orphans, or others in like condition, whose parents could not maintain them. They had to be between seven and eight at the time of their application, and must have previously attended an English school for at least six months. The names of Hutchesone and Herbertson still took precedence and applications had to be accompanied by a burgess ticket, by a certificate from the teacher in the school he had attended, by an extract of the boy's age from parish records, and by a certificate from a surgeon that the boy was free from any infectious distemper. In a laudable effort to be transparent, all such details were inserted in the local Glasgow newspapers.

A Special Committee of Patrons also delved into details of the state of the families of the different petitioners and a summary was forwarded to the Patrons. Parents were informed about details of the meeting being held to elect the boys, which boys and their parents were expected to attend. These were prepared in case the Patrons wished to see them and make further inquiry.

The curriculum of the School was somewhat remarkable for a charity institution educating children under twelve years of age. The boys were to be instructed throughout their four years at the School in the principles of religion, in learning to read English, and in Church Music. At the end of the first year, each boy was to be admitted to Writing, or even sooner if the Master judged him fit for it; at the end of two years and a half, the pupil was to be introduced to Arithmetic, or sooner if the Master judged him qualified; and each boy was to write a book of Arithmetic (to be given to him by order of the Committee of Education) in a fair hand, which he was allowed to take with him when he left School.

When boys had been four years in the Hospital School they were to be apprenticed to a craftsman 'according to the several dispositions of the boys'. Provision had also been made for any scholars, who would be financially supported at the Grammar School for four or five years. But these were few and far between.

The Schoolmaster, elected every year, was to be a person of 'good credit and reputation'. His hours were spelled out: from 1 April to 1 October, classes were to be six hours – 9 to 11 am; 12 to 2 pm and 3 to 5 pm; from 1 October to 1 April classes were to last five hours – 9 to 11 am and 12 to 3 pm. On Saturdays, classes were held all year from 9 to 12 noon; on Sundays, the Schoolmaster was to accompany boys to Church and supervise their behaviour there both morning and afternoon; and he was to continue with them, in the schoolroom, at least for an hour after public worship in the afternoon, and was to be employed in religious exercise and instruction. The summer vacation was to be two and half weeks in length.

A priority for the Master was to watch over the moral conduct and conversation of the boys as much as possible at all times. He was also expected to account for their appearance, tidiness and cleanliness.

Other issues of concern for the Master included the expectation that he would resort to the use of a substitute only in exceptional circumstances. He was forbidden to take any gratuity – all education was provided free. He was also committed to exercise a 'steady, uniform, and moderate discipline in the School".

The School Committee on Education was set up in 1786 and consisted of five Patrons (two of them being ministers) with two a quorum. It met five times a year to 'improve the plan of education and to superintend the execution of it' and to take care that the teaching hours were observed. Their remit extended to the attendance of the boys and the disciplining of the Master. Moreover, twice a year the Committee examined the boys and made a report on their progress, comparing their performance with previous examination results. From these the Committee was expected to give an opinion on how far the School was flourishing or declining.

In April 1800 the Patrons decided to allow the Master to reward distinguished proficiency with a premium of 10s sterling per boy, and diligence and good progress with smaller rewards. These payments had a twofold objective: to encourage the Master to be assiduous and to encourage boys to emulate their peers.

Established practice ensured that all boys in the Hospital School received on 26 April yearly a suit of clothes, consisting of a short green coat, a corduroy vest and breeches, one pair of stockings, one pair of shoes, a hat and two shirts. In November, they received another pair of shoes and stockings and the boys in their first year received an additional shirt.

On leaving School the boys received an apprentice fee (provided they had been apprenticed) which took the form of a suit of working clothes, consisting of a short green coat, and corduroy waistcoat and breeches, as well as two shirts, a pair of shoes, a pair of stockings and a hat. In the following year, provided their apprenticeship was going well, they also received a short green coat, a pair of shoes, a pair of stockings and a shirt. These completed the clothing allowances, but each boy on the Hutcheson Foundation also received £3 sterling annually in maintenance, and was supplied, without charge, with all of what was needed at School – books, paper, pens, ink and slates. The Committee of Education supplied every boy with a Bible and his 'book of Arithmetic' on departure.

The number of boys attending the Hospital School reached 48 in 1800, but this number was only reached by ending the custom of giving a year's maintenance to pay for apprentice fees as laid down by the Mortification.

James Douglas, Twelfth Master of Hutchesons' Hospital School (1786–93)

Unfortunately, James Douglas, who had proved one of the less abysmal teachers, had come and gone between 1786 and 1793. Previously he had been a private teacher of English nearby the Trongate. He had a good reputation and the Patrons raised his salary significantly. However, he resigned in 1793, annoyed that the Committee had forbidden extra payments, 'it being the meaning of the Founders that education shall be given free of all expense'.

Thomas's suggestion of organising the Hospital School in classes had been put into operation. Regulations of 1791 and 1800 describe the students as working in gradated[24] classes, boys of the same age moving through the School, while within each year-group further classes were created by ability and aptitude. Entrance regulations were extended – a boy had to prove he had attended an English school for six months; prove his health by medical line and his minister had to confirm that the youth was above seven but below eight.

The selling of the Hospital building in 1795 led to a hunt for a convenient schoolroom, and the Hospital School moved at least twice before settling in the new Hospital building in Ingram Street. The Patrons could take credit at least for saving the School,[25] rejecting both the offer of the old Grammar School site[26] as unsuitable for a school and never seriously contemplating closing it.

FOUR The Final Years of the Hospital School

By later in the eighteenth century, the Hospital premises were increasingly dominated by commercial enterprises. The whole of the ground floor was turned into shops and let, the lofts were rented to merchants in need of storage space and the garden rented to nurserymen. The only surviving image of the first Hospital frontage, from about 1794, showed a changed appearance, with the innovation of shop-windows and sign-boards disfiguring the original elevation. The second 'floor' or 'gallery' of the main building was entirely occupied by the large Hall, which was let, if not permanently, at least very frequently.

The back wing occupied by the School and the houses and rooms of those of the pensioners who resided within the walls were likely to have been the only rooms not shared with others. A highly successful Glasgow school teacher, William Dickson, was elected to use the fore-hall (fronting the Trongate) in March 1786. With business booming, he was soon taking on staff of his own and advertising in the local press. 'James Begg, Assistant to Mr Dickson, Teacher of English, respectfully informs the public that upon Tuesday 3 November (1789) at 5pm, he will open a private class in Mr Dickson's Hall, Hutchesons' Hospital, for instructing young Ladies and Gentlemen in Reading and Spelling; with the principles of English Grammar'.

The scholars were well provided for in the Schoolroom. In 1793 they used 60 Bibles; 20 New Testaments; 28 Psalm Books; 27 copies of *The Economics of Human Life*,[1] 23 copies of Perry's *Spelling Book*;[2] 41 English Collections; six large slates; eighteen small slates; three desks; nine forms and five inkstands. However, gradually the numbers in the School increased. After dropping briefly to 17 in 1760, the numbers reached 20 again in 1762 and were 23 in 1774. By 1790 the numbers had risen to 32, and by 1800 were up again to 48. Numbers hovered slightly below this level until increasing again, reaching 60 in 1812 and 80 in 1813. Again the numbers levelled off until 1820, when they reached 102. Another plateau was not reached until 1839, when numbers rose to 120, and then in 1843 when they reached 140. Numbers grew again, reaching 154 in 1844, and they hovered in the 150s and 160s. Between 1852 and 1866 the numbers remained in the 170s, and between 1867 and 1870 in the 180s. In 1871 a new peak of 208 was reached; the peak became 219 (1872), 235 (1873), 283 (1874) and in the final year of the Hospital School (1875) another peak was reached at 286.

The increasing value of the site led the Patrons to sell it, and the drawing of the rear of the Hospital (see picture reference 8) is reputed to date from the time of its demolition in 1795. The Hospital School was found temporary premises in the same locality and, by demolition day, only five female pensioners[3] were resident and needed rehousing.

The new Hospital was built between 1802 and 1805. It was built on the Hospital lands to the rear of the Trongate Hospital, which was now the entrance of Hutcheson Street into the Trongate. After the old Hospital was demolished, the School was maintained in unknown locations. The new Hospital, built in the Classical style by the architect David Hamilton, was intended as a memorial to the Founding brothers. The statues from Trongate were given a more prominent location within large niches on either side of the building's front.

Much better equipped by now, the School in the late eighteenth century had a governing body, the Patrons, who like Thomas were active in shaping an education allied to the best thought of their day, widening the curriculum and following Adam Smith in using 'incitements to emulation' (they did not call them prizes).

A number of former students who had been educated in the School by James Douglas met together in 1801 and decided to meet annually in a Hutchesons' Society. All members had to be 'of good moral character and be free from all bodily diseases altogether', and membership had to be terminated at the age of thirty-five.

Charles Thomson, Thirteenth Master of Hutchesons' Hospital School (1793–98)

James Douglas had been succeeded by Charles Thomson, who, despite working for a reduced salary of £30, seemed satisfactory, especially as the roll was maintained. However, in 1797 the Committee on Education reported that 'the day after the annual parade of the scholars in April (26th) they met and found the Schoolmaster had left the school without any intention of returning'.[4]

Quintin Bowman, Fourteenth Master of Hutchesons' Hospital School (1798–1800)

Quintin Bowman was immediately appointed fourteenth Schoolmaster, but problems of poor health and irregular attendance were recurrent issues until his death in 1800. Matters had not been helped by Regulations which enabled Bowman to employ a substitute teacher without informing the Committee except in case of sickness. The general result was a school in poor order, where boys were unable to answer basic questions on the *Shorter Catechism* and showed no progress in writing and arithmetic.

The Patrons responded by insisting that future applications for the post of Schoolmaster had to be accompanied by references from previous employers and more details on their qualifications. Successful applicants could expect a salary of £45, which was not far short of contemporary salaries at University and Grammar School.

Andrew Hamilton, Fifteenth Master of Hutchesons' Hospital School (1800–04)

Andrew Hamilton provided these newly required testimonials and was appointed from a leet of two, both of whom had attended University, although neither had graduated.[5] The Committee was pleased by the changes Hamilton introduced. 'Indeed the general look of attention and satisfaction of the boys, their order, peaceableness and aplicatioun, with the respect esteem and confidence which Mr. Hamilton's manner seem to inspire, promise in the future state of the School everything good and agreeable.'[6] Under him the first Grammar School bursary was awarded. But then, at the end of 1803 he left, probably to join the ministry. He went on to become Minister of the High Kirk, Kilmarnock, and died in June 1839 aged sixty-seven.

John Willock, Sixteenth Master of Hutchesons' Hospital School (1804–16)

John Willock was appointed the next Schoolmaster in 1804, and in 1807 he received a substantial increase in salary to £60 to keep him. He had inherited a roll of 48, but by his death in 1816 he had raised the number of boys to 80. He and the Patrons followed educational reformers Bell and Lancaster, whose system enabled the teaching of large numbers. Unfortunately, this created accommodation problems.

John Ferrie, Seventeenth Master of Hutchesons' Hospital School (1816–27)

John Ferrie was elected Master in August 1816. Born in 1794, he was not only a graduate of Glasgow University but he was also Chaplain to Glasgow University between 1822 and 1828. The roll of the Hospital School took another surge forward during his tenure, reaching 102 in 1820 (in the space thought only suitable for a maximum of 82). Matters deteriorated as cracks in discipline in the monitorial system appeared and Ferrie's health began to suffer. The Patrons responded by employing Andrew Kirkwood as an assistant, and he was to stay long after Ferrie left. When Ferrie did resign, controversially he was appointed Professor of Moral Philosophy in Belfast, despite being attacked by some leading Irish Presbyterians for heterodoxy.[7] Ferrie retained his post at the Royal Belfast Academical Institution until 1872.

Dux medals were introduced in the 1820s, marking a change in educational direction. The stress was now on emulation and competition, although there is some evidence suggesting that the culture of the School was slow to come round to this concept of education.[8]

Originally the Hospital School was to be on the first floor of the new building (above the hall), but in 1810 rising numbers led to it moving next door, to part of a 'mean, plain-looking building' originally intended for the Master. The house cost £720 10s but from the beginning was deemed unsatisfactory. Not only was it noisy, but generally inconvenient. Although it was three times larger than the Trongate Schoolroom, it struggled to cope with the increasing number of scholars to whom the Patrons found it possible to give education as a result of their profitable business activities.

John McArly, Eighteenth Master of Hutchesons' Hospital School (1829–61)

John McArly was elected Master in September 1829 and came from Crieff. The religious revivalism of the age resulted in an increase in his duties. Boys arriving at the school would be taught music by him. He was 'esteemed' and was the first Master to be called 'Headteacher'. His assistant, George McMillan, was appointed about 1837 and came from Huddersfield. In their two decades working together, the roll increased from 120 to 171. McArly and McMillan used monitors to help them offer a curriculum which was in advance of other elementary schools. McArly retained his post until November 1861, and died while Patrons were appointing a new assistant.

The only other teachers mentioned in the School Minutes were the singing teachers, beginning with William Brown, who joined the staff in 1793 and remained until 1825. He was followed by John Chalmers, who was given the additional duty (without pay) of accompanying the boys to church and ensuring they behaved well and participated in the proceedings.

As the total area of Ingram Street was only 92 square yards, the Patrons, after discussing the possibility of an extension, eventually decided in 1839 to build a new School in Crown Street.[9] Its site was chosen not just because Hutchesons' Hospital owned the land but also because it was in a largely undeveloped and quiet Gorbals district with good air and plenty of room in an open site. It was also designed by the fashionable David Hamilton. It was a multi-classroom school (with three schoolrooms, plus accommodation for the Master on the first floor, the wings being decorative. Classes were still a relatively new idea).[10] There was also a playground, showing the influence of David Stow, whose book *The Training System*, published in 1836, advocated playgrounds as 'uncovered classrooms'. The School was also at the forefront of modern methods in its use of monitors, designed to deal with the pressing problem of how to educate the newly burgeoning industrialised city populations. All in all the Crown Street School, which opened in 1841, showed a determination to give a Hutchesons' boy an education equal to the best in Scotland.

Progress was made in another area – that of uniform – in the mid-nineteenth century. In 1788 the Patrons had made another attempt to introduce daily wear of a 'decent Uniform of a drab colour', but further changes followed in 1791, 1793, 1836, 1842, 1852 and 1862, until the School adopted a uniform which was universally and consistently worn.

The consideration of the question of extending the benefits of the School and liberalising or modifying the conditions of the qualification of the boys, became imperative with the passing of the Act in 1846 which abolished the exclusive privilege of trading in burghs in Scotland. Its effect was to lower the status of applicants for admission, as it ceased to be necessary to be qualified as a burgess to carry on the business of merchant or tradesman. Thus very few of the class intended to be assisted by Hutchesons', viz. Merchant or Trades Burgesses, who had been in business on their own account and who therefore qualified themselves, according to the strict letter of the regulations, for receiving the benefits of the charity. Indeed, it was found that it was being monopolised by the children of journeyman operatives, whose practice it had been to enter as burgesses for no other purpose than to benefit from the different charities and incorporations of the City.

Finding the number of truly eligible and qualified applicants yearly diminishing, the Patrons extended the benefits of the Foundation to the grandsons of burgesses. Gradually finding even this insufficient, on 26 November 1855 they carried some resolutions explaining that applications could come from merchants, craftsmen and tradesmen who had worked for five years and fallen on hard times.

Thomas had also hoped that boys completing their literary education, if so inclined, should be instructed in trade through apprenticeships. He also hoped that Hospital boys would procure bursaries in the gift of the Town. In November 1807 David Knox, a scholar whose education the Patrons had carried on at the Grammar School, was sent to College and the Preceptor was requested to apply for a bursary for him, his fees for the sessions 1809–10 being at the same time ordered to be paid.[11] Two years later James Simpson was recommended to the Patrons of Baxter's bursary, and £3 was further agreed to be allowed him from the Hospital funds to enable him to pursue his studies at College. In 1846 and 1847, fees were paid for W. Douglas, who also, in the latter year, was allowed the sum of £8. In 1850, 1851 and 1860, fees were paid and an additional sum for books was given to the boys. If there were any doubts as to the legality of such measures, these were put to rest by the 1872 Act.

THE END OF THE HOSPITAL SCHOOL

The 1872 Hutchesons' Hospital Act gave the Patrons ample powers to promote, in almost any way, the cause of education in Glasgow 'as, from time to time, they may deem expedient, and warranted by the state of the funds at their disposal'. Firstly it defined the powers of the Patrons, and secondly regulated the application of the Hospital funds.

Prior to the Act, the Patrons were the Lord Provost, Magistrates and Town Council of the City, and the ministers of the ten Established or City Parish Churches. After passage of the Act the Patrons were to elect annually the Preceptor from among 'their own number'; they were to include the Lord Provost and Magistrates, the Dean of Guild, the Deacon-Convener, the Town Council and the Ministers of the ten Established Churches within the Royalty;[12] three persons annually elected by the Merchants' House of Glasgow; three persons to be elected annually by the Trades' House of Glasgow and six ministers elected by the Patrons, not being ministers of the Church of Scotland.

The Act also made important changes in the application of funds. The amount to be expended in future in pensions was not to exceed two-thirds of the Hospital revenue, nor to be less than one-half thereof. The same provision was made regarding the income from Blair's and Baxter's Mortifications, but in the case of Scott's the proportion was fixed at a half, and in the case of Hood's the whole revenue was to be devoted to pensions. There was no distinction made in the Act between male and female pensioners, except in the case of Hood's Mortification, the benefit of which was confined to unmarried females.

Power was given to apply the remainder of the revenue of the Hospital and its relative Mortifications, and one-third of the Hospital's capital, for furthering the cause of education. The Patrons would determine what actions were deemed expedient, and which would depend on the state of funds at their disposal and the educational wants or necessities in Glasgow.

On obtaining the Act, the Patrons lost no time in proceeding to exercise its powers, and as the Act itself indicated what should be done, their first steps were to enlarge the School in Crown Street and to establish a school for girls. The days of the Hospital School were coming to an end.

On 9 April 1875 a Committee of Patrons was set up; it reported on 26 October of the same year. It recommended that the School should comprise an Elementary and a Secondary, and that boys and girls be eligible for both, after passing an examination. With the exception of the Foundationers, the others would pay modified fees – still somewhat higher than those charged by the School Board in Glasgow in 1873. Only the Foundationers would be given clothing and they would be strictly limited to the children of the needful and deserving, who had carried on business or trade in Glasgow on their own account, with credit and reputation, but who, by misfortune, had been reduced in circumstances. This was confirmed by the Patrons on 22 November 1875.

In the Secondary Department, in which the higher branches of education were to be taught, the Committee recommended the institution of Scholarships, affording free education, to be competed for by pupils educated either in Hutchesons' or other schools; School Bursaries, confined to pupils educated in the Elementary Department of Hutchesons' Schools; and Bursaries at the University of Glasgow, to be competed for by pupils who had completed their course in the Secondary Department of Hutchesons' Schools.

The Committee explained the objectives behind the changes as, firstly, to connect the School with the University and to encourage promising youths, by scholarship and bursary, to attend University; and secondly, to meet the requirements of those preparing to devote themselves to mercantile, scientific or technical pursuits, or to prepare for posts in the Civil Service or other competitive areas. The Patrons wanted the fees to be higher than those in the Board Schools, but believed that its plans would only succeed if the fees were adjusted to ensure the education offered was within the reach of all classes 'who may be wishful to secure for their sons the advantages of the highest culture, and glad to sacrifice a little in its attainment'.[13]

'A STRONG AND SOUND GERM OF A SECONDARY SCHOOL'

In 1875 there were twenty-seven endowed schools in Glasgow, the largest number of charity schools in Scotland. However, only fourteen of them were inspected by the Government, and of these only four were deemed efficient. Hutchesons' was one of the latter. The Report on Hutchesons' School from Assistant Commissioner, Meiklejohn, summed up the School. 'This is a primary school of the highest class, with a strong and sound germ of a Secondary School in it. It would be most unfair to the School to characterise it only as a Primary School because, even in the subjects which are generally called primary, the methods Mr. Menzies follows, and the lines on which he works, seem to point everywhere to a "liberal" education and to pass beyond mere temporary "results". The teaching throughout appears to be informed with thought, and Mr. Menzies seems to be able to get intellectual training out of everything done in the School. The boys have a sound knowledge of principles in every subject, and use their own judgments in applying them. The feeling, too, of the School is excellent. A delightful quiet and order lived in the room – the order and quiet that come from everyone being busy and interested in his work. Each boy seemed filled with the sense that he had a great deal to do, and that others also were busy and must not be disturbed. There was no hurry or noise anywhere, but steady and tranquil diligence.'[14]

The year of the Report was also that of the publication of the original Prospectus, as the School started out on the Secondary School path, having been enlarged and remodelled and opened on 1 August 1876. It stated that the aim of the School was 'to reproduce, in its best form, the old Grammar School, where in former days a superior education was to be had at a moderate fee; where the children of country gentlemen, professional men, tradesmen and artisans, were educated side by side, and were prepared, either for the University or commercial life. Many of the best scholars were sent up from these Grammar Schools to the University, and many sent out from them have left their mark on the world.' This aim was reiterated in subsequent prospectuses.[15]

'Foundationers' were introduced – children of Glasgow burgesses whose parents had been reduced in circumstances. These continued the charitable tradition. Eighty scholarships offered free education for four years (open to boys from all schools including Hutchesons') and twenty-four bursaries (for boys from Hutchesons' Primary) offered free education and money payments from £5 to £15 per annum, and twelve University bursaries for four years offered for Hutchesons' pupils from £20 to £30 per annum.[16]

Meiklejohn[17] returned again in 1880 and issued the following Report: 'There is no question that there exists both in the Rector and in the Masters a desire to make every class and department in the School as perfect as human things can be.' However, this time he had a criticism that the class size, which reached eighty in some areas, was too large. Meiklejohn believed that fifty was large enough, but admitted that the School used little rote learning even with their large numbers. He approved of paper examinations and noted that Hutchesons' had four every year.

Meiklejohn concluded: 'so far as hard work, thorough and careful teaching, complete organisation, and a business-like working of the whole establishment are concerned, I do not think this School can be surpassed in Great Britain. The discipline and order are perfect; the organisation is like that of a first-rate man of war; and there is an atmosphere of vigour and purpose throughout the School. The Rector radiates energy, and it appears to me that the smallest boy in the place has the benefit of it. It would be difficult to find such results – results so level, and on so high a level – as reached in this School in Arithmetic, Mathematics, and English, in any other school in this country . . . The character of the work done is plainly visible in the fact that, the longer a boy has been at the School, the greater seems to be his mental power, and the better his mental habits . . . Though English Composition is not one of the strong points, the papers received by me from the forms VIa upwards (the last year of the Primary, or Preparatory School) were superior to those I was in the habit of having sent to me some years ago, from young men from eighteen to twenty-two, who were candidates for direct Commissions in the army . . . Each class seemed to move with one mind, and maintaining a healthy corporate life in a class is one of the highest successes of a high practical teaching skill.'

'If a school, then, is a place where a boy is to be trained in infinite pains-takingness, from this point of view I should say that Hutchesons' Grammar School is engaged in the serious business of making a nearer and nearer approach to this ideal. There is hard and careful work from the lowest to the highest form in the School; and the higher boys seem to have a strong and steady appetite and liking for this hard work. Probably the most just thing I can say of this School is that it satisfies in the completest and most satisfactory way the demands of the neighbourhood in which it stands, and that every individual boy – without exception – has the fullest care given to him. However lazy and careless he may be, he cannot escape the thorough organisation and arrangement of the School; he must work, and most of the boys work their hardest and do their best.'

Meiklejohn was so impressed with Hutchesons' that he independently wrote to the Preceptor, Archibald Gray Macdonald, making recommendations for the development of secondary schooling in Glasgow with Hutchesons' at its centre.[18] He suggested that schools should be public, that results should be available to parents and the community; that courses should be well organised and compulsory with some options in the later stages; that pupils should progress from one stage to another based on attainment; that fee-paying pupils and others should be taught together and examinations should be held at least twice a year, and should test the ability of pupils to apply the ideas and techniques that they had learned in new situations. As Meiklejohn moved towards persuading the authorities to adopt a more meritocratic schooling and society, it is significant that he saw Hutchesons' as the proper role model for such a change.

Crown Street was almost entirely reconstructed in 1876, to convert it into Hutchesons' Grammar School, a full secondary and elementary school. Fees were also introduced for the former (free elementary schooling having arrived in Scotland in 1872). Pavilions were created for the north and south wings and the original 'diminutive' tower was replaced by a handsome cupola and spire above the main entrance. This was considered both more elegant and more massive and imposing, and indeed formed a distinguishing feature in the locality. With rising numbers the original three schoolrooms were partitioned into eleven newly fashionable classrooms, soon labelled 'palatial palaces'.[19] They were all large, well-aired, properly ventilated rooms. The upper flat of the south pavilion housed the Gym. In a two-storey erection carried over a part of the playground, backwards to Rose Street, accommodation was found on the first floor for the Rector's office, a boardroom and the School library. On the second floor, the most spacious school hall in Glasgow was provided for collective gatherings of the scholars. Memorial windows (of the Founders) were placed in the eastern gallery.

The Rector had a commodious residence over two storeys. There was a new building to the rear, a T-shaped projection three storeys high, with the top two storeys supported on pillars over a spacious covered playground, estimated to hold 600 scholars. Space for drill work was marked out in lines and squares. There was extensive provision of lavatories.

No pains were spared to make Crown Street a 'model' building, based on German thinking which led the way at that time in school design. The change of name indicated the direction of ambition – to convey the School as now belonging to the centuries-old tradition of the Scottish burgh grammar school.

HUTCHESONS' GIRLS' SCHOOL

The Patrons had decided in 1873 to rebuild their Crown Street building, not to increase the number of boys, but to extend the educational benefits of the Hospital to girls. The question had first been raised as early as 1842, but efforts to take the issue further failed in 1847 and 1861. However, in 1866 Preceptor William Whyte began to pursue the matter more seriously, and in this he was backed by Rector Menzies. By 1873 they were planning for two separate schools, sharing staff but not classes. Whyte then sent Menzies and City Chamberlain Hill to do some field research. Their findings were a surprise. Generally female education was aimed at increasing the social value of a daughter, but nowhere were girls taught 'domestic economy' systematically. The Patrons decided that Hutchesonian girls should not only benefit from a literary education, but also be trained in womanly accomplishments, particularly 'economical cooking'. Their plans aimed at creating a model school not for the poorest classes but, like the boys' school, the children of respectable widows. Such radical thinking saw a future with much wider employment opportunities for women. There was also little argument about a mixed-sex school, despite the issue being a focus of debate elsewhere.

There were to be two Departments in the School – Elementary (soon to be called Primary) and Secondary, eligible to boys and girls. Fee-paying pupils had to pass the same exam as applicants for free places (Foundationers). Elementary Foundationers would have clothing provided, while Secondary Foundationers had their books bought. Bursaries were available for School and University places.

Rector Menzies believed strongly in free schooling, and the Patrons, too, were anxious to avoid the School becoming a middle-class institution. The High School in 1876 charged fees of £8 to £16, while Hutchesons' first fees were to be from £2 10s to £4 so that Higher Education was to be within the reach of all.

Despite all the planning, in two months in 1876 everything changed. Hutchesons' was suddenly offered the Gorbals Youth School[20] in Elgin Street, which was bankrupt, ruined by the cheaper education on offer at the Board Schools since 1872. This unexpected offer to the Patrons led them to change their original plan to educate both boys and girls in Crown Street, and determined the development of two largely autonomous schools for the next century.

Elgin Street was given a refurbishment. The result was a 'cheerful and tidy appearance'. It provided classroom accommodation for five hundred scholars with a cooking department – a large classroom with a counter for demonstration lessons. Nearby on a lower floor was the kitchen, which had been introduced for practical cooking work. It was given a new playground area, which had room for nearly 700 scholars, 'where the girls may frolic'.

The general view was that if Elgin Street was a success, which was expected, then establishments of similar character could be set up in the north, east and west of the city. There was little opposition to this, although Councillor William Brown held that creating a school in the south and neglecting districts like Camlachie and Bridgeton with their great poverty was unreasonable.

Both Crown Street and Elgin Street had a general inspection on 4 August 1876, and this was followed with a meal for between two and three hundred guests.

The first Prospectus advertising the opening of the Girls' School on 7 August 1876 laid down the aims of the School. It would make provision for the Higher Education of girls over and above elementary instruction. 'Special care will therefore be given to train them in all womanly accomplishments, and to impart to them a high degree of mental culture and refinement.'

The curriculum included 'Arithmetic, Book-Keeping, Telegraphy, Sewing and Cutting-out, Household Economy and Cookery, so as to give girls such an industrial training as will qualify them fitly to discharge their duties in domestic life or, if need be, to occupy positions of usefulness and profit, in the Post Office and Telegraph service, and in other establishments where female labour is in remunerative demand'.

'Foundationers' were introduced on the same basis as boys, and arrangements made to introduce sixteen bursaries for girls who had completed their course in the Primary department of Elgin Street.[21]

Fees were now to be paid quarterly in advance, a move away from the annual Parents' Evening in the Hospital School, when parents received their allowance and free uniform.

The buildings of Hutchesons' Grammar School and Hutchesons' Girls' School were opened and were an immediate success.

THE BALFOUR COMMISSION

By early 1883 there existed in some quarters the view that the Patrons of Hutchesons' Hospital had departed from the spirit of their Founders' intentions, and that educational assistance should be given to the class intended to benefit from them. This was strongly denied by Rev. Dr Robertson, who saw the School Board as responsible for primary education while secondary education should be provided for boys and girls of promise. It was not intended to give higher education to all. This was the basis of the Draft Scheme put forward by the Hospital in 1883 and defended by Preceptor Mathieson, Rev. Dr Robertson and Principal Douglas, before the Balfour Commission.[22]

Mathieson explained to the Commissioners that George Hutcheson's Bequest was charitable – two-thirds of the total – while Thomas Hutcheson's Bequest was partly charitable and partly educational, the latter being one-third of the total. The Commissioners suggested that Thomas had left more than one-third for education and this should have been followed.

The Commissioners disputed the need for 14 representatives from the Town Council (and only one from School Board) from a total of 23 on the Governing Body. There were concerns expressed by certain Commissioners about a Trust left for the children of poor parents and the problems they would face when their children would have to compete with those whose parents were of significant means. However, Robertson claimed that there was no way of restricting bursaries or competition without branding the scholar with the stamp of poverty. He held that if you restrict competition you do away with the honour attached to the bursary. When it was suggested that under the scheme operating many bursaries/scholarships were held by children for whom the Foundation was never intended, Robertson responded that 90% of parental fee-payers earned no more than

£150 to £200 per annum: for him the Schools were only middle-class to a limited degree.

The School Board's case was that the Hutchesons' brothers sole intention was to benefit the poor, and the word 'burgess' was only to be found once in all the deeds. All educational matters should be with the School Board, and the Patrons had no locus in such matters as establishing Higher Class schools. Professor Ramsay believed that the Founders wanted to give support to the children of 'decayed' master tradesmen. He believed that too much was being given to charity (pensions): given that the brothers had left 25,000 merks for education and 35,000 merks for charity, these sums should be divided annually more in the ratio of 5 to 7 instead of 4 to 8.

The Commissioners published their decisions in January 1884, and produced their Scheme on 5 March 1885. They separated the management of pensions from that of education. Ownership of the Schools and their sites was vested in a new body, the Hutchesons' Educational Trust, which was able to spend not less than two-fifths of net annual revenues of the Hospital, Blair and Baxter mortifications.[23] This annoyed the Patrons, who still favoured pensions over education. The governing body of the Trust was to be composed of 21 Governors, eleven representing the Town Council, three the School Board, two the Church of Scotland, two the Patrons, and one each the University of Glasgow, the Merchants' House and Trades' House.

The Commissioners spelled out the curriculum of both Schools, which were similar. The boys were offered Book-keeping, Mensuration,[24] and Greek; while the girls took Music and Domestic Economy. Otherwise both had English, Latin, at least two foreign languages, Mathematics, Drawing, at least one branch of Natural Science and Drill.

Both Schools would have Primary and Secondary Departments; Secondary would not begin until scholars were eleven years of age and there would be examinations for entry. The annual fees would be not less than £1 10s and £2, which were markedly lower than the High School's.

The Heads were to be graduates of a UK university and had control over the choice of text-books; methods of learning; arrangements of classes; school hours; and generally the organisation, discipline and arrangements of the Schools. They could suspend and expel pupils. They were in charge of hiring and firing assistants. Their salary was to be at least £500 per annum.

The Schools would have regular inspections from the Scottish Education Department. The Schools would each have a Foundation of 200 pupils. They would be from families of persons who had been engaged in business/ trade in Glasgow for some time or involved in promoting the prosperity of the city. The children would be orphans needful and deserving of assistance, or children of parents needful and deserving assistance and not in receipt of parochial aid. They had to pass an entry examination, and if there are too many candidates, they would be chosen by examination, conduct, attendance and progress. The Foundationers were to have their books and stationery free in Primary for four years.

The Schools would have not less than a hundred free scholarships to be awarded by competitive examination, and whose education took place in Hutchesons' schools or any public or state-aided school in Glasgow. Free scholars should attend the Secondary Department of Hutchesons', receiving free education for four years (with books and stationery). Not less than one-third of free scholarships were to be awarded among foundations, or those who possessed the qualification prescribed for Foundationers.

The Governors had to apply £400 per annum to establish bursaries, of value £5 to £10 per annum money payment, and free education and stationery. Not less than one-third of bursaries were to be awarded among Foundations, or who those who possessed the qualification prescribed for Foundationers.

The bursary system now introduced was very similar to that based on the Heriot's funds in Edinburgh. The Hutcheson Schools immediately attracted large numbers, though this early success was not maintained and the numbers were to fall drastically in the 1890s. Why? One reason was that the School's situation in the slums of the Gorbals deterred middle-class patronage, while another was competition from Higher Grade schools. Hillhead HS opened in 1885 in an area already crowded with secondary schools and charged high fees (£6 per annum); Glasgow Academy had moved there from the city centre, and charged £19 per annum; Kelvinside Academy opened in 1878 (£24 per annum), while Garnethill soon acquired a reputation for university successes and in 1894 it was converted into a High School for girls (with fees of £4 per annum).

The real secret of success for endowed schools was to combine moderate fees with social cachet and a reputation for high academic quality. The Merchant Company schools in Edinburgh and Hillhead HS in Glasgow pulled this off, but Hutchesons' was less successful in finding the right formula. However, Hutchesons' did play its part in making secondary education available to the lower ranges of the middle-class.

FIVE Recollections of the Hospital School

John Buchanan Monteith: *Reminiscences of My Schooldays in Hutchesons'*
School in Ingram Street from 26 April 1837 to 26 April 1841 Inclusive
(**written in 1901**).

'In the year 1837 – I was then eight years old – my father got me into
Hutchesons' School, he being a Burgess of the City, where I received my
education. The School was next to the Hospital in Ingram Street, Mr John
McArly our respected teacher. His house was above the School. The School
was a very large hall: the back half was narrow, the front wide. Mr George
McMillan[1] had the narrow half for his classes and Mr McArly had the front
for the advanced classes. There were three long windows at the front facing
Ingram Street. Underneath the School was a bootmaker's shop – the name
of Paterson; next to the School was the carriers' quarters where the Drymen
and Balfron Mail Coach started.

'The games we used to play most in the middle of the day were the
Rounders – we took Brunswick Street for it, being the widest; Prison Base,[2]
we took Hutcheson Street for it, and Smugglers, we used both streets. We
ran through the closes, jumping over the railings to get into our den before
the geg[3] would be taken from us. We had some battles with the Wilson
School and the Highland Society School, which generally ended with us
getting a good belting from Mr McArly as we were always among the first
to start the fight.

'The education we received was Grammar, Geography, Bible, History,
Collection-Counting and Writing. We had our singing days on Tuesdays
and Fridays. We got the best of education in these days. Mr McMillan was a
very severe master – he was not afraid to use the tawse. Mr (John) Chalmers
was our singing master. We had to go to the School on Saturdays as well as
on the other days, but we got away at one o'clock, and we had to go to the
School on the Sabbath Day at ten o'clock. When the Church bells began

to ring we got into our ranks and marched to the Old College Church off High Street. We walked in on each side of the pulpit into the long communion table seats, forenoon and afternoon. Dr Gibson was Minister of the Church then. In the middle of the day we went back to the School. On the way back we bought our biscuits from Mrs Hastie in Cannon Street at the corner of South Albion Street and ate them in the School.

'The Church was a very old-fashioned building. As you went in at the front door you had the Bellman standing inside the door ringing the old Bell. The pews we sat in were the two communion tables. They were very long and as they did not face the Minister we had to turn round to look at him. There were four monitors – two on each table – to watch to see if any of us were looking up during the prayer. Any who did look up were reported on Monday and were punished. We had all to be dressed in our uniform: a blue worsted bonnet with red and white checked tartan all round and red touries.[4] Our clothes were blue cloth jackets with brass buttons, corduroy trousers and vest buttoned together.[5]

'The clothes we received in the month of April were the full suit mentioned above. In addition to them we got one pair of shoes, two white shirts, two pair of stockings, two handkerchiefs, and a cravat. In October we received two white shirts, two pair of stockings, and one pair of shoes. We got our shoes mended every six months. Our shoes were all hand-made then. The half-yearly money we received was paid in April and October, thirty shillings each time. Our parents went with us to the Hospital to receive it. Mr McArly was present and the Preceptor as well. McArly had to report what sort of boys we were. We got always a good word from him in presence of the Preceptor. Most of the parents were all old scholars themselves.

'On the twenty-sixth day of April, that was our annual parade day,[6] we met in the School and got in front of the Hospital three abreast and marched with the other schools to the Church. Dr Paterson was Minister of the Church then. The procession was headed by the city officers with their halberds[7] over their shoulders, with their black satin hats, their red coats, their knee breeches, their black stockings and shoes with buckles on them. Behind them were the Lord Provost, Magistrates, Town Councillors, the Patrons of the Hospital, city clergy, and other gentlemen. Then came the different schools. The Wilson School – their uniforms were blue cloth swallow-tailed coats with flaps at the side pockets and big brass buttons at the sides and the back, corduroy trousers and vest, and blue bonnets.[8] Then Hutcheson (sic) School, Highland Society School, Trades School, and Miller's School, that was the girls' School.

'We walked to St Andrew's Church.[9] There were great crowds all along the streets looking at us as we were marching, a large number of police on both sides of the procession keeping the streets clear. Fathers, mothers, sisters and brothers all eager to see us, some of the mothers crying to their sons, "Ha, Johnnie, put your bonnet on right. It's a' tae the yea side like Gourock. Pit it on right and no' ha'e it that way".

'When we came out of the church we marched back to the Hospital. Each school went their own way. Our School always got their own dinner in the Hospital. The one who got the Medal[10] got seated into a big chair in front of the centre window facing Hutcheson Street, covered with green branches with oranges all round. He was elevated above the others. Our dinner was plum pudding, tarts, toddy, beer, and fruit. The songs we sang in the School we sang at the dinner. There was a balcony right along the north side of the Hospital where the ladies and gentlemen looked at us getting our dinner.

'In my second year the scholars were invited to go to Tollcross Estate and see the grounds there.[11] We got plenty of milk and buns. We rolled about on the grass and we all enjoyed ourselves well and got home in good time. Our next summer outing was in 1839 when we all went out to see the Old Botanic Gardens at the end of Sauchiehall Street. At that time Sauchiehall Street was considered as the street beyond Cambridge Street. All the way further out was a narrow strip of a road to the old gardens. It was just the country. There was an old farm on the left-hand side going west, and a fine old pump well up at the side of the farm, and an old broken down wall which ran along the road to where the Old Botanic Gardens were. Fitzroy Place occupies a part of the old gardens now.

'Any special day such as the laying of the foundation stone of the new School in Crown Street we walked in procession to Hutchesontown Parish Church in Hospital Street. After the service was over we walked in procession to see the foundation stone laid. That was in 1839. After the stone was laid we marched back to the Hospital and got our toddy and buns.

'The next special day we had was that of the Queen getting married to Prince Albert.[12] It was on a Friday, our Geography day. This day he (sic) had off his coat and started with the Geography. It was the first lesson he took and it was a big class. That morning he forgot to call the roll until an hour or so was past. I happened to be late that morning and one of the scholars was standing at the back of the door. He said to me, "can you say your Geography?" I said, "Not very well", so he said "Take my advice and don't go in or you're sure to catch it". I took his advice and I was not sorry for it. I saved myself a good thrashing. I took off my bonnet, threw it over my back and took out my Geography. I stood opposite Archie Livingstone and was learning my Geography when they were sent into the lobby. It was quite full in a short time. He commenced to call the roll. When our names were called, we just put our mouths to the keyhole and cried, "Here, Sir!" Just as he was done calling the roll in came Mr Chalmers to give us our singing. When the door was opened it was a rush to get to our seats. Our singing books were long, and one book served three. We had just sung a tune or two when in comes the Preceptor and says, "You will all be wondering at seeing me here today. You will all know that the Queen is getting married today, and I have come to join with you and drink Her Majesty's health and Prince Albert's. It gives me great pleasure to come and see you all so attentive to your lessons." There were a number of men who came in with baskets full of bottled toddy and rounds of buns. The toddy was served round in glasses on large trays with the glasses full to the brim, and we all drank the Queen and Prince Albert's health, long life and prosperity to them. After we drunk their health, the Preceptor joined with us in singing the Queen's Anthem and then he said to us we were not to come back till Monday. We had more than one glass of toddy before we left the School. That was in the year 1840.[13]

'The last special day I saw at the School was at the opening of the new School on the twenty-sixth day of April 1841. It was our Annual Parade and it was an extra day. There were the Lord Provost, Magistrates, Town Councillors, Ministers, and the Patrons of the Hospital, and many others all walked over from St Andrew's Church to the new school in Crown Street. The scholars were behind them. When we got into the new school we were told to go upstairs and see the grand dinner there. There were wines, grapes, and everything of the best, all laid out in the best of order on a very large oval table seated round with chairs. That was in the Hall above the School. We thought we had nothing else to do but to draw in our chairs and sit down and partake of the good things before us, and we gave their dinner every manner of justice. When Mr Chalmers came up to see what we were doing when we were all so quiet he took his walking stick and cane across our backs, when the noise got up. When the whole of the company came up to see what was wrong, to their dismay they just looked and saw what a fine table we left them. All they said was: "We might have known better. We have ourselves to blame." They seemed to have been quite content with our leavings. We were told to go downstairs and get our own dinner in the School – ours were never touched by them. That ended my four years in Hutchesons' School on the twenty-sixth day of April 1841.

'Little did I think that I would have lived till the age of seventy-three and receive from the Patrons of the Hospital a pension which they so generously give to old burgesses of the city. It is a blessing bestowed on me that I am recipient from that great fountain Head. My father, grandfather, and great-grandfather were all burgesses and received their education in Hutchesons' School.'

''TIS SIXTY YEARS SINCE'
An article in the School Magazine by An Old Boy (Dr Hutchison)

Part I

'This somewhat ambitious title will be recognised as the sub-title of the first of Sir Walter Scott's famous novels – *Waverley: or 'Tis Sixty Years Since*. It is chosen here as being exactly descriptive of the length of time that had elapsed since the writer closed his course at the School, and, as Dux for the year, occupied a conspicuous place in the annual ceremonial with which was connected the prize distribution of the year. That ceremonial has long been discontinued, and it may interest the boys of the Grammar School to know what a prize distribution was like sixty years ago. Even at that time, no doubt, the scholars enjoyed their summer holiday as much as do their successors in these days. It is not on record, so far as I know, how the length of the vacation was determined; but as a matter of fact, during the five years of my attendance at the School it was rigidly observed and extended to forty-five days (or six weeks and three days, as we always described it), from the middle of June till the first Tuesday of August. But this break-up of the School had no connection with the ending of the School session or with the awarding of prizes, nor had the opening on the first Tuesday of August anything to do with the opening of a new session. School terms, or terminal examinations, or House reports, or Leaving Certificates, were all unknown in those days, and the summer vacation was merely a break in the long and steady round of the twelve months' work.

'The great ceremonial of the School year in my time was observed on the 26th of April. The late Dr Hill, in his excellent *History of Hutchesons' Hospital*, in which a special chapter is devoted to the School, shows that the Patrons attached some importance to that date. It was deliberately chosen, for example, for the formal opening of the present School building in Crown Street, in 1841, "as being the day of the annual procession of the scholars". But not a word is said about the points from which and to which the procession marched each year, or how the procession originated, or what it was all about. Meanwhile the date may be noted – the 26th of April. Its importance may further be gathered from the fact that it marked the close of the School year, and the following day marked the beginning of a new one. About thirty boys each year bade farewell to the School on the 26th of April, after five years attendance, and thirty new boys (or thereabout) began a five years' course on the following day. We must go elsewhere than to Dr Hill's monumental work for the meaning and importance of the date 26th April.

'In former times, long before the days of School Boards or compulsory education, or even before the efforts of Rev. Dr Chalmers[14] to make education as nearly universal as possible through Kirk sessions, some merchants of Glasgow, upon whom fortune had smiled, left considerable sums of money for educating boys. Among these was Mr George Wilson, a native of Glasgow, and merchant in London, who in the year 1778 bequeathed to the city a foundation of this sort. As a result Wilson's School was founded, largely on the lines of that of the brothers Hutcheson. It was situated on the west side of Montrose Street, near to the Rottenrow, and in close proximity to another valuable educational foundation – the Highland Society's School. Both of these foundations disappeared as schools in the reorganisation of the educational endowments of the city that took place over thirty years ago. In his trust deed Mr George Wilson desired that the Governor and boys on his foundation should attend Divine Service one day in the year, and out of respect for his memory the Magistrates resolved that the procession of children educated in such foundations as those mentioned should take place on the 26th of April yearly, the anniversary of Mr Wilson's death. When that day should fall on a Saturday or Sunday the procession was to take place on the following Monday. "The procession," says Dr Cleland, a highly intelligent citizen of former days, who filled many public offices and has left behind him some very valuable records of city life: "The procession usually moves off from Hutchesons' Hospital to St Andrew's Church, at half-past ten o'clock. The Magistrates appear in full dress, preceded by their officers; the ministers in their gowns and bands, preceded by their beadles; the Governors of the various charities in black; the teachers in their gowns; the children, about six hundred in number, in their new dresses, decked out with evergreens and spring posies. After Divine Service, the scholars move off to their respective halls, where dinner of roast beef and plum pudding is provided for the children, and a cordial glass to drink to the memory of their beneficent founders. This very imposing spectacle excites great interest; the streets are crowded with persons of every rank, to witness a sight than which there is none more calculated to inspire the mind with gratitude to God."

'Hutchesons' School, with probably 150 boys, took the lead in the procession as being the most important educational foundation, and the others followed. The pupils met at the School at the usual hour in the morning. The prizes, as noted below, were distributed by 10 o'clock, when the boys were marshalled in lines of three each, the medal boy for the year at the head, wearing his medal, and supported on the right and left by the boys who came nearest to him in the competition for the medal. It was undoubtedly a proud day for the medal boy, who perhaps never forgot the 26th of April to the end of his days. The boys marched from the School to Hutchesons' Hospital in Ingram Street, where the other schools assembled to the number of six hundred, as Dr Cleland says, and marched to St Andrew's Church. Sixty years ago, Dr Runciman was Minister of the Church, and the preacher for the day. The sermon and even the text I have forgotten, but I have no doubt they were suited to the occasion. Some changes had been made in the ceremonial between the days recorded by Dr Cleland – Dr Cleland died in 1840, and his notes describe what was customary before 1825 – and the end of my attendance at the school in 1855. In my time the Patrons still retained the custom of clothing the scholars in a special dress, as is the practice of the Bluecoat School in London to this day. The school dress consisted of grey trousers and waistcoat and (unless my memory here fails me) a blue (Eton) jacket, with brass buttons, and a Kilmarnock bonnet. I have the impression that the Kilmarnock bonnet about the end of my time was giving away to the Glengarry cap. A new suit of these was provided yearly, in time for the annual procession or, as it was popularly known, "the parade". The "roast beef and plum pudding" had in my time given way to a pie, a tart, and an orange; and the "cordial glass", whatever may have been its ingredients in earlier times, had in my time descended to a quite innocuous tumbler of table beer. All was in keeping with the festive occasion. The walls of the larger of the two schoolrooms were decked with evergreens, and spotless linen covered the tables. A special seat of honour was prepared for the Dux of the year. The boys were seated at the tables on ordinary School forms, but the medal boy had a chair conspicuously placed, and decorated with abundance of flowers, and, according to a practice as old as the Pharaohs, he was favoured with a double portion of the mess.

'The prize distribution had taken place at the very beginning of the day, and it would perhaps be held to be on a modest scale compared with that of more recent times. But Mr McArly, the teacher of the time, who always held an honoured place in the memories of those whom he trained for the long period of thirty-two years, had a keen eye for what boys would read, and he made an excellent selection of prize books. I am still the possessor of some of these. If space allowed, I am sure the mention of all the titles and authorship of the books would make you wish to read some of them, even to-day. Everyone who was that day leaving the School was presented with a Bible. The Dux boy got his in two halves, handsomely bound in morocco. I possess only one of my halves to-day. The other was lost many years ago at a Sunday evening service. The Preceptor, of course, presided at all the ceremonies of the day. I remember well the kindly and genial appearances of Bailie – afterwards Preceptor – David Mackinlay on these and similar occasions. He held the office continuously for sixteen years – surely a strong proof of the high respect in which the citizens held him.

Part II

'At the close of that record of the fleeting glory that fell to the medal-winner on the 26th of April each year, reference was made to a more permanent and substantial part of the annual prize. This consisted of a four years' course at the High School, where the medal-winner received free education and books, and a small but very useful maintenance bursary. It has to be remembered that sixty years ago Hutchesons' School had a very limited curriculum compared with that indicated by its present curriculum. The teaching accommodation consisted of two large class-rooms, each capable of containing about one hundred boys, and the teaching staff consisted of two members – a head- and an under-master. There was obviously not much scope for teaching more than the three Rs – and the fourth R, religion, was by no means neglected – though Mr McArly, the principal master, frequently shortened his dinner-hour by fifteen or twenty minutes to give a few selected boys some drill in the Latin declensions and conjugations. Practically, however, the medal in Hutchesons' School sixty years ago was gained by a boy of twelve or thirteen years of age, and mainly for excelling in what in these more advanced days would be called the Qualifying Examination or the work of the junior school.

'It may be interesting to recall what a four years' course even at the High School meant sixty years ago. At that time Hutchesons' School and the High School were both administered by the same Governors, who were the Town Council, assisted, in the case of Hutchesons', by the ministers of the city parishes, one of whom at the time was also Principal of the University . . .'[15]

'The High School of the time was a modest and quite unpretentious building of two storeys, situated between John Street and Montrose Street . . . The main entrance was from the former, and led along a narrow passage, north of St. Paul's Church, to a playground – considering the time – of quite reasonable dimensions. The situation and surroundings of the School were far from attractive . . . [It was only in 1878 that the High School moved to Elmbank Street.]

'It now consisted of five large class-rooms, each capable of containing about a hundred boys, whilst a sixth room of about the same dimensions was divided for the classes of French and Drawing respectively. Still, it was a great step forward for an old Hutchesonian to find himself in a School among the sons of the foremost citizens, and a School in which there were two – albeit co-ordinate and quite independent – masters for Classics, a master for English, a master for Arithmetic, Geography, and Mathematics, a master for Writing and Book-keeping, a master for French, and a master for Drawing and Painting. A curious point was that among these masters there was no sort of co-operation except that they appointed one of their number as chairman in quarterly rotation to arrange any corporate business that might arise. There was no Headmaster or Rector, and there was no curriculum of study. Each boy or his parent might choose what subject was to be studied and what might be left alone. It was like dining a la carte in a restaurant . . . The whole arrangements were conducive to overcrowded classes, insufficient staffing, and entirely capricious and lopsided training for the boys. Here, for example, is the course through which I was put – on whose advice I know not:

First Year: Latin, two hours a day; Writing, Arithmetic & Geography – each one hour a day.

Second Year: Latin, three consecutive hours a day (one of them for Roman history); Writing, Arithmetic & Geography (with Astronomy), one hour a day each.

Third Year: Latin, two hours a day; Greek (one hour); Writing, Arithmetic, & French, each one hour.

Fourth Year: Latin, two hours a day; Greek (one hour); Arithmetic, French, Writing (half the year), Book-keeping (half the year) one hour each.

'I had no English, no Mathematics, no Drawing. Why, I know not, though it is not difficult now to see that it was somehow connected with the want of unity in the School, the want of a time-table, and the want of sufficient staff; perhaps also from a want of due oversight on the part of the Governors. Science as taught in the schools nowadays was then unknown, though Dr Bryce in his Geography classes gave some simple lessons on Geology and Physics, and by arrangement with Professor Nichol took us out on clear frosty nights to scan the heavens through the big telescope at the Observatory. In the senior English class, too, I have been told, Mr Bell gave elementary lessons on Physiology and Logic.[16]

'There was, further, a total lack of anything like corporate life in the School. There was abundance of activity in the ten minute intervals that were given each hour between classes, when the class-rooms were emptied, and the playground was covered with boys. Prisoners' base, cross tig, hokey-pokey, port-the-helm, were easily extemporised for short intervals but anything like School (much less inter-School) football, cricket, athletic sports, or anything that required some organisation was quite unknown in the High School, as it probably was at the time referred to, and for long after, unknown in any burgh school in Scotland. Dr Arnold's fruitful ideas in the importance of the varied phases of school life had not yet permeated School authorities and much less general society in Scotland.

'Still allowing for all drawbacks, as they appear to people who have lived through one or two generations of intense educational activity, the citizens of Glasgow were well satisfied with their principal School. In my time the school was crowded with boys, and those whose aim was to make progress in their work had excellent teachers. Any boy, for example, who wanted to learn French, by doing diligently the course of two years – one hour a day – could, under M. de Wolski, acquire a knowledge of French that would stand him in good stead all the days of his life. It was the same with Latin and Greek and the other subjects for which I was enrolled. It is, further, only fair to the Town Council to say that about the end of my time at the School doubts were beginning to arise as to the wisdom of some of the arrangements that had been made in 1834, and serious – but strongly opposed – efforts were put forth to unify the school, and to bring it up to the growing requirements of the time. These were eventually successful, and were entirely on the lines followed after 1872 by the new Governors of the School and their successors.

'"Hutchesons", too, has undergone great transformation since I entered it in 1850. By skilful management it is now recognised as one of the most important of the Higher Schools of the city. The advantages of its higher courses are not confined to one boy each year, but are open to all boys who care to make use of them.

"O fortunatos nimium, sua si bona norint"!'

John Hodge: *Workman's Cottage to Windsor Castle* (London c.1931), p. 7.

'As a matter of course I was sent to school, and the school chosen was the Gorbals Youths' School. I had not been very long in this school when it was closed down, because the Glasgow and South-Western Railway Company were anxious to have their own station in the heart of the city, and as a consequence of their scheme they went through our school. Arrangements had been made for building a temporary school, but as some delay occurred, the scholars were all sent for a short time (in 1866–67) to the Hutcheson Grammar School (sic). During this period of my schooling, the one thing which sticks in my memory is the lessons in elocution which we boys received. The teacher, whose name I cannot recall,[17] whether reading poetry or prose to us, made the words live. That tuition caused me to go in for reciting. This I assiduously practised. A few years later Penny Reading Entertainments[18] became the rage all over the country and my fame as a reciter got me many invitations, and I very soon drifted into singing comic and sentimental songs. Looking back, I oft-times wonder if the organisers of these functions had had to pay me, how many engagements would I have received?'

Charles W. Thomson: *Scottish School Humour* (Glasgow 1936), pp. 20–32. Charles Thomson was a pupil at HBGS from 1882 until 1888. He looked back on his time there half a century later.

Recollections of Pupilhood
'At the age of ten I was transferred to Hutchesons' Grammar School in Crown Street, Glasgow, and proudly bore for the next six years the designation of "Hutchie Bug" . . .

'A grand training-ground in general was Hutchesons' School, though it was rather sneered at by some of the "better class" students at the University as a School attended by the sort of fellows who did well because they knew they had to earn their living! It is a charge one can admit without a blush.

'Iron discipline reigned supreme, and the work was hard, but from Rector Menzies down there were men to inspire one for life with earnestness of purpose and with the habit of work that makes work a pleasure. Cameron, McInnes, Pringle, Mair, Caddell, Philp. Who could pass through the hands of such a succession without being fashioned as by the potter? Though the curriculum was severely Classical, we carried with us from the School not only a sound training in the University subjects, but a good knowledge of French, and a fair beginning with German, Dynamics,[19] elementary Chemistry and Book-keeping, which doubtless partly determined my whole subsequent bent towards modernism in education. As in most schools of the period, however, practical work was almost entirely neglected. Even in Mathematics we passed through Euclid[20] up to Books VI, XI, and XII, with the addition of Casey's *Sequel to Euclid*,[21] and Todhunter's *Trigonometry*,[22] without using a pair of compasses! Our circles were either drawn freehand or helped out by using the copper coins of the realm. The chief Mathematical teacher was very thorough, but there was not much "lift" in his manner . . .

'In our later years at School we owed most to a little "stickit minister"[23] named James Caddell, who was our Classical master. He had no degree, being useless at Mathematics, and he was paid a paltry salary in consequence. But he knew his Classics, and could pound them into one.

'The teachers were mostly men of good temper and cheerful nature, and there was not much play for that sort of humour which consists in "taking the teacher down" . . .

'"Froggie" – the French master – so earned my disapproval in general that I wrote a "poetical" lampoon about him. By design or accident a fellow-pupil allowed this to fall into the hands of our Science Master, Mr. Mair, and I lived for a fortnight in apprehension of the expulsion which would probably have followed had he passed it on to the Rector. But Mair proved to be a "sport", and nothing happened. Soon afterwards "Froggie" got into trouble with the law, and disappeared from the city.

'Of the other foreigners – Schroeder and Sonntag, the latter of whom succeeded "Froggie" – I have none but the pleasantest of memories. The former was one of the kindliest of teachers, and the wonder is that we never tried to impose upon him. He very seldom resorted to punishment, and when he did, he would expatiate on the disgrace to himself and to the culprit involved in such a breach of the harmony of things. Then he would let the strap fall on the boy's hand as softly as if it were meant for a caress. With almost any other teacher we should have laughed, but we understood Schroeder and loved him. He was a true German "of the antique mould".

'Sonntag was more lively, and more of a "slasher". He bore on his right temple the mark of a wound, whether got in a students' duel, or while hunting Swiss bears, we never knew. When he got angry the colour of the wound deepened, and his finger went up to it as if to say "Now, beware! Don't rouse the soldier in me!" But a grand little Switzer he was, and the Hutchie boys esteemed him as he deserved. When he went to Edinburgh his old pupils were indignant to learn that the boys there treated him badly, and probably hastened his early and lamented end.

'More than a passing reference is merited by our Singing Master, James Robson. We called him "old Robson" . . . but there was no suggestion in that "old" that we wanted a younger man.[24] . . . When he got the whole School gathered in the big Hall of an afternoon, and made the rafters ring with some stirring chorus, there were sounds awakened which re-echo to this day in many a heart. I well remember the morning of 5th February 1885, when he announced to us, in a voice quivering with emotion, the news that had just arrived of Gordon's death and of the fall of Khartoum.[25] We boys had much to be thankful for in learning our music from a man of feeling and a Scot . . . He taught on till 1906, when, at the age of 96, he informed the Governors that he was feeling the need for a rest, and retired to Roseneath . . .

'And then "the Drilly!" John Muirhead was an old Crimean veteran . . . The drill was largely "military", and was carried out with the help of carbines dating from Crimean days[26] . . . In the upper classes we proceeded to fencing with the single-stick, and the more skilful pupils were even entrusted with foils . . .

'In the case of the Rector himself, the brusque manner and commanding voice concealed a great amount of genuine kindness, and his nickname "The Bear" probably arose more from his shaggy appearance and rugged personality than from any condemnatory suggestion. With a self-sacrifice which we did not fully appreciate at the time, he used to take the highest Latin and Greek class for two hours on Saturdays. He was as particular about punctuality then as on a week-day . . .

'Nothing gave the Rector greater pleasure than to learn of the success of his boys at the University or in the varied walks of life, and to have the privilege of looking through his carefully preserved newspaper cuttings regarding old pupils was to have some idea of the glorious record of the Crown Street School . . .'

S I X   A Hospital School Timeline
1639–1885

COVENANTING TIMES 1639–51

National events were part of the back-drop of Hospital School history when it was founded. People in Glasgow were generally strong supporters of the Covenanting Movement.[1] George Porterfield was the leading figure in national Covenanting politics in Glasgow during the 1640s, while Thomas Hutcheson was a leading subscriber to the forces raised by Glasgow for the first Covenanting army. The Royalists fought back, and after their victory at Kilsyth in April 1645 the troops of the Marquis of Montrose plundered Glasgow and forced its surrender. However, Montrose was defeated at Philiphaugh, and Glasgow's Town Council was dismissed by the Covenanting leadership. Porterfield became Provost and Member of Parliament, 1645–51.

The Covenanting government in Scotland disapproved of the execution of Charles I in 1649 and proclaimed his son king, as Charles II of Scotland. Conflict with Oliver Cromwell and the English Parliamentarians followed. Cromwell came to Glasgow in October 1650 after his victory at the battle of Dunbar. He stayed in the Saltmarket at the home of Colin Campbell, a merchant and politician as well as being the Preceptor of the Hospital[2] from 1641 to 1647, and again in 1652–54 and 1664–65.

1639. George Hutcheson (c.1560–1639) in his Will provided for a Glasgow Hospital (home for the aged and infirm) and a 'Draft Contract' for founding a School.

1641. The building of Hutchesons' Hospital began, with additional funding for the School from Thomas Hutcheson (c.1590–1641), which was to provide for twelve 'indigent orphanes'. Thomas chose Colin Campbell, younger, a former bailie of Glasgow, to be Master and Collector and to take charge of the building.

1642. After the death of Thomas, Campbell was re-elected 'Maister' and continued in office until 1647.

1643. Archibald Edmiston, a burgess son of the burgh of Glasgow, who was both fatherless and motherless, became the first Hutchesons' pupil.

1643. Besides the amount already expended on the Hospital building, the institution then possessed £39,300 Scots, the interest on which of 6% brought in annual revenue of £2,358 Scots. However, further outlays in the erection of the Hospital buildings, amounting to £16,777 6s 8d diminished the capital to £22,522 13s 4d. This figure was essentially corroborated by an Inventory of Bonds belonging to the Hospital, recorded in the Patrons' Minutes of 1 January 1653 – when the Hospital building had been completed – and which gives the capital invested in bonds at £22,096 6s 8d.[3]

1647. The Hospital premises began to be let out commercially.

1648. Until this date pupils were funded and sent to a local 'Inglis' school.[4] Schooling began in the unfinished Hospital building in the Trongate with John McLay appointed as the first schoolmaster. Hutchesons' School began with the most up-to-date textbooks, the new *Shorter Catechism*,[5] which children were expected to learn by heart, and the New Psalm Book.

1649. An unprecedented amount of admission activity occurred and the School's roll reached the target of twelve boys. However, within the year only one remained.

1650. After the death of the Hutcheson brothers the Hospital Patrons began acquiring land to the north. The funds of the Hospital were also used to help buy land in the Gorbals for the Town and this led the Hospital into retrenchment.

1650. The building work on the Trongate Hospital was abandoned and the last Account paid. The building was never to be completed.

1652. Boarding ended for pupils in the Hospital wing where the school-room was located. The School was down to five pupils and closed, but private teaching continued in the building until the Town Council appointed another teacher in 1655.

1661. Boys were admitted again under the Hutchesons' Foundation. The Hospital Patrons were now distinct from the Town Council and were composed of twenty four individuals (twenty-one bailies and councillors and three Glasgow ministers).

1661. The Hospital building was being used for all kinds of storage.

1664. The title Preceptor was used for the first time (instead of Maister) and he took on the role of admonishing or, by precept, exhorting the boys. Although a position of honour and dignity, the post was by no means a sinecure and at first the Preceptorship was to be held for only one year.

1667. The full complement of twelve boys was enrolled under schoolmaster Robert Forrest. (Until 1712 the number of boys and old men provided for continued about twelve.)

1668. The Accounts show revenue of £2,709 15s 10d Scots and expenditure for pensions, Hospital repairs, salaries of Officers and charges connected with Gorbals of £2,111 11s Scots, leaving a surplus revenue of £598 4s 10d Scots, or £49 17s 1d sterling.

1690. The Town Council appointed bailie James Peadie and Peter Corbet to inspect the old men and the young men to see if the former were burgesses and the latter were burgesses' sons.

1690. School-master Robert Forrest was suspended from his office 'for some speeches spoken by him against the government'.

1694. The lands of Ramshorn and Meadowflat were bought by Hospital funds for the Town and by 1700 they had added £1,070 16s 8d Scots to revenue. Total revenue then was £7,695 4s 5d Scots and surplus over expenditure was £5,613 9s 11d Scots.

1700. James Sloss, a former bailie of Gorbals, took over the office of Preceptorship for nine years, giving up in 1710 from ill-health.

1715. The numbers had increased to sixteen boys and fifteen old men.

1718. The Patrons determined that any boy applying to enter the Grammar School had to be tested for English proficiency.

1721. All boys entering the School had to produce their father's burgess ticket before being allowed to enrol.[6]

1729. Preceptor Robert Alexander, merchant, having given good management since 1713, was rewarded for his service.

1737. From the mode in which the Accounts were kept prior to 1737, it was extremely difficult to give any regular or correct statement of the annual revenue and expenditure, or even a progressive view of its Stock. In these early accounts which, however, were most methodically engrossed in the Minute books, the Preceptor charged himself, but not always in any systematic arrangement or order, with the principal sums contained in the Bonds due to the Hospital, interest and rents, as well as outstanding arrears, frequently without distinguishing them from one another, or stating the years to which the arrears were applicable.

Moreover, previous to 1736 no valuation of the Heritable Properties and Stock was either made or recorded in the Preceptor's accounts, or in the Minutes of the Patrons. From 1736 a new system of accounts was begun and in September of that year the Stock of the Hospital was shown as £77,746 16s 5d Scots.[7] The accounts have fourteen old men receiving pensions; with fourteen boys at Hutchesons' and four boys being awarded apprenticeship fees; and three old men and four boys on Blair's Mortification.

1737. Widows and daughters of such persons as would have been eligible as pensioners were admitted to the benefits of the Hospital.

1740. Robert Buchanan, Writer, was elected to the new post of Hospital Factor for the Gorbals lands. He held this office until his death in 1758 when James Hill was elected his successor.

JACOBITES 1745–46

After James VII and II's deposition in England was confirmed in Edinburgh in 1689, those who continued to support the exiled Stuart king became known as 'Jacobites'. Most of these were Episcopalian or Roman Catholic and few were found in west central Scotland.

On 28 March 1708 the Principal and Professors of Glasgow University confirmed their maintenance of 51 men for 40 days to help defeat the threatened invasion by the French and Irish in support of 'James VIII'. This was confirmed in August 1715 when the threat arose again. George I was confident enough to reject the offer of help as unnecessary.

By 1745 Presbyterian support for the Stuarts had almost disappeared. During the rising of that year, the Whig, anti-Jacobite burgesses of Glasgow supplied only £5,000 in cash and £500 in kind in response to the Jacobite demand for £15,000 cess or land tax. Meanwhile the University Principal paid the wages of a pro-Hanoverian company of 50 soldiers.

From 26 December to 3 January 1746, upon its return from England, the army of Prince Charles spent a week in Glasgow, but gathered little support. However, Charles's review of his army on Glasgow Green showed that few had deserted during the march south. The Prince is reputed to have admired the city, but admitted that he had no friends there. Nonetheless he set up his headquarters in the Trongate in the Shawfield Mansion, one of the most splendid private residences in the city and home of the Glassford family.[8]

The Prince gave fine balls while exacting supplies of clothes and shoes, as well as monetary fines from Glasgow and Paisley to penalise them for their lack of support. Twelve thousand shirts, plus six thousand each of bonnets, waistcoats, shoes and stockings, were required of the city, These exactions did nothing to increase enthusiasm for the Jacobites. However, it could have been much worse, for Donald Cameron of Lochiel is credited with persuading the Prince not to sack the city.

The Prince and his army put on a good show for Glaswegians, including the 27 pensioners and 19 boys who nearby were enjoying their Founders' bounty at this time. Charles took particular care to dress with great elegance and to make sure the locals saw him and his army. However the most eagle-eyed would have spotted that when the Prince reviewed his troops, his men marched down one street and up another in order to appear a larger force than they actually were.[9]

On 17 January Glasgow militia fought alongside government forces at the battle of Falkirk, where they suffered heavy casualties in a Jacobite victory. However, at Culloden in April 1746, the Jacobites were finally defeated and Glasgow's Lord Provost, Andrew Cochrane of Brighouse (1693–1777), a wealthy tobacco merchant, went off to London to negotiate for compensation. This proved a difficult and prolonged process. It was not until 1749 that £10,000 was paid to the city from Treasury funds. Back home, Cochrane became a hero for rescuing Glasgow from insolvency and the esteem for him was such that Cotton Street, off George Square, was renamed Cochrane Street in 1787.

1776. Following his lengthy but successful tenure as Preceptor from 1736 until 1777, Andrew Cochrane had his portrait completed.

1779. A salaried Book-keeper was appointed for the Hospital.

1783. The curriculum for Hospital boys involved learning the principles of Religion, reading English, Writing, Arithmetic and Church Music.[10] This ensured the Hutchesonian was well-equipped for the world of employment.

1785. The Accounts valued Gorbals (at twenty years purchase) at £9,447 sterling and the total Stock value was £19,031 10s 8d sterling.

1786. The Patrons opened the School to twenty-four City foundationers, whose maintenance was paid. Such a move breached the Mortification.

An Education Committee was appointed 'to superintend and direct the education and management of the boys in the Hospital School'. It was irritated by the existence of so many different Mortifications which it was thought allowed unqualified boys to gain entrance.

1787. Classes were established in the Hospital School, with a proposed roll of 48, which included 32 on the Hutchesons' Foundation, four on Blair's and twelve on Scotstarvet Foundation. The 20 extra boys on the Hutcheson Foundation was made possible by ending the custom of giving boys one year's maintenance when they left School.[11]

1789. With increased numbers the Patrons believed that the £3 per annum given in lieu of maintenance was not enough without supplement from other sources. In effect such boarding out ensured that orphans were no longer admitted and entry would be restricted to boys with parents or grand-parents. This went against the Mortification and was deemed a necessary 'evil' by the Patrons.

1791. The Entrance Regulations were tightened up for educational reasons.

Thomas Hutcheson's requirement that an entrant should first be found capable of learning was revised. From this time on a certificate had to be produced proving attendance at an English school for six months. Moreover, the entrant had also to produce a certificate from a surgeon that he was 'free from any infectious distemper' and a certificate of age from his parish minister affirming that he was 'above seven . . . and not exceeding eight'. Having overcome these hurdles the pupils moved through the School in classes of the same age receiving education which progressed incrementally.

1794. The final division of Gorbals' lands was completed. The value of the Hospital's property in the Gorbals increased eight-fold between 1740 and 1821.

1795. Despite legal opinion and the opposition of the Preceptor, John Campbell, the Patrons went ahead and sold the Hospital building. They, however, did not close the Hospital School. On the contrary they supported its continuation and Campbell was told to look out for a convenient schoolroom.

1799. Following a decision to build the new Hospital in Ingram Street, work began, after three further years of discussion, in 1802.

1800. *An Abstract of Hospital Rules and Regulations* had Hospital classes engaged in gradated work (ahead of practice in the Grammar School). For the first time 'small annual premiums' were awarded to scholars who proved diligent and made good progress in their education.

At the beginning of the nineteenth century, the roll included 48 boys, 53 male pensioners and 73 female pensioners.

1800. The free Stock of the Hospital was understated in the Books by a considerable amount. Hill, the official historian of the Hospital and School, estimated that the total valuation should be £36,106 18s 9d sterling.[12] Expenditure included pensions for 53 men (£330 19s 8d) and 79 women (£514,06 0s 8d), with 48 boys' maintenance at £3 each.

1801. 'A number of persons, who were educated in Hutchesons' School by Mr. James Douglas, met together and resolved to hold an Annual Meeting.' They established a Friendly Society and its Hutchesonian members had to be of good moral character and be free of all bodily diseases. They also had to resign at age 35. The Society, with its membership restricted to former pupils, continued in existence until dissolved in 1912.

1803. John Sharp won the first bursary to the Grammar School.

1805. The new Hospital was completed by the architect, David Hamilton. It lay opposite Hutcheson Street. The School moved into the room above the 'Great Hall' soon after it was ready for use as a schoolroom.

1810. With numbers continuing to increase, the School moved from the Hospital to a building next door (on the east side) which had been intended for the Schoolmaster's house. The Schoolroom was on the first floor, with a shop on the ground floor and houses on the top floor (one of which was reserved for the Schoolmaster). One Patron was to call it 'mean or plain-looking', but its saving grace was a schoolroom three times larger than the Trongate basement. It accommodated some 82 boys and monitors, older scholars who were employed to help the one schoolmaster teach and super-intend such large numbers.

1820. Another significant increase in numbers and 102 boys were now squeezed into the room which previously had been deemed fit to take 82.

1821. A Royal Charter was obtained. It conferred on the Preceptor and Patrons 'the exclusive power, management and administration of the affairs of the Hospital' and especially 'power to make such bye-laws and rules, as they might think expedient, for their own government, and the management and distribution of the funds of the Hospital'. The Patrons framed regulations following what they believed as the spirit of the Founders' intentions rather than the strict letter of their Endowment Deeds. They also augmented charitable and educational benefits as revenue became available. However, appreciating that the benefits of the Hospital could be greatly extended they applied for statutory powers.

1825. An assistant teacher was employed and this increased the possibilities within the Schoolroom.

1827. The Patrons deemed the School building in Ingram Street too small and extremely exposed to noise and other inconveniences. They failed to purchase the Grammar School in George Street which was bought by Anderson's Institution.

1829. John McArly from Crieff became Schoolmaster and was the first to be described as 'Headteacher', partly because he had an assistant, George McMillan, from Huddersfield.

1829. The first dux medal was awarded in the School. The term had not been used before in the School's history.

1839. A Committee Report favoured building on the Hospital's lands in Crown Street in the Gorbals, despite this being outside the Burgh's boundaries.[13]

1841. The new School in Crown Street was opened on the day of Glasgow's annual procession of charity schools.[14] All paraded to St Andrew's Church. After the service the schools went their separate ways. It cost £4,236 8s4d and the builder was Robert Craig. The building provided 3,168 square feet of classroom accommodation; the 1866 Commissioners on Education described the School as 'a beautiful one' and the classrooms as 'admirably adapted for the purposes of teaching'. The 1841 School had three classrooms, each measuring 36 feet by 26 feet, accommodating, in 1875, 286 boys, while the Rector's dwelling house occupied the upper floor of the south division.

1842. The Patrons held that 'great good' would result if the benefits of the Hospital were extended to girls. This was a very early statement in national terms.

1846. The number of Patrons was increased to 60 (50 lay and 10 ministers).

1847. The Patrons set up a committee to look into the 'propriety and competence' of 'establishing a Female School' in the Crown Street building.

1860. Four Hospital boys at the Grammar School carried off between them fourteen prizes and a gold medal. (The gold medallist, John Hutchison, became the Rector of the High School, which had changed its name from Grammar School.)

1861. Thomas Menzies was appointed Headteacher. From his training in

Stow's Normal Seminary he learned 'simultaneous' (whole class) teaching. He commanded the attention of all boys on the same subject without monitors. He tested by asking questions at random so all pupils were engaged in simultaneous answering (one orally, the rest silently). To be effective classes needed to be relatively small in number, the teacher needed to engage constantly with the pupils and they needed to give him their undivided attention. This was the beginning of modern class teaching in the School.

1861. Another attempt to take forward female education failed.

1866. With Preceptor William Whyte and Rector Thomas Menzies on board the issue of a girls' school was actively pursued.

1869. The reform of endowments had not awaited the work of the commissions in Glasgow. They mostly took the form of free schools giving elementary education to the poor, a provision which was considered obsolete after the passing of the national Education Act of 1872. In the case of Hutchesons', the beneficiaries were supposed to be, in the first place, the sons of 'decayed burgesses, who had carried on business on their own account in Glasgow with credit and reputation'. In practice, they seem to have come from the artisan and small tradesman class. This had created controversy, and it was partly in order to clarify the position that the Trust had sought an order under the Hospital and Endowed Institutions Act of 1869.

The Hospital and Endowed Institutions Act gave Hutchesons' the right to educate girls. It also granted endowments the right to provide secondary education. However, by 1871 the Act was clearly a 'dead letter' and the Patrons decided to press ahead with their own Hospital Bill.

1872. Hutchesons' Hospital Act received Royal Assent. It defined the power of the Patrons and regulated the application of the Funds. The Patrons had the right to set up schools throughout the city, the right to provide secondary education, and the right to charge moderate fees. Pupils were then 'the children of respectable labouring people' and the School aimed at 'promoting the higher intelligence of our working classes'. The Act added twelve Patrons (three to be elected by each of the Merchants' and Trades' Houses and six to be elected by the Patrons themselves from the ministers of Glasgow not of the Established Church). In future, the amount to be expended in pensions was not to exceed two-thirds of Hospital revenue, nor to be less than one-half thereof. The same provision was to be followed with regard to the Blair and Baxter Mortifications. The Scott legacy was fixed at half, while the Hood money was all to be used for pensions.[15] The remainder of the Hospital revenue and one-third of the Hospital's capital was to be used 'for furthering the cause of education'.

1873. The Patrons decided not to enlarge the boys' roll and set about redesigning and refurbishing the Crown Street building. It took two years and cost almost double the original estimate – exceeding £20,000 – although the builder, Robert Craig, was the same as in 1841. The new buildings comprised eleven classrooms, a large hall and a gymnasium (the old Art Rooms 12A and 12B), while the Rector was provided with 'a commodious residence' in the north wing. Just over 1,000 boys attended the first new school session.

1876. Years of planning were reversed in two months when Hutchesons' was suddenly offered the Gorbals' Youth School in Elgin Street, which was bankrupt and financially ruined from the competition of the cheaper education on offer from the Board Schools set up since 1872. It thus became the Girls' School with James Lochhead appointed Head Teacher.
Ingram Street was redesigned, removing the original first floor in favour of a larger main Hall.

Both Schools – Hutchesons' Grammar School and Hutchesons' Girls' School – opened on the same day.

The renaming of the Boys' School was significant for the Patrons as they pointed out in the first Prospectus. They were claiming a position within the Scottish educational tradition.

The Schools charged fees markedly lower than the High School's, including free education for foundationers along with bursaries of various kinds, and were intended, according to the Prospectus, to revive the old kind of grammar school 'where the children of country gentlemen, professional men, tradesmen, and artisans were educated side by side, and were prepared either for the University or commercial life'. Although one aim was to 'connect the School with the University', special attention was given to 'the requirements of those who do not propose for themselves a University career, but instead rather to devote themselves to mercantile, scientific, or technical pursuits, such as mechanics, engineering etc, or to prepare for appointments either in the Civil Service, or other government employment, open to competition'.[16]

The Schools immediately attracted 1,002 boys and 728 girls, though this early success was not maintained.

1878. The numbers in the Schools doubled in the first year, and by 1878 there were 1262 in the Boys' School at Crown Street and 913 enrolled in the Girls' building in Elgin Street. Why were the Schools so popular? Partly because, with Hutchesons' the only secondary school on the south side of the burgh and city of Glasgow, there was no public provision; and partly because the Schools offered what parents wanted.

1880. The Liberal Government began to tackle mismanaged and moribund city educational endowments. A deputation from Hutchesons' Hospital met in London with Earl Spencer, Lord President of the Council, and his Vice-President Mundella, and followed this up with a meeting with the Lord Advocate, who proved receptive to the proposed modifications proposed by the Patrons. The most important ensured that not less than a majority of a governing body would consist of persons elected by a Town Council or other public body. With this proviso, which protected their own endowment, the Patrons supported the Government Bill provided their own endowment was not alienated.

Essentially the chief Scottish educational problem of the time was how to manipulate the intentions and resources of those pious Founders of the past so as to bring the secondary and superior education of the present up to the mark.

The Pension list comprised of 146 men and 1,017 women among whom was distributed £9,610 10s.

In the first year when pupils could go forward direct to the Glasgow University Bursary Competition, Hutchesons' Boys took the first three places, and another four were placed in the first thirteen.

1880. The Revenue Account included feu-duties of Gorbals which brought in £15,477 19s 3d sterling and had in surplus two thirds for pensions – £7,561 7s 5d and one-third for education – £3,780 13s 9d. The Pensions were paid to 133 men and 956 women and funeral charges were paid for 35 deceased pensioners.

For the education of 1,083 boys in the Grammar School in Crown Street, of whom 88 were Foundationers, 63 held Scholarships and 24 had School Bursaries, and from the sum of £4,376 17s 6d some £2,167 2s 6d was deducted for fees received.

For the education of the 719 girls in the Girls' School in Elgin Street, of whom 72 were Foundationers and 16 held School Bursaries, from the sum of £3,053.05/05d some £1921.10/00 was deducted for fees received.

The Accounts also made provision for the Allowances for School Fees of 61 boys and 22 girls – £91 8s 11d.

1881. The roll of the Schools was composed of 1,084 boys and 657 girls. A Special Committee of Patrons found that significant over-payments (in excess of the maximum sum permitted by the 1872 Act) had been made.

1882. The Education Endowments (Scotland) Act was passed. It aimed at providing 'one comprehensive scheme of endowments – for the benefit of the entire community'. The Commission set up under Lord Balfour of Burleigh found 1,187 Glasgow endowments and was not able to organise a majority of them. However, it set up two Endowment Trust Boards – the City Trust and the General Educational Endowment Trust – whose governing bodies overlapped with each other and with that of Hutchesons', and all three had the same Secretary, Revd. Lockhart Robertson. It left two major schemes outside – the Marshall Trust and Hutchesons' Hospital. Given its importance to Glasgow, Hutchesons' Hospital was allowed to submit a scheme for autonomy. To the annoyance of the Patrons, however, the Commissioners decided that not less than two-fifths of their revenue was to be spent on education. This was a considerable increase, for between 1835 and 1885 under a quarter of revenue was used for educational purposes.

1884. The Patrons were not reconciled with the intention to increase the amount to be expended annually on education. They went as far as the Court of Session before withdrawing following an adverse opinion from two eminent counsel. The Patrons said the funds were being used to subsidise parents who needed no aid, and being denied to pensioners who desperately needed it. The Governors said that the Schools were poor and the lack of pensions was a function of the Hospital's own mismanagement of investment.

1884. The Balfour Commission's First Report schemes for Glasgow were a defeat for the School Board, but together they offered a bursary system. The Schools were left much as before. The only important change at Hutchesons' was that scholarships which had formerly been open were restricted so as to favour the poor. This was attacked by those like Professor George Ramsay who favoured the principle of 'absolutely free and open competition'.

1885. Despite the objections from the Patrons the new Scheme was put into operation.

SEVEN

Heads and Principals of the
Modern Schools

Thomas Menzies: Rector, Hutchesons' Boys' Grammar School (1876–1902)

Thomas Menzies, nineteenth Headteacher of Hutchesons' Hospital School from 1861 to 1875, and first Rector of Hutchesons' Grammar School from 1876 to 1902, was born on 1 November 1828 at Leadhills and he received his elementary education in the village school. In time he passed through the University curriculum in the Old College in the High Street. Although not a graduate, he trained in Stow's Normal Seminary and he began his teaching career in the Gorbals' Youth School in Greenside Lane. After teaching in three further schools, he became Master at Dalmonach School, Bonhill, where he made the reputation which took him to St James's School, Calton, Glasgow.

In November 1861 Menzies ('The Bear'[1]) replaced John McArly as Head of Hutchesons' Hospital School, from a leet of six, chosen from 143 applicants. He was elected on the fifth ballot by 29 votes to 18. Significantly, he did not receive the support of the Preceptor David McKinlay, who was credited with the wise investments made during his tenure in office (1848–64). Following Menzies' appointment, McKinlay seems to have lost interest in the School.

The Head's salary was fixed at £320 per annum. On appointment Menzies immediately began pressing for, and on the retirement of assistant George McMillan in 1865, obtained, two teaching assistants. In return Menzies publicly committed himself to provide the 'sound elementary and commercial education' which the Patrons wanted.

Menzies inherited a roll of 171, with six others attending the High School of Glasgow, a convention that a number of Patrons had come to oppose, given the broadening of the High School's curriculum from the merely Classical which was now being mirrored at Hutchesons'. It seemed to a number that when Hutchesons' boys went to the High School it was only to find that they had already covered most of the work at Crown Street. Certainly Menzies took over an advancing school.[2]

The three teachers (i.e. Menzies and the two newly appointed assistants) enabled three classes to be formed in distinct classrooms.[3] This ensured whole-class teaching, setting by ability and dux prizes to the first in each class. The curriculum on offer was widened and included Religious Knowledge, which was no longer based on pure memory, but on 'analysis and Scripture proofs'; English (Grammar, Reading and Orthography[4]); Arithmetic and Algebra; Geometry; Letter-writing; Book-keeping; Geography; Vocal Music and Elementary Drawing. In 1867 Biblical History was added, while Menzies himself introduced and taught a before-school voluntary class of Latin, a signal of a new ambition towards secondary status.

The curriculum was also made relevant to Glasgow; for example Geography was taught through reference to Glasgow's trading links and was made relevant to earning a living. By 1869 systematic instruction in Science had been introduced as a means of updating the curriculum,[5] while Menzies also led the way in modifying teaching style and urged colleagues to abandon rote learning, which he rightly associated with large class numbers and the use of monitors.

The curriculum was delivered by a timetable with periods lasting an hour; and courses were expanded to last five years. Instead of accepting boys between seven and nine years of age, Menzies introduced a minimum entry age of eight (and a maximum of ten). The boys also had to pass an entrance examination and, once accepted, their progress in the Hospital was by results and attainment. Menzies tried to keep them for an extra year so that they would be old enough for employment.

In the Hospital days, the pupils received not only an education but also clothing and a sum for maintenance. In 1866, James Greig and Thomas Harvey reported for the Government on the 'state of education in Glasgow'. They found the original intentions of the Founders were still being carried out 'in their integrity'.[6] On examination the boys displayed a proficiency that was very gratifying, while accuracy and promptness of answers were equally pleasing. Writing was 'far above the average of most schools'.

Eleven years after Menzies' appointment, the Patrons of the Hospital were empowered by Act of Parliament (the Hutchesons' Hospital Act of 1872) to expand the original Scheme; the institution was to be no longer limited to foundationers, but was opened to the public as a day fee-paying grammar school for primary and secondary education up to university standard.[7]

During his tenure, the School was praised for its efficiency in the Report by J. M. D. Meiklejohn[8] for the Endowed Commission in 1874. The Inspector found 'the reading wonderfully good' and had never found it as good in any school 'either in England or Scotland'. The articulation and expression of the pupils were deemed admirable. Menzies had expended great efforts and set high standards for all his pupils in classes as large as eighty in size. He could also take credit for steadily increasing numbers, the Hospital roll reaching 286 in its final year, 1875.

Menzies was delighted with the glowing remarks about his school. The Patrons could now look forward to the creation of a secondary school, seeing it as a reproduction of a great burgh school of Scotland, the standard work on which had just been published by James Grant in April 1876.[9]

The aim of the Grammar School was to send out its pupils fully equipped for the battle of life, and Menzies did not forget the importance of physical culture; military drill and swimming received due encouragement. Indeed, including swimming in the curriculum was the Rector's idea, and Hutchesons' was the first school in Glasgow to put on such a course, on Saturdays.

The Rector himself took an interest in various forms of sport and was known as a very keen angler and an enthusiastic curler. He was, indeed, a well-rounded man, and was a member of societies of all kinds, from Burns Clubs to the Incorporation of Barbers and the Anderston Weavers' Society. He was a Justice of the Peace, and for many years an elder and Treasurer of St James's Parish Church, Great Hamilton Street.

Menzies also had a high reputation in his emerging profession. He was distinguished as a Latin and Greek scholar, with a partiality for the latter, and exemplified a rapidly vanishing era, which believed that a deftly turned classical quotation was the arbiter of literary elegance. He was also in the forefront of implementing changes in Arithmetic and Mathematics, giving special attention to the decimal system. His pupils were successful in all walks of life. His successes led to the award of the Fellowship of the Educational Institute of Scotland.[10]

His time saw significant change and Hutchesons' was transformed from a two-teacher, largely elementary charity school to a fee-paying secondary institution,[11] being at one time, in 1878, the only one on the south side of the city. By this time the Patrons generally believed that fee-paying resulted in a 'superior education' and promoted upward social mobility. Thus the charity tradition, aimed at bettering the poor, gave way to maximising advantage for the most able while the practice of apprenticing boys fell into disuse.

Meiklejohn returned to inspect again in 1880, expecting that the growth in school numbers would have resulted in a dilution of standards. However, his Report gave another highly satisfactory verdict on the School and its Head. Such positive comments by Professor Meiklejohn were confirmed in the results of the Glasgow University Competition Examination in November of that year when seven, out of the thirteen first year students who sat the exam, were from Hutchesons', including the top three.

There were, however, increasing concerns, as from 1891 the introduction of free local authority secondary schools diminished rolls for the first time since the beginning of the School. By 1900 the boys' roll was one-third of the 1880 figure and the girls' numbers had halved since the late 1870s. The Elgin Street School had become 'ill-ventilated, over-crowded, old-fashioned', and in 1897 the Governors, very short of funds, had to act and rebuild the School in order to receive a Government grant.[12] These were dark times.

Despite this, as Rector, Menzies continued to guide and direct the Grammar School till his retiral, which was soon followed by his death in his 74th year on 29 August 1902. The Governors appreciated his 'valuable services' in his long tenure of Headship. They understood how he had brought the School into the modern world. In doing so, Menzies had laboured faithfully, strenuously and with conspicuous success. However, not all of their decisions were palatable to him, especially in his last few years when discussions took place on the possible transfer of the School to the School Board.

James Lochhead: Headmaster, Girls' Higher Class School (1876–85)

James Lochhead was born in 1829 and was the first Head of the Hutchesons' School for Girls, taking office in 1876 when the School opened in Elgin Street. Like Menzies, Lochhead was not a university graduate. He followed the Madras System[13] and used pupil teachers. He widened the curriculum by adding Drawing, History, Geography, Singing and Grammar. He was renowned for his demands on girls and staff. By 1878 there were 913 girls in Elgin Street, which had been built for 500, and this led to profit-making. The press referred to the pupils as 'middle-class'.

The Meiklejohn Report of 1880 was also highly satisfactory, stressing the thoroughness of the work done and the high standard of efficiency attained. Meiklejohn commented on 'steady diligence and a constant endeavour on the part of each pupil to do her very best; perfect order and discipline, good habits, attention, (and) thoughtfulness were all apparent, even conspicuous in this School'.

'The Head-Master (Lochhead) appears to me to spare no labour or thought in bringing each department of the School up to the highest level, and in keeping it there. His vigilance is unwearied, and his insight into the character and powers of both teachers and pupils decidedly remarkable. In all the subjects in which Drill is paramount the School is nearly perfect; and every individual girl has her talents and habits influenced, by the work and organisation of the School. Everyone is caught in the net. I never saw a set of Examination papers of such remarkable neatness – not to say elegance – as those sent up to me by the girls in this School. The effect, both upon the habits and the characters of the pupils, of all that is done, is obvious, even to the superficial observer . . . Meanwhile we have a School that is of the highest value to the district of Glasgow in which it stands, that maintains a very high standard in all its work, that has a strong influence for good on all who belong to it and that trains to the best habits, while it develops the mental powers of all its pupils.'

Lochhead's School saw the girls beginning their course a year later than the boys – usually at about 10 years – and finishing a year earlier. Their school day was also shorter. In the first Primary class the girls took Sewing, then in the second, Sewing and Knitting, and in the third, Sewing, Knitting and Crochet.[14] Drill and Callisthenics[15] (instead of Fencing) began in Primary 2 and continued until the end of Secondary. The Theory of Domestic Economy was tackled in Upper Primary (when boys took Latin), allowing Cookery to be taught from the beginning of Secondary. Physiology[16] was added in the last year of Secondary in 1880. (Pianoforte and Swimming were the only extras in the Schools.)

Sadly Lochhead went home at lunchtime to his home at 17 Knowe Terrace, Pollokshields, feeling unwell, but collapsed and died suddenly there in the course of the afternoon of 25 March 1885. He was survived by his wife and their children (a boy and a girl, the latter of whom later joined the School staff).[17] His high expectations led to success in University Bursary Examinations and the School had prospered under his leadership.

Dr William Thomson BA: Headmaster, Hutchesons' Girls' Grammar School (1885–1914)

William Thomson was born on 6 February 1849. He was a native of Carluke but his family moved to Glasgow when he was a young boy of six. He was a pupil teacher in the Sessional[18] School in Bishop Street, 1863–67, and thereafter entered the Glasgow Established Church Training College, 1868–69. He was one of the best students. He supplemented this with a course at University, and during that time he acted as an assistant teacher in Macdonald Road School, Rutherglen. He taught for a couple of years in Lorn Academy, Oban, and then was assistant to the Mathematical master, Thomas Muir, at the High School of Glasgow, 1874–78. While there he took a BA degree from London University with Honours in French (First Class) and German (Second Class). He was then Rector of Dunfermline HS from 1878–85. During his time there it became one of the 'most efficient (schools) in the country'.[19]

In 1885 he was appointed Head of the HGGS[20] from the field of forty applications and soon proved to be 'original in his ideas'. He introduced ingenious and successful methods into teaching because he was an 'experimenter'. A special feature was the attention he devoted to the teaching of his own subject, Modern Languages. He strongly championed the claims of Modern Languages to be the equal of Latin and Greek as means of culture. According to the Inspector who visited the School in 1889, 'the principles on which Modern Languages are taught may be said to constitute a new departure. They are spoken, and spoken only, in the initiatory and subsequent classes'.[21] When formal Grammar was subsequently encountered it was not as a foreign but as a 'familiar tongue'.

Thomson thus gave languages, including Italian, a prominence not known previously. He raised English Literature to a higher plane and encouraged wide reading. The results in German were remarkable: in 1890–91 thirteen of the fifty-two Honours German passes in Scotland were awarded to Hutchesons' Girls. Thomson's successes can also be judged by the high number of his students who gained FCH[22] in Modern Languages at Glasgow University.

Other progressive innovations were Thomson's banning of homework for all except the senior Leaving Certificate class, on the grounds that learning should be fun, instead of homework consisting of a teacher listening to what the teacher had given the pupil to learn the previous evening. He also disliked the teaching and learning of material which the pupil could learn themselves and explain best on their own, with little or no assistance.

Having dispensed with formal homework in 1911 for three years Thomson confidently claimed that his methodology – aimed at cultivating initiative – not only did that in less time, but also resulted in the ability to pass examinations as a by-product. Sceptics were not always convinced by his argument that no homework actually meant more homework, as pupils showed initiative, power of planning and invention. A number of parents and staff opposed the measure, although this opposition abated when exam results did not appear to have been adversely affected. Much of the passion also died down when it was appreciated that what Thomson wanted was for the girls to set their own homework.

Thomson's vision included introducing 'Teaching' as a subject for senior girls and the setting of classes by ability not age, although this last measure led to some classes containing girls whose ages ranged from eight to thirteen. Higher Education bursaries became available for girls who wished to follow a 'Preparatory College Class' in the School. Young would-be teachers accompanied the Headmaster on his daily classroom visits, received tuition in the 'Art of Teaching' and occasionally had the opportunity to take a class under the Head's supervision. These developments were very advanced for the time, which tended to concentrate on allowing a student to teach for a full day and then restricting them thereafter to evening classes.

Thomson also understood the need to introduce a complete Primary department, on the grounds that parents usually wished their children to attend the same school for Primary and Secondary education. The Governors[23] took heed and the First Class in Crown Street Boys' School was restored from 1888–89.

However, Thomson had his arguments with important personages. Sir Henry Craik[24] disputed his methods in the teaching of Modern Languages and the first Secretary of Hutchesons' Educational Trust, Rev. Dr F.L. Robertson, was deliberately unhelpful because of a reference from Thomson for the post of Head of Edinburgh Ladies' College which Robertson failed to get in 1891. Thomson also had problems with parents when he made Latin and German compulsory to gain University entry. When this was challenged he then made Latin or Science the choice, but he was forced to offer Latin or German. Parents were now unconvinced of the need for a second language at all and so in 1909–10 he offered 'Latin or German, for those who are capable of a second language'.

Thomson also had his disagreements with Menzies. One issue between them was that of departmental organisation, which Thomson pressed for. However, Menzies and the Governors were lukewarm until Thomson showed it would avoid replacing lost staff. Even then, Thomson was only allowed to introduce a temporary scheme in 1891 and he had to wait until after the death of Menzies to make progress on this.

Thomson also had problems with state regulation of the School's accommodation, which led to new pupils being refused entry and some already in the School being asked to leave. With the Scottish Education Department threatening grant cuts, Thomson staged a vigorous campaign for a new School.

Fortunately, the Governors were allowed to borrow money by the Court of Session, and the Patrons offered a portion of land between Kingarth Street and Calder Street. Plans were accepted from the six submitted, and two years later, on 31 January 1912, the new Girls' Grammar School opened. It was designed by John Thomson (1859–1933) and Robert Douglas Sandilands (c.1860–1913). In general outline like a High Renaissance palazzo, flanked by two staircase towers with Baroque detail, including Vanbrughian[25] arcaded tops. It has glazed loggia to the central hall; above it are the large art-room windows; below, an insignificant entrance to the one-storey offices. It has a contemporary former domestic economy and gymnasium block (facing Calder Street) and Janitor's house.[26] It was opened by one of Scotland's greatest education experts, Lord Balfour of Burleigh. He held that Hutchesons' was the institution which provided the yardstick against which other Higher Grade schools in and around Glasgow measured themselves.

The building of Kingarth Street prevented the Hutchesons' Schools from becoming a 'class school', open only to the rich. It was a fine building[27] and attracted scholars to come back as teachers. However, the 'spacious edifice' created new problems in the rundown Elgin Street, where pupils had to be taught below ground level in a church across the street.

Thomson is best remembered for his onslaught on compulsory Latin as entry for University classes. He won this battle and was instrumental in founding University chairs in Glasgow in French and German.

Thomson wrote articles in learned journals. In 1905 he published a book, *The Basis of English Rhythm*, simplifying English grammar. However, although his ideas were accepted in Germany, the controversy about his work delayed the award of the Higher Degree of LL.D. from Glasgow University. He was active in the Glasgow Philosophical Society, and President of both the West of Scotland Teachers' Guild and the Association of Secondary Teachers. He also served on the Provincial Committee for the Training of Teachers.

He retired in December 1914 under new regulations which enforced retirement at age sixty-five. In his last major speech he described true education as fitting the youth of the country for the world after school. This called out for new approaches to problem-solving. Schools had to become places for independent and co-operative mental activity.

As an early adherent of Montessori,[28] Thomson adopted two of her educational mottoes – 'Do and ye shall know' and 'Be still and know', and had them engraved on the Assembly Hall in Kingarth Street. He died on 16 May 1925, aged 76. He was survived by his wife, three sons and three daughters; five of them graduated from Glasgow University; the sixth was an Associate of a London Institute of Engineering.

Robert Philp: Rector, Hutchesons' Boys Grammar School (1903–13)

Robert Philp was baptised on 28 February 1854 near Largo in Fife. His father was a corn merchant and an Inspector of the Poor. Robert attended Madras College, St Andrews, and was awarded 'merit' in the Bursary Examination and matriculated at St Andrews University in October 1869. He gained his MA after four years study on 30 April 1873. For three years he was an assistant master at Madras College. He was then Principal Teacher (Mathematics) at HBGS[29] between 1876 and 1902 and lived during that period at Scionbank Cottage, Rutherglen. His wife, Jessie, died young there in 1879. He joined the Edinburgh Mathematical Society in February 1885 but was unsuccessful in his application in 1888 to be Head at Waid Academy, Anstruther.

Philp was appointed Acting Headmaster of the Boys' School in 1903 and was paid an honorarium of £100 towards his new duties. It was not until 1907 that he was appointed full Headmaster[30] on £500 per annum.[31] He had to contend with more issues of accountability and interference in the forms of certification and inspections. Apart from the time he spent teaching at Madras College, his old school in St Andrews, Philp spent his career at Hutchesons'. He had developed a distinct style of teaching, preferring discussion among his pupils to reach a solution or make progress, rather than lecturing to the whole class. He was remarkably modern in approach, especially for a Mathematics master, and came to an agreement with Menzies that allowed him not to give places and prizes. When pressurised to fall into line he reluctantly restricted assessment to one major annual test, viewing it as a necessary evil.

In the early days of his Headship Philp was not in favour of homework, but this was another area in which he was forced to compromise. By 1904 he had gone to the other extreme, and HMI reported that the School policy ensured that even the most capable of scholars were expected to devote five hours every evening to home study.[32]

As a result of HMI threats to cut financial grants unless the School improved its sporting facilities, Philp had the large hall converted into a gymnasium, turning the previous gym into a cloakroom. An HMI Report saw these as 'welcome and much-needed improvements'. He also had a Science room fitted out as a modern laboratory suitable for experimental work. This led to improvements in both the curriculum on offer and the quality of Science teaching. The Inspectors approved the introduction of a separate specific Art room and Philp also found space for Manual Instruction (Woodwork), which entailed a workshop on the ground floor. The School Board provided an Instructor and the result was 'entirely satisfactory'.[33] The Inspectors thought the Art teacher, Frederic A. Weston, should use the workshop to develop the curriculum in further crafts. This finally was achieved in 1911, although only in the Primary School.

The introduction of new SED Regulations in 1908, restricting secondary class size to thirty and practical classes to a maximum of twenty, meant the need to find more accommodation at the School. This was done mainly by partitioning existing rooms, which in turn meant an immediate increase in the number of teaching staff.

Philp supervised other advances. Sport was developed with the acquisition of a football field; French teaching was reorganised; Latin was given more time which helped improve relatively poor results in the subject; both History and Geography teachers were pressed to introduce more interesting and stimulating content in their lessons; and under the new Mathematics teacher, Barr, Philp was pleased with the move away from old-fashioned theoretical teaching. However, despite HMI efforts, he failed to introduce French into the Classical side. Clearly, Philp could not change everything; he was slow to get rid of slates and pupil desks remained without back supports.

Philp supervised a gradual move to subject departments, with Principal Teachers and assistant teachers responsible to them. He followed HMI advice as closely and as quickly as he could. This led the SED to support the Hutchesons' changes financially and the roll of both Schools began to increase, despite the fast-developing local authority secondaries on the south side of Glasgow. Along with Thomson, Philp made the Schools difficult to close.

In spite of many educational difficulties caused by the relocation of population, reduced attendances and insufficiency of school buildings,

Philp carried on the School to the entire satisfaction of the Governors. He was the first Head to give all his time to administration. He died in office on 1 March 1913 in Glasgow.

Taken together, Philp and Thomson have gained the reputation of saving the Schools. The financial crisis which they faced led to a fall-out. The Governors of HET and Hospital Patrons went separate ways. Heads became more significant and as their status grew their Governors deferred increasingly to them.

The Schools were now in a strong position financially. By 1914 the original Hutcheson endowment of £4,017 and three tenements had grown to £600,000, providing income of £22,000. There were 1,700 pensioners and 1,200 scholars. The funds were so massive because Glasgow had grown so quickly in the nineteenth century; it was appreciated this would never happen again. 'The times appeared as propitious as could be for the building of a new Boys' School.'[34]

James Alexander McKenzie: Interim Rector of HBGS (1913)

James Alexander McKenzie was born in 1862 and gained his MA from Glasgow University in 1887. He taught English at HBGS from 1890 until 1915 and became Principal English Master. He was Interim Rector for five months following the death of Rector Philp in March 1913, but failed to become Head. In fact, although he showed both tact and vigour in a temporary post, he did not gain the support of a single Governor for his permanent appointment.[35] Instead he was appointed the Head of a Board School, Mathieson Street Public School, in 1916. He was unsuccessful again in a further application for the School's Headship in 1919.

William Joseph McVicar: Headmaster, Hutchesons' Girls' Grammar School (1914–27)

William Joseph McVicar was born on 13 November 1862. He began his teaching career at Ayr Academy. He joined the staff at HGGS, Elgin Street, in 1882 and completed his MA in 1887. He distinguished himself as a Classics student while at University and Professor Ramsay thought highly of him. He had long been his predecessor's right-hand man and had run the School on his many absences on School business, as well as being Principal Teacher of English and Classics. When Thomson was forced to resign on age grounds, McVicar followed him seamlessly into the office of Headmaster, despite the twenty-two applications for the post (and a short-leet of four).

McVicar was less of a radical than Thomson, and quietly dropped the home-lessons experiment, which the Inspectorate saw as a sensible move despite its apparent success. He was methodical, painstaking, scholarly and refined, and the staff welcomed his appointment.

When confronted with the 1876 objectives of 'a Higher Education' and 'womanly accomplishments', McVicar consistently confirmed academic standards as excellent and constantly stressed the breadth of interests the girls were encouraged to exhibit. In doing so he barely tolerated the continuance of the nineteenth century 'womanly accomplishments' and he showed little enthusiasm for 'Housewifery' and Domestic Science. He had no time for those who commonly referred to the HBGS as 'the Grammar School' while the HGGS was merely the 'Girls School' even if the name 'Grammar' appeared in both titles after 1886.

The main feature of his tenure was the importance he placed on 'social usefulness'. This was to prove an effective and lasting contribution to the ethos of the School, which was to become more inclusive with its emphasis on service to the community. During World War 1 the girls enthusiastically supported War Bond and Certificate Schemes[36] and raised £15,000, and with the female staff they became a 'huge Ladies' Auxiliary for the Supply of Comforts to the Troops'. They also included in their patriotic duty watching regiments march past on Victoria Road.

Such activities also helped McVicar to retain the idea of being a city school. The girls, staff and former pupils set up three play centres, one of them run solely by the girls. The original centre had been set up in the Tradeston district in order to provide an hour of enjoyment and healthy recreation for children who otherwise would be wandering the streets. Moreover, the girls decided to give up school prizes for the duration of the War and on its completion set up a Hutchesons Girls' Cot at the Sick Children's Hospital. The rationing of food at this time led the girls to giving a box of sweets weekly and an annual Hallowe'en Party to the residents of the nearby Hollybrook Special School. The Athenaeum hosted fund-raising 'entertainments' put on by the girls, and after the War a fortnight's 'knitting campaign' provided eight hundred garments, with thousands more from parents and friends for the Save the Children Fund. Literally scores of other good causes were helped by the 'Philanthropic Committee'.

McVicar was right to believe that this record was outstanding, and had much to do with the strong comradeship among the girls who organised the projects themselves. This goes some way to explain why the girls formed an FP Club before the boys and why the Schools remained open during the post-War influenza epidemic[37] when most schools in the country were closed.

One severe lack was rectified in 1924 when a School Magazine was published. Its substance proved to be much more than a revival of the 1914 Magazine, which had proved a very grave disappointment. The new publication was to do much more than continue the traditions of its predecessor, and immediately offered scope for abilities which were not displayed in the classroom. The first edition related the many directions in which the School had been active. A sale had raised £170 for the Glasgow University Students' Welfare Scheme; the Camera Club, now in its second decade of existence, continued to flourish under the guidance of Mr Wiseman (with McVicar as vice-president) and the new Art Club also owed much to the Head, who was its President. The formation of a choir to compete in the Glasgow Musical Festival was also a new venture for the School and a success (as it took second place). The Magazine also highlighted the success of the FP Club, with hockey, badminton, tennis and swimming all prominently on offer.

When he retired in 1927, a Governor of HET, Rev. D.B. Kyles, held that the School 'had never stood higher in prestige'.[38] Certainly McVicar himself was held in high regard by staff and pupils. At his retiral McVicar was presented with an 'upright grand gramophone' by the staff, along with 'valuable etchings' from the pupils; and from the Old Girls' Club he received 'his portrait, a wallet full of notes and an autograph album containing the signatures of about five hundred pupils'. He was deemed to be 'cultured, kindly and always just', qualities which made him an ideal headmaster.

The building in Kingarth Street had room for 750 and was, throughout McVicar's time, always over-subscribed. He found space to teach Nursery in the Housewifery bloc. He continued to promote a University education for the girls, and this did not involve Domestic Science. It was not surprising that he and his girls thought such subjects were an aspersion on mothers. The girls did well: in 1924 six were among the distinguished hundred in the Glasgow University Bursary Competition.

McVicar will be remembered mostly for being strong on ethos and 'social usefulness'. The result was a school thoroughly committed to the community. McVicar moved the School in the direction Gillies was taking the boys, and both established a tone which was to last. 'Pa' died in October 1937.

(William) King Gillies: Rector, Hutchesons' Boys' Grammar School (1913–19)

William King Gillies was born on 20 March 1875 and was educated at Speir's School, Beith, and Glasgow University where he took a FCH in Classics in 1895 and where he was also the Logan Medallist and Snell Exhibitioner. He went on to take a FCH in Philosophy at Balliol College, Oxford. He taught Classics at Greenock Academy, Campbeltown Grammar School and Perth Academy, before becoming Senior Classical Master at the High School of Glasgow in 1904.

On the death of Philp in March 1913, the Governors of HBGS interviewed the four internal candidates. James McKenzie, a highly commended Principal of English, was made Acting Rector[39] but the Governors believed they should appoint someone with a 'more striking public presence'.[40] William King Gillies was their choice. McKenzie deserved a Headship and was appointed Head of Mathieson Street Board School. He was the first to benefit from a reciprocity agreement between Hutchesons' and the Corporation.[41] Both sides believed that the former should be ahead of the latter, but both should firmly be City schools.

The Governors saw Gillies as an outstanding personality when they appointed him in September 1913 to replace Philp. He was the third Rector and twenty-first Head. The Governors saw his mission as raising the School's academic and social standing. He was comparable to the very best schoolmasters in the country, and his fierce discipline was a shock to the system after Philp's 'kindly easy manners'. For the Governors it was a tragedy that their new Rector only stayed six years before moving on to become Rector of the Royal High School in Edinburgh. The boys at Hutchesons' saw him as 'awesome', but his innovations were not all welcomed. He was a slim, energetic figure who hurried hither and thither with his 'flying gown' his hallmark. He also wore a mortar-board and his staff wore gowns.

Gillies guided the School through the difficult War years. He proved not to be a narrow Classicist, despite publishing a Latin Reader (Verse and Prose) in 1908. However, he retained the traditionally Classical character of the School but encouraged with equal zeal the organisation of full Modern Languages and Science curricula. He increased the School roll, doubling the size of the post-Intermediate Department, helped by holding fees at 1893–94 levels. He developed the Combined Cadet Force, the Rugby Club, the School Choir, the Literary and Debating Society and the School Magazine.

Such extended activities owed much to his drive. He even had time to introduce the School Council.

Founding a Cadet Corps had been one of his first actions, and was warmly supported by the enlistment of 54 boys.[42] In 'drilling order' by January 1914, the Corps' first public appearance followed two months later at the unveiling of the bronze busts of the Founders, commissioned by the Patrons.[43]

The School could now begin to compete with the High School Corps. It was open to thirteen-year-olds and upward and had over a hundred members by December 1915. The boys competed in musketry and signalling, attended annual camp near Skelmorlie, were affiliated to the Cameronians, worked as flag-sellers, took part in processions, attended funerals, and, most importantly, the Corps was a recruiting agency. By Prize-giving Day in June 1916, 430 FPs were in the forces, 107 of commissioned rank. At least 715 served in the War, ten of them teachers, and by the end of the War 140 had been killed.

The Hutchesonian had appeared irregularly since the beginning of the century, but it ceased altogether in 1909. It was important, however, to Gillies that it be revived. It had a particular role for him in shaping the public conception of the School and its activities. It had a good story to tell and did so from December 1915, mostly containing news relevant to the School. It was published twice a year.

The game of Association Football was played at the School from 1895 when educational regulations allowed such expenditure. Once a field was found for the School, success followed. Hutchesons' won the Scottish Secondary League and Cup in 1907 and 1908. Meantime, ground difficulties delayed the introduction of rugby until eventually, in 1917–18, Allan Glen's School offered Titwood every Tuesday afternoon. However, the standard of School rugby remained disappointing, while the Association game could boast of two internationalists – Marshall and Lithgow both played in the international against Wales at Swansea, which the Scots won 2–0, and in the international at Hampden Park against Ireland, which the Scots won 5–0. There was real concern that the 'wrong' sport would win out. To ensure that it did not, Gillies announced at prize-giving in 1919 that rugby would be the official School game. Cricket and swimming were the other major sports.

Another important decision was made at this time. When in the early years of his tenure the 'Old Boys' had been circulated about creating an FP Club, there seemed little interest. It was a different story in 1919. The Club's existence and the scale of its growth in the post-war years had much to do with the Rector and the spread of activities from the School.

Why did Gillies leave in October 1919 after only six years? It seems most likely that he took the Hutchesons' post on the understanding that a move for the School was being planned. The Trust publicly confirmed this in 1914, and HMI Reports consistently demanded accommodation improvements. By 1919 Art, PE and Science were acutely affected by the situation. The Governors knew how close Gillies was to leaving. Hence, he was given an increase of twenty per cent in his salary, and this on a scale rising to £800 per annum. Unfortunately, his mind appears to have been made up and leave he did, disillusioned with the lack of progress towards a new School building.

He left a Classical School with a strong athletic bias and this legacy was to last for over half a century. His immediate successor, J. C. Scott, was appointed to embed the many innovations which had been introduced.

King Gillies was awarded an honorary degree (LL.D.) from Glasgow University in 1929 and received the tribute that he had maintained the Classical ideal in Scottish education and had pursued the tried method which, at the same time, built up the character of the School and qualified him to perform well his work in the world.

A former office-bearer of the Classical Association of Scotland, he took a prominent part in the work of the Educational Institute of Scotland, which conferred the honour of Fellowship upon him in 1917. He was FRSE, and in November 1941 was appointed Grand Secretary of the Grand Lodge.

He retired from his post as Rector at the Royal High in Edinburgh in March 1940, having spent two fruitful decades there as one of the 'great Rectors of modern times'.[44] Sadly he was admitted to Edinburgh's Royal Infirmary on 1 October 1952, after being knocked down by a tramcar, and died there on 15 November of that year. He was survived by his second wife and by his son and daughter of his first wife.

James Caddell: Interim Rector Hutchesons' Boys Grammar School (1919–20)

James Caddell joined HBGS as a pupil in 1865 and was Dux in 1870. Following the custom of the time he went on to the High School before graduating from Glasgow University and Divinity Hall. He became a member of the Classics staff in 1882, teaching Latin and Greek, and completed 38 years' service before retirement. When Gillies resigned, the School faced another Acting Rectorship. The Governors turned to Caddell, who was a formidable figure and renowned for his discipline. He was Interim Rector in 1919 while the Governors found a replacement for Gillies. He died the following year in September, shortly before he was due to retire.

Dr John Charles Scott (J.C.): Rector, Hutchesons' Boys' Grammar School (1920–32)

John Charles Scott was born in August 1872 in Ireland and had his early education in Carlisle Grammar School before entering Glasgow University, where he gained a FCH in Classics in 1894. He taught at Glasgow Academy as Classical Master from 1894 until 1919, when he moved to Hutchesons'. He was a figure who earned high respect in the community and in the two schools which he served. He was the fourth Rector of the School.

At Glasgow Academy he had become almost a legendary figure, 'pugnacious, witty and debonair, bustling about in knickerbockers every Wednesday afternoon, wet or fine, cheerfully organising games for a hundred and fifty or two hundred noisy shouting boys by sheer enthusiasm mixed with a great deal of shrewdness and knowledge of Rugby football'.[45] When he went to the Academy, football and cricket and games generally were in the doldrums and things needed wakening up. J. C. Scott woke them up and achieved a transformation.

There were 34 applications for the post of Rector and the Governors interviewed five of them:

David Anderson MA MC – Senior Mathematics Master at HBGS
Alexander Ross Cumming MA – Rector, Hermitage Academy
Thomas Keen MA BSc – Head of Modern Languages, High School
    of Glasgow
Peter Ramsay MA BSc – Head of Mathematics, Watson's College
John Charles Scott – Classical Master, Glasgow Academy.

Scott arrived at Hutchesons' in time to face two major problems in the immediate post-War years. The first was whether the School was still entitled to grants, with School Boards being replaced by Local Authorities. This was settled by Glasgow giving over £22,000 and the SED contributing another £6,000. The other issue was that of teachers' pay. Traditionally a teacher at

Hutchesons' was paid by personal request and as a result many anomalies crept in. In 1919 new national scales were introduced and the wage bill at Hutchesons' rose markedly. Fees, unchanged for twenty years, doubled in Crown Street and rose substantially at Kingarth Street.

Scott was disappointed at his first set of Glasgow University Bursary Examination results in 1920, which were perhaps a reflection on the numbers leaving at the end of Form V. This state of affairs was particularly difficult given the as usual 'excellent' results of the Girls' School. Scott turned a blind eye when a number of Fifth Formers decided to enter the Competition, and Hutchesons' made a much better showing in the List. He was not slow to tell the Governors and the newspapers of this 'revival'. By September 1921 he was claiming that 'no School in Scotland had a better record'.[46] As for the Leaving Certificate results, he told the *Glasgow Herald* that they 'surpassed anything in the recent history of the School'.[47] In 1923 the Boys had twice the number of bursary winners as any other school, with six in the top 25, despite the dreadful condition of Crown Street. In 1926, with the School top of the bursary list again, with eight in the top hundred, Scott was almost blasé and held that 'he would far rather see many trying to acquire for themselves a well-balanced education, giving mind, body and spirit all their due proportions of attention and development in the endeavour to make useful citizens than produce a few champions in either the academic or athletic sphere'.

Despite working hard at School, many pupils found examination work difficult and both Schools catered for the academically less able. The majority of Hutchesons' boys did not go to University on leaving School but instead went straight into paid employment or attended institutions such as Skerry's Commercial College, which offered special courses to prepare for Civil Service appointments down to quite humble levels. Scott regretted that promising pupils left School without fulfilling their academic potential.

At Hutchesons' Scott was much involved with the corporate life of the School and put a great deal of emphasis on the work ethic. In his first year he took over the new rugby fixture list of his predecessor and promoted cricket, both played at Cartha Club's grounds in Dumbreck Road. Scott used his networking contacts to enable the School to use Ibrox, the football ground of Rangers FC, for its Annual Sports' Day between 1920 and 1924, and followed this up with the use of Hampden Park in 1925 and Allan Glen's School's Bishopbriggs Ground in 1926.

Scott was very quick to raise the issue of sporting accommodation, and was tenacious in his efforts to solve the problem. Only a year into office he publicly rebuked his Governors for a lack of effort in looking for an athletics field. His relentless work on this ensured that on 4 June 1927 the eighth Sports Day was held on the School's own ground of Auldhouse. The Old Boys from 1923 played their part and the Patrons were also involved. Fundraising continued beyond purchase to pay for the development of the 10.5 acre ground near Mansewood, Pollokshaws. The field was levelled and drained, pitches were laid out, a new pavilion was built with a groundsman's house and equipment purchased. Even the HMI saw the securing of a playing field as 'the outstanding event of the year'.

Scott built on the innovations of Gillies and widened extra-curricular activities. Golf and badminton appeared, as well as a Country Dancing Class, an Ambulance Class, a Chess Club and a Radio Club. He brought back Drama, began an orchestra and encouraged choirs. He saw an increase in senior pupils taking Science. Not all was success however. The supporters of Association Football continued to grumble and it took till 1924–25 for the grievance to peter out. Scott had made his reputation with rugby at the Academy and he was determined to do similar work at Hutchesons'. But he only began to make real progress in 1923–24, and even then that proved a false dawn. Lack of success plagued rugby until daytime use of Auldhouse was introduced into the timetable in the later 1920s. This was followed by the appointment of Donald MacLennan in 1931 to the Science staff of the School, but in many respects it was his coaching of School rugby from 1934 which was to be of great significance.

Swimming too was in decline but a new House system – despite the lack of imagination over names – Bruce, Burns, Scott and Wallace[48] – helped the cause of Games. A swimming gala became an important annual School event and in 1929 was shared with the Girls'.

Scott wound up the now poorly-supported Cadet Corps in 1930, believing that organised Games, the new prefect system and Gymnastics classes were good substitutes.

A new school uniform dated from this period. The colours of red and green were those of the Town and this choice was another way of Scott's cementing that all-important relationship. A School song by FP staff member Robert Bain also appeared.

The War Memorial was unveiled, with Gillies in attendance, in 1921, by former pupil, John Buchan, who had been coached by Scott for his University Entrance.

Scott's discipline was fierce, especially in the Secondary. He used the strap often, as was the norm in this period. Despite this, reports of the time mention a generally relaxed, even happy atmosphere in the School. Moreover, Scott knew every boy by name and made an impact by speaking individually to all boys when school reports were issued.

Scott was an elder in the Church of Scotland and a member of Glasgow Corporation. He was also a Councillor and Bailie, having been elected as a Moderate member for East Partick in 1922.[49] He was Convener of the Business Committee of Glasgow University and sat for twelve years on the University's Court. He was made an honorary Doctor of Law in 1929. He retired in 1932 at the comparatively early age of 60, devoting himself to public works. He became an OBE in 1954 and died in March 1955 aged 82. Scott left a school with better than ever Leaving Certificate and Glasgow University Bursary results and one recognised as a leader of Glasgow's city schools.

Margaret Kennedy: Principal, Hutchesons' Girls' Grammar School (1927–48)

Margaret Kennedy was born in 1883, the daughter of a local doctor, and was an outstanding pupil at Perth Academy. She went on to have a brilliant academic career and graduated with FCH from Edinburgh University in Modern Languages in 1906. She twice gained the George Scott Travelling Scholarship.

Margaret Kennedy taught at Leamington Spa Secondary Girls' School, and between 1908 and 1927 she was Principal Teacher and Lady Superintendent at North Kelvinside Higher Grade School. She narrowly missed being appointed Head of the High School for Girls in 1926, but for a short period she was PT in Hillhead High School. Before coming to Hutchesons' she had worked her whole career in local authority schools. She was the only leeted candidate with extensive experience of a Higher Grade School in a working-class district, and Glasgow Education Authority intended her for the most prestigious headships. She was a leading figure in the Western Division of the Modern Language Association and was its President for a number of years. A member of the Franco-Scottish Society, she was bestowed the French honour of Officier d'Académie. She was the author of a number of textbooks for teaching French, and had acted in an advisory capacity to the BBC on their talks in French.

Her application for the post at Hutchesons' was a mere page and a few lines, but in it she explained that her current job in a large school encompassed many of the duties which would ordinarily fall directly to a

Headmistress, being devolved from her Head to her. She therefore had had a unique experience in dealing with the girls in matters of conduct, of application to their lessons, of physical health; advising them as to the courses of study in school and when leaving school for the University or Colleges and discussing possible careers; the taking of Scripture with the fifth and sixth year classes; oversight of the girls' athletic interests, hockey and tennis; the arranging of all social functions and the dealing privately with cases of necessity and the disposing of funds contributed by the staff for such cases.

She explained further her 'large part' in the 'making of the following year's Time-Tables, settling time allocations to subjects, arranging senior girls' personal subject-groups, and deciding with the Head of the Classical Department who was fit to take two languages as well as English'. She held that it was on 'the grounds of this administrative experience' and also the fact that she had experience in an English as well as in a Scottish secondary school that she applied. She promised 'to maintain the high prestige of the School and to foster the best interests of the pupils'.

The fact that her Leamington experience was not in an exclusive private school and that North Kelvinside was situated in a working-class district strengthened her application with the Governors, who wanted their Schools to be in the mainstream of Scottish education.

Perhaps it should be mentioned that there had been some 'agitation' to appoint a woman to the Headship of the Girls' School from June 1926. The Law Agent of the Governors took legal opinion as to the position in both schools, especially in the Girls' School, appreciating that McVicar would reach his 65th birthday on 13 November 1927.

In the event Kennedy was one of four women in the leet of six from 32 applications. They were:

David Anderson MA – Rector of Dalziel HS, Motherwell
Agnes Borland LLA BA – Head of Modern Languages, Bellahouston
  Academy
Esther M. Legge MA – PT English/History at HGGS
William J. Merry MA DLitt – PT English at Whitehill Secondary
Annie S. Robertson MA – Head of French, German and Spanish at
  Dumbarton Academy

Margaret Kennedy was appointed the first woman Principal.[50]
Finding the academic curriculum fully developed, she widened opportunities for the less academic girls. She added Commercial (Secretarial)

Subjects to the curriculum and reorganised and extended Domestic Science. She ensured that Art, PE, Music and Geography were all on the general curriculum. She established the Kindergarten, introduced two infant classes, enhanced the Library and stressed good citizenship. The School remained a teacher training centre, now known as a Centre for Preliminary Training in the Art of Teaching, with the Principal as Mistress of Method.

She began a Sports Day (on the athletic ground opposite Kingarth Street), brightened the School uniform, organised many overseas trips and introduced debates and dances with the Boys' School. During World War 2 she began a Girls' Training Corps. She supervised the transfer of pupils in war-time to Sanquhar, then Dalry, and was disappointed when the Milton Park experience was discontinued.[51]

She retired in November 1948 after twenty-one years as Principal, and in her final year the Girls' School gained the largest ever number of Leaving Certificates. She was 'certainly one of the great Headmistresses of her generation'.[52] Much of what she had introduced to the School became an integral part of it: for example, the uniform, the crest, the Garden School and the Library.[53] It was not surprising, then, that in 1948 the City of Glasgow met more than half of Hutchesons' expenditure and provided substantial additional grants to the HET.

Margaret Kennedy made constant improvements to her already superior structure. Governors were presented with a stream of suggestions. When thwarted she waited for the right moment and delivered a powerful response. When asked to justify the continued employment of an Elocution teacher, she waited some six months and then told the Governors that she recommended that all the girls should take the subject.[54]

She had a strong staff with only three male teachers, and all the major departments were run by women. In 1928 her staff at Kingarth Street was twice the number at Crown Street. She used them well to open up the world to the Girls and the Magazine carried numerous articles about their experiences and the insights gained. The variety was as impressive as the number.

Miss Kennedy died in November, 1957.

W. Tod Ritchie: Rector, Hutchesons' Boys Grammar School (1932–45)

W. Tod Ritchie was born in December 1880 and was an outstanding scholar at Speir's School, Beith, where he was Dux Medallist. He took double Honours in History and Classics at Glasgow University in 1904 and won the

Ewing Medal. He edited Dunbar's poems and the Bannatyne Manuscript of medieval Scots verse, and did academic research in Oxford and London, before studying further afield in France, Germany and Italy. His focus was on Scottish history and literature. He was keen on athletics, winning a Blue,[55] and on cricket, playing for West of Scotland CC, and was still turning out to play at the age of fifty. He was also in HM Forces.

Ritchie began his teaching career at Lanark Grammar and moved for further experience to Helensburgh before taking up Rectorships at Alloa Academy (until 1923), Jordanhill College School (1923–31) and North Kelvinside Higher Grade School (1931—32). He seemed ideally qualified to become Rector of the Boys' School in 1932 as a scholar-athlete (as the press labelled him) and certainly his background put him firmly in the burgh grammar tradition of which Hutchesons' was clearly a part.

Despite his remarkable curriculum vitae, Ritchie only just made it to be Rector of the School. The Special Sub-Committee which recommended his appointment had been tied at 6–6, and needed the casting vote of the chair, Sir Charles Cleland, to reach a decision. There was also annoyance in some quarters that not enough information had been given to the Governing Body about Ritchie and the other candidates, and it did not help that the Committee did not advertise the post, thus restricting the field unnecessarily. Ritchie had been the only candidate invited to interview and he was asked 'only a few questions'. The row led Glasgow Education Authority shortly after the appointment to rule that all Hutchesons' appointments must be made from the Corporation 'list' or 'submitted for the approval of the Corporation'. 'Being a City School meant playing by the City's rules'.[56]

From his first days in post, Ritchie took up what was to be his consistent theme – the need for a new School building. He thought Auldhouse would be the ideal place to build, seeing it as an uncovered classroom, and suggested Hutchesons' follow the example of Watson's in Edinburgh and move to the suburbs.

Another important issue of the time was left to a new Commission, which had been set up to investigate the position of the endowed schools and which had the power to change their operating schemes. As the Commissioners had to take note of the effectiveness of existing schemes, the Governors were content with the status quo and dismissed any suggestion of reform. The Hutchesons' Schools were deemed an integral and vital part in the city's schooling. In the event, in 1935 the Commissioners set up two schemes – the Glasgow Educational Trust and the Hutchesons' Educational Trust (HET). Reorganisation meant more money was available and the

Commissioners ordered £25,000 to be put aside in a building fund. Ritchie was a step closer to getting his new building.

By 1939, land for a new Boys' School had finally been secured. The new School would provide 'a central institution for Secondary education available to the whole City, to fit in with the scheme of education for the City'.[57] Auldhouse had been found unsuitable for building and now a ten-acre site at Crossmyloof Station, close to all forms of transport, was the favoured location. Optimism ran high and the Governors asked Ritchie 'to draft a curriculum for the new conditions'. He responded by suggesting a practical side for those boys who did not wish to pursue a Classical course.

However, things began to go wrong. The original estimate of £90,000 proved insufficient – partly because the projected roll had been raised to 875 instead of the original 700. Ritchie was asked to accept substantial reductions in the plans, which he refused to do. The plan passed to the SED whose support was dwindling. For them the sums did not add up. However, it was World War 2 which put paid to Ritchie's ideas and his plans for building. Crown Street was given another quarter of a century lease of life, Crossmyloof was turned over to allotments and the architect's proposed competition cancelled.

With the outbreak of war, Education Authority Schools were closed and Kingarth Street was designated an 'Assembly School' to facilitate evacuation. The Girls were sent off to Sanquhar while the Boys' building was closed. The Governors were able to get both Schools re-opened by partitioning rooms and using sand-bags up to the ceilings. Fifteen air raid shelters were built in the Boys' playground. By Easter 1940 normality was restored in both Schools and was maintained for the rest of the War.

Ritchie returned to another theme – examination results. In 1934 he had publicised a 100% pass in the Leaving Certification Examinations. During the War, following the Glasgow University Bursary Competition of 1943, Ritchie claimed that academic standards were 'a little above their average', while in his final year in 1945 the Boys' had a new record, with fifteen in the top 100, in the Competition.

Such results were mirrored in Kingarth Street, and both Schools were regularly turning away many more applications than they could cope with. In 1943 Crown Street rejected 250 boys. Nonetheless, Ritchie prided himself in also knowing every boy's name – and pupils would remember him blowing in and out of classes with his gown billowing behind him, dispensing some wisdom on route.

Ill-health forced Ritchie to retire on 10 September 1945. Known as 'The Beak' to the boys and 'Tod Almighty' to the staff, Ritchie preached on 'teaching of the all-round pupil' and in 1944 he instituted a prize for that purpose. He also sent memorial cards to the parents of the 82 Hutchesons' FPs who died in the War.

Ritchie was fifth Rector (twenty-third Head) of the HBGS. He fought long and hard but unsuccessfully for a new building. Nonetheless, he fitted well into the Hutchesonian tradition. When in 1934 the City Council sought to take over the management of the Schools and their funding entirely, the plan was to spread the benefit of the Hutchesons' education to those who could not afford the fees.[58] This had echoes of the Trust Scheme in the later nineteenth century to develop a chain of Hutchesons' schools throughout the city. It was supported then by the Reverend Dr F.L. Robertson, the first Trust Secretary and Secretary of the two Endowment Boards in Glasgow, who had seen the Heriot's Trust in Edinburgh set up a school in every parish before state involvement following the 1872 Education Act.

Towards the end of World War 2 in one of his last addresses as Rector, Ritchie said that unless they could raise privately half the capital required for the new school, then the School would be handed over to the local authority. Ritchie seemed comfortable with such schemes. He did not fear for the future if fee-paying was ended or retained, although he would regret the loss of meritocratic access to the best education. He died in 1955.

James A. Watson ('Steamy'): Rector of Hutchesons' Boys' Grammar School (1945–55)

James A. Watson was born in June 1890, a native of Aberdeenshire. He qualified in Honours Classics at Aberdeen University in 1912. He served in World War 1 with the Black Watch and Gordon Highlanders. He taught as First Assistant in Classics in Queen's Park Secondary School. In 1930 he became Master of Method for Classical students at Jordanhill Training College, and in 1932 was appointed Principal Teacher (Classics) at Hyndland Secondary School with the remit of creating a Classical Department there. He moved to the post of PT (Classics) at Hutchesons' in 1937, and in 1945 became the first Head since Philp, to be appointed from within the School. Unlike a number of other Scottish endowed schools, internal promotion to the post of Rector was never a Hutchesons' tradition.

From the seventeen applications a short-leet of seven (including Watson) was drawn up. The others were:

1. James H. Filshie MA BSc – Headmaster of Riverside Secondary
2. James Barclay MA – PT English at Albert Secondary
3. Walter Dick MA BSc – PT Science at HBGS
4. David H. Knox – PT English at HBGS
5. John A. Muir MA – PT Classics at Jordanhill College School
6. James Paterson MA – PT Classics at the High School of Glasgow.

James Watson was appointed unanimously from the Corporation list, being seen as a safe pair of hands in difficult times.[59] He was sixth Rector, and twenty-fourth Head, and remained in office for a decade until 1955.[60]

Probably the most disappointed applicant was David Knox, for he had fully expected to succeed Ritchie. The Governors, however, favoured the Classics specialist, which Watson certainly was, to lead the foremost Classics school in Scotland at that time. Although thwarted, Knox apparently bore no grudge against Watson, whom he admired, and Knox served him loyally as Depute Rector from 1946 until 1950, when he achieved his own promotion and became Head of Hamilton Crescent Junior School (and then Strathbungo, retiring in 1957). The headship of a junior secondary school, however, must have been small consolation in the light of the post he really aspired to and expected to obtain. Like most of his contemporaries, Knox had the respect but not the affection of his pupils.

During Watson's tenure, the Boys' School was frequently described in the press as a Classical school whose raison d'etre was to dominate the Glasgow University Bursary list. In his first year as Head, the Boys had a new record, with fifteen in the top one hundred; in 1952 they had seven of the first eleven, while in 1955, his last year, the School repeated the 1945 results.

It seems that Watson's academic priorities were those of the Classicist purist, and Greek was soon regarded as a subject chosen by his successful students in the Bursary examinations. By the time of his retirement, the Boys' School was accepted as the leading Classics school in Scotland. This confirmed what Glaswegians had thought for a considerable time, viz. it was Hutchie for Classics, Allan Glen's for Science and Glasgow High for Law.

In these days the Glasgow Bursary List was widely publicised in the press, with Hutchesons' and Hamilton Academy usually competing for the top places. Only Allan Glen's rivalled them. The *Evening Times* on 30 June 1955 in its editorial entitled 'How does Hutchy (sic) do it?' concluded that an official Government investigation should be undertaken for the good of everyone's education. This followed the first four places being taken by three Hutchie boys and one girl; and of the first eleven, seven (four boys and three girls), attended Hutchie.

Watson prodded his Governors in efforts to keep the School up to date. He failed initially, however, to persuade them to introduce the post of Depute Head, although this was achieved when the Local Authorities introduced the position into its schools. Continuing his theme of improving staff arrangements and status, he pressed for Principal Teacher rank for those leading the Music, Geography and PE Departments, which did not present for certification. Watson also urged the appointment of PTs with responsibility for both the Boys' and Girls' Schools. Such changes were contested by the Governors, who wanted to save money by keeping the fees low and staying within Corporation regulations on staffing.

Watson appreciated how the post-war situation made talk of building a new school increasingly unlikely. In his final days in office he was quoted as saying that 'generations of Hutchesonians had come to regard the subject of a new school as a quaint but harmless myth'.[61] Nonetheless, he played an important part in helping the School and FP Club erect a small grandstand at Auldhouse in 1953. It was opened by Watson in May 1954, during the first great years of Hutchesons' rugby under Roy Smith and Willie Wilson.

The highlight of Watson's time as Rector was his organisation of the School's Tercentenary Celebration in 1950. The validity of the date was based on the very dubious authority of the old School song, the first line of which held that 'in 1650 the school began'. However, Rector Watson worked hard to make sure no one thought of the 1950 Celebration as anything other than fully justified. Although Aberdeen Grammar School abandoned their proposed 700th Anniversary scheduled for 1956 when doubt was thrown on its foundation date, the oldest Hospital School in Scotland, George Heriot's, went ahead with its Tercentenary Celebrations in 1959.

Hutchesons' week of Celebrations began with a service in St David's (Ramshorn) Church, after a march from the School to the Kirk. On Tuesday, there was a Governors' Dinner in St Enoch's Hotel for the City Fathers and eminent educationalists. On Thursday, the entire Boys' School was bussed to the Trossachs. On Friday, a reception was held in the City Chambers and the historical affinity between the School and Glasgow was confirmed. The week ended with the School Sports at Auldhouse.

Watson secured the School's reputation as a centre of academic excellence. He had a long retirement. He died in June 1975.

Miss Isabella Gray McIver: Principal, Hutchesons' Girls' Grammar School (1948–73)

Isabella Gray McIver joined the HGGS as Principal following the retirement of Margaret Kennedy in November 1948. She had wide experience as both teacher and promoted teacher in Scottish schools. As a pupil she had attended Old Kilpatrick Public School and Clydebank High School, and went on to achieve FCH in Modern Languages at Glasgow University in 1931. After a course at Teacher Training College in Glasgow she was appointed teacher of French at Muirkirk Higher Grade School, Ayrshire, in 1933. From 1934 until 1945 she was an assistant in the Modern Languages Department of Ayr Academy. Afterwards she was appointed Principal Teacher of Modern Languages at Royal Academy, Irvine, where she founded a French club. In 1946 she gained a French scholarship to the University of Besançon. McIver was one of the four ladies leeted for the Principal's post from fifteen applications in October 1948. Elsie Forrest was the internal candidate, but despite her many qualities she was only an assistant Classics teacher at the time. Indeed so were the others – Elizabeth Dougary of Gillespie's School in Edinburgh, and Elizabeth Stewart of Glasgow High School – but all were on the Corporation's Mutual Eligibility list. McIver took her chance and the post was hers.

She pioneered an oral approach to language teaching a generation before it was accepted practice, and this was a very different approach from Miss Kennedy with her textbooks and class work. McIver backed the introduction of a four-term year and abolished the use of hats for S3–S6 girls. She planned the Music building, and is given credit for improving Primary accommodation and Biology laboratory facilities. She retired in January 1973, a legend in her own lifetime, and, gifted with the ability to get her own way on just about everything, she made the Girls' School a centre of excellence which grew to almost twice the size of the Boys' School (1,000 to 600). She aimed the girls at high-achieving futures in male-dominated spheres.

During her period in post, Art and Music became basic subjects, studied by every girl in the School. James Reid's concerts were highlights, with hundreds of girls singing, and his successor, Alan Graham, was responsible for a great development of orchestral work. In the opera, 'Dido and Aeneas', presented in 1970, the combined resources of the Art, Music and Needlework Departments were united to produce a work of such a standard that it will not be forgotten by those who took part in it, or saw it.

New courses were begun: in particular, the School embarked on the experiment of a six-year primary followed by a seven-year secondary. Generally, pupils and parents appreciated the wider choice of subjects which resulted. In addition to their specialised subjects, the Sixth Form followed a programme of General Studies, in which Science, Art, Current Affairs and Homecraft played a part.

The tutorial system was established so that every pupil from second year onwards was assigned to a member of staff who followed her School career, advised her when difficulties arose and reported them to the Guidance specialists, if further help were needed.

School journeys started up again in 1949; since then hundreds of girls, supervised and instructed by members of staff, have gone to France, Switzerland, Austria, Germany, Norway and Greece, and with the English Speaking Union (ESU) to America.

The Literary and Debating Society flourished. The Burns Supper was an important date in the school year. Teams acquitted themselves well in the ESU inter-school debating competitions, and twice the School won the Balfour Trophy, awarded to the best team in Scotland.

Mountaineering became almost a school subject. Every year, under Donald Crabb's guidance, about three hundred girls reached the summit of some peak within reasonable distance from Glasgow.

The girls continued to show concern for others. Each year the Philanthropic Committee, composed of staff and pupils, distributed between £300 and £400 to various charities; this was the product of weekly voluntary contributions. Funds were raised by Friday 'tuck shops', run by each class in turn; for special occasions seniors organised Coffee Mornings and, for extra-special occasions, Fêtes! Four classrooms in the playground, and the furnishing of the new Biology laboratory, were largely paid for by the girls' efforts with, of course, the support of staff and the girls' families.

All of the Sixth Year constituted the School Council: divided into committees, the girls worked for the School and for others outside. They helped with the annual collections of nuts and apples at Hallowe'en, and of clothes and toys at Christmas for less privileged children, and went themselves in groups to work in a club for mentally handicapped young people.

Meetings with the Boys' School became more frequent: there were joint debates and dancing classes, there was co-education in Russian, Spanish, Dynamics and Biology. And then, in 1974–75, the plunge! Primary 5 and 6 and First Year Boys were taught at Kingarth Street; Third and Fourth

Year girls at Beaton Road; in 1975–76 all pupils of Second Year and below attended Kingarth Street, while all years above that, attended Beaton Road.

McIver had a national profile, and indeed was more prominent nationally than any Hutchesons' Head before her. She joined the Executive Council of the EIS in 1946, and also in that year she was appointed President of the Western Modern Languages Section. She became a member of the first Scottish Certificate of Examination Board, was a Governor of Jordanhill Training College and was elected by the teaching profession to the first General Teaching Council of Scotland.

She was a formidable character. Shortly after her appointment to the HGGS, a primary member of staff complained to the Governors that the Principal was forcing her to teach First Year Latin. The Governors backed McIver.[62] Perhaps it was not surprising that her relations with teaching staff led to 'some discontent'.[63] To be fair she was probably very aware of the actions taken by the Director of Education and the Council against Frances Barker, Principal of the Girls' High School, whose relationship with her staff 'never fully recovered from the disputes of her early years in office'.[64] In the case of McIver her Governors decided that two women Governors would deal with the matter best. The two Governors tried, and failed, to meet with the Principal. After five months they gave up and the matter was closed. There would be no repeat of the problems experienced by Frances Barker.

In her last years in office McIver strongly supported the amalgamation of the Schools, determined that the Girls' School would not be swamped. She need not have worried. She did her job well and had ensured the Schools grew accustomed to each other. She died in November 1976.

John Muir Hutchison: Rector, Hutchesons' Boys' Grammar School (1955–66)

John Muir Hutchison, born in 1901, was a son of the manse and attended Whitehill School before attending Glasgow University with a bursary in French. He had a distinguished academic career, achieving certificates of distinction in every one of his classes in French and German, and in Latin and Political Economy. He also gained prizes in Old French and Roman History, and the prize for the most distinguished student of the year in French Language and Literature. He graduated with FCH in French, German and Latin, and also took the degree of Licencié ès lettres at Paris.

He conducted adult classes in French at Glasgow University for the WEA, and was a member of the Glasgow Panel who handled the Leaving

Certificate examinations during World War 2. He was Secretary of the local EIS Modern Languages Section for over twenty-five years, a member of the EIS Central Modern Languages Committee and a member of the committee of the Franco-Scottish Society. He also found time to be Voluntary Educational Organiser for a youth centre in Bridgeton for seven years.

He taught in Woodside Secondary School, was Principal Teacher of Modern Languages at the High School of Glasgow (Boys) and at HBGS, the latter between 1936 and 1947, then spent nine years as Depute at Whitehill Senior Secondary School. He found himself on a leet of three from fourteen applications. His two rivals both had experience teaching at the School. Robert Ferguson and Ninian Jamieson were serious contenders, but it was Hutchison who was appointed seventh Rector (twenty-fifth Head) of the School. He became the fourteenth Scottish Head to gain membership of HMC in June 1964.[65] Outside the classroom he was active in sport, especially golf, and he organised and led many school journeys abroad; he also acted as Treasurer of a variety of clubs and societies.

Although Hutchison's values were the same as those of his predecessors, he felt it necessary in 1957 to make statements of what could formerly be assumed. His Six Aims appeared on classroom walls in the new building in 1960:

To seek for truth, through research and clear and honest thinking.
To appreciate beauty, in nature and in art in all its forms.
To develop a strong, healthy body, controlled by a clean, healthy mind.
To respect differences, whether they be differences in age, economic levels, educational levels, nationality, creed or colour.
To consider our fellows, and to use our talents, skills and knowledge to serve others as well as self.
To know the will of God, and to do it.

Hutchison knew the ethos intimately, and his Aims encompassed what he believed already existed and would be lived as they always had. It seems probable that his work on a statement of values led to his initiation of a Founders' Day.

He oversaw the move from Crown Street to Beaton Road – with the Junior block opening in 1957 before the full opening at Crossmyloof in 1959. During this exciting period, Hutchison's painstaking attention to detail secured many improvements in the original plan for the new School, although limitations of finance vetoed some desirable features, in particular a swimming pool. Nonetheless, the new building made possible an expansion of the Primary School which contained six classes instead of the former four. At the same time the upper forms of the Senior School grew, which enabled twice as many examination candidates as before. The 1955–56 session opened with a roll of 680, while the 1965–66 session began with 837.

Hutchison liberalised the curriculum. Three more Principal Teachers were added to middle management – in Physical Education, Geography and Music. Geography was studied to Sixth Form level and Music became a full Certificate course. Modern Language candidates were enabled to take Latin, while Classical pupils could take French. Art was also developed and offered a variety of activities. The School was quick to adopt the new approach to Mathematics and also pioneered the 'alternative syllabus' in Science. In so doing, Hutchison built up Science to rival Classics. This did not go down well in some quarters, for many were concerned about, and regretted, the threatening of Classics.

Even the long-established subjects were affected by the progressive outlook from the top of the School. In English, group teaching was introduced, set home readers disappeared, and a more fluid curriculum was enlivened by an infusion of modern literature.

The School Office also benefited from Hutchison's attentions, one of his innovations being a more efficient and less laborious system of filing and registration. He took a close interest too in ground improvements at Crossmyloof and Auldhouse.

Academically, Hutchesons' kept up its standards: in the Glasgow University Bursary Competition the School took 124 places during his decade in post. On the social side, the School's clubs and societies were too numerous to allow weekly meetings to be held, and the Annual Concert became a major occasion. He introduced a Founders' Day in 1961 reminding the school community of its debt to the past. Width had been cultivated as well as depth.

Under Hutchison's leadership the School acquired a balance without loss of traditional strength. Hutchie was still a stronghold of Classics, but other subjects were competing strongly for parity.

Although modest, Hutchison proved to be a gifted musician and had a very good baritone voice. He lifted the rule requiring seniors to wear caps. He was painstaking in the tasks he took on and was always the gentleman. He gained a Fellowship from the EIS. He died in 1989.

Peter Whyte MA MEd: Rector, Hutchesons' Boys' Grammar School (1966–78)

Peter Whyte was educated at Shawlands Academy, where he was School Captain in 1930–31, and Glasgow University, where he had qualified in Mathematics and Physics with Honours in 1935. He taught from 1935 at Kelvinside Academy and Jordanhill College School, but war service in the RAF[66] interrupted his Mathematics teaching in the latter, after only a year, in 1939. He returned to Jordanhill and remained there till 1950 and then was appointed Principal Teacher Maths and Depute Rector at the High School of Glasgow, before being becoming eighth Rector (twenty-sixth Head) of HBGS in 1966[67] until 1976, and of the amalgamated Schools until 1978.

He was seconded in 1969 by the SED to go to Malaysia for the first term (without salary) as he was an international expert in the new Mathematics of the 1960s. He was involved in the production of textbooks which helped transform the teaching of Mathematics in Scottish schools. He was also involved in making TV programmes for teaching. He served on the Mathematics Panel of the Scottish Certificate of Education Examination Board.

Whyte's appearance and bearing were always appropriate. He was diplomatic, dignified and discreet. He was approachable and supportive. His interests included golf, curling, dancing, gardening and photography.

Whyte arrived at HBGS when an educational debate was heating up on the continuance of fee-paying in secondary schools. From 1945 local authority schools became entirely a charge on the rates, but an anomaly remained in the form of 'grant-aided' schools, which included Hutchesons'. They were concentrated in the towns, especially in Edinburgh and Glasgow and had resulted from the reorganisation of educational endowments in the later nineteenth century. They, however, had served as part of their local authority's educational provision ever since.

By 1966 Glasgow's secondary provision was made up of 25 comprehensives,[68] 22 senior secondaries, including five fee-paying, and 28 junior secondaries, but a rebuilding programme to replace all the senior and junior secondaries within five to seven years was in place. The five fee-paying schools whose grant came from the Corporation – Glasgow High, Girls' High, Notre Dame, Hillhead High and Allan Glen's – were invited either to join the local authority schools or to go fully independent.[69]

The nine 'grant-aided' schools – HBGS, HGGS, Jordanhill College

School, St Aloysius, Kelvinside, Laurel Bank, Westbourne, Craigholme and Park – expected to be approached for discussions, but instead in 1967 the Labour Government froze their grants, pending recommendations from the Donnison Commission which had been tasked to advise on how such schools could be incorporated into comprehensive reorganisation. However, it was not until March 1969 that the Commissioners visited Hutchesons' and met with Miss McIver and Acting Rector Arthur Meikle.[70]

The unexpected return of a Conservative Government under Edward Heath in June 1970 did not solve the problem, but at least improved the financial situation. Grant-in-aid was restored, but in future it was based on 40% of expenditure instead of the historic 60%. The Governors reacted quickly, and a Special Committee was set up in May 1971 to consider the future of the Schools. Both Whyte and McIver attended its meetings, and when asked to submit proposals they produced, in less than three weeks, exciting plans for a co-educational primary and secondary school, a single Hutchesons' Grammar School. In detail, Kingarth Street would accommodate Primary I to Secondary II, while Crossmyloof would house the remainder of the School. The merger date was set for 1975–76.

Meantime, the new Labour government of Harold Wilson delivered an ultimatum in 1974 demanding that each of the 'grant-aided' schools decide whether to become a local authority comprehensive or a wholly independent school. For practically all the schools involved, the latter course appeared to offer the better option. But for Hutchesons' the situation was different. Despite having more in common with the Corporation fee-paying schools than any other institution, now there was no other school remaining of this type, the priority for its Governors was keeping alive in Glasgow the idealism and effectiveness of the city tradition,[71] even now that it had been decided to go completely independent.

Following the amalgamation of the Schools in August 1976, HMI inspected both primary and secondary departments. The total roll was 1,721 pupils, of whom 507 were in the Primary and 1,214 in the Secondary. They were drawn from a wide area of West Central Scotland, the great majority coming from the southern residential suburbs of Glasgow and from Eastwood District. Staffing was generous, especially in the Secondary where 83 full-time members of staff were employed (with national guidelines stipulating 75.5 members of staff). The School was deemed fortunate in having a staff who were highly qualified, who exhibited a rigorous professionalism in the exercise of their craft, and who gave considerable time and energy to support the wide range of extra-curricular activities provided for the pupils.

Within the various subjects the level of the pupils' work was high and the courses were well organised. Judged by the criterion of results in the external examinations, there could be no doubt that the School was achieving the high academic standards to which it aspired.

The process of amalgamation was a continuing one, and the School organisation of management had to be adapted to serve best the interests of the combined School and enhance the opportunity for effective dialogue on the curriculum within the School and within the subject departments. In this way the scope and quality of the sound learning which the School already provided continued and indeed improved.

Whyte retired when he reached his 65th birthday in December 1978. He had inherited a successful school, and knowing the Glasgow scene and its schools he ensured that under him this success was continued. He reached 100 years of age in December 2013.

Arthur E. Meikle: Interim Rector of HGGS (1969)

Born in 1910, Arthur E. Meikle was a former pupil of Queen's Park Secondary School, where he won the Gold Medal in English. He graduated from Glasgow University in English Literature and Language in 1933. He taught at Drumoyne and Petershill before serving in Whitehill Secondary School, where remained from 1939 until 1956. He became PT (English) at HBGS in 1956 and added the role of Depute Rector in September 1965. He was Interim Rector for the first part of 1969 while Rector Whyte was in Malaysia. He retired in June 1975. He was a talented violinist who conducted the Glasgow Teachers' Orchestra from 1953 until 1962. He was later the President of the School and Club, and was the only member of staff other than an incumbent Rector to be a Governor of the HET. His hallmark in all these positions was his avuncular gravitas. He was a clear, incisive thinker, and a meticulous organiser and administrator. He had the respect of the pupils and was well-liked as well. Even the staff with very different perspectives had only good things to say about Meikle. From his time as an English teacher at Whitehill he was remembered for 'quiet courtesy, sympathy and knowledge'.[72] He was Founders' Day Speaker in 1979. He died in 1993.

Jessie G. Knox MBE[73] MA: Acting Principal of HBGS (1973–76)

Born in 1912, Jessie G. Knox joined the HGGS Classics staff in September 1949 and was promoted to PT Classics, succeeding Miss McKendrick, in

1955. She gained an MBE in the New Years' Honours list. She was promoted to the new post of Assistant Head Teacher (Curriculum and Guidance) in 1971. She was Acting Principal from 1973 until April 1976, after which she retired. She contributed much to the very complex educational project of amalgamation that was carried out at this time. She proved an effective promoted teacher, was very communicative and with her sound educational ideas she was quite progressive. She was, however, criticised widely by staff in the Girls' School, who feared the results of merger.

Dr (David) Gilmour D. Isaac: Rector, Hutchesons' Grammar School (1978–84)

David Gilmour D. Isaac was born in Pengam, Wales, the son of a primary headmaster, whose father had been a miner. He attended Sir Edward Lewis's GS and won a Music scholarship to Jesus' College, Oxford, but studied Modern History. He won a Blue for soccer.

He taught History at Edinburgh Academy and was a Tutor and Housemaster. He was then Head at King Henry VIII Grammar School at Abergavenny, which had merged with the High School for Girls. With 1,800 pupils it was the largest school in Wales. He gained a PhD from Edinburgh and became Head at Marr College, Troon, a post he held for a decade. He became ninth Rector (twenty-seventh Head) at the School in January 1978. He was the first Rector since Ritchie to have previous experience as a Head.

There were 44 applications for Rector, a long-leet of 11 and a short-leet of four. He was interviewed with three others on the leet[74] and was 53 years of age when appointed. His wife came from Edinburgh. He brought much expertise to developing and improving the management of the amalgamated Schools, transferring S2 to Beaton Road, paving the way for the whole of the senior school to be under one roof, and appointing a Head of Lower School to Kingarth Street, so giving a stronger sense of identity.

He believed in challenging pupils and was a firm and caring upholder of the School's values. His educational watchword was 'stretching'. On appointment, he held that his first aim was 'to get to know the pupils and the School. Insistence on quality in education will continue to be the prime consideration of Hutchesons". He supported Mrs Fotheringham's vision of computing by installing 14 BBC B computers and peripherals in a newly converted laboratory at a cost of over £10,000. This was the first networked computing laboratory in any West of Scotland school.

Isaac inherited a large School which was not yet balanced or united. There were two staffs, two sites and two cultures. Beaton Road had been built for 800 boys, but the girls and boys had to share the same building. But should they be in the same classroom?

HMI returned again to the Secondary department of the School in September/October 1981. They had much advice to offer. Despite improvements in accommodation and resources, many staff were excessively peripatetic and the need for economy had limited the breadth of experience offered in some subjects to the pupils. Although the Secondary was exceptionally generously staffed, relationships were tense in some subjects. A more varied pedagogy and greater differentiation were recommended, and staff needed to stimulate the many very able pupils. There was still much to be done to ensure the amalgamation was a success, e.g. a review of differential provision for boys and girls in games had to be undertaken, since current practice did not appear to meet the requirements of the Sex Discrimination Act of 1976.

Unfortunately, Isaac did not have much time to deal with some of these matters. He was forced to resign in June 1984 as a result of the pain he suffered from neuralgia. He had been reserved, cultured and courteous. He had admired the School and its traditions and had appreciated the diligence of his staff, for he too was committed[75] and hard-working. He died in June 2003.

Isaac was an important Rector in Hutchesons' history for, from the first, he supported the move to independence. It had no future as just another City school. Rightly he galvanised the staff and laid down the route-map for the School to follow on what he saw as the only way to preserve the Hutchesons' ethic.

Paul V. Brian: Rector, Hutchesons' Grammar School (1984–85)

Paul V. Brian was born in 1942 and was a former pupil of Perth Academy. He graduated in Pure Science from Edinburgh University and spent a year at Heriot-Watt University studying Biochemistry. A brief spell in industry was followed by two years on the staff at a boarding school in Switzerland. After teaching in Edinburgh he moved to Garnock Academy, Kilbirnie, Ayrshire, in 1971. He was promoted in 1977 to become Assistant Rector at Marr College, Troon, and again when he became the first Head at the new Gryffe High School in Houston, Renfrewshire, in 1979. He arrived at Hutchesons' in 1984 with a considerable reputation in the maintained sector behind him.[76]

He was the first Rector since Hutchison to have come from a local authority school. However, Hutchison's background was that of a senior secondary, while Brian was committed to the comprehensive.

In October 1965, Circular 600 had been issued by the Labour Secretary of State, William Ross, giving guidance to Local Authorities on how to reorganise secondary education in Scotland on comprehensive grounds. From then on Hutchesons' positioned itself very much as the last bastion of senior secondary values. The evidence from applications and roll numbers, and the continuing high academic success, suggested that a significant number of parents supported them too. The Governors had done what they could to keep the School open to the talents and had already ended foundations, scholarships and bursaries awarded purely on merit, making them available on affordability grounds alone, for parents who could not meet the fee cost.

It should have been no surprise, then, when Brian's educational and management perspectives met with suspicion, even opposition, from a number within the School. Before his first term in office had ended, Brian had to explain to the Governors, chaired by Professor R.B. Jack, why the complaint regarding his introduction of 'comprehensive education' was ill-founded. Since taking up his post he had not, he claimed, made any major changes affecting education in the School. Nonetheless, before December 1984 was over, Jack had received a letter signed by eight Principal Teachers in the School, expressing grave concern about the School's future.

Adverse publicity deepened the crisis, as teaching staff resented the register introduced by Brian in which teachers had to explain their reason for leaving School during non-teaching time. It seemed to some staff that signing out took away a degree of professional responsibility. For others it seemed a move towards making the School more like the maintained institutions which Rector Brian had experienced.

When Jack and his Education Convenor, Dr A. J. Howie, met the signatories of the letter of complaint and the other senior teachers of the School on 15 January 1985, the Chairman took great pains to spell out that Brian had been chosen as Rector 'because they (the Governors) felt he was the person best suited to lead the School to independent status and that he enjoyed the full support of the Governing Body'. Nonetheless, a series of allegations regarding the Rector was discussed one by one.

By March 1985, a fundamental rift was still apparent, although when Brian talked of staff resistance to his measures he told the Governors that, given the backing of the Board, he was confident that in time all problems could be satisfactorily solved. This optimism was misplaced, partly because the Rector's agenda was so extensive that his proposed measures affected all of the staff in one way or another, and often adversely. In the case of perhaps the most controversial, tampering with the traditional successful timetable and replacing it with five periods of one hour in length, even Brian appreciated that it needed the support of all staff for such a radical change to work.

On 12 June 1985 Jack reported to his Governors on the problems affecting the School which had received widespread press publicity, and had resulted in a considerable number of letters from parents demanding an early meeting. He also told of a petition submitted to the Board signed by about 400 parents calling for a meeting. Some 76 teachers employed in the School had also presented a petition expressing doubt about Mr Brian's appointment. The Chairman then went on to detail what, in his view, were the main areas of concern to parents and staff, namely, the loss of authority and credibility by the Rector, his commitment to 'academic excellence', the breakdown in relationships with staff, and that Brian was perhaps seen as an instrument for implementing 'state sector philosophy' in the School. The Rector responded at length and remained optimistic. After he had left the meeting, Jack told of his invitation to Sir Roger Young, Principal of George Watson's, Edinburgh, to advise the Governors as to how the difficulties might be resolved.

On 24 June at a further Board meeting, Professor Jack announced Brian's willingness to resign from his post as Rector, to prevent further damage to the School's reputation and to his own standing. After lengthy discussions the Board accepted Brian's resignation with effect from 25 August. Brian had resigned as a result of the 'damage being done to the School and to its reputation by adverse publicity, particularly in the press'.[77] He returned to a comprehensive Headship in the state sector in October 1985 at Biggar High School.[78]

Why then did the Governors appoint Paul Brian? It seems that the Hutchie Governors, able and experienced as they were, had little idea what they wanted from a new Rector. They ran a Glasgow School that felt its values of traditional academic education were under attack from a new educational orthodoxy. Nonetheless, with the Governors' support and approval, Brian initiated certain changes, but there was no time to judge their appropriateness or effectiveness, because the conflicts which led to Brian's resignation at the end of the 1984–85 session largely neutralised whatever might have been achieved. At the same time they helped bring to light a number of other deep-seated problems facing the School. It was in this situation, before appointing a new Rector, that the Governors asked Sir Roger Young to produce an educational consultant's report on the state of the School.

Young held that the problems were not of Brian's making, for documentation from the previous Rector, Isaac, held that 'It was evident to me [that] real power in 1978 lay not with the then Rector . . . but with Senior Staff and Heads of Department who had assumed directive powers in a quite amorphous body riddled with intrigue and vendetta'.[79]

He, as Rector Brian had before him, stressed the need for the general upgrading of the existing accommodation and facilities and he also stressed that in his opinion the Schools had never really been amalgamated into one unified and integrated community. He laid down a thorough programme of educational objectives which the new Rector, when appointed, would work from. By June 1986 the Governors had also agreed to the setting up of the Joint Consultative Committee (JCC) which would in future lay the basis for better communication between the Board and staff.

The huge strength of the School, through all the confusion and muddle of a problematic merger and the subsequent illness of the next Rector and then the row over Brian, was the amazing focus of the staff on teaching their pupils. There were a great many outstanding classroom teachers who saw their teaching as really important and just got on with it, whatever else happened. They carried the others in this attitude, and the School was able to function.

Miss Janet C. (Nita) Murray: Interim Rector, Hutchesons' Grammar School (1985–86)

Janet C. Murray took a FCH in English and taught at Albert Senior Secondary before joining the English staff of HGGS in November 1950. She was appointed Head of Department in 1964, and Assistant Rector in 1973. She then replaced Miss Cowan as Depute Rector in August 1979. Following the departure of Rector Paul Brian, for one year she became Interim Rector (reverting to Depute thereafter). She was the first woman to head a co-educational HMC school and the first Head since Rector Philp to have spent an uninterrupted career in Hutchesons' service. Academically gifted and a fine teacher, she was a constructive and progressive supporter of amalgamation. She handed on to her successor, David Ward, a strengthened School in good heart.[80] She died in October 2001' in her eightieth year.

David Romen Ward: Rector, Hutchesons' Grammar School (1986–99)

David Romen Ward was born in Newcastle in 1935 and received his primary education at St Mary's School in Melrose, before moving south to complete his schooling at Sedbergh, where his father was a housemaster and, later, Depute Head. After less than a year studying Science at Emmanuel College, Cambridge, he switched to History, and graduated MA in that subject in 1957. His main sporting interest was rugby, and he played for London Scottish for a short spell. He took a PGC in Education at Cambridge, but opted instead for graduate training with the South Eastern Gas Board. However, he gave this up and followed in his father's footsteps by taking up a History post at Winchester College.

He served eight years teaching History and Economics at Wellington; eight years as Head of History and Politics at the City of London School; spent four years as Deputy Head of Portsmouth GS; six years at Hulme GS, Greater Manchester, and finally twelve years at Hutchesons'. He was the first Head not to have taught in Scotland before his appointment. An author of history books, his leadership was marked by his tremendous work-rate and a good memory for names and faces.[81]

Ward waited a year and watched before introducing any notable change: from then he wasted no time. Energetic and experienced, he brought to Hutchesons' ideas that were fresh to a School that had always been a Glasgow school.

The School was outstandingly successful academically under him, and he led the major building programme which transformed Beaton Road, making it fit for the future. The new fifteen labs of the Science Block, the rebuilt North Wing, the Corridor Link, the Infant School at Kingarth Street, the Sports Hall, the Library and Resource Centre, together with, outside the campus, the new hockey pitches and changing facilities of Auldhouse, all owed much to him. In addition, he strongly supported the development of new Departments – Technology, Computer Science and Drama. His partnership with Chairman Derek Mason and Bursar Ian Tainsh resulted in new facilities enabling Hutchesons' to compete at the highest level.

In 1991 the School commemorated its 350th birthday, taking 1641, the date of the laying of the original foundation stone, as its beginning. Ward saw the value of making Former Pupils proud of their School. A data base was established and Anne Brown was appointed FP Registrar. As part of the Commemorative Week, Dux Medals were awarded to those who had failed to receive their prize from 1942 to 1957, when the awarding of medals was suspended as a result of the shortages of the time.

Ward's interests were wide-ranging, curricular innovations reflected that. His enthusiasm did not flag. He was well-prepared for the frequent planning meetings. Before he arrived, Hutchesons' was synonymous with University of Glasgow success. During his time, sights were aimed much further afield. The Secretary of the Trust was replaced by a Bursar, Ian Tainsh, and the Governors found the money for this change. Ward retired at the end of session, 1998–9.

Ward was a particularly important Rector of the School. Although the agenda he pursued had been laid out in some detail by Sir Roger Young in his Report, Ward still had to deliver, which he did so effectively. There was never any possibility of a repeat of the Brian episode. It was clear what was needed – providing the necessary facilities for the new very large mixed School. Allied to this, but separate, was the issue that there had not been much effort to create a mixed school, rather two schools under one roof at Beaton Road.

The pastoral structures of the two schools – via Form Masters in the Boys' School and via different years in tutor groups in the Girls' School – were just given up because of the difficulty of combining them. The Form classes were separate Boys and Girls, while a number of subjects were taught separately including English. The PE Departments were not combined and the staff rooms were separate. Another important difference was that in the past the staff in the Boys' School moved into and out of the School, looking for promotion and change. In the Girls' School the appointments were very much for life with little movement, and marriage was frowned upon if members wanted to stay in post. What Ward achieved in a crucial decade for the future of the School was the fusing of the two cultures.

John Geoffrey Knowles BSc MSc FRSA: Rector, Hutchesons' Grammar School (1999–2005)

John Geoffrey Knowles was born in Loughborough in June 1948. He spent his early years on the Wirral peninsula, before going as a boarder to St Bees School on the Cumbrian coast. He read Physics at Manchester University, followed by a Postgraduate Certificate in Education at Worcester College, Oxford, and a London University MSc in Theoretical Nuclear Physics.

He began his teaching career at Mill Hill, an independent boarding school in north London. A spell at Wellington College in Berkshire was followed by eight years as Senior Science Master at Watford Grammar School. Returning to the north-west in 1984, he became Vice-Master of Queen Elizabeth's Grammar School, Blackburn, before his appointment as Headmaster of King Edward VI Five Ways School, Birmingham, in 1990.

During his tenure as Head there, his school became fully co-educational, making it the only mixed grammar school in the West Midlands. Before arriving in Glasgow he was Chairman of the Association of Heads of Grant Maintained Schools; Chief Examiner for Nuffield Physics at A-Level; and Chairman of IMPACT, the south Birmingham Education Business Partnership. A keen musician, he had a particular interest in the music of Elgar, singing and playing the organ as well as writing record reviews and CD booklet notes. In 1998 he completed a part-time Theology course at Queen's College, Birmingham, and was ordained as a Church of England minister.

Knowles was another 'outsider' who had not taught in Scotland when he was appointed Rector of Hutchesons' in 1999. However, he continued with his wide interests. He was at the helm when, in August 2001, Laurel Park School became part of Hutchesons', and for the first time the School had a site north of the Clyde. This revived memories in some quarters of the nineteenth-century ambition for a city-wide chain of Hutchesons' Schools. The thinking behind this merger was to supply secondary pupils from the north, but this did not happen, as Laurel Park parents proved not to be keen to embrace the Hutchesons' academic ethos and saw better options for their children than travelling across Glasgow. In retrospect, the merger was a mistake, but perhaps an understandable one, given the competition for independent schooling in Glasgow.

His achievements in his five and a half years as Rector were the restructuring of pastoral care, with an increasingly closer and supportive relationship between pupils and staff; the progress on staff professional development which became an integral part of teaching life; the move toward a more inclusive, participatory management style, a departmental mentoring programme and the establishment of working groups to involve staff in reviewing and revising policies; and the embracing of the digital age with his legacy of some 630 computers over three sites, 27 interactive whiteboards, and a smart website of incredible further potential. Pupils and staff rightly expected to be electronically able and IT-literate, and as a result a stunning revolution had taken place in a short time.

The Fotheringay Centre, the converted Congregational Church adjacent to the School, was commissioned and fitted out under Knowles and he achieved much, for Music and Computing in particular. However, although Knowles appeared friendly, unfortunately and unjustly he was regarded with suspicion by some of his new colleagues on the grounds that he was English, Anglican and Evangelical. In 2003–4 there were differences within the School on examination results, discipline and relationships, and Knowles left in 2005 to take up a new career south of the border.

Graham Watson Armstrong MacAllister MA: Interim Rector (2005)

Graham Watson Armstrong MacAllister joined HBGS in Primary 5 in 1952 from Radleigh School in Clarkston, and left in 1962 to attend Glasgow University. Having graduated in History he taught at Shawlands Academy before joining the staff at Hutchie, a post he retained until 1971. His successful teaching brought him to the attention of the Education Committee of Glasgow Corporation, and under the Mutual Eligibility Scheme it was decided to transfer him to Whitehill Secondary School as Head of its large, successful History department. In 1973 MacAllister was interviewed at Hutchie by Rector Peter Whyte, Principal Isabella McIver and Depute Jessie Knox, and was appointed to the first joint Head of Department post as the two Schools began the process of amalgamation, during which he was responsible for the integration of the two History Departments.

In 1979 the Governors appointed him Assistant Rector, a relatively new and developing role. He helped orchestrate the 350th Anniversary Celebrations and was responsible for Prizegiving until his retirement in 2008. He was given the post of Interim Rector in 2005 when his knowledge of the School was to be invaluable. In retrospect it is clear how important he was in preparing the way for the new Rector. Certainly, Rector Greig appreciated how indispensable MacAllister was, and paid tribute to his knowledge, wisdom and loyalty. Moreover, MacAllister remained after the new Rector's arrival for another three years to help him in his tasks.

MacAllister was awarded a G and THA in 2010 for his outstanding contribution to HGS. He remained involved as a School Governor until 2014, and as President of the 1641 Society plays an important role in encouraging alumni around the world to reconnect with the School.

Dr Kenneth Muir Greig MA PhD: Rector, Hutchesons' Grammar School (2005–)

Kenneth Muir Greig was born in 1960 and educated at George Heriot's, where he was School Captain and Joint Dux, at Worcester College, Oxford where he gained a First in Natural Science (Geology) and at Edinburgh University where he gained his doctorate, also in Geology; his personal academic success made him a natural leader of schools. He was an Exploration Geologist with British Petroleum, 1984–7, before teaching Mathematics and being a Housemaster at Christ's Hospital, 1987–93 then Head of Mathematics and Director of Studies at Dollar Academy 1993–2000. He went on to be Headmaster at Pangbourne College, 2000–05, a co-educational boarding and day school in Berkshire. He was the unanimous choice of the Governors for the post of Rector at Hutchesons', and took office in August 2005. His background and diversity of experience both north and south of the border were powerful assets, especially his secondary schooling at Heriot's, which gave him an immediate understanding of the ethos of Hutchesons'.

The post interested him, as he wanted to lead a more academic school and he was attracted by the idea of coming back to Scotland, where he felt he understood what it would take to strengthen and improve a school like Hutchesons'.

He found the School to be everything he had hoped for. Academic excellence was squarely at the heart of it, and the pupils had an impressive focus and self-discipline regarding work. Inevitably as a new head he saw things he felt should be done differently, but that was not a criticism of any previous regime. He found staff, Governors and parents who were ready to work hard together. He tried to clarify the management structure, and included more people in decision-making, and that bore fruit in several areas, notably the articulation of the School's core values, which turned out to be very similar in essence to those which had been in existence many years before.

In 2008, after three years in post, Greig set out a statement of the Values of the School. This was the first attempt of any Rector to do so since John Hutchison's Six Aims a half century before. As he said:

'I hope by now that most pupils and staff are aware of the six values that underpin our academic curriculum: Honesty, Resilience, Independence, Curiosity, Creativity and Compassion. These were arrived at through a period of consultation with subject departments several years ago, and represent the sort of qualities or characteristics that we hope a pupil leaving Hutchesons' will have gained during their time here with us, through their academic studies.

'There are clear dangers in trying to summarise a complex educational process in six words, just as there are dangers for any organisation in producing a 'mission statement' phrase or slogan. The full richness of what a child experiences during their time with us can end up being rather trivialised, and at worst the words themselves can immediately be reduced to a kind of cliché. But it is important to know what a school 'stands for' and although I feel sure we would all have an instinctive feeling of what makes Hutchesons' unique, it is not always easy to articulate that, and I think these words help us.

'It is important to realise that although this list of values arose out of the academic curriculum, they apply to the curriculum in its widest sense as well. They are the values behind every aspect of the curriculum we provide, and of the community which the school represents. It is surely a good aspiration that we might all represent a curriculum which aims to be honest in its dealings with people, resilient in the face of difficulties, independent of spirit, curious and keen to explore new ideas, creative in how it makes things happen and always compassionate to others.'

Dr Greig has experienced significant challenges during his time at Hutchesons'. He quickly closed Hutchesons' Primary at Lilybank Terrace, recognising that it would require significant investment to bring the fabric up to the standard of other parts of the school, and the pupils were absorbed into Kingarth Street with an ongoing commitment to smaller class-sizes there.

Another issue escalated when the School failed the Charity test as one of a group of ten schools at the pilot stage. However, the clarity which Hutchesons' gave to the detail of the process made it easier for other schools to pass when their turn came. It also gave a timely reminder of the need to attract intelligent pupils from a wide range of backgrounds, and to increase the financial support available to them, in keeping with the spirit of the School's original foundation. The School became more truly meritocratic in admissions than it had been for some time and was more diverse as a result, another strength.

The Rector was proudest of the fact that the School not only remains at or near the top of the examination league tables every year, and this is done by keeping the level of challenge to pupils high, helping them to do difficult subjects well, and encouraging them to take six Highers at one sitting where possible. The school's leavers progress to university with good qualifications and an understanding of how to succeed with academic work.

In recent years there has been a growth of pupil interest in learning about other cultures around the world, and a growing sense of responsibility to others less fortunate than them. This goes alongside the encouragement given to take part in wider interests such as sport or drama, where excellence is also shown on a School and national level. All of which helps to make Hutchie's leavers more rounded people, and gives them confidence that they will succeed at university and beyond.

EIGHT   Recollections of the Modern
          Schools: Hutchesons' Girls'
          Grammar School

Janet W. Millar taught English in HGGS from 1885 until 1923, when she retired. In her article in the *School Magazine* in 1946 she 'Called Back Yesterday'.

'(On) a day early in August, 1885 . . . I found myself mounting, with a trembling heart, the steps of the old School on Elgin Street, on my way to an interview with William Thomson, B.A. (Lond.), lately come from Dunfermline High School. His first words, as he scrutinised me through his glasses, were, "You are very small," which I parried with the parody, "I am indeed, sir, but I cannot help it."

'After the usual preliminaries as to former career and qualifications he suddenly suggested a specimen lesson. Why this should have caused such consternation, it now seems hard to understand. Presently I plucked up courage when on putting the somewhat foolish question, "Shall I take off my hat?" I was met with a look of absolute helplessness and the rejoinder, "I don't know."

'Thus early I had discovered the Achilles heel in this strong man who could face the most intricate mental problems, but stood helpless before a practical one.

'With courage restored I followed him to a classroom with a gallery accommodating some sixty to seventy and was asked to give a lesson in Arithmetic – my weakest subject.

'Determined not to run the risk of error in working a sum on the blackboard, I launched into a talk on the origins of weights and measures which evidently gave satisfaction sufficient to bring a request that I should show myself again the next morning at nine a.m. Thus without any formal written appointment I became a member of "that glorious company", the staff of the Girls' School, an employee of that ancient and honourable institution, the Hutchesons' Educational Trust, and laid the foundation of a

136

long, unbroken (although I cannot honestly say unruffled) friendship with Mr. William Thomson, until his death in 1925.

'Of all the members of the staff at that date, only one besides myself, Miss Helen Sharp, is still alive and in good health in her quiet Clydeside home. During her whole career she was lovingly associated with the little ones, always in happy fellowship with her colleagues, though somewhat overshadowed by the more virile personality of her older sister – Flora – "The Duchess". By their nicknames or pet-names, one can always read a teacher. Flora was for many long years a pillar of the institution. A disciple of the old School with its tradition of "Work while it is yet day", she laid a firm foundation of character for hundreds, I may safely say, thousands of girls who still rise up and bless her . . .

'A few men were on the (staff) list but gradually disappeared, leaving only Mr. Ormiston to teach Mathematics with the aid of copious quotations from Shakespeare – a sugar coating for the pill perhaps. Fate had unkindly interfered with his career, and left him an embittered little man, with impoverished health and an irascible temper . . . All the same, he was a very capable teacher, and died sincerely mourned by both pupils and colleagues.

'Our "visiting masters" included that notable and portly personage, Mr. Muirhead, the Drill Sergeant, a Crimean veteran with a proper stentorian voice. Besides his professional work, he was useful at School functions with his "Charge of the Light Brigade". To enjoy that performance to the full one could not do better than read the works of the late Frederick Niven, the novelist. He was a pupil at the Boys' School, which appears in more than one of his works, dealing with middle-class Glasgow in the eighties and nineties, for example, in "The Justice of the Peace" and "Mrs Barry". Glasgow has recently erected a tombstone to him, and Canada is preparing a memorial to be unveiled in the autumn. Herr Schroeder, the German master, in spite of prolonged residence in Scotland, still "pretended", when I "professed" so many books or pages to a coming examiner; whilst Monsieur Janton, the French master, delighted to watch the girls "divvel-up". Both were fine men and excellent teachers. Mr Hanbridge, the Drawing master, was growing somewhat feeble by that time, but he still succeeded in getting beautiful designs for book-covers – his pet speciality. Mr Harrower, the elocutionist, was very affable, with an impressive air that befitted his subject. His text-book of pieces was well known all over Scotland, and its influence made itself felt in unexpected quarters.

'The first Singing master I remember was William Miller, an enthusiastic exponent of the Tonic Sol-Fa system. He prided himself on what some considered s strong resemblance to Shakespeare. His successor was the genial and popular Mr. Reid.

'In somewhat tardy recognition of the fact that ours was a school purely for girls, the authorities appointed Mrs Black, the pioneer in Domestic Economy for Schools.[1]

'Hitherto, teaching in that department had been left entirely to the mother in the home, but schools were ignorant of such training. In well-to-do families an "engaged" daughter might take twelve lessons in Higher Cookery at a price corresponding, but that was the only concession, whilst to train a girl of the artisan class properly to cook a dinner was a "wasteful and ridiculous excess". So to Mrs Black one must give the credit of foreshadowing the Domestic Economy School of today. She came every Friday afternoon to give a demonstration to some one hundred and twenty girls packed into a double room classroom with sliding doors. Is it to be wondered at that Mrs Black, who though a good cook, was not a trained teacher and anything but a disciplinarian, should lose control of the mass, and that Miss Turnbull, who hated to act policeman as much as I did, dreaded and loathed the Friday afternoon?

'All too brief was the meteor flight across our sky of James MacMillan. Although a brilliant classicist, he shared the same fate as the rest of us and taught different subjects, so it came that one day I found myself sharing the same classroom – so scarce was our space – teaching a small class of first years Latin while he was busy with English pupils over Macaulay's "How Horatio kept the Bridge". Presently I signed to my girls to close their books and listen to the masterly exposition of the poem enriched by his classical lore. It did them more good than Latin accidence.

'After a time I noticed him limping and enquired after a supposed accident, but my enquiries were not encouraged. On his return next session the limp was more pronounced and he had collapsed by summer. After a year or two of suffering he passed away . . .

'Years afterwards, J.M. Barrie, in one of his very few public speeches, referred to his School fellows and University friends, singling out Sir John Struthers, Chief of the Education Department, and James MacMillan, "with the most brilliant intellect I ever met".

'My appointment was followed shortly by that of Rev. Dr J. L. Robertson who became Secretary to the Hutchesons' Educational Trust from 1885 to 1892. He was followed in this post by William H. Macdonald. Outside his professional duties Mr. Macdonald was a well-known figure in Glasgow society, in high repute as an after-dinner speaker as he had an inexhaustible source of good stories and was a polished "raconteur". During the Great War he was induced to publish a collection of these, price one shilling. It proved an inestimable boon to the forces . . . He was a devoted friend of the School and a prime favourite with the girls.

'His successor, Mr Hall, equally devoted in all that pertains to our School, is still in office, so that in all these seventy years there have been only three secretaries of the Trust.

'In 1886 three outstanding members were added. Miss Ingleton, Mr. McVicar, and Miss Lochhead.

'Miss Ingleton, successor to Mrs McCready, filled the post of Lady Superintendent. Miss Lochhead, the daughter of Mr. Thomson's predecessor, Mr. Lochhead, was made assistant to Miss Ewing, head of the Sewing Department, and Mr. McVicar, distinguished Classical student and Greek medallist, soon assumed the position of First Master. Miss Ingleton's duties were not too clearly defined, but were supposed to include the oversight of the "morals and manners" of the girls, a post more necessary in those days with more men on the staff.

'Her work in the early days was largely secretarial, until the increasing demands for statistics necessitated the appointment of a secretary. The first to hold that post was Katherine Alexander, a former pupil, and sister of Miss Mabel, still the honoured head of the French department.

'Her successor was Jenny Borland, another FP, who retained the post until her marriage when, however, she did not change her name. She still does yeoman work in the FP Dramatic Club as one of the leading ladies.

'Miss Ingleton's gentle influence was felt not only during schooldays but in the after-life of many girls who kept in close touch with her long after they passed into the wide world.

'Our Janitors were outstanding characters. The first, Mr. McKechnie, an indefatigable worker, did not last long. No other messenger ever went to town and returned as swiftly as he. My picture of him is that of a figure seated by the gong filling up the few spare moments he ever had in mending the broken frames of slates. Later came Mr. Munro, a Highlander from remote Ross-shire, with true Gaelic pride and temper, but exceedingly clever with his hands. He showed me once a very beautifully finished sideboard, intended for his new house. He also renovated for me a bust of Milton which had lost an eye in the old school and had its nose damaged in the "flitting" to the new School.

'All these belonged to the nineteenth century, which was slowly but far from peaceably drawing to a close. Amongst other problems we had the evergreen Irish Question, the aftermath of the attempted Home Rule Bill which succeeded only in wrecking the Liberals, and creating the new Unionist party.

'Glasgow, at that day, was full of Irish, especially Fenians, who employed their leisure in laying bombs around our public buildings, notably the gasometer not far from our own doors. Happily, the munitions were poor or the conspirators inept, as no widespread destruction followed, but . . . they kept the public nerves on edge . . .

'As the years slipped by, the School increased to such an extent that the Governors were compelled to add a large wing extending east to Pollokshaws Road. So, early in the twentieth century, we found ourselves with two staffrooms, several additional class-rooms, a second and more spacious staircase and a third flat occupied by a much larger Drawing room and a cloak-room for the highest class. This added space made way for more staff, so in the first decade, we welcomed the appearance of Miss Bain, with her vivacious Celtic temperament and keen civic consciousness, to take charge of French and Miss Murray, with the calm, dispassionate atmosphere of Mathematics and the mountains. Her arrival settled what, for many years had been a weak spot in the curriculum. With her musical ability she brightened many of our social functions.

'The following year brought Mr. Wiseman to introduce for the first time a Science Department. Hailing from the north, he brought all its tonic virtues and very soon made his weight and helpful hand felt, not merely in his own department . . . His first assistant was a former pupil, Mary Simpson, now Mrs Glen. She was amongst our earlier University graduates as by this time "Gilmorehill" had opened wide its doors to women, and our girls were not slow to respond to the invitation. Her marriage removed her to England for some years, but on returning to Glasgow, she attached herself firmly to her old School and is still an unquestioned authority on the career of many members who have slipped from our immediate ken . . .

'Previous to 1895, largely through the efforts of Miss Galloway, Glasgow University had provided a kind of ante-room for women where they could be tutored in the various subjects, but in that year a great step forward was made and two women had the degree of MA conferred on them. In the following year Jeanie McJannett was the solitary woman graduate, with the first prize in Logic.[2]

'Naturally for the first few years the Arts Course attracted our girls until other avenues opened and Dorothea Lyness became our first Medical . . . For several years she practised successfully as Doctor Elizabeth until her marriage with a minister in the east end, where she did much good work amongst the poor. Later in life she unfortunately, though not unexpectedly, cast in her lot with the militant suffragettes, and became "known to the police" in a case of arson. Her death, which occurred a few years ago, evoked a very appreciative article in the pages of the *Glasgow Herald*.[3]

'The militants had by that day become a power, indeed occasionally a menace . . . The Pankhurst family were at the helm, and the mother just released from prison under "the Cat and Mouse Act" was, in spite of the prohibition of the City Magistrates, billed to address a mass meeting in St. Andrew's Hall. The girls of the highest class were permitted, at Miss Ingleton's request, to attend to see "history in the making". From them came very varied accounts of the event. Mrs Pankhurst had barely stepped on the platform, decked with large pots of aspidistra, the Glasgow palm, when the police re-arrested her. A wild uproar ensued and, according to certain spectators, lady members of the platform party were seen brandishing chairs in the face of the burly policemen – whether offensive of defensive was not clear.

'The additional wing added early in the century had, owing to our rising numbers, become quite inadequate, so the Governors once again had to face the problem of extended premises, which they did by building the new school in Kingarth Street. The architect was a son of "Greek Thomson" whose Greco-Egyptian Church in Queens Park was burned by German bombs towards the end of the latest war. Sheena Thomson was one of our distinguished Science students.

'It was somewhat of a trial to older members of the staff to leave Elgin Street for the spacious edifice in Kingarth Street, but very soon we settled into the spacious surroundings and possibilities of an extended curriculum. The annexe to the west of the playground gave space in its lower storey for a fully equipped Domestic Science department with laundry, kitchen and Dining Hall. Upstairs housed a suite for housewifery and a spacious Gymnasium with every appliance. The first of these brought us into happy contact with warm-hearted Miss Beattie, and the latter with the vigorous and athletic Miss Neilson, under whom the domain of sport had a beginning.

'A long and lofty hall in the centre of the main building now afforded scope for many functions till now unattainable, and for morning-prayers, hitherto conducted in separate class-rooms. For several years at this service, led by a small orchestra, I sheltered under the bronze wing of George Hutcheson, whose bust, with that of his brother Thomas, a gift from the Governors, helped to adorn this hall, while the other decorations included copies of old masters collected by Mr. Thomson, and photographs of the three headmasters, James Lochhead, William Thomson and William McVicar. The latest additions are an oak table and chair for the platform gifted by the late Miss Lochhead in memory of her father . . .

'Barely had we settled down in our new surroundings when a shadow began to creep over us at the thought of parting with our much esteemed Head, Doctor Thomson, who under the Superannuation Scheme was due to retire in 1914. Through all these long years he had devoted himself body and soul, to the interests of the School and the advancement of Higher Education, for he was a born educationist, who like the pioneers of other causes, was exposed not merely to lack of sympathy but to hostile opposition. This last arose perhaps in his younger days from a lack of tact in his relentless, sometimes almost ruthless, search after truth.

'Amongst his first opponents were members of the University, who, still under the monkish hand of mediaeval days, objected to his onslaught on compulsory Latin in entrance to its classes, and at the same time to his crusade for modern languages. He carried the day, however, and was largely instrumental in founding Chairs in French and German. This was the first of three great education movements engineered by him.

'The other two aimed at the simplification of English Grammar and resulted in the production of a weighty volume on Rhythm. One aim in the latter was the abolition of the clumsy and absurd attempt to squeeze the lines of English verse into Feet, fit mould only for Latin and Greek. His new system of measurement included an adaptation of the Tonic Sol-fa system . . .

'Dr. Thomson's efforts after simplification of English grammar were frequently nullified by the restless mentality that urged him to probe behind the surface of words so that, even if he simplified in one quarter, he complicated in another, but certainly he succeeded in clearing away much meaningless verbiage . . .

'Largely through his weighty volume on Rhythm, the authorities of Glasgow University awoke to the fact that in their community was a man of power, whom Germany, at least, delighted to honour, so, much to our satisfaction and gratification, they conferred on him the degree of LL.D.

'In June of 1914 he retired, still full of plans for the advancement of the School and dreading the prospect of unemployment, but very soon his thoughts were diverted into a new channel when War was declared on August 4th. His three sons all joined up and he, like everyone else, was plunged into the fears and anxious forebodings of four years. The whole School, teachers and pupils alike, resolved itself into a huge "Ladies' Auxiliary for the supply of Comforts to the Troops". The heavy work involved was occasionally relieved by an odd half-hour's permission to stand in Victoria Road and see a regiment march past. Conscription was not then in force and these parades were staged to attract volunteers in the forces.

'The deep regret and fear of changes which haunted the staff over the departure of Dr. Thomson were somewhat mitigated by the appointment of our old and tried colleague, Mr. McVicar, as Headmaster. For many long years, he, as First Master, had borne the burden of the practical work of the School, such as time-tables and the increasing demands of government for statistics. In Leaving Certificate work he had the responsibility for English, Latin and German until specialisation forced him sorely against his will to relinquish the last-named of these to Herr Oswald. The latter was a "live wire" both in work and play, the girls finding him a great acquisition in our social functions as a skilled pianist and yodeller.

'Miss Forbes next robbed Mr. McVicar of his beloved Latin but not for long . . . However,) his appointment as Headmaster compelled Mr. McVicar to hand over English to Miss Esther Legge, recently retired. She came as a bright particular star to capture, not only the ears but the hearts of the girls, and raised a monument to her own memory by resuscitating the School magazine until its enforced stoppage by the War just lately ended. In this successful venture she was substantially aided by the business acumen of Miss Currie.

'As a man, Mr. McVicar was the antithesis of Dr. Thomson, a master of detail rather than an educationist. One may safely say that he knew the name of every girl in the School, and had an intimate knowledge of all that happened in daily life. No drone was ever tolerated in his class; no effort physical or mental was ever spared nor did any outside interest, except perhaps that of his Church, ever divert him from his immediate duty.

'Never was there a more living exponent of the Scripture admonition "Redeeming the time". Firm was the hand but kindly the heart that moulded so many generations. Especially for the little ones he showed a marked partiality, and exercised such an attraction that latterly his room became a centre of daily pilgrimage to those little mites bearing individual problems . . . He retired in 1927 and died a few years later leaving a widow with whom he had shared all the joys and sorrows of his School life . . .

'Another true friend of the School . . . is Mrs Thomson, who has mourned her husband since 1925, when he passed away leaving three sons and three daughters, who have done distinguished work in education and medicine.

'So the days passed until the shadow of my own retirement began to overhang the scene of many long and happy years, until in June, 1923, I said "Goodbye" to my old life, and became one of the great mass of unemployed.'

Anna Buchan (O. Douglas), in *Unforgettable, Unforgotten* (London 1945) pp. 46–7. Anna Buchan was an early pupil at Hutchesons' Girls'. She did not stay long.

'After a couple of years at Queen's Park Academy (Glasgow), Willie and Walter joined John (her brothers) at Hutcheson's (sic), and I was sent to the corresponding school for girls. John gained a scholarship in his first year, and the other two did quite well also, but – with shame I confess it – I was the dunce of the family.

'It was not so bad in a little private school where nothing much was expected of one, but in a big school, one of a crowd, I simply sank to the bottom. Algebra and Mathematics I *could not* understand; any but the simplest of sums left me helpless. Besides being naturally stupid, I must also have been careless and inattentive, not listening unless I was interested, and when exams came my sins found me out . . .

'My ignorance was certainly not the fault of my English teacher, Miss Flora Sharp, who was a most efficient instructor of youth. She did not, however, suffer fools gladly, and had the sense to see that if a child sets herself not to learn it is labour lost trying to teach her. I can see her now, with her iron-grey fringe and piled-up hair and rigidly neat figure, eyeing me sardonically as I sat resisting education. Years later when I happened to be lecturing in Glasgow I was aware of something vaguely familiar in a front seat. It was Miss Sharp, still smiling sardonically.'

Charles W. Thomson, from *Scottish School Humour* (Glasgow 1936). Charles Thomson taught at HGGS from 1898 to 1901 and at HBGS from 1892 to 1895; he wrote about his time there in 1936 in 'My Assistantships', pp. 44–59.

'Wishing, mainly for family reasons, to return for a time to the west, I applied for a language post in Hutchesons' Girls' Grammar School, under my old Governors, and found there very congenial and happy work for three years under Wm. Thomson, B.A., the leading protagonist at that time of modern languages, and one, therefore, with whom I found much in common . . .

'I learned from Thomson the value of trust in his assistants on a headmaster's part – a lesson which I firmly held on to in later years . . . There was no corporal punishment, and a kindly free-and-easy discipline prevailed, but one which required distinct grit in the teachers. The pupils gave a new teacher about a month with every encouragement to show his paces. If in that time he had gained their confidence, all was permanently well. If not, he (or she) might just as well look out for another place. One man, who had found difficulty in a very good mixed school, wrote and asked me whether I would advise him to apply for a post in the girls' school. I honestly replied, "Certainly not. If you had trouble in yon Academy, you need not try Hutchie Girls!" However, to his sorrow, he risked it, and as his pleading with the pupils for better treatment was pathetic but vain, he hurriedly went off to teach children outside of Europe . . .

'Mr. Thomson was, above all, a gentleman. He had had some rather unpleasant differences with Professor Ramsay,[4] who was one of the Governors. Hearing this, a Glasgow lawyer who was publishing spiteful lampoons on Ramsay called at the School in the hope of extracting from Thomson some tit-bits for his next brochure. He was very promptly shown to the door . . .

'Before taking farewell of Hutchesons' Girls' School, I may remark that from the Governors of the School, alone of all my employers, I twice received the pleasant surprise of an unsolicited "bonus" in appreciation of my work.'

Reminiscences of Miss McKendrick, HGGS from August 1916, from the *Centenary Magazine* of 1976.

'When in August 1916 I was interviewed in the office of Hutchesons' Educational Trust for the post of assistant teacher in the Girls' School, one wall of the rather dingy room was adorned by the framed text of one of the platitudinous precepts of the American, Elbert G. Hubbard, "A smile is worth a thousand a year, then smile, damn you, smile." I was shocked and was not very sure that I wished to be appointed!

'However, September saw me installed in School as a member of staff. I found that I had come among colleagues who added to a devotion to their work a freshness of outlook and a lively interest in the issues of the time which were a constant source of wonder to me.

'I must pay a special tribute to Mr. McVicar, the Headmaster of the School. He was indefatigable in the performance of his duties and was possessed of an amazing energy, as was displayed by his frequent sorties, with gown flying, along corridors and into class-rooms where he could show knowledge of the lesson being taught in almost any subject.

'In those days changes of staff were rare, except for matrimony, and women gave up teaching on marriage. I should add that even at that time we had men teachers in the departments of Science, Art, Music and German.

'In the First World War, School was active in many of the efforts, which became necessary to alleviate hardship among the non-combatants, also providing comforts for troops on service and entertaining the wounded in hospitals in Glasgow and neighbourhood.

'Armistice Day 1918 affords more lasting memories. The end of the War came unexpectedly, and on Monday, November 11, a day of brilliant sunshine, we went to School and attended morning service as usual. Hostilities were to cease at the eleventh hour. In time for that moment we again gathered in the Hall, were told by Mr. McVicar that the War was over, sang Psalm 124 (second version) and, after a prayer of thanksgiving, were dismissed for the day, many of us to join the throngs of dazed, but thankful, people who walked aimlessly through the streets of Glasgow, too stunned for "mafficking".[5] For the rest of the week we spent only a few hours each day in School, being released thereafter to follow our own devices.

'That Armistice Day found the School with a flag-staff, but no flag to betoken our rejoicing. A shipping firm in town provided us with one, with which, in spite of its unfamiliar hue, we were well pleased. What was our chagrin to learn that passers-by in Pollokshaws Road wondered why Hutchie was flying a plague flag!

'Later in the same month a well-known Inspector of schools came on his lawful business. He offered the girls in one class of the Primary School their choice of the themes for an essay. "How I spent Armistice Day" and "The Blessings of Peace". One damsel, having opted for the second topic, wrote "German biscuits will soon be back in the baker's, but they will be called 'Empire biscuits'".

'A feature of School life in the summer was the class picnics, organised by the girls themselves. On those Saturdays the sun always shone as we travelled, sometimes by rail to the Clyde coast, sometimes by rail and steamer as far as Ardlui. Mothers, as always, provided generous supplies of food and we returned to town in the evening "tired but happy" (no mere cliché this!) However, the proliferation of the motor-car in the 'twenties, making roads unsafe for pedestrians, put an end to such outings.

'Before the War was declared in 1939 extensive preparations had been made for the evacuation of children from the cities as bombardment from the air was expected to take place immediately. Our School was allocated to Sanquhar in Dumfriesshire. We left Strathbungo Station on the afternoon of Saturday, September 2 (the day before the declaration of war) on our journey into the unknown.

'When we arrived at Sanquhar Station we found nearly the whole population of the Royal Burgh lined up in welcome on both sides of the road to the Academy. There tea was provided for us, and in due course we were taken to our various havens of refuge, some in the town, others on farms in the outlying rural area.

'I was one of those in the second category and was conveyed by car to a sheep farm among the hills, having been put in charge of three of the group of boys from Crown Street who had been added to the number of evacuees from the Girls' School. When our hostess came out to greet us, she could not conceal her disappointment saying, "I wanted a wee lassie". However, her disappointment was short-lived, and next day, when some of our fellow Hutchesonians had resort to their evacuation rations of a packet of biscuits and a tin of corned beef, we enjoyed a dinner of roast duck and trifle.

'By the spring of 1940 very many of our evacuees had, for one reason or another, returned home, and the whole scheme was abandoned in June of that year.

'Of all the schools in Scotland which provided accommodation for evacuee children and their teachers, Sanquhar Academy, I would venture to assert, was outstanding for the generosity and consideration of the Rector, Mr. Philip Mackie, and his staff, some of whom vacated their comfortable class-rooms for dingy and draughty improvised substitutes in various buildings in the town that we might be better accommodated . . .'

Hutchesons' Girls' Grammar School, 1917–24, by Margaret R. Alston.

'The School building in Kingarth Street was only a few years old when, on a mid-September afternoon in 1917, I first made my solitary entrance via the West door. I was overwhelmed by the atmosphere of calm, by the dignified beauty of the open-arched Hall, and particularly by the polished wood floors throughout the School. The name and fame of the School had not been unknown to me, having had an aunt at the School in Elgin Street and a kinsman a fellow classmate of Johnnie Buchan's, but here was something very different from my (albeit limited) experience, with its uncluttered walls, windows, doors, shelves, one felt one could not but "Be still and know" in such surroundings. The first door on the left as I entered was my P6, with the wonderful Miss Mary Smith. This was also the Singing Room, where, outside, sparrows chirruped the whole year through, their only rivals the swifts announcing the arrival of Spring as they swept past the top corridor classroom windows.

'I was greatly impressed by the order of things – personal desks, pigeon-holes, classroom pegs and the carefully arranged rows of desks around the Art Room thrones. The third Art Room at that time had been specially designed as a Craft room, with special tables, water and gas supplies, bellows, apparatus and tools for metal work – none, sadly, ever put to use, though we offered to stay behind to be taught.

'Prayers in the hall each morning were an occasion. Originally, there was no platform, Mr McVicar standing precariously on a bentwood chair – to the great concern of his colleagues. The word 'colleague' was new to me, and when Mr McVicar said he would have to consult his colleagues on some matter. I visualised them as tomes of wisdom in his large bookcase.

'The School day finished at 3.15pm and we had generous holidays – at least a fortnight at Christmas and Easter, and two months in the summer. We also had skating holidays. Although we thought that Mr McVicar waited until the thaw before granting them, at least we did not have (as once happened in the Boys' High) to make the request at Prayers, at short notice, and in Latin.

'We even had a holiday to go picking wild flowers! This surely could have been only for the Primary School's participation. In my Primary 6 days, in this competition, the prize was, fairly, won by an arrangement beautifully displayed in a basket (the latter, we felt, giving it a distinct advantage over our prosaic jam jar efforts). One of my recollections of those early days is of a total solar eclipse. A somewhat apprehensive Mr McVicar allowed some of us to go out into the playground with darkly smoked-over pieces of glass. It was not the darkness that gave us cause for concern, but the utter frigidity! It was a lesson in itself and we were very quiet for the rest of the day.

'There was no School uniform as such, though a hat of some sort was always compulsory. How we should have enjoyed, and worn with pride, the later blazer and the return from *Luceo non Uro* to *Veritas*.

'In the Senior School the first three years were known as Intermediate and after the third year as Post-Intermediate or Secondary. Each Form Mistress had her own classroom and the door had a lettered nameplate with her name, class and subject taught. There was a certain ambiguity when a nameplate would declare Mr Reid, Singing; Mr Wilde, Drawing (at a later date I changed that to Art). Even in Sixth Year, we marched in twos, in lines between Captain and Vice-Captain, not only to and from Prayers, but from class to class.

'I cannot note too highly the quality of the teachers we had. Though many of them had heavy home commitments, their participation in the School's support for good causes, and concern for others, was one of the best lessons we learned. We contributed weekly to the Cot Box (originally named for our support of a cot in the Sick Children's Hospital). There were always good causes in need of assistance. Apart from wartime needs, there were famines and earthquakes in Russia and Japan – a former teacher's mission in Africa, and mine disasters nearer home. These were the days too, when female teachers were paid less than the men and had to retire on marriage.

'I cannot remember a teacher ever being absent despite adverse weather conditions or distance to travel (with two travelling daily from Greenock). They didn't ever seem to desert us (unless to die or marry a minister). There was a later date during a General Strike when several came, delivered in a van, under a canvas labelled Ripe Bananas. They even took time to fill my large autograph book with paintings, sketches, photographs and original verse. Miss Buist, who was our Form Mistress in the First Year and taught English, not only took us to the usual theatrical, musical and other events, but had the whole class (in two lots) to a party in her home. In those days, too, there were the Summer Term Class Picnics – which must have ruined many Saturdays for our teacher "guests".

'The photographs have long since faded, but I did have one of Mr and Mrs McVicar drinking tea, sitting on the cobbled "beach" at our First Year Picnic at Rhu, while another snap showed teachers and pupils running a race on the road at Inverkip with heads entirely covered in brown paper bags. Fortunately, for our "guests" and possibly the rest of us, due to a succession of wet Saturdays and other interests these events petered out after the Fourth Year.

'Our PT kept pace with our scholastic training. In P6 our activities were not limited to "Hips Firm" or climbing "Ribstalls".[6] We played football on the pitch at lunch time, with a real football, and learned to swim at Gorbals Baths on Saturday mornings.

'The back playground was lined-out for tennis – at a time when the whole facade of the building was ablaze with Virginia creeper and the Calder Street boundary lined with trees and rhododendron bushes. Across Kingarth Street our pitch extended over the whole length from Victoria Road to Pollokshaws Road, affording us the space for two hockey pitches, a tennis court and clubhouse, as well as an adequate area for Sports Day. Our First Year (1918/9) class did not play hockey – there was not a hockey stick to be bought in the whole of the country. Instead, we played netball and later badminton, practising in the chilly precincts of the local Scottish Rifles Drill Hall. At one time the University Ladies' Team were all ex-Hutchie girls. In the year following ours were the hockey experts, and the year after them held the first of our Scottish Junior Tennis Champions. At Christmas time we had flowers, holly and mistletoe, laurel, ivy, for our window ledges (but no trashy paper chains). On the final day of term, after prayers, each class supplied entertainment for the others of their years and, should the concerts finish early, we danced in the Hall till the official closing time.

'Towards 11am on Armistice Day, we were summoned by the usual bell to the Hall for Mr McVicar's announcement of the signing of the Armistice. We sang "O God of Bethel" and were free for the rest of the day. I do not recall any cheering, but I do remember thinking "I shall never forget this day".

'These were the days of guidelines to us from Home, Church, School. There were no "teenagers or adolescents" speaking and acting with all the assurance of their own infallibility. Though we may, in our day, have told our parents they were "old-fashioned", their example stood us in good stead, unchallenged by TV standards.

'It was said to one of us, "it was easy for you, you knew right from wrong". Maybe not – but at least we gave it a try.'

Joyce Reid (Class of 1945)

'I went to Hutchie at eight years of age in 1935. My memories are mixed because I didn't really like school, but it wasn't just Hutchie. I didn't even like Sunday school. I found Kingarth Street intimidating after the single storey primary I had attended. The grand, dignified building, the height of it, the heavy stonework, the twin staircases and tier upon tier of classrooms it seemed.

'The Headmistress was Margaret Kennedy – a most capable, clever woman – rather strict, I think – whose French textbook was a teaching classic. To a young child, Miss Kennedy's grey hair put her into the "granny" category. I was summoned to her room once to be reprimanded and she was not a bit like my granny. Teachers also had a uniform, wearing black gowns, with varying degrees of style, and a face honourably covered in chalk dust. My first Teacher in Primary 2 was charming, young and as I remember married. I had assumed the profession was celibate and female, but there was a male teacher – the music master. Primary classrooms were all along one side of the ground floor and beyond them – outside – were the school toilets. I don't know why I hated them – white-tiled, big doors, but I did.

'Secondary pupils were elevated to the classrooms on the first floor. The top floor was the creative area. The sewing room was pleasant, but a project for every girl to make a summer dress to wear at the end of term was a hard task for someone hopeless with needles of any kind. On parents' day I moved so carefully for all my seams were still in their tacking threads. The Art department with high studio windows and Greco-Roman plaster casts had the memorable Miss Tebbutt.[7] An artist herself, she went on to teach at Glasgow Art School and was a contemporary and friend of Joan Eardley.[8]

'The war came, of course, four years later. A lot of panic about city children being evacuated to the countryside, even Canada. Hutchie must have closed for some of the School evacuated to Ayrshire. Those of us who did not went to our local secondary, in my case, the newly built Eastwood, now Williamwood High. My single memory is of being taken to the school kitchen and shown how to boil potatoes. Perhaps we were supposed to be qualified to then deal with emergency rations if we ever had to take to the fields. Thousands of children on mainland Europe had to do just that. The period did not last and we were back at Hutchie, I can't remember much change at School. but there must have been. Gas mask boxes had to be carried. I don't recall an air raid siren sounding during school hours, but there were several at night at home. An Anti-aircraft gun was on top of a hill in Clarkston and fragments of its exploding shells would clatter onto our bungalow roof and be found in the garden the next day. One of the teachers left to join up and visited the School in her Wren's Officer's uniform, looking so smart we all wanted to do the same.

'I left Hutchie in the summer of 1942 when my family moved to live in Glasgow. Compared with surburbia, the West End was a war zone. I have always been grateful to my parents for sending me to Hutchie, for whatever sacrifices they made, because in spite of my dislikes and difficulties, something of its fine education sunk in. I did not miss the irony when later in life I became a teacher.'

Sheila Ferguson (Class of 1947)

'I am indeed one of the older girls having been evacuated from the Primary during the War but not to Milton Park as my aunt had a large house in Perth and instead of being advised to take refugees from the Channel Islands I was dumped on her with another cousin.

'Of course I started in the year of the renowned Margaret Kennedy of the French Grammar fame and finished off with Miss McIver who was not well liked. My wide general knowledge I totally attribute to the quality and passion of most of the teachers. Miss Hyslop instilled in me a lifelong love of our world and made it so exciting and fortunately I have been able to explore much of it. The physical discipline of Miss Howie (the one with a lisp) encouraged my interest in sport and I loved swimming and tennis. My passion was to enjoy a lifetime of climbing and hill walking at which I attained my Gold Medal and taught the skills and map-reading to many in the club. The dreaded Miss McKendrick. Also Miss Walton – History, not too much fun there. The Miss Cockburn who taught English and Shakespeare so colourfully.

'What really reached me and ended up the love and success of my life was Art. Miss Sheridan who was regarded by most of us as being quite mad racing along the corridors gown hanging off and Mrs Alston, who did not teach Art in any way inspiringly, did not lead me to following what I wanted to do later on after a good career in Commerce. I went to university and attained my diploma and sell most of my work from commissions – I just love it – better late than never. I understand the new Art department has moved forward successfully. One of my sons took Higher Art at Hutchie and has a prosperous career in design, advertising and distribution in Europe; he lives in Barcelona. I recall being a difficult and extroverted pupil and encountered too many scraps which required me to write and memorise chapters from the Bible like *Corinthians* 2.'

Hutchie in Wartime: 1940–44 as remembered by Sheila Willis (née Kilbey)

'Like many children war changed my life. When it began I was living with my parents in Bushey, Hertfordshire, just north of London, and I attended a private school in the area.

'In 1940 my father was asked by the Admiralty to work on the river Clyde in Glasgow in connection with the war work being done on the river. So, in August of that year we set off on the long journey to Scotland.

'We stayed for a couple of weeks at the house of a business friend of my father's, and then we managed to find a rented house in Clarkston, a few miles south of Glasgow. To find a school for me was the next thing to be thought of as the autumn term was about to commence. My parents were advised that Hutchie would be a good choice, if they would take me. So, on a morning early in September we arrived at Kingarth Street for me to sit an exam and to meet the Headmistress, Miss Kennedy.

'I found everything about the School quite formidable and as a result did not do very well at the exam. However, because of our circumstances I was accepted and was to be a pupil in form 4B, which was in the Garden School. Leaving the main building, we crossed the playground where air-raid shelters were being built alongside the railings, and were taken round to the Garden School.

'Having been accepted, my mother and I set off for the School outfitters Copeland and Lye[9] in Sauchiehall Street, Glasgow, to buy the necessary uniform which was very varied. At that time of the war, clothing coupons had not been issued but were reported to be on their way. I was kitted out in a navy gym slip, a grey long sleeve blouse, a white blouse with a square neck for Gym with a pair of black gym shoes, also a pair of black shoes with cross-over bars for Scottish country dancing. For outer wear there was a navy raincoat, a heavy winter coat and a navy velour hat to match with the School badge in the middle of the hatband, but best of all was the blazer in a lovely shade of blue with the full crest of the School on the pocket. I had never had so many clothes in my life.

'I was all set up, but not raring to go, however the next Monday morning I set off on the bus to go to Form 4B. It had rained during the night and the roses were all dripping wet in the garden but once inside the building it was quite cosy. We had a very nice teacher, Miss McDonald who was very kind to me, giving me a lot of attention as I was well behind the other children in the class.

'I seem to remember that because of the winter and the threat of air raids we did not stay in the Garden School longer than the autumn term, and we were moved into the main building. During the spring term it was very dreary and sometimes cold in the classrooms and we used to wear mittens to keep our hands warm. Netting was put up at all the windows in case they were blown out, also to protect the pupils from shrapnel.

'The next class I went to was 5B but I must say that class life was not very easy for me. I was not very good at Mathematics, I only knew about English History and other than Mary Queen of Scots, knew precious little about Scottish History. Geography I loved, also Art but that was about it. I was not very interested in Games until I played netball.

'By this time we all had gas masks, to be carried at all times, but a lot of us had problems in getting them to work properly, so a man came to visit the School to show us how to adjust these troublesome masks. In this day and age it is difficult to conceive what interest it aroused having a man come into a classroom in an all girls' school, never mind fixing gas masks.

'Our day began at nine o'clock in the morning and finished at three o'clock in the afternoon, this was because of the short hours of daylight in the winter time. From what I remember the winter of 1940–41 was a very cold one and in early spring, the Germans who had overrun Norway had easy access to Scotland across the North Sea and were starting to bomb the Clyde area. As I mentioned, our air raid shelters were at the back of the main building in the playground and we used them for air raid practice. Long benches had been placed inside but they were dark and cold, a teacher came with us and carried a lamp. Instructions were given on what we should do, in the event of us coming under attack. Girls in the senior classes joined the A.T.C. and were kept very busy.

'Time passed and I made friends and eventually moved into senior classes and life became more interesting. One of the key points of everyone's day was Assembly, held first thing in the morning. The School had an excellent little orchestra which played the hymns for us on the platform in the hall, the centre of School life. After hymns we had prayers and the School announcements were given out by Miss Kennedy, also various items of news from the theatres of war. All in all, we kept up very well with what was going on as odd items of news were incorporated in our School work as well.

'One of the things we were much involved in were the various war charities such as "Mrs Churchill's Aid to Russia Fund", which was very much needed in the siege of Leningrad in 1942, when the citizens were dying in their thousands in the streets from starvation. Another was "Mrs Churchill's Aid to China Fund". We were given collection boxes on Friday mornings, then wearing our school uniforms and a special label to show we were authorised collectors, collected round the area we lived on Saturday mornings. We returned the money to school on Monday morning which was added to the main School collection.

'In winter 1942–43 terrible cases of injuries were reported as the wounded returned home from various theatres of the War. A number were so disfigured that they were unrecognisable to their own families. Miss Kennedy told us of an old mansion in the country which had been purchased so that some of them could have a permanent home after they had left hospital. They would need medical attention and to be looked after as long as deemed appropriate.

'We had a large Domestic department at the School, which consisted of a laundry and a cookery section, both next door to each other opposite the luncheon room. My class was asked to wash some very long curtains which were to be given to the home. They were very long indeed, awkward to manage, and it took two girls to get each curtain into the sinks, then three to get them out because they were very heavy when they were wet. They then had to be dried and ironed, but that job fell to another class. A great many people gave whatever they could to furnish this home. It was a wonderful idea and met a great need at the time.

'Glasgow was heavily bombed, particularly Govan and Clydebank, the raiders being helped by the light nights and the silver ribbon of the Clyde which threaded its way through the valley. The School fortunately came through unscathed.

'I think those of us who were at School at the time, irrespective of age or circumstances, were inspired by the hymns we used to sing at assembly in the mornings, some of the old Scottish paraphrases, also an inscription from Psalm 46 *Be still and know that I am God*, which was on the wall of the Hall. Miss Kennedy excelled in guiding the School through a difficult period of its history, and I am pleased to have been a part of it.'

Corrie McNeil (Class of 1951)

'Six years as a pupil of Hutchie from II to VI – a lot of memories! Morning assembly whose legacy is knowing by heart the words to so many wonderful hymns to this day. The 'Be still and know' plaque. Mr McVicar, whose face is as clear to me today as it was on the many mornings I stood in the Hall. Fifty years after leaving School, I can still picture Miss McKendrick in her room at the end of the upstairs corridor opposite Mr Gowan's room and Miss McKay and Miss Coburn and Miss Sheridan in whose Art room I seemed to spend an entire term drawing a box from different angles. I recall the end of term dances in the hall – the girls on one side, the boys from several different schools, not just the Hutchie boys, on the other. After one year's dance pupils from a school, which shall remain nameless, were banned after some of the boys were caught smoking in the cloakrooms. The memories are like a kaleidoscope, a collage, video clips unconnected and springing up in a jumbled sequence.

'There is, however, one abiding memory – My first day. I came to Hutchie in 1945 having previously been a pupil at Morrison's Academy in Crieff with a pupil number less than 250. I remember sitting with my mother outside Miss Kennedy's room when the bell for assembly rang, watching the classes pouring down the stairs on either side. Because there were railings then I could see what seemed to be a never ending stream of legs hurriedly descending the stone stairs. I was awestruck and horrified at the sheer numbers – thousands it seemed to me. I can see them yet and hear the noise of their feet on the stone stairs. I thought then I could never cope with a School as big, but I did and managed to become one of those thousand very soon.

'I have never been convinced that schooldays are the happiest of our lives, but in retrospect they were fun, full of friendships, carefree on the whole (except on the run up to examinations) and yes very, very happy – well the memories, rose-coloured maybe, are anyway.'

Kathleen Miller (Class of 1951): Primary 2 to 6th Year

'On moving to the south side of Glasgow from the West End in February 1939 I was accepted into Hutchesons' Grammar School to start in Primary 1 in September. As a result of the War, I was evacuated with an Aunt, Uncle and cousins to the Isle of Bute then Roberton, Lanarkshire, to a one-teacher school with an open fire, slate instead of jotters and no uniform. My parents were notified that I would forfeit my place if I did not take it up in September 1940. My father built an air raid shelter and I came home to start in Primary 2 with Miss Malvenan in the wooden Garden School building . . . Happy memories of Mr Reid and singing in chorus for Gilbert and Sullivan productions. Playing 1st XI hockey, thanks to Miss Howie for three seasons – 1948–49, 1949–50, 1950–51, last year as captain. Having Miss McKendrick as form mistress in 6th Year, "Hurry up – no running in corridors!" Weekend youth hostelling with Miss Currie, in Borders Eildon area for Higher Geography. Travelling to Paris, France in 5th Year soon after the War, seeing bullet holes and French female guides who dived under tables when aircraft passed over head. As a result I passed my Higher French and still visit a French friend.

'Hutchie was one of the happiest periods and friendships continue to this day. It was a perfect base for life, be it farming, government career and travelling. I was amazed how many teachers still remembered me a few times I have managed to attend reunions.'

Sandra Young (Class of 1956)

'Earliest memory is of the entrance exam. The hall seemed very big and I was asked about colours! In September 1943 I began in the Garden School with Miss Scott – a garden, a sun dial and lots of small chairs and warm bottles of milk and pinafores.

Progressed through Junior school with various teachers, Miss Waddell, Miss Howie for Gym and finally Miss Newlands who was young and fun. Enjoyed most of it, although I remember a lot of competitiveness. I was always in trouble for talking and spent time outside the classroom doors hoping the headmistress was not passing at the time. Two head teachers – Miss Kennedy – who was kindly and Miss McIver who was terrifying as was Miss McKendrick. I didn't like school dinners and usually managed to get home for lunch. We had lots of fun in the playground and a very nice janitor called Mr Smith. We had lavatories outside the main building Senior school.

1A1 with Miss Knox was great and we had her for three years. I enjoyed Chemistry and Maths but remember lots of homework. Miss Cockburn for English. I remember many of my classmates some with me from five years old as we arrived in Miss MacDonald's class, and some in senior school. I left Hutchie in 1955.'

A Hutchie Girl Remembers – Sheena Culling (née Rodger). She attended HGGS, 1952–7.

'My mother came with me for the first two days as I'd never travelled alone to the city before, taking an hour by bus and tram from beyond Kirkintilloch. Twenty girls in brand new uniforms hung their brand new hats and coats in the cloakroom. Our Form Room on the second floor was a Science laboratory and we perched on back-less wooden stools. The home-grown First Year classes of 1A1, 1A2, 1B1 knew the system and took Latin as well as French. 1B2 and 1B3 formed "the others" learning French only. And we in 1B3 became the only class EVER to keep both the same Form Mistress and the same Science lab, as form room for four long, consecutive years.

'Miss Ross greeted us, explained that the first bell was three minutes to nine and six minutes later, the bell would ring to go to "prayers". As one thousand students filed SILENTLY from their classrooms down the stairs, I was impressed beyond description at the sound of two thousand feet-on-the-move to the Assembly Hall. The four piece orchestra played quietly, Miss McIver swept in, tall (so she seemed) in a straight black gown, straight grey hair. She announced the hymn and accompanied by the violins and piano, one thousand voices sang, imprinting our brains and minds with music to last our entire lives. Twice a week a Form Six Prefect read from the Bible. Occasionally Miss McIver delivered a sermon on "Wearing-your-hat-till-you-reach-home". She read out the sports results, sounding aggrieved if the First XI had not won at hockey the previous Saturday.

'*English*. Shakespeare of course. Dear Miss Mackay, with snowy white hair, was Form Mistress to the Sixth Form, always. Would we ever get there? Dickens; Thackeray; such serious books written for a previous age. Ploughing my way through *A Tale of Two Cities*, I found that having to write a summary was totally daunting . . .

'*History*. Miss Hyslop; poor old "Sloppy", we were cruel in our nickname for her.

'*French*. Miss Mayne had a frightful strabismus; this squint meant it was not clear to whom she was directing her gaze. Mrs McKellar was sarcastic and addicted to wide-open windows even in winter. She spluttered wetly on the first row of students due to ill-fitting dentures. "If you don't want to learn, there's a waiting list of girls who want to get in." She insisted on a formal French lesson on our last ever day of Form five. "Because of the clever ones returning for Highers after the summer."

'*Art*. Wonderful equipment. I won a bronze medal in the Schools' Competition at the Art Gallery. Mrs Alston was a kindly teacher.

'*Music*. Mr Reid, who led our four piece orchestra on the piano, let us sing "The Lorelei" and "Santa Lucia". Wonderful compositions. He also said loftily: "The Glasgow children speak THIS way; but Hutchie girls speak . . . THIS way!" Elitism at its best/worst.

'*Sport*. Freezing in a huddle on that hockey pitch, while Miss Howie in a long coat explained the finer points of "defence" and "dribbling". This eleven year old hated it but equally, some loved it. I'd never seen a Gymnasium, a wonderful revelation and good fun.

'*Domestic Science. Sewing*. Six of the eight sewing machines were TREADLE.[10] I can hardly believe I'm writing that. We made small sampler books; Embroidery; patching on various materials, "Make them INVISIBLE, girls!" Miss Crockatt was always gentle as she said "Take it out", meaning my work had to be re-done and I used to think of her when I mended my children's clothes with less than perfect stitching.

'*Cookery*. We used lard and suet and butter with abandon, the war years having produced underweight twelve year olds. The results were absolutely scrummy.

'*Laundry*. We washed and starched by hand and the twenty flat-irons were heated by gas, cleaned on sand, cleaned again on an asbestos cloth (are my lungs OK?). No temperature setting and so we had to wet a forefinger and lightly tap the hot iron and to the degree of "hiss" as to whether cotton or delicates could be pressed. "You're the first person to refuse to test the iron," said the teacher. I deemed it to be far too scary an action.

'*Science*. Our intellectual and unbelievably sarcastic Form Mistress was also our Science teacher, four periods a week, for four years. I felt sick every Sunday and Tuesday evening because of "double Science" next morning. And for Form mistress, Miss Ross was also responsible for one period a week of "Religious Instruction". Openly atheistic, she used this time to belittle a different girl each week, attacking her apparent lack of knowledge of an equation or some other aspect of our current Science lessons. She whipped herself up into a rage with a voice that went lower and lower with sarcasm. She didn't need to shout to terrorise us . . .

'Certainly, every school has some built-in horrors. But in my final year, Fifth form was a real pleasure; it was with incredulity we found that Miss Noble was our Form Mistress, and we each had a proper desk in a standard classroom. And in five years I'd changed from a timid country girl to a confident traveller, hopping off trams to investigate enticing shops whose lights reflected on the wet pavements while starlings chattered in the darkness above.

'I suppose, as anywhere, the real influence was "the girls". As I didn't live near ANY of them, contact outside School was very rare. Their accounts of boy-friend dalliances exuded confidence (which they may not have felt) aided possibly by frequent film-going and TV exposure. I was ten when I first saw a film and we never had TV . . .

'Returning from Australia in 1975 with daughters aged six and four, I was keen to show my old School to them. I thought they'd be as impressed with our wonderful Gymnasium as I had been. Passing the changing rooms, I saw . . . BOYS! No one had told me Hutchie was now co-ed! I still blush remembering the shock of discovery . . .'

Ann Watkin (Class of 1967)

'I have so many happy memories of Hutchie. The best memories relate to the many friends I made while at school. So many of these friendships have endured the years and I treasure them still. I also loved hockey which was a great help at Hutchie. My memories inevitably involve Miss Howie and her devotion to the game. She was a disciplinarian but a gifted teacher.

'My recollections of the academic side of life are varied. I recall being shouted at by Miss Murdoch and Miss Knox, being encouraged by Miss Shearer and Mrs Maxwell and being kindly smiled upon by Miss Campbell. Like most girls I was terrified of Miss McIver, though I was to discover a softer more understanding side in my last year at school.

'In my final year at school I was School Captain which was an amazing experience. I recall being quite terrified at the prospect of reading a lesson on Founders' Day at Glasgow Cathedral and making speeches in public. Little did I realise that these experiences would be quite so valuable to me as I took up some high profile jobs in later life. Nothing was ever as nerve wracking as those Head Girl Responsibilities! Hutchie was the best possible training ground to coping with what life throws at one later on.'

NINE Recollections of the Modern Schools: Hutchesons' Boys' Grammar School

James Cowan: Boyhood Memories of Mount Florida, in *From Glasgow's Treasure Chest* (Glasgow 1940), pp. 332–335.

'Of my schooldays I have mixed memories. Most of the children on the terrace[1] went to Queen's Park School, which was quite near; but I was sent to a small private School at Myrtle Park, kept by Moses Park, assisted by two maiden ladies, and his brother-in-law. I still clearly remember my first day there, because of the feeling that I was not fairly treated. Having spent the forenoon with a certain amount of boredom, I was asked whether I would like to stay for the afternoon, or go home. I chose to go home; whereupon it was decreed that I should remain. As this seemed to be quite unfair, after having been given the choice, I judged that further argument with such people would be useless, so I promptly kicked the astonished lady teacher in the shins, and marched off home.

'Apart from that first day, my memories of that little school are pleasant. The teaching was excellent, and though Moses Park maintained discipline, he was a kindly man . . . After two years or so at Moses Park's school, I went to Hutchesons' Boys' School in Crown Street. This meant a walk of nearly two miles every morning. We carried our lunch with us as well as a heavy bag of books, and walked home again after 4pm . . . and there were other boys, who just as cheerfully, covered the distance twice daily, from Cathcart – a mile and a half more each way . . .

'I was not fond of School, and was glad to leave it at the age of fifteen. Nevertheless, I have pleasant and grateful memories of at least three of the teachers at Hutchesons' who took some pains to make our tasks less irksome than they might have been. Thomas Menzies was the Rector.

'The Prize-Giving day was always a great occasion. The Drawing and Writing prizes usually fell to me; but seldom any that required real brain work to win. The highlight of the day was always "The Charge of the

Light Brigade", recited by our drill-master, Mr Muirhead, who was a great favourite. He was a veteran of the Crimean War, and we always watched for the moment when he drew his sword and made vigorous passes and lunges, as he "sabred the gunners", and when "Into the mouth of hell, rode the six hundred" we could never restrain our cheers.

'Quite a few boys in my class, and the one above me, attained to different degrees of celebrity in later life; but I shall mention only two. John Buchan – who was to become so famous a writer, and ultimately Lord Tweedsmuir, was always a class ahead of me, so I did not come a great deal in contact with him, though we often enough rubbed shoulders, so to speak, and frequently shared in the same games. I met him only once in later life, when he gave a lecture on mountaineering, in his father's church in Bedford Street, on the south side of Glasgow; but unfortunately, his time after the lecture did not permit of much conversation, and the subject of our experiences at Hutchesons' School had to be left over in the hope of a future meeting, which, however, was destined never to take place.

'Frederick Niven, who became a novelist of distinction, was in my class. He was a pleasant boy, good at Drill, for which he usually won the prize, and he was sometimes singled out from the rest of us by the drill-master as an example of how to do things smartly. Though Fred Niven was destined to achieve fame with his novels of Glasgow, he only impressed me in those days as a good fellow to play with.'

John Buchan left HBGS in 1892 to attend Glasgow University. He became probably the School's greatest FP. In *Memory Hold-the-Door* **(London 1945), pp. 30–1, he remembered his school days.**

'I never went to school in the conventional sense, for a boarding school was beyond the narrow means of my family. But I had many academies . . . When we migrated to Glasgow I attended for several years an ancient grammar school on the south side of the river, from which, at the age of seventeen, I passed to Glasgow University.

'Had I gone to a public school I might have developed into a useful wing three-quarter in the rugby game. Otherwise I don't think I missed much. I and my brothers were, I fear, incapable of what is called the public-school spirit. While devotees of the open air we lacked interest in games, and had few of the usual boyish ambitions. We had no wish to run with the pack, for we were absorbed in our private concerns. School to me was therefore only a minor episode . . . I never felt the shyness and repression of the small boy which I have read of in school stories. At my various schools I had my ups and downs, but they mattered little and were forgotten in an hour . . . Looking back, I seem to have enjoyed my schools enormously. There I mixed on terms of comradeship and utter equality with children from every kind of queer environment . . . Even at my later schools the School played but a small part in my life. It was an incident; a period of enforced repression which ended daily at four in the afternoon.'

David Kerr left the HBGS in 1920 and passed on his memories of the School during World War 1.

'My admission to Hutchesons' Boys' Grammar School in Crown Street at the age of eight coincided with the outbreak of the Kaiser's War in 1914. I was in the Junior Department of the School for three years and I was fortunate to have two very good teachers during that time.

'From 1914 to 1916, I was with Miss Campbell. She taught us to recite from the "Song of Hiawatha" by Henry Longfellow, and she took us to a performance of "Peter Pan" by Sir James Barrie at the King's Theatre. She taught all subjects, including Gymnastics at which she was quite the expert. From 1916 to 1917, I was with Miss Galt. She taught us to recite the poems of Robert Burns, and she took us to Cathkin Braes for a picnic. There were no prizes for reciting Longfellow's American Indian epic, but for reciting "Tam o' Shanter" etc we received book prizes.

'In September 1917, I was promoted to the Upper School where each subject was taught by a different master, so that we did not get to know them like Miss Campbell and Miss Galt. The exception was James Caddell, who had us trembling with fear because of his excessive use of the tawse. When he died in 1920, he was replaced by a tall young man named John Keay – more a lecturer than a teacher – and just the opposite of "Jimmy" Caddell (who was short in stature) but the most effective teacher I have ever known.

'Staffing was not the only School problem during the 1914–18 war. The rooms were lit by gas, which frequently required the attention of John Glennie, the janitor. Heating was by open fire which added to the sulphurous smog outside. Some boys tried to escape the fog by travelling to School in a tram car. They found the top deck of the trams crowded by men smoking "thick black" tobacco, and the lower deck occupied by women on their way to work, knitting socks for the soldiers in response to a Red Cross appeal.

'Food was poor in quality, and so short in supply it had to be rationed. In the autumn of 1917 the School was closed for two weeks because of an influenza epidemic.

'There was little in the way of organised Games out of School. A disabled Science teacher called John Drimmie could do little more than hand out footballs and check that he got them back. Because of the absence of organised sport, some boys spent their weekends gathering and cleaning sphagnum moss for the Red Cross to use as field dressings. In the summer vacation other boys did National Service on farms in the East Kilbride and Carmunnock areas.

A speaker told us about the War Savings effort, the forerunner of the present National Savings Bank. Some of us were persuaded to visit a War Savings exhibition in George Square. There were tanks there and soldiers in steel helmets, but it was all spoiled by heavy rain.

'On Armistice Day, 11th November 1918, the teaching staff at Crown Street disappeared, but the boys wanted to do something to mark the occasion. They decided to march to the Girls' School in Kingarth Street. They lined up four deep outside the School in Crown Street and marched off singing wartime songs, such as "Pack up your Troubles in your Old Kit Bag". When they arrived at the Girls' School, they found that all the girls had gone home, so they gave the few teachers who were left three cheers and then dispersed.

'I felt there should have been something spectacular to mark the occasion. I remembered the procession of tramcars decorated with coloured electric lamps for the Coronation of King George V in 1910 – but that was not the mood of the people in 1918. They were very glad the war was over, but the next morning they were back to work as usual.'

Professor J. Joseph attended the Boys' Grammar School, 1926–31, and provided these recollections of his time at the School.

'The School building was in Crown Street between Cleland and Cumberland Streets in the heart of the slums of the Gorbals and was begrimed like the surrounding tenements. Crown Street formed part of one of the main north-south roads in Glasgow and going north led to a bridge across the Clyde. Eventually it became continuous with the High Street. I think the site was chosen because it was on a main street and Hutchesons' Educational Trust being a charitable organisation wanted to provide a grammar school for the poor.

'The School was set back from the road behind railings and had a central part with a main entrance and two wings. Only important people such as teachers and visitors were allowed to use the front entrance. There was a gate at each end of the railings and pupils walked along the alley at the side of the School to the rear of the main building to enter the main part of the school from the back. Each wing also had a rear entrance. The Assembly Hall of the School was on the second floor and ran backwards at right angles to the central part of the main building. The hall was supported by pillars and formed a colonnade down the middle of the playground. One could enter the back of the hall by a staircase on each side. The main staircase led up from the entrance hall to a mezzanine floor under the main hall. The Rector's and his secretary's rooms were on this floor and beyond them were two classrooms. Inscribed on the wall of the landing (on the next part of the stairs) was the list of Duxes of the School dating back to 1829.

'There were classrooms on each side of the ground floor hall. To the left of the main door a large gong, 60 cms wide was used to indicate the end of a teaching period as well as the beginning of classes after the lunch interval. School Notices were put up on a Board on the right.

'The wings had classrooms on the ground, first and second floors. The ground floor room of the north wing was used as a canteen and also sold soft bread rolls with jam in the morning interval and lunch time for one old penny. The staffroom was on the first floor of the north wing and on the few occasions when I caught a glimpse of the inside of the room, little was visible because of the smoke from cigarettes and pipes.

'The desks for pupils were arranged either in long continuous rows or as rows of single desks; the seats had no backs so that one could lean backwards only on to the desk behind. All the individual places had ink wells filled regularly by the janitor, John Glennie, and fountain pens in the 1920s were not very common. Most of the blackboards were fixed to the wall but some rooms had mobile blackboards because of the lack of wall space. The teacher had a high desk with a lid containing a box in which he kept his personal property which always included a leather strap (the tawse) for inflicting punishment.

'There was no central heating when I went to Hutchesons' and the classrooms had coal fires. I associate these with the teachers standing with their gowns held over one arm and their backs to the fire while they warmed their bottoms. I think the main hall had large gas metal heaters. About 1929 central heating was installed and consisted of large black inelegant 10 cm. diameter pipes running along one or more walls at ground level. Some classrooms had smaller pipes at ceiling level.

'The main hall was quite impressive because of its size and height and the large wooden rafters holding up the roof. The front entrance from the staircase led to a platform which extended along the whole width of the hall. It was about three steps high and not more than three or four metres deep. The hall was large enough to accommodate the whole School for morning assembly and prayers – twenty two classes, four junior school and eighteen senior school drawn up in rows with the youngest at the front. At the back of the hall there was a stage about one metre high and sufficiently deep to put on a play. The stage did not extend the whole width of the hall and on each side there was a small room. One was the Gym Master's and the other the sixth year form room and could just about accommodate the ten to fifteen boys in that form.

'The hall was also the Gymnasium and had parallel bars along the whole length of the hall below the Gothic windows. Climbing ropes and rope ladders were suspended from the ceiling on each side and these were raised out of the way when not in use. There were transverse beams at the back of the hall in front of the stage and various pieces of equipment (buck, horse, mats, low benches, basketball nets) were kept on the stage. The floor of the hall was marked out for badminton which was played only by the masters, the sixth form and some FPs.

'When I went to Hutchesons' in January 1926 there were three junior School years. Apart from one teacher in the senior school, the four teachers of the junior school were the only women on the teaching staff. Entry to the senior school was by examination in December/June while junior school entry was by examination and age although I do not think there was a great deal of competition for places for the latter.

'The senior School had six years, the first three years with four form classes and fourth and fifth years with three form classes and a sixth form of ten to twelve boys who stayed on to sit the Glasgow University Bursary Competition. There were about 450 boys in the School, with each class having about thirty boys. Forms 1A, 1B, 1C and 1D were arranged on a strictly academic basis with 1A the most able. 1A and 1B were taught Latin and 1C and 1D French so that a slight rearrangement was possible at the end of the First Year. Three of four boys, the worst academically, were moved from the A to the B class and the best three or four went from B to A. A similar transfer between C and D took place. Form 2A did Latin and Greek, 2B Latin and French, 2C French and German and 2D only French. To the best of my knowledge no pupil was asked what he wanted to do either at School or in the future. Thus one's fate in School was partially sealed in the first year and completely at the end of that year as far as the subjects studied were concerned. The School's attitude was that the best pupils did Classics and no choice was offered. One consequence was that the sixth form consisted of pupils who had done Latin (five years) and Greek (four years). It was rare for somebody from 5B or 5C to go into the sixth form and even more unusual for a pupil to continue with Science after the third year. Since I knew that I would be studying Medicine, I asked the Rector unofficially in the street whether I could do Science instead of Classics and he assured me that the Medical Faculty at the University preferred students who had done Classics at school. And that was that. One may say that the facilities for doing Science after the third year were poor but that only reflected the policy of the School.

'Hutchesons' was a private School and had its own hours, holidays and fees. School began at 9am with assembly and prayers for the whole School in the hall. There were seven periods per day each of about 45 minutes, with four in the morning 9.15am till 12.15pm and three in the afternoon 1.00pm to 3.00pm. In 1927 or 1928 a new policy was introduced in order to have a longer period of time for games on a Wednesday. On Tuesdays, classes went on to 4pm and on Wednesdays they stopped at 2.30pm. Unlike the local authority schools we were given the whole of July and August for our summer holidays.

'The Rector always presided over Assembly and stood in the middle of the front of the platform with some of the teachers lined along the wall behind him. A prefect read some verses usually from the Old Testament, the Rector then said a short prayer followed by the whole School reciting the Lord's Prayer. This was followed by another short prayer by the Rector who then made his announcements. On the opening day of term the Rector himself read Corinthians 1: ch 12 v 1–13 (Though I speak with the tongues of men and of angels . . .). The religious part of assembly raised some problems. The great majority of pupils were Presbyterian and there were a fair number of Jewish pupils. Attendance at assembly was compulsory and a Jewish boy could be absent only if his parents personally requested this. During my six and a half years at Hutchesons' I can recall only the son of Glasgow's senior rabbi and one other boy being given permission to be absent. Prefects were on duty to see that all boys attended and that boys excused were at School at nine o'clock and remained at the back entrance until Assembly finished.

'In addition to prayers at Assembly the first period on a Monday morning was devoted to Religious Instruction. During this time the Jewish boys sat as a separate group and did some of their homework. Jewish boys did not go to School on a number of Jewish festival days. However, the absence of Jewish boys created problems for teachers and provoked envy in other pupils. Socially the Jewish boys tended not to mix with the other boys. Some of them lived nearby in the Gorbals while others lived in the better parts of Glasgow but were well known to each other. Inevitably the Jewish boys formed a separate group. In many situations being different is enough to evoke hostility. However, I can recall only one boy in our class who was overtly anti-Jewish.

'If there were any regulations about punishment I as a pupil certainly did not know them. Teachers as well as the Rector were allowed to punish pupils with the tawse applied to the palm of the outstretched hand. The type of strap (hard or soft, solid or divided end), the number of times the hand was struck and most important the force with which the strap was wielded were determined by the teacher. As far as I know, no rules were laid down but "six of the best", three on each hand were generally regarded as the maximum. Pupils were punished for misbehaviour such as talking in class, being late, not doing homework and I regret to say for not being able to learn something.

'The intention was that only the palm of the hand was struck. Some teachers insisted that the sleeve of the jacket be pulled down over the wrist. The strap could produce a large weal on this part of the hand because unlike the palm the skin of the wrist is not attached to the underlying tissue. A child going home with a large weal on his wrist was likely to upset his parents. Sometimes the teacher missed or hit only part of the hand, whether this counted depended on the teacher. Usually another attempt was made. Withdrawal of the hand was fairly common in which case the hand may be held on the desk for another attempt. Sometimes the teacher insisted on the left hand being strapped so that the writing hand was not affected. On the whole the strap was not used a great deal and its use became less frequent in the higher forms.

'Since physical punishment of children by teachers in Scotland is now illegal one may ask what I recollect were the effects of knowing one could be punished for all sorts of offences at school. On the whole I think fear of punishment was only a minor deterrent with regard to general discipline and behaviour. It is true that we got to know which teacher would make little effort or no effort to check homework and if homework was neglected it would be that teacher's. As a rule we were always attentive and well behaved in class.

I wholeheartedly support the banishing of the strap (and cane) from schools. I am well aware of the argument that fear of physical punishment can be a great deterrent but there are different and better ways of persuading people to behave well. Lines were frequently used as a form of punishment. As far as I can remember detention was rarely if ever used. I suspect that this form of punishment was inconvenient for the teachers.'

Hugh Paterson was a pupil at HBGS, 1933–39, and wrote of his experiences in *Veritas* **2002/3.**

'There were six bursaries and six scholarships in each year beginning in S2. About sixty pupils must thus have had free schooling. I cannot have cost my parents very much for my Hutchie education! I left from the 5th year at the end of session 1938/9. I had been first in all subjects and had taken eleventh place in the Glasgow University bursary in 1939. So, despite pressure from the Rector, W. Tod Ritchie ("the Toad", to irreverent pupils), I decided to go straight to University. My runner-up in 5A, Ian Thomson, stayed on and duly became Dux (You had to be in Sixth year to qualify). The Rector had applied pressure already, telling me that as a 5th Former I was not entitled to the special tuition given to the 6th Year Bursary candidates. I entered myself and proceeded without the tuition. Mr Ritchie was peeved.

'In fact, I rather admired Tod Ritchie. More a Great Bear than a Toad. He had a habit of perambulating the School and "taking over" the lesson. Teachers grinned and bore it, we pupils tended to welcome the break. Mr Ritchie, we thought, stretched the longbow with his tales of his own career: he'd written a manual on Rifle Drill for the Indian Army, he'd run some remarkable race in Germany and he'd edited medieval Scots manuscripts. I checked and found it was all true. With his height, his burliness, his "piggy" eyes, his sudden squealing laugh – he was a formidable figure: a Johnsonian character. At the end of his life, in retirement, he was tutoring some lass for University entrance when he was diagnosed with terminal cancer. He made sure that, although in pain, he completed his tuition. She passed. Maybe the trumpets sounded for Tod Ritchie on the other side . . .

'I remember many Hutchie teachers and pupils of the 1930s. I still have a 'panoramic' photo of the entire School, staff and pupils. In Primary 1, I was taught by Miss Ferguson and Miss McCalman (Jeanie). Many years later when my own three children became Hutchie pupils I met Miss Ferguson at a parents' night. She must have been in her 90s, but she remembered me and my classmates. Miss McCalman would be in her mid-twenties when she taught us. She was beautiful and altogether a nice person – we worshipped her. And so did the School Captain, a tall Sixth Former, who used to come into Miss McCalman's class to talk to her. In due course Miss McCalman and the School Captain married and went to farm in East Africa. This romance had a happy ending . . .

'I remember Ian Campbell (Art teacher) well. He inspired in me a (passing) enthusiasm for illustrating manuscripts in medieval style. The Principal of Art, Mr Thomson, had been a camouflage artist in World War I. We could always divert him from serious lessons by asking questions about that war.

'Dr Gavin Hood (Mathematics) was respected as a formidable scholar. But he was quite over the heads of his pupils. My own Mathematics teacher, "Bulldog" Eric McDonald, was more down to earth. I actually asked for *Mathematics for the Million* for my prize one year! The rest of the class thought I was mad.

'I resisted the Rector's invariable prize choice of *Tales of a Grandfather* (we thought he must be getting a cut from the publishers!) and asked for a Greek dictionary (the Junior Liddell and Scott – which I got).

'John Drimmie ("Gammie") also taught me Mathematics. His room was on the ground floor near the front entrance in Crown Street. The gong was outside the classroom door; often (if the Jannie wasn't at hand) it fell to a boy from JD's class to go out and pound the gong to sound "lousing time" at the end of the morning or the School day.

'JD's room had a coal fire which had to be tended. And JD had to beware lest his gown sweep towards the flames. (Many of the staff wore gowns, some even mortarboards. Tod Ritchie was never without both. The mortarboard covered his Kojak head). JD (called "Gammie" because of his stiff leg from a war wound) was deaf and had a very loud voice. Some of the more daring used to make sotto voce remarks. In 1946–48, JD (back from retirement) was my colleague in King's Park Secondary.

'By then he had some sort of hearing aid. His voice was as loud as ever but no one was getting away with sotto voce. JD was heart-broken when his only son was killed in North Africa in World War II.

'Of the Science teachers "Puggy" MacLennan was very popular with us pupils. Poor Mr Langley (too nice a man) was unmercifully ragged. I remember "Big Bill" Finlay inserting the end of a hose into Mr Langley's pocket and turning on the tap. Tod Ritchie in person administered the Lochgelly.[2] My own Science teacher was Walter Dick. No nonsense with him. I recall him once convulsed with laughter. He'd been instructing us how to write up an experiment. He told us to write "comments" in the margin. A pupil handed in his Science notebook with the whole experiment written up in the margin!

'The Music Department has a hard row to hoe. The trouble was that it was not an examinable subject; pupils looked on it as mere recreation. Dr Pritchard, I knew to be a respected musician (he composed and arranged), but he found my class entirely philistine. We would bellow out "There is a Tavern in the Town" adding our own amended words. The Pope's name was often taken in vain. Sectarian days, even in Hutchie. Mr Ward ("The Wart") who succeeded Dr Pritchard was a very small man. That did not help him with us. Tod Ritchie took us in hand. He did not teach Music but he could wield the tawse on a whole Music class if necessary.

'My teachers in the English Department were "Soapy" Sommerville, "Pony" (David) Milne and the Principal, Mr Knox. "Soapy" could be bitingly sarcastic but I liked him though. He set high standards. He made a bad career move by going for promotion to (I think) Adelphi Terrace. When I became a teacher myself (of Classics then History), I spent the winter of 1944/5 on the Hutchie staff filling in for a teacher on war service. Anxious as he was to get away from Adelphi Terrace and return to Hutchie, "Soapy" would come into our staffroom at lunchtime. He obviously much regretted his move.

'"Pony" Milne was a gentle man (and gentleman). He had Leftist leanings which put him at odds with his chief, Mr Knox, who did not scruple to instruct us boys when election time came to advise our parents to vote Tory and dish the Reds. Knox had commanded Indian troops in World War I against the Turks. He had strict ideas about the "lesser breeds". His standards were high, his discipline strict. When the Higher results came out he belted failures . . . But Knox knew his stuff.

'He co-authored *Barclay, Knox and Ballantine*, for long an invaluable aid to the understanding of the English language. He told us that in his opinion English language had gone sadly downhill since Thackeray and Tennyson. He would personally never read a "modern" novel. "Modern" poetry too was rubbish. At least this provoked us and made some of us react. I myself even began to write verse (first in the *Hutchesonian* during my editorship).

'Robert F. Hepburn ("Heppie") also taught me English. Red-haired and vigorous (I remember him belting our whole class for not having learned the meaning of "eschew"). Heppie still played rugby (for his native Dunfermline). He died from a sudden heart-attack during a match.

'Another member of the English staff who also died with a sudden heart-attack was "Tubby" Smith. English teacher in two senses for he was the only southerner on the staff. He was also my History teacher. In those days History and Geography were not taught by specialists, the English Department was expected to do the job. "Tubby" had a high stress level. He would foam with indignation at an answer that fell short. "Tubby" was also renowned for stamping his feet when in a rage.

'In the Classics Department, "Daddy" (John) Clarke was the softest-spoken teacher I ever had. You had to strain to hear him. Consequently his classes were held in the profoundest silence. (It did not work for me when I became a teacher.) Daddy's foible was an interest in Bushido (the way of the Warrior). He could be diverted by carefully placed questions about Japan.

'T.C. Dorian also taught Latin (I had him for French). He had a fearsome reputation as disciplinarian and pupils trembled when hearing he would be teaching them. With this reputation he was very seldom challenged, even by the toughest. When I became his colleague at the end of the War I found him a very nice person. His method of getting our interest in French, I remember, was to prescribe thrillers in the language for our reading.

'Robert Q. Ferguson [who left in 1920, a one-time Dux] taught us Latin. Dozy boys would have their backsides jabbed with a sharp pencil. Ninian Jamieson [who left in 1921, another Dux] taught me Greek. He was a dab hand with bits of chalk. His aim was unerring. The offender's forehead or cheek would sting as Mr Jamieson flicked the chalk. Or the chalk would fly past as a warning and out the open window.

'Miss Borland, the dragon School Secretary, chided him for his extravagance. Mr Jamieson got his chalk stick by stick, not box by box. Miss Borland was herself a character. She looked on supplies as almost her own property to be dispensed most grudgingly and at long intervals. When she retired a large stock of supplies was discovered which she had been squirreling away for many years.

'In those days teachers were paid their salaries in notes and coins in an envelope on the afternoon of the last Friday of the month. They had to go in person in their turn to the Office where Miss Borland would count out the money.

Stained glass window in the grand restaurant of Hutchesons' Bar & Brasserie, which is located in the Hutchesons' Hospital building in Ingram Street; after a painting by Scougall. George Hutcheson was the founder of Hutchesons' Hospital (then meaning a home for the old and destitute). His was the first personally funded charitable institution in Glasgow.

Stained glass window in the grand restaurant of Hutchesons' Bar & Brasserie, which is located in the Hutchesons' Hospital building in Ingram Street; after a painting supposed to be by Vandyck. Thomas Hutcheson was the founder of Hutchesons' Hospital School. His younger brother, George, wrote a Draft Contract for a school but it was left to Thomas to endow the School.

George Hutcheson's Kist, or chest, contained all George's financial dealings. It was kept in the Trongate immediately adjacent to the Tolbooth, centre of the City's administration. [Royal Faculty of Procurators]

'Partick Castle' is shown here as a late eighteenth-century ruin. It was built for George Hutcheson in 1611 as the country-house of a landed laird. George took a very personal interest in its design and construction. It was demolished in the 1830s. [©CSG CIC Glasgow Museums and Libraries Collections]

The Monument of Thomas Hutcheson and Marion Stewart at Glasgow Cathedral. Situated to the right of the main entrance it was built in Jacobean style and paid for by Thomas's widow. Thomas was buried beside George in the family sepulchre in the Cathedral. [Image courtesy of SNS Group]

The Trongate Frontage of the first Hutchesons' Hospital in 1794. It is the only surviving image of the Hospital. [By permission of University of Glasgow Library, Special Collections]

The earliest image of the Glasgow skyline from the south-east by John Slezer in 1693. The fourteenth-century bridge in Bridgegate was demolished in 1845 and replaced by the Victoria Bridge. The first steeple to its right is that of the Merchants' House, built in 1659, after the style of Hutchesons' Hospital, and the next steeple is that of the Hospital itself. [National Library of Scotland]

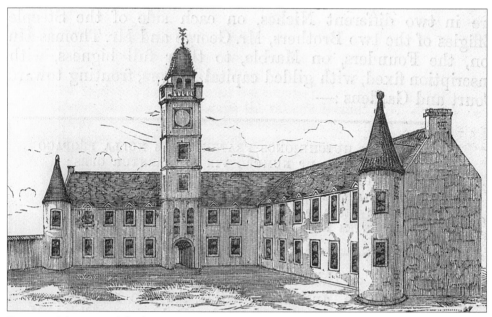

Drawing of the Hospital (back view) reputed to have been completed at the time of its demolition in 1795. [©CSG CIC Glasgow Museums and Libraries Collection: The Mitchell Library, Special Collections]

The new Hospital was built between 1802 and 1805 on Hospital lands to the rear of the Trongate. It was designed by David Hamilton (1768–1843) and the style was a mixture of French Neo-classicism and English Baroque. The drawing is from a booklet created for the opening of the Girls' School in Kingarth Street and can be found in the School Archives. There is no record of who drew it.

Thomas Menzies was the nineteenth Headteacher of Hutchesons' Hospital School, between 1861 and 1875, and the first Rector of Hutchesons' Grammar School from 1876 until 1902. [*Weekly Herald* 6 September 1902]

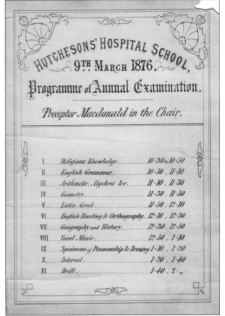

HUTCHESONS' HOSPITAL SCHOOL,
9TH MARCH 1876,
Programme of Annual Examination.

Preceptor Macdonald in the Chair.

I	Religious Knowledge	10·30 to 10·50
II	English Grammar	10·50 . 11·10
III	Arithmetic, Algebra &c.	11·10 . 11·30
IV	Geometry	11·30 . 11·50
V	Latin, Greek	11·50 . 12·10
VI	English Reading & Orthography	12·10 . 12·30
VII	Geography and History	12·30 . 12·50
VIII	Vocal Music	12·50 . 1·10
IX	Specimens of Penmanship & Drawing	1·10 . 1·20
X	Interval	1·20 . 1·40
XI	Drill	1·40 . 2·—

The first Programme of Annual Examination (14 May 1877) of the Grammar School.

'Magnificent Pavilions' (*Glasgow Herald*) – The Rebuilding of Crown Street, 1876, to make it Hutchesons' Grammar School, a full secondary as well as elementary school.

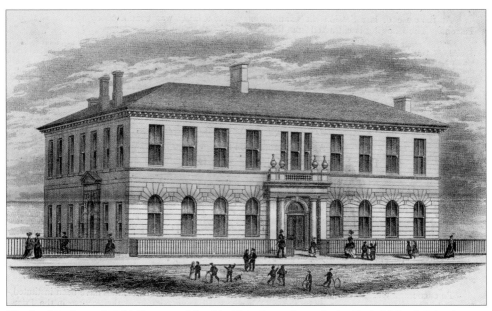

The first Hutchesons' Girls' Grammar School in Elgin Street, formerly the Gorbals' Youth School.

James Lochhead was the first Head of the Girls' School, 1876 to 1885. He took office when the School opened in Elgin Street.

(Dr) William Thomson was appointed Head of the Girls' School in 1885 and proved an innovative leader until his retirement in 1914.

Head Thomson and the staff of the Girls' School c.1907.

William Joseph McVicar joined the staff of Elgin Street in 1882 and as right-hand man to Dr Thomson succeeded him in Headship between 1914 and 1927.

Characters from the Boys' staff – Muirhead, the Drill Sergeant at School for forty-three years.

Characters from the Boys' staff – Robson, Singing Master until the age of ninety-six.

Characters from the Boys' staff – Hanbridge, the Drawing Master.

'Gym or PT or PE in its transformations (we called it "Drill") was supervised by the "Sergeant". Ex-Army Sergeant Instructors often filled these school posts; qualified teachers came later. Drill was distinctly Army-style. Every Wednesday my class and others left school at 2.30pm for Auldhouse. Rugby was on the menu but when Mr Jamieson's back was turned (for he was our rugby coach) we'd revert to soccer.

'The only Asian pupil in Hutchie in my time was a Japanese lad (son of a diplomat) who proved himself a fine gymnast. From 1900 or so, Hutchie always had a sprinkling of Jewish pupils. They were exempt from Religious Instruction but it would hardly have mattered had they attended. For RI it was not. When Ninian Jamieson took us for RI he simply dished out copies of the Vulgate; RI turned into a Latin lesson. At Morning Assembly, prefects in rotation began reading from *Genesis*, chapter 1, verse 1 and kept on day by day, week by week, month by month, until after some years the last verse of the Old Testament was read. Then they started again. I do not remember that we ever reached the New Testament! Jewish pupils hardly needed to opt out.

'The Jewish pupils had a double burden – Hutchie during the day and evening "Shul" for Hebrew Studies in their Turriff Street premises (just north of Eglinton Toll). Languages taught in Hutchie itself were Latin, Greek, French and German. In 4A I was allowed to add French to the Latin I'd had since 1A and Greek since 2A. In those days a Greek class might number two dozen. Latin too survives. I'm glad that the Classics do retain a toehold in Hutchie.

'The Boys' School was for boys, the Girls' for girls. And never the twain should meet except at the joint Annual Dance. I remember the dance in 1939. Too many of the boys were faint-hearted; the girls had to invite a contingent of boys from the Glasgow Boys' High (our deadly rivals) to make up the numbers.

'Hutchie had about thirty Foundationers (poor lads o'pairts); we thought of Glasgow Academy, Fettes or Loretto as being the real snobs, not us. At one time there was some needle with the Gorbals' kids around us. If we kicked a ball out of the playground into Rose Street at the back, some urchin would appear and snaffle it before one of us could climb the massive gate. There was great poverty around. The contrast between well-dressed us and almost ragged them was painfully obvious. Could the School have done anything to bridge the gap?

'I do know of one Gorbals' lad, Ralph Glasser, who was accepted as a Foundationer and later became an Oxbridge academic and author. I myself became friendly with a working class family, the Reids, who lived in a Crown Street tenement opposite the School. The contrast, so near and so obvious, radicalised Hutchie pupils, such as James Maxton (and myself). Hardly likely to happen in Beaton Road! I do hope though, that current pupils, without the ever-present Gorbals' challenge we had in Crown Street, aren't unthinkingly bereft of social conscience.

'All in all (though missing the girls) I have good memories of Hutchie in the 1930s. It had excellent staff, excellent teaching, and congenial classmates. Rebel though I was I'm glad I went there.'

Ronald E. Baker joined the staff of the English Department at HBGS in Glasgow following World War 2. Following his retirement he wrote an article for *Scottish Field*, published in July 1999, called '*Old Hutchie*', in which he recorded his memories of the corridors which echoed the clatter and chatter of pupils.

'Hutchesons' Boys Grammar School in Glasgow's Crown Street is now demolished, high-rise flats occupy its original site where in 1650 the brothers George and Thomas Hutcheson opened its doors to "Twelf mail children sons of decayed burgesses of the City of Glasgow to be educated according to their several dispositions". Ever since, with greatly increased numbers and a change of role to a fee-paying School, it has retained its tradition for hard work.

'In those early days of the post-war years it was the only school in Scotland to have a full Greek class for six years, besides concentrating on the teaching of English, French, Latin, Mathematics and Science. In the Glasgow University Bursary Competition of 1949, fourteen Hutchesonians obtained places in the first hundred. It was said that even His Majesty's Inspectors were a little nervous when their turn came to visit Hutchesons'.

'But old Hutchie was not a daunting place. Certainly every boy having passed his entrance examinations started in first year with two hours' homework each night and that increased as he advanced in his studies, but the boys were a happy, wildly cheerful lot. Not all of them were academically brilliant but motivated presumably by teaching staff and parents expecting realistic returns from the comparatively light fees they paid. They settled down to work in the hilarious, almost eccentric, atmosphere of the School.

'The building itself was a bit peculiar. It looked more like an old mansion house in what was once a quiet Glasgow suburb with wide streets and elegant dwellings.

'Classrooms had an odd habit of opening one into another and had high plaster ceilings with old-fashioned cornices, great open fireplaces and ancient wall cupboards that clung tenaciously to work records of Hutchesonians from another age.

'Each morning Alfie (Leitch), our janitor, lit a huge fire in each of the fireplaces stoking them up during the dinner hour. On particularly cold days boys were sent out to bring in fresh coal supplies. Naturally teachers stood near the blaze to keep warm, some even stationed their blackboards on the wide hearths. It was a common sight at morning Assembly to note that the entire teaching staff had singed and tattered flaps.

'For a pedigree School our staffrooms were a disgrace, real Dickensian stuff. The lower staffroom, which the more junior masters frequented, contained a coke boiler, a chipped sink, a collection of old enamel coffee mugs, a storeroom with hundreds of books and jotters and a boarded up window. Boarded-up because bricks were so regularly thrown through it by local youth that Alfie finally got fed up and plunged us into semi-darkness.

'The School could barely have functioned without Alfie. Alfie was large in all ways, fat, red-faced, cheerful and unfailingly helpful to anybody new in the School. He practically lived in the junior staffroom, could get you shopping bargains at all the cut-price shops around the Gorbals or take a line at short notice to the bookie. Hampden Park was just up the road and whenever there was a match Alfie, by reciprocal agreement, would leave a note beside the kettle asking us to ring the bell for him at four o'clock.

'The School had a Secretary of course. Miss Borland, an indispensable member of staff who sat upstairs all day in her tiny office labouring over an ancient typewriter. Her sense of dedication became even more evident at exam times when she was supposed to cyclostyle the papers but instead became so engrossed in answering the questions herself first that frequent and frenzied trips had to be made to her office before she could be persuaded to part with them.

'For some obscure reason she also resolutely refused to call Latin and Greek by any name other than "Gibberish". "You taking 3A for Gibberish this morning Mr Jamieson?", she'd ask as Ninian strolled past en route to his classroom.

'"I am," Ninian would agree mildly to the alarm and bewilderment of any newcomer who happened to be around. Our Greek master lived and breathed the subject he taught to the extent that he couldn't be bothered with any other.

'No old Hutchesonian is ever likely to forget Islay Shanks, one of our English masters given, when time allowed, to lecturing his classes on anything that particularly interested him. Old Scots words, steam engines, the making of haggis, all these things fascinated him. But Islay's greatest and abiding interest was the poetry of the Gaelic Bards.

'Hutchie was blessed with more than one memorable character. Our Mr Thomson taught Art and with his classroom windows a mere six feet away from those in the opposite row of tenements this might have proved a little inhibiting to some teachers. It did not worry Tommy in the slightest. He merely got his class going, opened the window and exchanged cheerful salutations with various ladies watching his class and "a guid hing oot the windae".

'Then there was Mr Langley who took Science and whenever time and opportunity presented itself, he had the boys checking up on the science of popular thrillers. Was it actually possible that some trick could have been made to work – or a certain poison dropped in a cup so that the victim would suspect nothing and drink it?

'Our pupils, though they may have had to concentrate for the most part on the Classics, were nevertheless aware of the everyday life that went on around the School. The bank across from us for instance suffered more than once from grab and run merchants until the manager invested in a large dog. And twice to the delight of the entire school it sailed through the air and sank its teeth in a wrist that strayed too far and refused to let go until the arrival of the nearby polis and the black maria.

'On yet another memorable day the manager from the South Side sawmills was mugged. At least that was his attacker's intention but unfortunately for him, he was unaware that his victim was a judo expert. The incident therefore lasted a mere six seconds, just long enough for the mugger to fly through the air and hit the side of a passing tramcar with a resounding dunt after which, when the cheering had died down, those pupils with unobstructed views went back to their *Iliad* with renewed energy.

'There was no lack of enthusiasm for Physical Education in Hutchesons', at least that is, among the pupils. Teaching duties also included the supervision of Games so Thursday afternoons saw most of the senior School at the Auldhouse playing fields near Thornliebank. There was a housing scheme on one side, the canal and railway on another and a cemetery at the top side. The fields were big enough to take six rugby pitches all of them occupied, with each game supervised by two masters trying to cope with apparent miracles and the most unlikely infringement of rules. In summer it was tennis and cricket played in Queen's Park.

'That was old Hutchie in the forties: the best academic teaching in Glasgow, the funniest staffroom, the scruffiest building and the brightest pupils you'd find anywhere.'

Duncan Graham in *Sunset on the Clyde: The Last Summers on the Water* (first published 1993; paperback 2005), Chapter 2 – 'Tantalising Glimpses, 1946–52'.

'The years between the war and my student days were spent not unprofitably in educational terms and might have been even more so had my thoughts not wandered so often to the Clyde. Girls were to figure only later. Fortunately, the school I attended believed in the generous application of physical stimuli to encourage study. Today it is fashionable to spare the rod and send for the psychologist but not at Hutchesons' Boys' Grammar School, Gorbals, Glasgow in the late forties. Six out of ten for spelling was the threshold – five marks were likely to lead to five marks on the hands, administered with clinical, magisterial efficiency. In the Latin class the slowest division of four declensions and conjugations got three apiece on a good day. As seats varied daily there was a hideous scramble to avoid the row with the spotty youth who stuttered – the stop watch the size of a turnip was not calibrated to allow for human frailties.

'Hutchesons' was a hard school in every way. It was fee-paying, but £2.10/- a term was affordable with the result that pupils were drawn, by ability alone, from the leafy suburbs of Glasgow's south side, the aspiring housing estates like Kings Park and from the Gorbals itself. There were few snobs since their parents preferred to pay much more for what was possibly much less at Glasgow or Kelvinside Academies. Contempt was mutual. Today's rugby players could teach us nothing about the black arts. We usually lost to those schools in scoring terms, but not at maiming and gouging. I suspect that if we had been better off, my outlook would have been different.

'My parents used to explain that the building in Crown Street had been there before the Gorbals, when the city was still "dear green fields" – on the south bank at least. I have to say that it was very hard to envisage this. Both Crown Street and Cumberland Street, which I walked every day from the tramstop in Bridge Street, and the Gorbals Cross area provided a vital part of my education. It was that last sordid, decaying but vital phase before the planners and "improvers" shook the life out of the place. But it was the people who walked and shuffled along Crown Street who were my real education . . .

'Collisions and altercations led to the fruitiest of exchanges which mingled interestingly with the wise words of the principal teacher of English and author of the grammar book used then in most Scottish schools, Daddy Knox, whose room was on the front overlooking Crown Street. Iron discipline prevailed: years later he confessed to me he had often heaved the tawse with suppressed laughter too. He did not do so the day he found the initials DG carved on a desk in room 9, his wee empire. I was modestly proud because John Buchan, the author of *The Thirty-Nine Steps,* had left his initials embedded in Crown Street wood . . . It is best to draw a veil over what happened next . . .

'Culture was acquired more by accident than design at Hutchie. The curriculum was narrow. English, Mathematics and History for all. Then the class-system operated – Latin and Greek for the high fliers; Modern Languages for the middle of the road, and Science for the positively obtuse. They had the best of it, becoming doctors or accountants – in one case Glasgow's biggest turf accountant, and all made money. The top lot got arts degrees and were living proof that you do not become richer by degrees. Real education was largely accidental – absorbed from a few Mr Chips who had seen life and been in the war. The History master had been captain of a destroyer in the convoy battles in the North Atlantic. When he was demobbed and recruited to Hutchie, he was adjudged too inexperienced to run the School book-store! Today's educationalists who talk of curriculum breadth and studying ten subjects at least, will note that we made do with no more than a passing acquaintance with the arts or even DIY skills. The only visual aid I ever saw was a tattered wall map of ancient Greece, from which either the mice from the open fireplace or an errant youth had amputated the Peloponnese. In spite of that, Ninian Jamieson, the Classics master, brought alive a world so remote from our own lives as to seem quite unreal . . . He would stand in room 19, toothbrush moustache bristling and Brylcreemed hair glistening, his ample posterior bent into the fire toasting while we shivered . . .

'Long before I left the place I had resolved that no child of mine would endure the ordeal of a Scottish classical education, but looking back I can see the gains – an ability to work hard under pressure and a lively social conscience. However, memories of my life and privileges compared with the boys and girls I saw every day in Cumberland Street, shoeless and inadequately clad for the ravages of a Glasgow November here left a lasting impression. Children from whatever background deserve the best of educations. Sadly, even today it is better to be born with a silver spoon in your mouth!

'Nowadays both the Gorbals and Hutchesons' have changed beyond belief. In both cases much of the poverty and bleakness have gone. Both have lost something too. The new Gorbals could be anywhere, the new Hutchie is just another over-sized good school in a characterless building in Pollokshields. When I delivered the Founders' Day Address in Glasgow Cathedral a few years ago, I tried to remind today's pupils that without daily immersion in the Gorbals of the past, their experience of life was sadly lacking. Collecting for charity is a poor, if worthy, substitute for seeing poverty and fortitude at first hand.'

Graham Watson Armstrong MacAllister spoke at the Prizegiving on 29 June 2005.

'My own connection with Hutchie goes back to Crown Street in the far-off world in 1952 when, as a wee, nine-year-old boy with dark, thick, wavy hair I sat the formidable entrance examination for primary 5. I remember vividly the experience. Mr Kane, Miss Ross, fellow entrants, now lifelong friends, the austere, dilapidated environment and telling my mother that I certainly did not want to go to Hutchie. For I also had had The High School entrance experience which I found much more user-friendly. However, my parents with obvious foresight and realising that Auldhouse was much nearer our home than Anniesland, chose Hutchie for me, and here I am fifty-three years on with an almost lifetime of association with Hutchie; as a pupil, former pupil, a probationary teacher here in Beaton Road, junior member of staff, special assistant teacher, and exciting time away as Head of History at Whitehill in Dennistoun to return as Head of History in both the Boys' and Girls' School, leading to amalgamation and co-education in 1976, assistant Rector for twenty-five years, depute Rector and finally interim Rector with the responsibility of taking care of the School at this critical time.

'Amazingly I have known and worked with nine Rectors and Principals, seven Chairman of Governors, eight Bursars/Secretaries and Treasurers to the Governors, innumerable members of the teaching and support staff and countless generally inspiring and wonderful young people and their parents. Little did my parents know that their decision in 1952 would lead to almost a lifetime of involvement in the Hutchie community.

'We must never undervalue or neglect the special community life of the School. The thread of tradition and service, which I recognise through half a century, has brought us to the vibrant and successful community of today.

'Please forgive the historian for indulging a little in the Hutchie past but we are fortunate to have a long and still evolving tradition, it is part of our being. I do remember clearly the spirit of the school in the 1950s, a bygone age. It was a school stern and somewhat narrowly focused with the emphasis very much on rigorous hard work spurred on by able if strongly authoritarian teachers who, in their own inimitable way, achieved for most pupils at least their academic potential.

'Indeed I recall Prize-Givings in the dark high-beamed gym hall of Crown Street lined with wall bars, climbing ropes and rope ladders, our daily instruments of physical torture, the narrow platform, the clock over the central doorway, civic dignitaries with golden chains, ladies all in hats, the remote, aloof figures of Chairman and governors, along with the silver-haired, impressive Rector, the singing of metric psalms, named prizes still awarded today and the frenzied climax of the announcement of the usually just-released results of the University of Glasgow Bursary Competition and the regular Hutchie triumph of places at the top of the list and significant numbers in the first hundred awards. This was very much seen as a league table of success in those days. Like all such measures of success it masked the individual success of so many pupils whose own achievements, although not on the bursary list, were nevertheless very real.

'I believe that what I learned from my schooling was to try my hardest, to work regularly and honestly, to achieve my very best, to aim to survive a fairly harsh regime but I do recall fondly a real sense of School community and pride. We loved the decaying School building, the idiosyncrasies of many teachers, the inspiration of success of senior pupils, the fascination of the surrounding world of the old Gorbals, a district now twice rejuvenated and yet never again to see the unique local community life which was swept away by the modernist civic planners of the Sixties.

'The School was very much a real part of the Gorbals community supporting in various ways local needs, for example in memorable all day Saturday Jumble sales where the most amazing queues formed overnight almost the length of Crown Street. Similarly the Girls of Kingarth Street were involved in community work with support for hospitals through the Cot Box scheme and regular collections for and visits to Childrens' Homes. A thread of involvement in and care for those about us has strengthened over fifty years and is an integral part of School ethos and life today . . .

'The Hutchesons' story over the past fifty years and indeed throughout its three hundred and sixty four year history is very much of the School community flourishing in its particular time in history, of continuity and change and survival through centuries of social, political and economic evolution. As we stand at the gate of a new Rectorship, and look forward to a new chapter, it is important to remember and appreciate that the School, Governors, Rectors and staff have promoted fundamental change over the years with determination and with foresight and energy ensuring survival and ongoing progress. Over the past fifty years each term of office of Rector or Principal brought distinctive and necessary change.

'My first Rector, James Watson had established Hutchie as the leading Classics School in Scotland. He was a firm, self effacing man who praised and encouraged all honest effort and is remembered with respectful gratitude for his personal interest and indeed he knew us all by name. The School reached the heights of academic success. Nevertheless the Governors were aware of the two cultures debate, and the increasing importance of the growth of Languages and Science in the curriculum. The appointment of John Hutchison as Rector, controversial at the time, brought to the School an unassuming but principled man, alert of mind, wise and cautious who ended the Classical/Modern division and ensured that the School's record in Science rivalled that in Classics. His progressive outlook encouraged changes in subjects widely and the School emerged strengthened and acquired balance without loss in tradition.

'Principal McIver of the Girls' School, small in stature but impressive in presence, with her keen logic and outspoken comments was an educationalist ahead of her time and indeed of the Boys' School. New methods in almost every area were pioneered, tested, adapted and put into very successful practice. Whilst she endeavoured always to ensure the distinctive and progressive strengths of the Girls' School and to promote the fullest educational opportunity for women, she was also remarkably a strong advocate of amalgamation and co-education. Both John Hutchison and Isabel McIver saw significant expansion of the Schools.

'Rector Peter Whyte inherited the School at a time of acute danger . . . A brilliant and internationally recognised teacher of Mathematics, Peter Whyte brought a calm, courteous presence, with powers and careful organisation. The Public Schools Commission of the late Sixties had the remit to advise on how schools such as Hutchie could be incorporated into comprehensive re-organisation as grant in aid was withdrawn. In the face of the government ultimatum of becoming a local authority comprehensive, to go wholly independent or to close, the Governors in 1971, along with Mr Whyte and Miss McIver, took a daring initiative and produced a plan for a co-educational primary and secondary independent school. In the mid-Seventies, Peter Whyte, along with the Acting Principal, Jessie Knox, embarked on the very complex educational project of amalgamating the schools with purpose, verve and success and out of despair a new strength emerged, embracing the best traditions from both schools.

'Dr Gilmour Isaac's time as Rector was clouded by ill-health but he brought to the School the realisation of independence, and began the process of true integration. His leadership and his careful promotion of the best of the distinct Hutchesons' traditions in academic scholarship, sporting, artistic and musical success ensured continuity in the emerging co-educational School.

'Paul Brian's troubled months as Rector were indeed a transient period. His ideas for reform of the curriculum and modernisation were perhaps not well articulated and over hastily introduced and thus he was misunderstood, but in longer time most of his ideas were implemented and indeed overtaken. Temporarily the school was disrupted and uncertain of the way ahead. Miss Murray's caretaker time restored some calm and confidence and the School embraced enthusiastically the future again under new Rector, David Ward. Along with the relative financial plenty of the Assisted Places Scheme, his years brought unparalleled expansion in pupil numbers, in teaching and support staff, in fine buildings and facilities, in broadening further the educational experience with new subjects and activities, really strong academic success, the fostering of relations with former pupils and the development of the Bursar's Office to manage a multi-million pound business. In many ways it was a special time of purpose and success.

'Change continues to be an inevitable ingredient of our modern world. This past session has undoubtedly been a time of significant change. John Knowles, Rector for five and a half years, left in December to take up a pastoral and educational post in the diocese of Chester . . . In our large school, he implemented smaller teaching classes in many subjects and smaller form and pastoral groups. John Knowles brought the successful revolution of the electronic age to the classroom and administration, the merger and the creation of our new Primary at Lilybank Terrace, huge moves forward in staff professional development and mentoring, a much more inclusive participatory management style and much besides.

'This session has also brought continuity and success. In August our pupils achieved a vintage set of examination results...We continue of course to provide pupils with much more than academic excellence. Pupils have a wide and healthily balanced education to prepare them well for future life and to take their place as well as well-rounded citizens. Our aim is to ensure that the provision of education for each young person is targeted to that individual's needs focusing on our core values of academic attainment and individual personal and social development, realising to the fullest each individual young person's potential . . .

'The range of co-curricular opportunities is incredible . . .

'I report on a strong and successful community, some nineteen hundred young people, our raison d'etre, our inspiration – taught, encouraged and fostered by some two hundred and thirty teaching staff and some hundred support staff back up . . .

'School life is enriched by the interest and involvement of the School Association and the 1957 Group. The former, in a good-natured challenging way encourages the Rector and the School to be more accountable to parents. I have valued that experience! The latter continues a forty eight year tradition of fundraising and supportive interest . . .

'I suggest that Hutchesons' can further serve society by promoting a balance of values:

Excellence and achievement
Enterprise and imagination
Autonomy and leadership service to the wider society
Personal self worth . . .'

Professor Thomas Noble left the School in 1964. In 1999, he wrote about his reminiscences of the change from Crown Street to Beaton Road some four decades before in 1960, in *Veritas*, 1999, pp. 18–19.

'Farewell, Crown Street . . .

'It is a shock to realise that it was all of forty years ago this summer that HBGS moved from Crown Street to Crossmyloof and the gleaming new building opened by Sir Thomas Innes of Learney, the Lord Lyon, King of Arms.

'I was one of the last intake at Crown Street in September 1958 and, along with most other boys who had not attended the Hutchie primary classes, I was registered in Form 1D. Form 1A was the Classic stream, studying Latin and (from second year) Greek; 1B was a kind of hybrid, taking Latin and French; the "C" stream (which I joined in Second Year) took Modern Languages (French and German); and the "D" stream, Science.

'The 1D form room – Form Master, the inimitable Willie Wilson – was up the back stairs at the south end of the building. An enormous Victorian classroom had been divided in two by a large wooden partition and we sat with our backs to it, facing the fire. The room was heated by a real coal fire and the class prefect for the week had the duty of bringing up more coal to keep the fire going through the day. The blackboard ran across the top of the mantelpiece and, on cold mornings, Willie Wilson would stand with his back to the fire, facing the class, his gown gathered on his right arm, his hands in his pockets, heating his posterior.

'He had his own peculiar wry sense of humour. We had two Millars in the class, so my friend Alasdair Millar[3] promptly became "Turner", and "Turner" he remained . . . He never raised his voice or used his belt. His technique was to appeal to us man to man. "Look here," he would say, "Come off it! We're all working class, aren't we? Doesn't your father work?"

'"Now, look," he would remonstrate with the little pan loaf suburbanites. "You pronounce this verb 'ferr', not 'fair'. Just as in 'A rerr terr at the Glesca ferr.' Right?"

'"Acutes," he would explain helpfully, "slope towards Crown Street [to our right], graves upwards towards Florence Street." (No wonder we could never remember when we got to Crossmyloof!)

'The day would start, of course, in the Assembly Hall, which doubled as the Gym and the formidable Roy Smith would call us to order before the rest of the staff entered. Form 1D was right at the front, under the Rector's nose. Up at the back of the hall, the Hutcheson brothers stared down at us from their stained glass windows. Occasionally, when Jack Bolling (the Music master) was absent the Depute Rector – affectionately known to generations of Hutchie boys as "Papa Chang"[4] – would lead the praise. On these occasions, it was always the 124th Psalm . . .

'On Remembrance Day, the Psalm was, of course, the set praise and, for the last time that November, we remembered the war dead in the old building they themselves had known.

'"Papa" was not the only revered member of staff to be awarded a nickname. Sometimes the origins were obvious to us new boys. In some cases it was because of a surname shared with a famous cartoonist or singer. In others, it was a certain resemblance. "Chang" was so named after the Chinese leader (or was it his habit of narrowing his eyes?) "Papa" being added when "Mama" came to teach along with him. "Commie Joe" in the Science Department kept on preaching the virtues of Russian science; "Long John" was obviously tall; but where did "Ponty" come from? I never worked that out.[5]

'On Friday mornings we had Art during the first period. ("Art!", Willie Wilson would rasp scathingly, "You don't do 'Art'! 'Drawing' you mean!" Since the dinner money had to be collected, "Charlie" Charleson, the one-armed Head of the Art Department, would simply stand and chat to us. At least, that was what we thought. He was an amazing conversationalist and actually gave us very clever lectures in aesthetics and design. Occasionally, he demonstrated his amazing skill with his one remaining arm by throwing his belt and hitting a ball of paper thrown up in the air by someone at the far end of the room. Along the corridor, nervous laughter could be heard from Jack Bolling's room, as he terrorised his class with his war-club! His technique worked marvellously, for he had an enormous senior male choir voice.

'The Art and Music rooms were at the north end of the building. The Junior School Scripture Union used to meet there, and the legendary "Boss" Meiklejohn would come to take it. Our English classroom was two floors above that, right at the top of the north stairs. (In later years, I was fascinated to discover . . . that in the 1880s that top floor had been the flat where the then Rector Menzies lived.)

'At lunch time, we went out the enormous gates at the end of the cloisters and crossed Florence Street to an old church building where Glasgow Corporation school lunches were served; often mashed potatoes, floating in thin mince, with some sad cabbage, followed by steam pudding with a dollop of custard. After School, a packet of crisps for threepence or a cream "snowball" kept the hunger pangs at bay . . .

'Tuesday afternoons were interminable. We had five periods lasting till four o'clock (when other schools finished). Normally, classes finished at 3.15pm. On Thursdays, classes finished at 2.30pm, and we ran through the Gorbals to catch a tram to Auldhouse for rugby practice. The competition was fierce to get seats upstairs in the little compartment at the front above the driver. Sitting there, masters of all we surveyed, we rattled and swayed our way along the cobbled street all the way out to the green fields of Auldhouse.

'The old building was basically T-shaped. The top of the T was the main range of buildings running south to north and fronting on to Crown Street. The stem of the T was the assembly hall, doubling as the Gym with its climbing ropes suspended from the great varnished wooden rafters. On the storey below the Hall were the Rector's Office and two classrooms and below that, the cloisters. In the new building at Beaton Road, the cloisters below what was originally the Gym (now the Library) were designed especially as a memento of the old building. By 1958, the fabric of Crown Street was crumbling, but it is funny to think that such a solid old building only now exists in the memory.

'. . . *Hello, Beaton Road!'*

'Only members of staff came in through the great front door at the foot of the grand staircase. There stood the gong, which duly resounded at the end of each class period. At morning interval, we still all received our bottle of milk. There were, of course, no showers in the Gym (not even a changing room!) so that unforgettable ambience of the old Corn Street building was pervaded by stale sweat as well as stale milk, coal dust and smoke, and the ingrained dirt of old buildings.

'It was a strange experience to meet all the same people the following September in the gleaming new building. Junior pupils were not invited to the official Opening Ceremony, but I went anyway, and slipped in at the back door of the Assembly next to the new War Memorial to hear the Lord Lyon tell his audience in his strangulated treble voice that "facts are chiels that winna ding!"

'Yet the new building really belonged to us. We gazed with awe at the beautiful wooden panelling; groaned at the ineffective modern heating system; examined minutely the Hutcheson brothers in their stained glass windows (for so long, far above us, but now brought right down to our level). We identified the buildings in the Assembly Hall mural and peered into the two lily ponds for goldfish. The smell of new varnish, new wood and new books indicated a new chapter. The new chairs scraped along the new floors when we stood up to speak in class, and the order was given that we no longer had to stand to speak. The wood panelling in the corridors was threatened by the buckles of our cases, bulging with books, and we were ordered to "walk on the left, with bags on the right". School lunches were now cooked on the premises – with a choice of menu – and there were changing rooms and showers.

'Old things had passed away and the new had come. It had been given to us to enter the promised land.

'I didn't see much of Willie Wilson that year, but he paid his annual visit to morning Assembly. I had been given the task of handing out hymn books to the staff. "No thanks, Noble," he said, "I'm trying to give them up."

TEN   Timeline of the Modern Schools

1885. The new Scheme for the reorganisation of educational endowments in Glasgow separated the management of pensions from that of education. A new body, the Governors of Hutchesons' Educational Trust (HET), was separated from the Royal Incorporation of Hutchesons' Hospital. Ownership of schools and their sites was vested in the Trust. Funds still came from the Hospital, which continued to control the investments (although Governors could invest from their allocation). The Governors consisted of twenty-one persons, eleven elected by the Town Council, three by the School Board, two by the City ministers, two by the Patrons, and one each from the University of Glasgow, the Merchants' House and the Trades' House. Such a composition showed how far the school was still perceived as a Glasgow School. The Secretary of the Trust, Rev. Dr F. Lockhart Robertson, was to be paid.

With the handing over of the Schools in Crown Street and Elgin Street to the HET the direct connection of the Patrons with Education was terminated after an administration of almost 250 years.

William Thomson was appointed Headteacher of the Girls' School (until 1914).

Under the 1885 Scheme fees were raised considerably. The roll consisted of 825 boys and 567 girls.

1886. The Girls' School was renamed the Girls' Grammar School.

1887. The Patrons petitioned Parliament for a return to the 1872 revenue arrangements. The Petition was fruitless.

1889. The first National Leaving Certificate was introduced. Hutchesons' (Boys and Girls) pupils achieved 50% more passes than the national average, despite not being selected for examination and despite the Boys having a course one year shorter than usual.

1889. HET demanded far more rigid economy.

1890. The rolls had declined to 596 boys and 475 girls.

1890–93. In the Glasgow University Higher Certificate for Women some 36 were awarded and 15 were won by Hutchie Girls.

1891. Fees were abolished in all Scottish Council-run schools for pupils between the age of 5 and 14. Hutchesons' roll fell dramatically.

   The Trust nearly went into the red and was only saved by an Income Tax repayment and a Bursary underspend.

1892. HET claimed a portion of the Equivalent Grant which was to be applied to secondary schools. Awards were made to both Schools and the Trust was given representation on the new Burgh Committee on Secondary Education.

1892. The Girls were very successful in the Honours Grade Examinations; one-eighth of the successes nationally were in English, French and German.

1892. Lockhart Robertson died.

1893. Following the reduction and abolition of fees in other schools the Boys' School cut fees at the top of the School from 40s to 21s.

1894. *The Hutchesonian*, the first School Magazine, was produced. It was printed monthly and priced a penny. It urged masters to dress like those in better-class schools; it urged the Governors to provide a proper gymnasium and called for a playing field, an athletic track and a cadet corps. The Girls were not much involved.

   A Scheme was accepted by the HET to improve accommodation for the Girls in Elgin Street.

   The Patrons, still smarting at the 'injustice' of the 1885 revenue arrangements, petitioned the SED under Henry Craik. The Petition proved fruitless.

   The lands of Camphill, 60 unfeued acres adjacent to Queen's Park and 'one of the most valuable possessions of the Hospital' had been bought by the Hospital in 1865 and was sold to the Town Council to extend Queen's Park for £35,000 below the market price.

1895. With far more free education available the Patrons – the whole Corporation of Glasgow, numbering 77, and 22 others – including ministers of the Established Church and representatives of the Merchants' and Trades' Houses – pressed for more to be spent on pensions. They met with representatives of the leading endowed educational institutions of the city but received no encouragement. A Statement was also rejected by Lord Balfour of Burleigh.

1896. The number of fee-paying pupils were 301 boys and 315 girls and the total amount collected in fees had dropped from £4,144 (from both in 1885) to £2,477. Moreover, since the introduction of the 1885 Scheme, places had to be offered to a minimum of 200 foundationers but the numbers could not be realised. The Governors observed the schools moving in a direction which left them open to criticism, and their concerns at the drift made for an uncertain defence. 'Complaints were loud about the gentrification of the Schools.'[1] It was believed that boys from public elementary schools had 'great difficulty in fitting in', which by further discouraging working-class applicants made it even more likely that few scholarships would be awarded to 'outsiders'.

1897. James Macfarlane, an HET Governor, proposed transferring the Schools to the School Board. The initial reaction was cool. The School Board had no means of conducting the Schools more economically and would need the transfer of the whole of the Hutchesons' endowment. It also envisaged a reduction in fees and a reduction in the status of the Schools. Despite this a Special Meeting of the HET voted 5–3 to proceed with the transfer.

1899. After eighteen months of discussion it appeared that the School Board had agreed to take the Schools, but legal opinion held that such an action was likely to be rejected as the funds of HET were being sought for a purpose which would have the effect of relieving the taxpayers of a burden imposed on them by Statute. The School Board moved to a more 'neutral' position on the issue and the HET Governors began to investigate the possibility of a Private Bill to get rid of the Schools.

1902. A low point was reached in numbers: the number of fee-paying pupils in the Boys' School sank to 161, and in the Girls' School to 213. It was a very competitive market – with Glasgow Academy, Kelvinside Academy,

Garnethill and Hillhead HS all in an area already over-provided with secondary schools.

1903. The Governors prepared a Private Bill, but a new School Board decided to have nothing to do with Hutchesons' under the terms agreed by their predecessors. By this time it held that there was ample accommodation for all the scholars likely to be brought forward. Indeed, it already had under its jurisdiction sufficient room for all the scholars if these Schools were closed.

The roll in both Schools began to rise, thanks mainly to the work of Rector Philp of the Boys' School and Head-teacher William Thomson of the Girls' School. Ten years after the failure of the proposal for the School to be taken over by the School Board, the roll had gone up in the Boys' School by more than 300 to 480. The upward trend was to continue during the first part of the inter-war period, and by 1928–29 the roll had reached 573. However, the deterring conditions (as they were for many parents) of locale and premises and the economic difficulties of the time acted strongly during the 1930s as a brake on the recovery process, and by the outbreak of World War 2 numbers were down to 514. Indeed, there were times during the 1920s and 1930s when the School was under-populated in the sense that there were some available places not taken. The end of the War changed all this: by 1948–49 624 boys were in attendance, and ten years later the 800–mark was passed (of whom 600 were secondary pupils. After a further ten years, the roll had reached 870, of whom again about 600 were secondary pupils). Factors in this increase were the opening of new buildings and the School's growing academic reputation.

1904. Despite having the support of all the Patrons and fourteen Governors, the Hutchesons' Educational Trust Bill was abandoned. Lord Balfour of Burleigh had spoken out against changing the proportions of revenue which had been fixed in 1885.

Further Hutchesons' legislation was prevented by a continuing series of failed Government Bills to re-organise Scottish secondary education (up to 1908).

1908. The long-awaited Education (Scotland) Act had been passed, permitting if not guaranteeing the continuance of endowed schools, and centralising the various Government grants into one Educational Fund from which schools might draw. The Governors sought borrowing powers from the Court of Session.

The Governors faced tightened state regulation of School accommodation.

1909. Faced with the threat of grant cuts the Governors began a search for a suitable site for a new School. The SED gave them an ultimatum.

1910. The Court of Session amended the HET allowing the Trust to raise loans.

1912. The new Hutchesons' Girls' Grammar School was opened by Lord Balfour of Burleigh in Kingarth Street. It cost £43,000 to build and accommodated 240 Junior pupils and 660 Senior pupils. It was built on Hospital land of 7,012 square yards and consisted of 22 classrooms, 3 Art rooms, 4 Science rooms and labs, 2 Music rooms, a gymnasium, a dining hall for 150, a library and janitor's house. It was lit throughout with electricity (which would not follow in Crown Street until 1927).

1914. The first Girls' Grammar School Dux (gold) medal was presented by Sir Thomas Mason, a former Dean of Guild, although the Dux had been awarded since 1885–86.

The Kingarth Street roll almost doubled that of the last Elgin Street roll (758 to 440).

The first Girls' School magazine was produced.

With funds in the black the Trust pledged to build a new Boys' School on the plot opposite the Girls' School. HET set up a Committee to investigate the cost of a new Boys' School but World War 1 and its aftermath intervened. It was estimated that a well-equipped school would cost approximately £50,000.

The bronze busts of the Founders were unveiled by Lord Strathclyde. They were executed in triplicate: one pair was gifted by the Patrons to the Girls' Grammar School; another pair, the property of the Corporation, was placed in the Kelvingrove Art Galleries; while the third pair adorned the Hospital Hall.

Two new Heads took office – William McVicar (1914–27) in Kingarth Street, and W. King Gillies (1913–19) in Crown Street. Under McVicar the domestic side of the Girls' curriculum was played down and the School saw itself 'as an important feeder of the University'. Gillies set the path for the next half century of Boys' education, stressing academic excellence and introducing rugby and cricket.

1918. Post-war there was no money for rebuilding. However, a relationship of partnership developed with the new local authority covering now the County and the City of Glasgow. Authority representatives had been in the Trust since 1908. Glasgow was now subsidising the Schools, as part of its educational provision.

With the War moving to a close, the Governors reneged on their promise to build a new Boys' School. This led to the resignation of the Rector, King Gillies.

1919. J.C. Scott was appointed Rector (1919–32).

1920. The first Boys' Grammar School Sports Day was held.

1921. The War Memorial was unveiled by John Buchan in Crown Street. Buchan was the first president of the FP Club.

1924. Revival of an independent Girls' school magazine.

1927. Miss Margaret Kennedy, the first female Principal (1927–48) took office.

The Auldhouse Sports Ground was opened and managed by the School and Club Trust (successor to the FP Club).

1929. The Girls' School Crest was licensed.

Glasgow University honoured the Boys' School by making Rector Scott a Doctor of Law; former Rector Gillies likewise; a former pupil, Rev. M. Scott Dickson, a Doctor of Divinity, and a staff member, Gavin Hood, a Doctor of Science.

A new Commission was established to investigate the position of endowed schools, but the Hutchesons' Schools were confident that they would be endorsed as a significant part of the City's schooling. By 1932 the Town Council was debating the financial balance to the City of taking over the Hutchesons' Schools. Fortunately, they had staunch defenders in former Rector James Scott and Sir Charles Cleland. Despite the Labour Party's control of the Council since 1932 it was never convinced that it wanted to take over the Schools.[2]

1932. W. Tod Ritchie (1932–45) appointed Rector.

1937. Under the provisions of the Educational Endowments (Scotland) Acts (1928–35) a new Scheme was prepared by the Commissioners and this received Royal Assent in 1937. Under the terms of the arrangements a new Governing Body was constituted[3] and at its first meeting this Board elected John M. Biggar as Chairman and declared its intention of making progress with the proposed new Boys' School. The Trust allowed for substantial sums to be put into a new building fund for a new Boys' School. The Commissioners also set up the Glasgow Educational Trust and the three Boards of 1885 became two in 1937.

1938. The SED approved of the Governors' proposal to acquire the site at Crossmyloof. Within eighteen months the site had been acquired at a cost of £12,500, financial difficulties had been solved and early arrangements were moving smoothly. It was estimated that the new building would cost in the region of £165,000. The enforced delay which followed was deemed a 'major disaster for the School'. Come the War, Crossmyloof was turned over to allotments.

Education Authority Schools were closed while Kingarth Street was designated an 'Assembly School' to help in evacuation. Hutchesons' girls were evacuated to Sanquhar while the Boys' School was closed. Fifteen air raid shelters were built in the playground. By Easter 1940 the normal programme was resumed in both Schools and maintained for the War's duration. However, Crown Street was bombed in March 1941 and closed for two weeks.

1942. The distribution of Dux medals stopped through lack of materials (and not resumed until 1957).

During World War 2 both Schools were over-subscribed.

The Girls' Training Corps was established (there was no OTC).

After withdrawal from Sanquhar, Miss Kennedy arranged to use Milton Park House, Dalry, Kirkcudbrightshire, as a boarding school for evacuated children. However, her exhaustive plans came to grief on legal grounds, viz. the educational portion could only be spent on education in Glasgow.

1943. Ritchie began the One Thousand Club to help with the rebuilding – 'a thousand genuine believers at no more than £100 a head'. The idea did not work.

Glasgow Corporation announced its intention to abolish all fees in schools it controlled or influenced (however, it dropped this pledge in 1948).

1945. James Watson (1945–55) was appointed as Rector with the mission to make the Boys' School 'the leading Classics school in Scotland'. The highest-ever number of Leaving Certificates were recorded in each School.

1947. HMI Report: Boys – with roll of 600+; dining arrangements inadequate; new Rector maintaining 'the traditional vigour of its academic and social life'; HBGS had a 'wide and well-founded reputation for sound and scholarly work'.

HMI Report: Girls – with a roll of 883 HGGS had a 'fine reputation for spirited endeavour and solid achievement'.

1948. Miss Isabella McIver (1948–73) was appointed Principal.

Dr James MacCallum had been Treasurer and Law Agent to Hutchesons' for 41 years. In his Will he left the Trust £4,000 on condition that the Governors began building within five years of the War's end. Legal advice was taken on how to interpret that date. Finally, in 1952, the Privy Council ruled that the War ended on 9 July 1951, so the Governors had until 1956 to start building. By 1953, £500,000 was the estimated cost of a new school, which was beyond the School's ability to repay. However, the SED agreed to support the building of a Junior School for 240 boys, costing around £50,000, and this was acceptable to the Corporation.

1950. Tercentenary Celebrations held taking the date based on Robert Bain's lyric in the School Song.

1951. Another Commission on Educational Endowments – the Taylor Report – supported Scottish endowed schools. 'We are satisfied that so long as these schools maintain the individual characteristics and worthy traditions which have long been theirs, and play their part in association with normal public provision in meeting the educational needs of the community, even though they have to depend on substantial assistance from public funds to do so, it would be a disservice to the Scottish[4] educational system to deprive it of the variety and quality they provide by suggesting any sweeping and radical alterations to their position.'

1952. The Governors instructed the School Buildings' Committee and the Finance Committee to make preliminary investigation into the possibilities of commencing the erection of the new Boys' School. Early estimates of cost were in excess of £500,000. It was back to the drawing-board.

1954 The Grandstand was erected at Auldhouse.

1955. John Hutchison was appointed Rector (1955–66). He made Science the equal of Classics and widened extra-curricular activity. He was a strong believer in the wishes of the Hutchesons' brothers that 'none were to be excluded through lack of means'.

1955. In the Glasgow University Bursary Competition seven places in the first twelve went to Hutchesonians, Boys being 1st, 2nd, 4th and 7th; the Girls occupied 3rd, 9th and 11th places.

1956. After four years of difficult negotiations, the Governors, chaired by Councillor John Stewart, confirmed the contract for the first phase of the building, comprising Junior School, Janitor's House and playing fields. Work on the new school at Crossmyloof had begun.

The Girls' School roll reached 1,000, while the boys stood at 600 as pupils were not admitted until Primary V.

Fee-levels were lower than all but one comparable Scottish school – Robert Gordon's College in Aberdeen.

1957. The 'Junior Block' at Crossmyloof was ready for occupation. Given the tortuous course of negotiations this, according to Rector Hutchison, seemed 'little short of a miracle'.

The '1957 Group' was founded – its members proved indispensable fundraisers. Each of the original fourteen members had to bring in an extra member, who then had to do the same.

1959. Glasgow Corporation ended the Mutual Eligibility Scheme despite the use made by the Corporation of Hutchesons'-trained teachers in promoted posts throughout the city. However, the Corporation reconsidered and produced a 'revised' scheme.

1960. The new School was opened by the Lord Lyon King of Arms, Sir Thomas Innes. It consisted of a Junior School of six classrooms and

Gymnasium providing for 240 boys, and a Senior School of twenty-three classrooms including two Geography rooms, five Science rooms and preparation areas, a Botany greenhouse, four Art rooms, a Music room, and a Gymnasium, providing for 660 boys. It cost £438,000 (including site) and was designed by Boswell, Mitchell and Johnston (of Glasgow). 'Like Trongate in 1641, Crown Street in 1841 and 1876 and Kingarth Street in 1912, Crossmyloof in 1960 was in the forefront of fashion.'[5] The Governors reluctantly raised the fees by the largest amount since the 1920s, in the Senior School from £27 to £45. The rolls dropped, especially in the Girls' School. By 1971 fees were five times what they were in 1960. Nonetheless, the Schools increased in size, the clientele were not financially privileged and academic standards were maintained.

1961. The first Founders' Day took place, in Glasgow Cathedral. It was another Hutchison innovation.

1966. Peter Whyte was appointed Rector (1966–79). He oversaw the amalgamation of the two schools. He prepared the School for independence and widened the curriculum.

Where would we place the Schools in social terms?[6] Hutchesons' Girls' was decidedly B2, reflecting the considerable body of B2 citizens residing in Glasgow's south side and beyond it to the south, with only the much smaller Craigholme as an alternative. Although up to four or five decades ago Hutchesons' Boys' had, it seems, some not inconsiderable representation of B3 homes, even of C1 homes, there appeared less of this and at this point the School is predominately B2. As with the Girls' School this is to be expected given the lack of competition on the south side, which gives it a monopoly of middle-class south-siders not wishing their sons to travel into, or to the other side of, town. However, the Boys' has more B3 parents than the Girls'.

1970. The Crown Street building was demolished. It had been used by the Ministry of Labour since 1959 (as Elgin Street had before it).

1971. Whyte and McIver proposed a plan for amalgamation.

1973. The SED maintenance grant for 1974–75 was frozen at the 1973–74 level (£201,875); HET estimated expenditure exceeded estimated income by £73,000 (excluding further increases in teachers' salaries); the fees were increased by £65 and economies discussed. The Houghton Pay Award in 1974–75 for teachers and the frozen grant resulted in a deficit of £98,000, and fees were increased by £62. It was in this situation that the Labour Government decided to phase out grant-in-aid over five or six years. The Governors had a choice of going independent or becoming a comprehensive school. Reluctantly, the Governors determined on the former, wishing the Governors to retain their own Board outwith local authority control. In 1975–76 expenditure was £706,530 with income at £686,000 and fees now at £318 p.a. and the school roll dropped by 62.

1974. Payment for Crown Street was received.

1975. The composition of the Governing Body of the HET was changed: it was to be made up of 17 nominated Governors and not more than 3 co-opted Governors.

1976. The amalgamation of the two Schools took place.
  The Centenary of the Girls' School was celebrated.
  Corporal Punishment guidelines were accepted by the Governors. The abolition took place in September 1987.
  The combined School became fully independent: forced on the Governors 'in despair' by the withdrawal of the block grant, to be replaced first by a grant-in-aid, then by the Assisted Places scheme in 1981–2 on a declining curve, to disappear in 1986.

1978–79. Fees now £470 p.a.; by 1979–80 fees £524 p.a.; by 1980–81 fees £657 p.a.; by 1981–82 fees now £760 p.a.; by 1982–83 fees £861 p.a., and APS £82,500, with 93 applications.

1979. Dr Gilmour Isaac was appointed Rector (1979–84). He implemented major organisational changes.

1981–82. The Assisted Places Scheme (APS) was introduced by the Conservative Government. In its first year 74 Hutchie pupils were awarded £345,000.

1982. An analysis of SCE results in prominent Scottish schools in the *Glasgow Herald* showed the dominance of Hutchesons' GS.
  The Hospital building in Ingram Street was sold to the National Trust for Scotland.

1984. Paul Brian appointed Rector (1984–85). His resignation accepted by the Governors 'with great reluctance and sadness'.

1985. Miss J.C. Murray appointed Interim Rector (1985–86), the first woman to head a co-educational HMC school.

1985. The 1975 Statute was amended: the Governing Body was now to compose of nine nominated Governors – two from Church of Scotland Presbyteries; two Patrons (including one minister not from the Church of Scotland), and one representative from the Glasgow University Senate; Merchants' House, Trades' House; Glasgow Educational Trust and the University of Strathclyde Senate; and not more than five co-opted Governors with education experience. The lack of representation from the local authority showed how completely divorced the School now was from Glasgow.

1987. David Ward was appointed Rector (1987–99). He made vital improvements to the building, in planning, funding and over-seeing the construction of a new Science and PE blocks.

1980s. Building work included Art Rooms and a large Music room with ancillary rooms. This is now the corridor to the Science building. Also four classrooms for Social Subjects were created on the North ground floor. This single-storey corridor was demolished and replaced with the three storey North Wing.

1990. The Foundation Stone of the Science building was laid along with a time capsule prepared by pupils.

1990. The launch took place of the 350th Anniversary Appeal.

1991. The new Science Block was opened at Beaton Road by the Rt Hon. the Lord Tombs of Brailes, Chancellor of the University of Strathclyde and chairman of Rolls Royce plc.

The School celebrated 350 years of excellence.

After eighteen years of struggle a Public Inquiry ensured that the School gained twenty acres of land adjacent to Auldhouse (while it lost the Kingarth playing field which the Patrons wished to develop). All the School fields were now concentrated in one area under one management, linked to the Former Pupils.

1994. The new Infant Department building was opened at Kingarth Street by Lord James Douglas Hamilton M.P., Minister of Education, Scotland.

1994 saw the infilling of the open Cloister corridor at Beaton Road, creating a suite of new classrooms, offices and storerooms.

The thirteen offers of places from Oxbridge was an 'unprecedented number'.

Hebrew was offered as a curriculum choice.

1995. The demolition of the former Classics corridor and completion of a new three storey North Wing including facilities for Economics, Computing and IT management.

The HMI stressed the School's 'outstanding examination results'.

The APS gave £488,000 to support 159 pupils.

Of all S5 Scottish pupils gaining 6 As in their Higher Grade examinations, 40% of them were from Hutchie.

1996. There were 173 pupils on APS.

This session some 32 Jewish children attended the School.

1997. The opening of the Sports Complex by Ally McCoist of Rangers F.C. at Beaton Road. Total cost of £1,530,000.

A record 16 Oxbridge candidates applied.

1998. The Sir Alexander Stone Foundation funded the purchase of the Boesendorfer piano for the Assembly Hall.

1999. The new double-decker Library with flexible learning suite was opened at Beaton Road by Harry Reid, Editor of *The Herald*. It used the most modern of technology.

The growth of the Music Department noted, from 1993 when 116 pupils were taking private Music lessons in School until 1999, when 451 pupils and 20 staff were involved in the programme. Moreover, some 600 pupils were now involved in extra-curricular music.

John Knowles was appointed Rector (1999– 2005).

The rededication of the War Memorial, which is now placed indoors in the Library corridor.

2001. The opening of Hutchesons' Lilybank Junior School.

The Lilybank story began in the late autumn of 2000 and the early months of 2001. An approach was made in total secrecy by the Governors of Laurel Park School to three other independent schools in Glasgow to explore the possibility of merger. Falling pupil numbers and rising costs had placed in serious jeopardy the future viability of Laurel Park School. All girls in Laurel Bank and Park School had merged four years previously (bringing the combined school up to 550 girls; but by the end of the century the roll was under 400).

The Governors and Rector of Hutchesons' were interested in the possibilities of an alliance and presented an outline plan in December 2000 to develop the Laurel Park site in west end Lilybank Terrace as a second co-educational Hutchesons' Junior School. The Laurel Park Board then found Hutchesons' proposals best suited to their wishes for the future, which included the provision of a stable financial future, continuity of the use of the Laurel Park buildings as a school, uninterrupted educational provision for the pupils, and protection of the whole Laurel Park staff.

The following months saw intense discussions in Hutchesons' on legal and employment issues, educational matters and property. A firm decision to go ahead was agreed and a legal agreement was made with the governors of Laurel Park. Unfortunately, despite confidentiality agreements, information was leaked to the press prior to the final decision. This aroused much ill-founded speculation, anger and some difficulties.

Despite these problems the two schools merged in August 2001 under the name of Hutchesons' with the Laurel Park girls only primary immediately becoming Hutchesons' Lilybank Junior School. Such an arrangement was a break with single-sex educational tradition and could not expect to be popular amongst all Laurel Park parents. However, a commitment was given that current Laurel Park primary pupils would be able to finish their primary education in the Lilybank Terrace building. Secondary girls were promised unchanged arrangements for session 2001–2002 except that they would have access to the wider educational provision offered by Hutchesons'. All Senior Girls transferred to Beaton Road in August 2002.

Hutchesons' Governors hoped to maintain through Lilybank a strong intake of pupils eventually crossing to Beaton Road for their secondary education, and also to widen geographically intake sources for the future.

Hutchesons' also became owners of the Lilybank buildings in the West End and the extensive Anniesland sports facilities. All Hutchesons' parents were to have their choice of the two primary schools, and the intention of having two primary streams feeding into the secondary school from both sides of the River Clyde was a realisation of a long-forgotten nineteenth-century aspiration for a series of Hutchesons' Schools throughout the city. While Hutchie promised a continuation of the highest class of education to the Lilybank community, Laurel Park brought a gentler tone to Crossmyloof, one more suited to the new century and changing ways of educating children.

Norman Malvenan, Assistant Rector at Kingarth Street, moved in August 2001 to Lilybank to be in charge of the Junior School. Subsequently, he was appointed Depute Rector to create a new co-educational primary school after the senior Laurel Park girls and staff moved to Beaton Road. For the next three years he adapted and changed the curriculum to create parity between the two primary schools.[7]

Capable, personable and approachable, Malvenan worked hard to produce a vibrant and happy school community. However, a disappointingly low number of Laurel Park parents took up the Hutchie offer.[8] Significant numbers of girls instead went to Kelvinside, Craigholme and Belmont, which began to take girls.[9] The Hutchesons' Governors became increasingly concerned about the long-term viability of Lilybank becoming a sustainable second feeder school providing a strong intake of pupil numbers and of good academic potential. Also the true costs now considered necessary to provide appropriate accommodation and equipment were disproportionate in the future overall property budget for the whole School.

Soon after his appointment, Dr Greig and his Governors made the decision to close Hutchesons' Lilybank Junior School in the summer of 2006. Thus, despite considerable genuine effort and financial investment by Hutchesons', some eighty years of education at Lilybank Terrace sadly came to an end.

2001. An analysis of SQA results by point of entry showed that the best results at Higher Grade were achieved by pupils who entered Hutchesons' at Primary 1 stage.

The unveiling by Lady Stone of the Sir Alexander Stone Memorial Windows created for the Library by John K. Clarke and funded by Lady Stone and the Alexander Stone Foundation took place.

SQA Examination Results:	Scotland	Hutchie
5 Highers at A Grade	707	31
6 Highers at A Grade	35	25
6 Grade A Highers at Band 1	1	1
7 Highers at A Grade	17	11

Two Higher pupils received the top score in Geography and Human Biology.

S6 numbers reach 200.

2002. The opening of the refurbished and extended Dining Room, Beaton Road with Founders' Room, classrooms and supporting facilities on the widened first floor above. The Art Rooms were redesigned on the third floor, returning the Art Department to where it had originally been placed in 1960.

2003. With the rebuilding of Williamwood, some concern that state schools are becoming more competitive. Pupil numbers struggled to reach moderate targets set.

It was noted that Glasgow Academy was to appoint a Chief Executive in order to free up the Rector.

2004. The Fotheringay Centre was opened by Terry Waite CBE, President of Emmaus, and the Lord Provost of Glasgow, Councillor Liz Cameron. It incorporated the existing Congregational Church, complete with internal stained glass window and red Glasgow sandstone walls. The former church hall was converted into an auditorium with collapsible seating. This has been described as 'Architecture at its best, incorporating the entire music centre, with practice rooms in the crypt and all manner of exciting performance space, plus the computing centre – for computing lessons rather than for use as an alternative teaching area.'[10] (The Church cost £150,000 in 1999.) School roll was 2,003.

SQA results: four pupils gained seven Highers; 77.4% of pupils gained five or more Highers; 61% of all passes were A Grade; such results were the best since they were compiled for the first time in 1993. They took the wind out of the sails of those criticising standards in the School.

2005. Graham W.A. MacAllister was appointed Interim Rector, the first Former Pupil to be given charge of the modern School.

2005. Dr Kenneth Greig was appointed Rector.

2006. The Primary Schools at Kingarth and Lilybank were inspected – no weaknesses were found in the Curriculum, Teaching and Learning, Educational Standards and Support for Learning.

2007. A new S6 Tutorial System was introduced. Each Form Tutor was to be responsible for a maximum of five pupils.

54 pupils received Bursary assistance, which resulted in a failure to pass the Charity Test. The role-model was the High School of Dundee, with 137 pupils from a total of 1,000 receiving financial support. (The value in terms of income was 6.3% at Dundee; 5.4% at Hutchie.)

2008. The unveiling in the Secret Garden of the late Sir Alexander Stone Memorial Sculpture created by John McKenna.

The opening in Kingarth Street of the new Primary Library and Donors' Glass Wall by Dr June Gow MA PhD (class of 1950) from Vancouver.

2009. The world-class Alix Jamieson Stadium at Beaton Road was opened by Alix Stevenson (née Jamieson) (class of 1960). It incorporated an Astroturf hockey pitch and international training standard Tartan athletics track.

2010. School roll was 1,514.

2011. Hutchesons' named Scottish Independent School of the Year by the *Sunday Times*.

Hutchie now passed the Charity Test.

2012. The new state of the art Drama Studios at Beaton Road were opened by Richard Wilson OBE, the actor.

2014. The Governors are now not more than 20 in number; representatives of – Glasgow Presbytery of the Church of Scotland (2); Senatus of Glasgow University (1); Merchants' House (1); Trades' House (1); Patrons of Hutchesons' Hospital (2); Glasgow Educational Trust (1); Senatus of Strathclyde University (1); FP Club (1); School Association (1) and no more than nine co-opted.

2014. The refurbishment of the Assembly Hall took place.

ELEVEN FPs Who Rejoined the School Community

This chapter includes profiles of those who attended the Schools and came back to give service to them in later life. It includes FPs who joined the teaching and non-teaching staff of the Schools and a number who joined the Governing Body.

Joseph (Joe) Adams left the School in 2003 and, after a gap year in Africa, graduated from Glasgow University in Mathematics. He joined the Mathematics Department of the School in 2011.

Hamish Aitchison MA BA (born 1943) was one of three brothers to attend the School. He joined HBGS Geography Department (from John Neilson Secondary) as Head of Department in August 1980, and left in August 1985 to be PT (Geography) at Upton GS, Slough.

June Alexander BSc left HGGS in 1967 and graduated from Glasgow University. She lectured at Motherwell College and returned to teach Biology in 2000, from which she has now retired.

Katherine Alexander was the first Secretary to be appointed in the HGGS. She was the sister of Mabel Alexander.

Mabel E. Alexander (b. 1886) gained an Honours degree in French and German and joined the School staff in 1934. She became PT (Modern Languages). She died in post in July 1950.

Margaret R. Alston (née Wilson) (1906–2010) left HGGS in 1924 and returned as a member of staff in 1946. She retired in June 1971.

Margaret M. Anderson BSc (née Macdonald) was a pupil of HGGS who left in 1949. She returned and spent 24 years in the Biology Department, retiring in June 1996. She took forward a new Learning Support Department, specialising in the teaching of English as a Foreign Language.

Elaine Bain (née Shearer) joined HGGS in S1 in 1961, leaving in 1967. She qualified in Biology from Glasgow University in 1972. Her career took her to Hillhead HS, Craigholme and Motherwell College before she returned to the School staff in 1988. She was a talented violinist. She retired in 2009.

Jean C. Bain MA was an FP who joined the Junior School staff in 1954 from Langton Road Primary, Pollok. She was appointed Infant Mistress in 1963 and continued in post as Assistant Head in the combined School from 1975 until 1987 when she retired. She died in March 2014.

Margaret (Maggie) Bain (née Bruce) (1876–1940) left HGGS as Dux in 1891. After studying in France for three years she returned to HGGS to teach in the Primary Department, then was promoted to teach French. She left when she married Robert Bain (FP, former teacher and writer of the school song).

Robert ('Wee Bain') Bain (1865–1955) was a poet and playwright, best known for his play *James First of Scotland*. A former pupil of HBGS, he took his MA from Glasgow University in 1886. He taught at Kilblain Academy, Greenock, before returning to join the staff between 1890 and 1901 to teach French, German, English and Latin. He is remembered as the writer of the School Song (1921).[1] He was Principal Teacher of English at Morrison's for thirty years until his retirement in 1936.

Robina Barr (1902–97) left School in 1921 and returned to teach Mathematics in HGGS. She left in 1952 to become Woman Advisor at Gartcraig School.

Muriel Beaton (née Calder) was a pupil of HGGS between 1949 and 1959. She returned and taught for 25 years in the English Department. She was a Senior Teacher in the combined School. Her interest in mass media led to Media Studies being added to the curriculum. She retired in 1997.

William (Bill) F. Bedborough left the School in 1960 and joined the History staff, 1965–68, before moving on. He then taught at Hamilton Academy; Bellshill Academy; was AHT at Arbroath Academy; Deputy Rector at Galashiels Academy and then Rector of Forfar Academy and Head of Jordanhill School.

Christopher S. Begg (1930–2004) left HBGS in 1948 and was outstanding as an athlete at School. He was Sports Champion, and played in the 1st XV and 1st XI. He was on the staff of HBGS, 1959–70, before moving on to Cathkin HS.

Richard Benn MA attended the School, 1981–86. He returned after study at Glasgow University and a year teaching at Williamwood Secondary, Clarkston, to teach English at the School in 1998. He developed Media Studies. He left in 2004 for a school in Brussels.

John Biggar (1944–98) left School in 1962 and returned to teach Mathematics from 1966 until 1971. He became PT (Mathematics) at Renfrew High School. He was a keen local historian and ran a successful Local History Society in the School.

Carol A. Biggart (née Hutchison) left School in 1975 and took a degree from Edinburgh University. She was Chair of the School Association. Following six years as a Governor of HET she became Development Manager in 2013.

(Andrew) Douglas H. Binnie (d. 1992) was at HBGS from 1935 until 1941. He returned, as a member of the English staff, in 1954, departing in 1964. He became Education Officer in Glasgow Division and then Assistant Director of Education for Renfrewshire.

George Wilson Blair MA BSc (b. 1890) was an FP who left HBGS in 1908 as Dux and graduated from Glasgow University in 1913. After teaching at Hyndland School, he returned in 1921 to join the Mathematics staff of HBGS. He left in 1926 to become PT (Mathematics) at Glasgow High School and later, from 1952, was Head of Govan Senior Secondary School.

(Dr) Frank Blin CBE (b. 1954) left HBGS in 1971 and was awarded a G and THA in 2009. He has been Chairman, Carduus, since 2012. He was Executive Chairman Scotland at PricewaterhouseCoopers from 1998 until 2012.[2] He was awarded a doctorate in Business Administration from Strathclyde University. He was chair of the School Appeal Committee in 1991 and is a past member of the School's Board of Governors.

William Blue was born in 1873. An FP, he was HBGS Dux and First Bursar in 1889 in the Glasgow University Bursary Competition out of 149 candidates. He gained a distinguished MA degree in Classics. He taught at Dryfield Public School before he was appointed to the staff of HGGS in 1896, resigning in August 1900. He also taught at Jedburgh and was a Modern Languages teacher in Elgin, where he died age 43 in December 1916 of a ruptured appendix.

Jenny Borland, the Rector's Secretary, was an FP and held her post from 1916 until 1949, when she retired.

Margaret A. Borland left HGGS in 1981 and returned to teach Primary in Kingarth Street in August 1986.

Ephraim Borowski left HBGS in 1967 and graduated with FCH in Mathematics and Philosophy from Glasgow University. He went to Oxford University as a Foulis Fellow. He became the Head of the Philosophy Department in Glasgow University. He served as a Governor of the School, 1990–2010.

David B. Brown (b. 1938) attended School from 1951 until 1956. He graduated MA LLB from Glasgow University and taught in Penilee Secondary before he returned to teach History and Geography at Hutchie from 1968 until 1971. He went on to be a PT (History) at Renfrew HS, an Assistant Head at Stonelaw HS and Rector of Dunfermline HS, from which post he retired in 1998.

(Dr) Karen M. M. Brown (née Ness) left School in 1976 as Dux. After gaining a FCH in Physics she became Chief Executive of the Institute of Photonics at Strathclyde University. She was Founders' Day Speaker in 1997. She is a former Governor of the School Board, 1998–2002 and was awarded a G and THA in 2014.

David A. Brunton left HBGS in 1961, and taught at John Street Secondary. He was appointed PT (Art) in April 1987. He coached the 3rd XV for sixteen successful seasons. He retired in 2005.

Aileen Burns (née Mitchell) left HGS in 1983 and took a degree from Strathclyde University. She joined the School Office in the Primary School in 2007 and is now Admissions Registrar at Beaton Road.

James Caddell attended HBGS from 1865 until 1870 when he left as joint-Dux. He dedicated himself to HBGS and teaching. He was on the staff of HBGS for thirty-eight years and in 1919 he was Interim Rector for a few months. He died in September 1920.

Marjorie M. Campbell (1915–2009) MA LRAM left the School in 1932 and joined the staff of HGGS, where she remained from 1937 until retirement in December 1979. Although she taught in both Primary and Music Departments, she increasingly concentrated on the latter.

Charlotte Caplan left HGS in 2000 and took a degree in Modern Languages at St Andrews University. She taught abroad and in East Renfrewshire. She joined the Primary staff in 2012.

Helen D. Carswell (née Galloway) (1925–2008) was a pupil in the HGGS, 1930–39. She gained a FCH in Physics and taught for eighteen years in the School's Physics Department.

Alison J. Chapman joined P1 as a pupil in 1952 and left in 1965. She joined the Primary staff in 1970 (teaching P2 and P3) and taught in the Primary School for 38 years. She was one of the original Housemistresses (Argyll) in 1989. She retired in 2008.

Sara C. Cockburn (b. 1916) attended HGGS, 1928–34. She took a FCH in English and joined the staff in 1941, teaching English and History. In 1960 she was promoted to PT (English) at HGGS and in 1964 she took a new appointment as lecturer of English at Craigie College, where she developed a course in Scottish Studies. She retired in 1977.

John ('Johnnie') M. Cocker (d. 1953) was a pupil at HBGS in 1882 and went on to graduate MA from Glasgow University in 1891. He then returned in December 1892 as a member of staff at the School teaching Modern Languages (mainly French), Latin, English and Mathematics from 1892 until retirement in January 1933.

(Prof.) John Muir Cochrane Connell was born in 1954 and left HBGS in 1972. He became a Governor from 1999 until 2003. He has been Vice-Principal and Head of College of Medicine, Dentistry and Nursing, University of Dundee, since 2012.[3] He was awarded a G and THA in 2013.

(Elinor) Muriel Cooke (née Halliday; Logan) (1924–2012) attended the class of 1941. She studied at Glasgow University and gained an Honours degree in Mathematics in 1944. She taught both RE and Mathematics at the School, becoming PT of the former. She helped organise a tea party every year for former members of staff of HGGS. (She married Hugh Logan in 1953 and Rev. John Cooke in 1986.)

(Dr) Ellen (Elspeth) B. Cowan (1914–92) was Dux of HGGS in 1932 and gained a FCH in Modern Languages and another in Education. She became PT (Modern Languages) and Depute Principal at HGGS in 1960,[4] then Depute Principal in the combined School from 1975 until 1980 when she retired. She was President of the FP Club (Ladies) in 1961 and became Honorary President. She was the Founders' Day Speaker in 1984.

(Aileen) Muriel Crockatt (1921–2012) left HGGS in 1939 and joined the staff in 1949 teaching Needlework until retirement in June 1986 as PT (Home Economics). She was renowned for her wonderful Annual Exhibitions of pupils' handiwork.

Edith F. Currie (1910–2000) was educated at HGGS, Glasgow and Oxford Universities. She taught in England before becoming PT (Geography) at the HGGS between 1945 and 1952. She went on to become Headmistress of St Margaret's School for Girls in Aberdeen in April 1952.

Mina Currie retired from her post as Senior Teacher (Arithmetic) in the Primary in May 1941 having reached the age of 65. Her business acumen helped Miss Legge to produce the School Magazine.

(Rev.) (Mary) Agatha Danson (née Turner) (1915–2007) attended HGGS, 1924–32. She served on the Board of Governors, 1991–2002.

Moira Davidson was an FP of HGGS. She taught for 31 years in the Primary before she retired in June 1993. She was involved in a number of extra-curricular activities including badminton and SU. From 1986 she ran the Primary Library and was later appointed Senior Teacher.

Alastair Kennedy Denholm DUniv, FUniv, FCIBS FEI (b. 1936) was a pupil in the School, 1948–53. He worked in the Clydesdale Bank PLC from 1953 until 1991. He was a Governor of the School from 1996 and Chairman of its Board between 2003 and 2010. He was the Founders' Day Speaker in 2003.[5]

Annie Dick (1910–2000) MA (Hons) attended the School between 1919 and 1929, leaving as Dux in the latter year. She returned to teach English (and History and Geography) at HGGS, 1938 until June 1954, before moving to the then Westbourne School for Girls as PT (English) and remaining there until her retirement in 1975.

David Dobson left HBGS in 1963 and became a Quantity Surveyor with Doig and Smith and a member of the Property Committee. He was Chair of the HET Governors from February 2010 until September 2013.

Andrew Donald (1882–1959) represented Hutchesons' Hospital on the Board from 1950 and succeeded Bailie John Stewart as Chair of HET Governors in March 1956. He took his MA (1905) and BSc (1906). He was teacher and lecturer and between 1924 and 1954 was Depute Director of Education in Lanarkshire. He was a member of Glasgow University Court.

(Dr) Rachel I. Douglas (née McDonald) was Dux of HGGS in 1950, and in 1975 she joined its staff in Chemistry, retiring in June 1989. She involved herself in a wide variety of School activities.

Margaret M. Dunbar (1941–65) joined the HBGS in August 1959 and took full responsibility for the School Office in 1961. She died in a drowning accident while bathing on holiday in Scarborough in August 1965.

Andrew Dunn (1937–2004) left the School in 1955 and later returned to teach in the Mathematics Department in 1962. He left in 1968 to work with IBM on computers. He became a leading figure in Scottish rowing.

Robert Queen Ferguson (1902–70) left School as Dux in 1920 and took a FCH in Classics at Glasgow University in 1924. He taught at Hamilton Academy and Shawlands Academy before returning to teach Classics at HBGS in 1928. He remained until 1947 when he became PT (Classics) at Jordanhill College School and then Head of Hillhead High School.

Alison Fielding (née Arrol) left School in 1972. She returned to teach Geography for six years before becoming PT (Geography) at Craigholme.

Gordon B. Finlay (1923–99) attended HBGS, 1935–40. He returned and taught in the Boys' Primary, 1955–73, before becoming Head Teacher at Gartsherrie Primary School, Coatbridge.

(Dr) Isabel D.B. Finlayson (née Simpson) (1916–2006) Dux of HGGS in 1933, took a FCH in English. She was the most distinguished woman graduate in Arts at Glasgow University in 1937 and won all the major prizes of the day. She returned to teach at the School, 1938–39. She completed her PhD on Scottish education and became Head of Langside Centre of Child Guidance.

Elsie Forrest (1904–97) left HGGS as Dux in 1921. She enjoyed accelerated progress through the School and was Dux before her seventeenth birthday. She took FCH in Classics at Glasgow University and was awarded the John Clark Scholarship for Classics and the Herkless Prize as the best female student in 1925. She taught at HGGS, 1925–50 and then became PT (Classics) at Bellahouston Academy.

James P. Forsyth (1909–96) left HBGS as Dux in 1927 and gained a FCH in Mathematics/Physics from Glasgow University in 1931. He taught Mathematics at Shawlands Academy, at HBGS from 1938 until 1943 and became PT (Mathematics) at Leith Academy in June 1943. He went on to become HMCI in the SED in 1962. He was the Founders' Day Speaker at Glasgow Cathedral in 1972.

Kathleen A.J. Galbraith (1924–2007) was Dux medallist in the HGGS in 1943 and returned as a primary teacher there from 1955 until 1970. She took up the Headship of Radleigh School, Clarkston.

Ian Gall left in 1967 and was the Premises Manager at the School from April 1998 until retirement in 2012. He was involved in various projects – Libraries; Dining Hall extension; Fotheringay Centre; Lilybank Terrace and Drama block. He was a third-generation Hutchesonian.

Mary Glen (née Simpson) (1878–1955) left HGGS in 1895 as Dux. She graduated MA from Glasgow University in 1900 and became assistant to Harry Wiseman in Science. She was an Honorary President of the FP Club.

Thomas W. Glen (1910–2004) MA BD MEd left the School in 1927. He took a FCH in Mathematics/Natural Philosophy at Glasgow University. He taught from 1940 in the High School of Glasgow and was known as an enthusiast for 'Moral Rearmament'. He was appointed PT (Mathematics) in HBGS in 1955, retiring in June 1975. He was also a very successful curling coach.

Mary D. Gordon (née Currie) MA was an FP of HGGS. She taught at North Kelvinside Secondary School and returned to HGGS in February 1906. She moved to Science and the then new laboratories owed much to her planning. During World War 2 she was in charge of Science. She returned to teaching late in life at Albert Road Academy.

(Prof.) Duncan G. Graham (b. 1936) CBE (1987) was a pupil at the HBGS from 1947 until 1954. He was a member of the History staff of the School from 1962 until 1965. He became Senior Deputy Director of Education in Strathclyde, 1974–79. From 1988–91 he was Chair and CE of the National Curriculum Council in England and Wales. He was the Founders' Day Speaker in 1990. He wrote a number of educational publications.

Mary (Marette) Grewar (1934–2011) left HGGS in 1952. She joined the staff in 1971 and was APT (English) between 1977 and 1994.

Sheila Gunn (née Burleigh) left School in 1981 as Head Girl. She became a partner in the legal firm of Shepherd and Wedderburn and was a Governor of the School for ten years. She gave the Founders' Day Address in 2006.

(Rev.) C. Douglas Hamilton, an FP, joined the Board of Governors in 1964 and was Vice-Chairman between 1975 and 1987.

Keith Hamilton left the HBGS in 1969 and went on to Dundee College of Education. He served 22 years as PT (Music) at Park Mains School in Erskine, returning in August 1996 to HGS as Director of Music. He later joined Duncanrig School.

Lesley Hart (née Hunter) MA MSc FRSA MBE left HGGS in 1966. She became Director of Lifelong Learning at Strathclyde University and represented the University on the School Education Committee, 2005–10.

Joyce Blythe Henderson (1932–2011) left the HGGS in 1950 and returned for spells on the PE staff between 1954–62 and 1972–93 (as PT) which totalled 29 years' service. She was a hockey internationalist and an international hockey umpire.

Jacqueline Hill (née Boyd) left the School in 1991 and joined the French/Spanish Department in 1998. After almost 12 years she took up the post of Head of Modern Languages at Queen Margaret College, Wellington, New Zealand.

(Dr) Alastair J. Howie (1917–96) left School as Dux in 1934 and came fourth in the Glasgow Bursary Competition. He gained FCH in Mathematics and Natural Philosophy in 1938. He became Dean of the School of Mathematics, Physics and Computer Studies at Strathclyde University. He was a Governor of HET, 1975–85.

Howard C. Howie (d. 1977) was School Captain in 1932–3 and joined the Science Department of HBGS in November 1950. He promoted baseball, chess and cricket. He left in 1963 to join Wellshot Secondary School as PT (Science).

(Dr) John Hutchison attended the School in Crown Street from 1849. As Dux medallist there (in 1855) he followed the then custom of attending the High School for four years as a reward. He went to Glasgow University in 1859 on a bursary and joined the teaching staff of the High School in 1866. He became Head of the Classical Department in 1901 and was Rector there from 1904 to 1909. He retired following fifty-four years of connection with the High School as pupil and teacher and was gratified to be handing over an efficient institution to his successor. He died in February 1924.

A. Gordon Jamieson MA left in 1960, graduated from Glasgow University and taught in the Primary School, 1970–82. He was appointed Assistant Rector (of Primary in 1982) and then in 1987 Depute Rector. His task was to integrate the School: as there was no Boys' intake in P1, while Boys dominated intake from P5. Under him the curriculum widened and he encouraged coherence and a common philosophy. He was keen on ornithology. He retired in June 1998.

Ninian A. Jamieson ('Ninny') (1902–73) left School in 1921 as Dux and First Bursar in the Glasgow University Bursary Competition. He won the Blackstone Medal in Greek at Glasgow and gained a FCH before teaching Classics at Whitehill and Queen's Park Senior Secondary, 1926–35. He joined the School as an assistant in 1935 and was PT Classics 1945–56 (as well as Deputy Rector). His Department of Classics was particularly commended in the Secretary for Scotland's Report to Parliament in April 1955. In October 1956 he became Headmaster of Paisley Grammar School.

Ronald Jamieson DA ARIAS ARIBA FRIAS attended HBGS, 1939–46. He became an architect and was a Governor of the School, 1995–96.

Jane McClure Jardine-Forrester (née Allison) (1878–1932) attended HGGS from 1890 until 1894 when she left as Dux. She took her MA from Glasgow University in 1898 and taught in Galashiels before joining the HGGS staff in August 1900. She was the first President of the FP Club.

Ian Jessiman (1929–2008) left HBGS in 1947. He captained the School Rugby XV in 1946–7 and played for Glasgow Schools. He qualified in Law. He was Secretary of the FP Rugby Club; President of Hutchesons'/ Aloysians, 1977–80 and 1994, and President of the FP Council, 1987–9. He was also a Governor of the School.

Joseph Kane (1912–2000) won a scholarship to the School which he left in 1930. He proved a polymath, being qualified in Arts and Humanities and then Mathematics and Science. He returned to the School as a Science primary teacher in 1946 and he was promoted to the new post of Assistant Rector (Primary) in 1957.[6] He retired in June 1975.

Iain Keter joined the School in Primary 5 in 1963 and left S6 in 1972. He took a BA degree at Strathclyde University in Accountancy and became a qualified CA. He joined the Trust Office as Bursar and Clerk to the Governors of HET in February 2007.

(Frank) Douglas (MacDonald) Kinnaird BA CA attended HBGS, 1963–72. He qualified as a CA in 1978 before establishing his own company, based in Scotland, in the field of recruitment consulting for senior executives. He was a Governor of the School, 1999–2001.

Gillian Kyle (née Inglis) attended HGS, 1974–82. She served on the Governing Board, 2002–2003. She was a nurse by profession.

Sheila Lang (née Thompson) left the School in 1976. She took a degree and joined the PE staff in 1981. She captained the Scottish Women's Hockey XI.

Alison Lawson (née Marshall) was the first full-time Drama teacher in HGS. She taught for six years, leaving in June 1997 to go overseas. She created the climate in which it was possible to make Drama an academic subject of study at HGS.

Philip M. Leckie left the School in 1965 and graduated at Glasgow University. After moving to Lanark GS, first as PT and then as AHT with responsibility for discipline, he returned to HGS to teach Geography and Modern Studies and was promoted to the new post of Director of Studies, which he held from 1988 until 1998, when he became Depute Rector at the High School of Dundee.

(Dr) Jean C. Lees MBChB FRCA (née McMillan) left HGGS in 1959 and helped introduce safe anaesthesia into the Cameroons. She was the first President of the FP Club and achieved a G and THA in 2007. She was a Governor of the School, 1997–98. She gave the Address on Founders' Day in 2013.

Helen R. Leitch (née Sutherland) (1931–2005) was Dux of HGGS in 1949 and returned to teach Modern Languages between 1956 and 1958. She was President of the FP Club in 1980. She was a highly influential figure in the teaching of Modern Languages in Scotland for over thirty years. She was the Senior Lecturer in Modern Languages at Jordanhill College of Education. She was the Founders' Day Speaker in 1982.

Helen Lennox (née Marshall) left HGGS in 1970. She returned to teach Primary in August 1990 and retired early in December 2005.

Sheila Leslie (née Anderson) left HGGS in 1967. She joined the Home Economics Department part-time in 1988 and taught at both Kingarth Street and Beaton Road, specialising in Crafts, especially sewing and dress-making, fashion and fabric. She retired in 2009.

Marjory Liddell (née Duff) (1913–2004) left the School in 1931 but returned later to join the primary teaching staff. She retired in 1973.

Ronald Livingston left HBGS in 1971. He returned from Eastwood HS to teach Mathematics between 1988 and retirement in 2013. He proved a polymath with a profound enthusiasm for Mathematics.

Rachel Loudon graduated from Glasgow in History in 1994. She returned in 2001 to Glasgow and became a Primary 7 teacher at Lilybank Terrace.

Mary H. Lowe MA was an FP who joined the Primary staff in 1924 and left in 1931 to become a missionary at Blantyre Mission Station, Nyasaland.

Margaret S. McConnell (née Reid) (1913–2011) left the School in 1930 and took a FCH in English in 1934 at Glasgow. She gained both Herkless and Logan Prizes and a scholarship to Oxford. She returned to teach English in the HGGS between 1965 until 1979 (when she retired).[7] She was an early specialist in Creative Writing and published fifteen romantic novels under the pseudonym Margaret Simpson. (Her elder daughter, Elizabeth Yearling, was Dux of HGGS in 1962.)

John McCrossan left HGS in 1999 and took his degree from Glasgow Caledonian University. He joined the Primary Department in 2001.

E.R.A. (Mona) MacDonald (1903–95), an FP, returned to the staff in 1936. She taught in Primary and also took secondary English classes. She retired in 1964.

Jessie O. Macdonald (née Ramsay) (1910–2004) left School in 1928 and taught English briefly in the School from October 1933 until February 1934. She retired as Headmistress of St Denis School, Edinburgh.

Anne E. MacDougall was a pupil in HGGS, leaving in 1923. In 1928 she achieved the top FCH in French/German at Glasgow University. As a part-time teacher she joined the staff of HBGS in 1951 – the first lady to join the secondary staff of the Boys' Grammar. She went full-time in 1953 and retired in September 1966.

Tom Macdougall left HBGS in 1962 and after teaching History became Advisor in History in Glasgow and Assistant Director of Education for Strathclyde. He was appointed in April 1996 to the new post of School Development Director. For four years he was much involved in the Legacy campaign and left in May 2000.

(Rev.) John Alexander Coull MacKellar DD (1875–1958) was minister of Kinning Park, 1903–10 and Cathcart Old Church from 1910 until 1958. He spent 21 years on the Board of HET.

Zoe MacKenzie (née Howieson) attended HGS, 1981–4. She took her degree from Glasgow University. She became President of the FP Club and has served on the Development and Marketing Committee of the Governors since 2014.

John S. McKie left the School in 1957. He joined the Classics staff in June 1967 and became PT (Classics) of the combined School in October 1973. He retired in 2004.

Eileen A. McLean (née Smith) (1948–2012) attended the HGGS from 1953–65 and became an international swimmer. She taught Home Economics from 1979, becoming Head of Department in 1986, and Examination Officer in 2005. She retired in 2008.

Helen M. McMillan (1917–79) was Dux of HGGS in 1936 and gained a FCH in French/German. She was on the staff of HGGS for 35 years, retiring in June 1979 and dying in August of the same year. She was a former President of the FP Club.

Peter Cairn McNaught MA MLitt. (b. 1925) was a pupil at the School, 1934–43. and in 1954 joined the English (and History) Staff. He was Asst. Vice-Principal at Moray House before becoming Principal of Craigie College of Education, Ayr, 1968–88. He was Founders' Day Speaker in 1977.

John McNee (1918–99) left HBGS in 1936 as Dux. He taught Classics at HBGS, 1955–65 and became Rector of Bellshill Academy.

Elizabeth (Elsie) McNicol (1920–2005) left HGGS in 1938. She returned to teach J2 at Kingarth Street on the retirement of Alexandrina Scott. She became Infant Mistress at Westbourne School in 1965.

Fiona Macphail left HGGS in 1971 and took degrees at Edinburgh and Strathclyde Universities. She was a teacher at Laurel Park until 2001, when she moved to HGS as Depute Rector. In February 2015 she was appointed Depute Rector – Head of Primary.

James S. Macphail (1925–2015) was an FP who left School in 1943 having been Captain of the 1st XV. He went on to become Captain of the 1st FP XV, President of the FP Rugby Section and President of the FP Club. He was also an engineer in his family's company. He served 17 years on the Board and succeeded Bob Jack as the twenty-fourth Chair of the HET 1987–97. He was awarded a G and THA in 1998. He was succeeded by Derek Mason.

Ewen Mackie attended HBGS, 1966–74. He became a QS and Director of a Property Investment Management Company. He served as Convenor to the Property Committee and on the Nominations Committee of the Governors.

Williamina P. Main MA (1893–1972) who had been Dux of HGGS in 1913, spent thirty-six years in the Modern Languages Department of HGGS, teaching mainly French. She retired in January 1954.

Anne M. Malvenan, an FP (1909–94), left HGGS in 1926. She joined the teaching staff in 1937 and was Infant Mistress for thirty-two years. She took pupils through the transition in HGGS from Garden School to the 'Big' School, retiring in December 1969.

Alistair Marr BA CA attended HBGS, 1967–75. He became a CA and has been a Governor since 2011, serving as Convenor of the Finance Committee. He runs his own consultancy business.

Mary I. Stewart Martin (1908–2000) left the HGGS as Dux in 1926. She returned to teach English.

(Rev. Prof.) John Mauchline DD (1902–84) was Dux and Mathematics Medallist at HBGS in 1919. After his MA and BD from Glasgow University he gained FCH in Semitic Languages and won a number of scholarships. He was Professor of Old Testament Language and Literature, University of Glasgow, 1934–72, and Principal of Trinity College, Glasgow, 1953–72. He joined the Governors in 1948 and was the 21st Chair from 1964–75. He was the first Founders' Day Speaker in 1961 and spoke again in 1970. He produced a significant number of publications.

William Allan Gibson Middleton (1927–99) left HBGS in 1944. He returned to teach in the Primary between 1958 and 1965. He became Depute Head Teacher at Thornliebank Primary School and later Strathblane Primary School.

Janet Miller (née Clark) (b. 1950) attended HGGS, 1955–67. She went to Dunfermline College gaining a Diploma in PE, 1970. She covered for maternity leave before becoming an assistant PE teacher on the staff, 1974–81.

Anne R. Morrison (née Lloyd) MA left HGGS in 1962. She taught in Africa before joining the English department of HGGS, which she left in January 1975.

Jan Murdoch (née Wilson) RGN left the School in 1984. She returned as School Matron in 1998.

Jane Niven was appointed to fill the Modern Languages vacancy in HGGS in September 1914.

Fiona Organ (née Robertson) was a pupil of HGGS who left in 1965. She joined the staff In Beaton Road in 1979. Throughout her twenty-seven years as Geography teacher she retained her enthusiasm for her subject and job. She retired in 2006.

Marion Osler MA (Hons) joined Miss Bain's Primary 1 Class in September 1959 in 'The Garden School' and left HGGS in 1972. Her first teaching post in 1978 was at Park, where she became a Senior Teacher with responsibility for Transition. She remained during the mergers. She initiated and was the driving force behind the successful Big Writing Scheme. She retired in 2013.

Jennifer (Jenna) Park (née Allan) left HGGS in 1958. She taught PE and was PT at Jordanhill College School and John Street Secondary School. She joined HGS in 1988 and was permanently employed from 1990. She retired in 2001.

Robert (Roy) Pinkerton left HBGS in 1963 and taught Classics in the School for only five weeks in May/June 1967. He became a lecturer in Classics at Edinburgh University.

Thomas C. L. Pritchard, an FP, gained an MA and BMus and became Teacher of Singing at the HBGS in 1925. He left in 1936 to go to Bellahouston Academy. He was given a Doctorate of Music from Edinburgh University in 1938 for his work as a composer and his research into the Viennese School of Music.

Lisa Queen left HGS in 1999 and took an Honours degree at the RSAMD, joining the School Drama Department in 2012.

E. Jane Rae (née Stewart) (1955–2009) left the School in 1973 and was appointed Music Administrator for the School in 1994.

Allan Ramsay BA CA attended HBGS, 1964–73. He became a partner in McLay, McAlister and McGibbon LLP. He was a member of the Governing Body, 2003–12, serving as Convener of Finance and latterly Vice-Chairman.

Elspeth Rose (née Crosbie) left HGGS in 1957 and took FCH in Geography at Glasgow University. She taught at Paisley GS for sixteen years. She joined the Geography Department on a permanent basis in 1985, becoming a Senior Teacher in 1990. She moved to Guidance and from 1998 was Assistant Rector with responsibility for Higher Education liaison. She retired in 2001.

Judith Russell (née Brown) left the School in 1987 and took a Psychology degree at Glasgow University. She returned to teach Primary in 1999.

Alexandrina C. Scott (b. 1895) MA BA was Dux of HGGS in 1912. She spent all her teaching career on the teaching staff of the Girls' School: beginning with Spanish (in which she took a FCH) in the Senior School in August 1916 and then as the Head of Infants from October 1938. She retired in June 1959 after forty-three years' service.

Elizabeth H. Sharp DA left HGGS in 1948. She joined the Art Department of HGGS in February 1972. She took early retirement in June 1985.

Jack Silverstone attended HBGS, 1956–64 and took his degree from Strathclyde University. He is now a retired IFA and has been a Governor of the School since 2010.

Roy W. Smith ('Wee Roy' or 'The Pocket Hercules')[8] (1912–99) joined Hutchie as pupil in Primary 5 in 1924, leaving HBGS in 1930. He returned on the staff as Games Master, 1947–73 and PT (PE), 1957–73. He taught every boy who passed through the School in a quarter of a century for most of that time, as he was the only Games master. He tolerated nothing but the highest standards and was blessed with an astonishing memory for names and faces. He retired in December 1973. He inspired his children, Alan and Eileen, to enter the teaching profession.

Arthur H.V. Smyth (1913–2005) left HBGS in 1931 and joined the Classics department in December 1946. He left in February 1949 to become PT (Classics) at Hawick HS.

Alexander (Sandy) L. Strang left HBGS in 1969 as Dux and Captain of Cricket. He read Classics before turning to English at Churchill College, Cambridge, where he also gained a Soccer Blue. After a short spell at Hillhead HS he taught at the School from 1974 for almost thirty years, initially as teacher of English, then Head of English (from 1981, following Miss Shearer, the first PT of the merged departments of the School) and from 1987 as Depute Rector. He resigned in August 2003.

Charles W. Thomson (1871–1948) attended HBGS from the age of ten in August 1882 until he matriculated at Glasgow in 1888 coming fourth in the Bursary Competition. He graduated in 1894. Meantime he had already returned to HBGS as a member of staff in 1892 and also taught at Rothesay Academy (1895–7); George Watson's (1897–8); and HGGS (1898–1901). He became Headmaster at Grangemouth Higher Grade School (1901–4); Rector at Larkhall Academy (1904–12) and Buckie Secondary (1913–34). He was President of the EIS, 1933–4.

Isa(bella) Waddell (b. 1893), MA, the sister of Mary, FP, taught in the Primary in Kingarth Street between 1918 and June 1957.

Mary Waddell (b. 1891), MA, FP, came from Lorne Street School and taught in the Primary, mainly P4, in Kingarth Street from 1924 until April 1956.

Jean Walker (née Anderson) (1928–2006) was Dux in 1947 and a Governor of the School, 1992–3.

Winning Webster (née Rough) (1906–99) left the HGGS in 1922 and returned to teach Drama.

Helen Wright attended HGGS, 1958–71. She became President of the FP Club and served on the Development and Marketing Committee of the Governing Body, 2009–10.

Agnes M. Young BSc was a FP who was a member of the Science staff, 1926–35, and took the new post of Senior Mistress and Women Advisor of the HGGS, 1941–64.

TWELVE Biographies of Senior Staff

The short profiles in this chapter include staff who have been promoted to posts such as Year Tutor and Head of Department or, particularly in the case of Primary staff, have given long service. Also included are members of the non-teaching staff and important Governors.

Staff who are Former Pupils of the Schools are to be found in Chapter 11 (which includes FPs who return to do service for the School) or Chapter 13 (which includes all prominent FPs).

Rectors (and Interim Rectors) can be found in Chapter 7.

An asterisk indicates a present member of staff.

Eva M. Aitken (née Killner) joined the Modern Languages staff of HGGS in 1956. She became Assistant Principal in the Department but retired owing to ill-health in 1984.

*Valerie J. Alderson was educated in Perth and qualified at Queen Margaret University with a Dip. Drama. She joined the staff as Head of Drama in 1998.

David Anderson (b. 1885) took a FCH in Mathematics and Natural Philosophy in 1907 at St Andrews University and was appointed Senior Mathematics teacher at HBGS in 1915. He was Captain of the School Cadet Force. He won an MC in October 1917 for 'conspicuous gallantry' during World War 1, adding a Bar for similar actions in November 1918. He became Head of Dalziel HS, Motherwell, in October 1923.

W. Fleming Anderson was the ninth chair of the HET, from 1906 until 1915. He was a Governor for nineteen years and Convenor of Finance. He died in March 1915. The building at Kingarth Street owed much to his advocacy.

Isobel Anderson opted for early retirement in June 1997. She had served in the Mathematics Department for a number of years and was appointed Assistant Principal Teacher in HGGS in October 1974.

Moira Anderson taught Modern Languages from 1980, became a Senior Teacher in 1990 and Assistant Principal Teacher in French in 1992.

Catherine Andrew taught Chemistry for twenty-two years before retirement in 2001. She was a Senior Teacher.

*Colin Bagnall took an MA degree in History at St John's College, Cambridge. He taught at Merchiston Castle School for five years, Leighton Park School in Reading, Dollar Academy and was PT (History) at Stewarts' Melville. He became Depute Rector (Director of Curriculum) at the School in 2006.

Marion Baillie (1922–2010) taught in John Street School and Govan High School before spending twelve years from 1950 on the staff of HGGS teaching English/History. She became Head at Morrison's (1965–71) then Dean of Women at Jordanhill College of Education.

Jessie G. Bain (LLA)[1] taught French in Stirling HS and then in HGGS from 1905. She became PT of French and retired in August 1934. She pioneered residence abroad.

Frances Barker (b. 1901) was Dux of Hyndland Secondary School and completed a FCH in French and German in 1923. She taught Modern Languages at Bellahouston Secondary, HGGS and Jordanhill College School. She ended her career as Principal of the High School for Girls.

Thomas Barr (b. 1860) MA BA taught Mathematics at HBGS from 1887 until 1915. He became Headmaster at London Road Public School.

William Battison was a Visiting Master of Phonography (Shorthand) at the HBGS from 1889 until 1909.

George Walter Baynham (b. 1832) produced a number of books including *Elocution* (1873). He was appointed to HBGS in December 1889.

Joyce Beattie taught at Perth Academy and St Margaret's School in Edinburgh before joining Laurel Park in 1997 as Assistant Head. After the merger with the School she became Head of Career Development and Higher Education, and then in 2009 Depute Rector with the same remit. She retired in 2011.

Matthew Bergin graduated from Sheffield University. He spent seven years at George Watson's College before he joined the School as Head of Economics and Business in 2005. He moved to be Head of Economics at Strathallan in 2014.

*Elizabeth M. Bertram took her degree from Glasgow University. She joined the Modern Language Department in the School in 1990 and became Head of Department in 2006.

James Beveridge resigned from HGGS in March 1896 when he was appointed Headmaster of Linlithgow Academy.

John M. Biggar was a former Lord Provost, a Governor from 1929 and Chairman of HET Governors from 1937 until 1943 (the fifteenth Chair).

William Blackwood ('Wee Joe') taught in the English Department, 1946–58, being promoted to the post of Special Assistant. He became PT (English) at Glenwood School.

(Capt.) Dougald Blue (b. 1878) took his MA at Glasgow University in 1900. He became Classical Master at the High School of Glasgow in 1910 and developed a Cadet Corps there. He was offered and accepted a similar post in HBGS in 1913 and was instrumental in forming the School's OTC. He joined the 3rd Cameronians, Scottish Rifles and was killed in action in France in May 1915.

Alexander Bonar CM taught at Maxwell School, Kinning Park; was Headmaster of Rigside School, Douglas, and between 1873 and 1914, when he retired, he was a member of staff at HBGS teaching English, Latin, French and Mathematics.

M. Marion Borland was School Clerkess for thirty-three years, retiring in 1949.

George Brabender was a Groundsman at the School from 1980 until his retirement in 2014.

Steven J. Branford joined the School as an RE and Classics teacher in 1979 and became Head of Religious Studies. He retired in 2014.

*Susan Breckenridge graduated in painting from Edinburgh College of Art. Following time at St Aloysius she became Head of Art and Design in the School in 2005.

*Graham F. Broadhurst took his degree at Glasgow Caledonian University and joined the Modern Studies Department in 1991 and took over as Head of Department in 1998. He was in charge of staff absence cover and was an Interim Depute Rector in 2005.

Anne Brown MA was FP Registrar for the decade of the 1990s. She created a database of over 12,000 contacts. The George and Thomas Awards to outstanding achievers from Hutchie was an idea she initiated.

Magnus A.M. Brown came from Keil School in August 1980. He left HGS in June 1996 to become AHT at Glasgow High School. He had proved a committed rugby player and coach.

William Brown became the first Music Master at the School in 1793 and he remained in post until 1825.

Norah Brunton was School Office Manager for 25 years and retired in December 2010.

Jane Bulloch (1971–2011) joined the staff of the School in 1995 and as Senior Librarian she was a major influence on the design of the Beaton Road Library.

*Jonathan Caddy was Dux at Kilsyth Academy and qualified in Physics and Philosophy from Edinburgh and Glasgow. He joined the Computer Services Department of the School in 1994.

*Jimmy Cameron was School Janitor from 1957 until 1986, first in Crown Street and, latterly, at Beaton Road and is currently its Manager.

Archibald ('Monkey') Campbell joined the Primary staff of HBGS in 1908. He recorded those who fell in World War 1.

*David G. Campbell, MA (from Dundee University) and MEd and MSc from Glasgow University, joined the English Department of the School in 1997. He became a Year Tutor and was appointed Depute Rector (Career Development and Higher Education) in 2011.

John Campbell of Clathic was Preceptor of the Hospital from July 1777 until April 1800. He opposed the sale of the old Hospital building but a majority group of Patrons pushed ahead with the sale between 1788 and 1795. The new Hospital was built in Ingram Street.

*Eileen Carey took her degree at Glasgow University and joined the School in 2010, becoming Head of Classics in 2012.

James W. Cathcart joined the Geography Department of HBGS in September 1961. He became Head Teacher at Cathkin HS.

John Chalmers was appointed Music Master at the School in 1825. He was expected to lead a hundred boys through Glasgow twice a day on Sunday and to see 'that they join properly in the psalmody'.[2]

D. Bruce Charleson became PT (Art) in March 1953 in HBGS. He designed the souvenir plaque marking the 1953 Coronation, gifted to all boys in HBGS, and also the 1960s interpretation of the School Crest. He retired in 1964.

*Catherine Chisholm was educated at Paisley GS and Strathclyde University. She joined the Mathematics Department in 1997 and is now Head of Career Development and Higher Education.

*Calvin C. Clarke was educated at Northampton GS and Newcastle University where he graduated BSc in Geography. He became Head of Geography at the School in 1993. He initiated the current international links with India, Malawi, Tanzania and Botswana.

John Clarke MA gained a War FCH Classics degree from Glasgow and joined the staff of HBGS as PT (Classics) in 1928. He left in June 1937 to become Rector of Paisley Grammar School.

(Sir) Charles Cleland was thirteenth Chair of the HET, from 1928 until 1935.

C.M. Close became Secretary of HGGS in 1960 and retired from the post of Senior School Secretary in November 1985.

Robert J. Collins taught Music at HBGS from August 1959 until January 1980 (and was PT from 1965 until 1980[3] and PT of the combined Schools from 1976).

Irene Colvil taught in the Primary Department between August 1986 and April 2013. As a Senior Teacher she developed the Mathematics curriculum at the Primary School.

Peter Colvin spent his whole teaching career at the School in the Mathematics Department, joining in 1977. He became Senior Teacher (for S1 and S2) and retired in 2010.

(Dr) Sue Cowling joined the School in 1994 as an Assistant Rector, became Depute Rector (CDHE) in 2003 and retired in 2008.

Donald J. Crabb MA BA (b. 1918) supervised the introduction of Geography into HBGS. He designed the Geography rooms in Beaton Road, but when the Departments were separated Crabb stayed at Kingarth Street. He became PT for the combined schools from 1976 until his retirement in 1980.

John B. Craig joined the Classics Department of HBGS in January 1923 and left five years later for the High School of Glasgow. Latterly, he was PT (Classics) in Hyndland School, retiring in 1957.

Joseph Craig MA BA became PT (Modern Languages – French and German) in July 1905 in HBGS. He retired in November 1936.

(Capt.) William T. Craig (b. 1882) joined the Mathematical Department of the School staff in June 1912. He was commissioned in the Cameronians, First Rifles, and was killed in France in October 1918. He was the fourth member of staff to be lost in World War 1.

Nan Crawford MA MEd BA joined the staff of HGGS as PT (History) in 1965. She became Assistant Principal (Curriculum and Guidance) at HGGS in 1971 and retired from this position in 1991.

Eleanor Cunningham was educated at the Girls' High and Glasgow University. She joined the Mathematics Department in 1973 and retired in 2001.

Margaret M. Currie MA gained FCH in Modern Languages at Glasgow University in 1920. She joined the HBGS staff in 1926, retiring in 1951.

Irene Davis taught Modern Languages and Latin between 1982 and her retirement in 2014. As a Senior Teacher she was in charge of Primary Languages in Kingarth Street.

*Ross R. Dewar joined the PE Department in 1999, later becoming Head of Boys' PE.

Walter Dick (b. 1893) was appointed to the Science Department in HBGS in 1915. He was promoted to PT (Science) in June 1931 and continued in that post until he died in April 1951.

James Dickson BSc joined the Geography Department as PT in HBGS in September 1959. He left in November 1967 when promoted to Head of Finnart Secondary, Greenock.

James H. Dickson was the sixth Chair of the HET, from 1900 until 1903.

Ethna Doig trained as a CA and became Bursar of Laurel Park in 1997. Following the merger in 2001 she joined the Trust Office as Assistant Bursar responsible for Finance. She was joint Interim Bursar in 2005–06 and left in 2009.

Andrew Donald became Depute Director of Education in Lanarkshire, 1924 until 1944. He joined the HET Governors in 1950 and was elected Chairman in 1956. He was the eighteenth Chair from 1956 until his death in December 1959. He was responsible for negotiating the loan needed to complete the building of the Primary School.

Thomas C. Dorian MA took an Honours degree from Aberdeen University in 1924. He taught Classics and French in the HBGS,1927–46, and in 1946 became PT (Classics) in Pollokshields Senior Secondary School.

Adam Dougall joined the staff in 1950 and was promoted to APT (Guidance) in 1972. He retired in 1977.

Andrew G. Dougall spent seventeen years in the PE Department from 1974 as APT (Guidance).

Eric L. Drever BSc joined the Science staff in 1963 and became the first PT of Chemistry in 1967. He left in 1972 to become AHT at Hillpark.

John Drimmie qualified MA from Glasgow University in 1914. He was wounded on the Somme. After World War 1 he joined the school staff as a teacher of Science and Mathematics, leaving in 1940.

Irene Drummond (née Allison) taught French and German in the School from 1960 for 37 years. Latterly she held the post of Senior Teacher and left the School in 1997.

John Morton Duncan taught the Advanced Class in the Elementary Department of the HBGS between 1873 and 1878. He became Headmaster of Erskine Public School in 1896.

Maurice T. Duncan BSc taught in HBGS, 1960–68, and was PT (Physics), 1973–89, and PT in the combined School, 1975–89, after which he retired.

Alexander Dunlop was formerly Head of the English Department in the School and spent twenty-four years on the staff – 1987 until 2011. His book, *The History of a Glasgow School,* was published in 1992.

Eva Dunlop (b. 1901) MA BSc joined HGGS as PT Science in 1948 and introduced Higher Grade Physics into the curriculum. She retired in 1961.

*Graham Dunlop took his degree from Heriot-Watt University and joined the PE Department in 1998, becoming a Year Tutor in 2015.

Myra Dunlop (née Blake) retired in 1992 after twenty-one years in the Music Department.

*Alexander Eadie graduated from St Andrews University and joined the School in 2012 from Paisley GS where he was PT (Maths). He was appointed Head of Mathematics in 2015.

Robert R. Eadie MA ('Two-gun Eadie')[4] took a FCH in Classics at Glasgow University. He taught at HBGS from 1946 to 1954 (when he left to become PT at the High School, 1954–6). He returned as PT (Classics) and remained in that post from 1956 until September 1973 when he retired.

David Elstone joined as Assistant Rector in the Geography Department. He was a cricketer of some note and a member of the MCC. He left after six years in 2006 to become Head of Hymer's College in Hull.

(Dr) Noel Evans took FCH in Modern Languages at Edinburgh and her PhD at Glasgow. She taught at the School from 1977 and was promoted to AHT (Higher Education) in 1991. She retired in 1998.

Jane A. Ewing took up her post of teacher of Sewing in the HGGS in 1879. She retired after twenty-six years' service in December 1904.

Hugh Ferguson (1931–2008) joined Hutchesons' Art staff in 1973. He served for almost twenty years. He was a Year Tutor when the post was created in the School.

*Gillian Fergusson graduated with MA and MEd from Glasgow University. She was appointed a Depute Rector (Pastoral) at the School in 2012. She came from the High School of Glasgow.

Janette Ferris joined Laurel Bank in 1986 and remained Infant teacher until the merger with Park in 1996. Under her leadership the Nursery expanded and she continued to run it after the merger with Hutchesons'.

(Bailie) William Fife was the fifth Chair of the HET, from 1897 until 1900.

David Finnie was Janitor at both Primary and Secondary Schools for twenty-seven years, leaving in 2012.

Mary Firth took her degree from Edinburgh University and joined the

English Department in 1993. One of the first Year Tutors to be appointed, she retired in 2011.

Mairi Fisher MA taught in the Primary Department from 1974–1995.

*Mary H. Flannigan graduated from Glasgow University. She joined the Modern Languages Department in 1997 and is currently a Year Tutor.

Renza Fordyce was the ubiquitous, long-serving stalwart of the 1957 Group. She retired in 2001.

John Forsyth resigned as Elocution teacher in HBGS in October 1904.

John G. Forsyth taught Mathematics at the School, 1955–62. He became Rector of Coatbridge High School.

Joan Fotheringham taught in the Mathematics Department between 1974 and December 1992. In 1993 she took the new post of PT Computing. When she retired in 1999 the subject was split into IT and Computing.

*Sheila Frame taught Geography at Park and was promoted to PT. Following the first merger she became Head of Modern Studies. She was External Examinations Manager until her retirement in 2012 and is now Chief Invigilator for the School.

Ian L. Fraser studied Classics at Oxford and taught at the School between 1959 and 1964. He became Assistant Director of Education in Edinburgh and ultimately Chair of the Scottish Examination Board (SEB).

Nick Fraser was educated at Robert Gordon's College and Aberdeen University and taught French and German at Stewart's-Melville. He was appointed in 2000 to take up the post of Head of Modern Languages and modernised the School's biggest department. He left in 2006 to become Academic Deputy at Magdalen College School, Oxford.

Robert J. Furness was appointed as Head of Technology in 1995. Originally from Melbourne, Australia, he established a new department from scratch, and it continues to grow following his retirement in 2013.

Mary Teresa Fyfe was PT (Mathematics) at St Bride's School, East Kilbride, before she was appointed Head of Mathematics at the School in 1995. She won a Gold Medal from the Royal Society in 2013 in recognition of her contribution to Mathematics enrichment for school pupils. She retired in 2015.

(Dr) Rona H. Gaffney lectured at Glasgow University before joining Hutchesons' in 1986. She was promoted to Senior Teacher in 1995 and Head of History in 1998. She retired in 2012.

Edward George joined the HET as a junior in the School Office in 1920. He was Secretary and Treasurer of the HET from November 1950 until he retired in 1971.

*Helen Gibson was employed as a primary teacher in 1988. She became Head of Stuart House and was appointed Depute Rector (Upper Primary) in 2015.

Duncan Gillies was appointed Head of Classics in 2006 from Bradfield College. He moved to become Academic Deputy at St Peter's School, York, in 2012.

John Glennie, School Janitor, was appointed to the janitorial post at Crown Street in August 1891 and retained the post until his sudden death in December 1934. He struck the School gong and those who failed to appear for the first gong of the day were taken by him to the Head to be belted.

James Gowans taught Mathematics at Kingarth Street between 1936 and 1948. He went on to become Head of Hillpark Secondary School.

Louise M. Graham was a former pupil of Craigholme. She joined the Primary Department of the School in 1975. She was the first Housemistress of Montrose House and retired in 2011.

Rod Grant joined the Primary Department in 1998. He completely revised the School's Language Curriculum. He taught P7 until 2005 when he was appointed Head of Clifton Hall School.

James Gray completed twenty-eight years as an elected Town Councillor in 1907. He was a Treasurer of the City and was elected Preceptor by the Patrons of the Hospital.

Dorothy Green taught Home Economics at the School from 1998 and was Head of Department from 2008 until her retirement in 2013.

*Gillian Green graduated from Heriot-Watt University and joined the PE Department as Head of Hockey in 2012.

John Guild took up supervision of the upkeep of Trust properties in 1962 and retired from the post of Clerk of Works to HET in 1981.

James B. Hall entered Trust employment in 1918 and was the (third) Secretary of HET between 1923 and his death in 1950.

Jeremy Hall graduated in Theology at Durham University and completed a PhD in Philosophy at Glasgow. He arrived at the School in 1998, taught Philosophy before moving to Newington College, Sydney, Australia, in 2008.

John Hall taught at HBGS from 1881 to 1891, leaving to take up the post of Headmaster at Drymen, from which he retired in 1926.

James E. Hanbridge was the Elgin Street Drawing Master. He was appointed in July 1894 and worked until he was seventy.

Alex Harbison was Janitor of the HGGS, 1951–64. He left to become Head Janitor at Craigie College, Ayr. On his retirement in 1975 he was awarded the BEM in the Queen's Birthday Honours List.

Moira Harrison joined the Modern Languages Department in 1980. She became a Senior Teacher in 1990 and APT (French) in 1992. She retired in 2002.

*Ian Harrow took a degree at Glasgow University. He joined the Economics and Business Studies Department in 1989 and became a Year Tutor. He was appointed Head of Community in 2014.

Thomas Harrower was well known as an elocutionist whose text-book was used throughout Scotland. He taught Elocution in the HGGS and practised in Glasgow from his premises in Bath Street and Bothwell Street in the 1890s until his death in December 1924.

Carolyn Hatfield was appointed to the Senior Staff of the Primary in 1992 and became Depute Rector (Lower Primary) in February 2001. She retired in 2015.

Christine Haughney was Head of Calderwood Lodge, Scotland's only Jewish primary school. She was appointed Depute Rector, Head of Primary, in August 2010. Unfortunately she retired for health reasons in 2014.

*Adele Henderson (née Page) took her degree at Edinburgh University and joined the History Department in 2004. She is currently a Year Tutor.

J. Douglas Hendry taught Chemistry at HBGS from 1963 for five years, leaving in December 1967 to become PT (Chemistry) at Hermitage

Academy, where he was promoted to post of AHT. He was killed in a climbing accident in 1972.

George Herriot served on the HET from 1893 and was its tenth Chair, 1915–19.

(Prof.) Paul Hirsh taught for ten years in Modern Languages in HBGS, 1888–1898.

(Dr) Gavin M. Hood qualified as an MA with FCH from Glasgow University in Mathematics and Natural Philosophy in 1914 and then added a BSc with distinction. He joined the Science Department of the HBGS in 1919 and remained until November 1938 (being awarded a Doctor of Science in 1929) when he became PT (Mathematics) at Victoria Drive. In 1942 he became PT at Allan Glen's.

Henry (Harry) Murphy Hood (1922–2003) was a Glasgow journalist who became Editor of the *Evening Times* in the 1970s. He and his wife, with no Hutchie connection, gifted their entire estate to the School.

*Rosemary Housley took her degree from Strathclyde University and joined the School as Head of Computing in 2000.

Eleanor M. Howie (b. 1908) was appointed to the PE Department in 1940 and retired in August 1973. She was PT of the Department and showed great expertise in training athletes and hockey players.

William B. Hutcheson MA BSc gained a FCH in Mathematics and Natural Philosophy at Glasgow University in 1922. He taught at Hyndland School before joining the Mathematics staff in HBGS in 1927. He was PT (Mathematics) between 1943 and 1955, and was appointed Deputy Head when the post was created in December 1951. He became Head of Govan Secondary School in 1955.

Agnes H. Ingleton was appointed Lady Superintendent in the HGGS in 1887, successor to Mrs McCready, Matron. Her job description encompassed 'the morals' of the girls. In 1911 she allowed the senior girls to be excused classes to attend a Suffragette rally in George Square. She retired in August 1921. Her maxim was 'Dignity and Discipline'. A lectern was presented to the School in memory of Miss Ingleton.

George Pratt Insh (1883–1956) MA was a History master, HBGS 1910–23; Principal Lecturer in History, Jordanhill Training College, 1923–45; and

President, EIS, 1938–9. His publications included *The Company of Scotland Trading to Africa and the Indies* (1932) and *The Darien Scheme* (1947).

*Anne Jack graduated from Glasgow University and joined the Modern Languages Department in 1977. She was an APT and Middle School Year Tutor before becoming Timetabler for the Secondary School in 2006.

(Prof.) Robert (Bob) Jack (1928–2010) was a well-known corporate lawyer in Glasgow. He was Professor of Mercantile Law at Glasgow University, 1978–93. He was twenty-third Chairman of the Governors of HET, 1980–7.

Tim Jacobs was Chair of the School Association, 1986–89 and a member of the Board of Governors.

Douglas Jamieson (1911–2002) ('Wee Dan') was appointed to the Mathematics staff of HBGS in 1954. He stayed three years and during that time took over School cricket. He became Second Master in Hydepark School.

Louis Janton taught Oral French in the HGGS from February 1887, but by 1905 the HET had a preference for female staff in the Girls' School. Janton published a number of French textbooks and readers between 1895 and 1928 and also taught at Allan Glen's.

Joseph Chesser Jessop (1892–1972) saw service in World War 1 (India, Egypt and France). He taught English/Classics in Selkirk HS, HBGS (1920); Brechin HS, and retired as Head of Lossiemouth School, 1933–58.

Manjit J. Jheeta took degrees from Himachal University, India. She joined the School in 1979, becoming Head of Biology in 2005. She retired in 2014.

Wendy Justice (née Fraser) joined the School as Assistant Director of PE in 1994. She became Director of PE in 1996. An outstanding hockey player and coach she won numerous international hockey caps. She became Head of PE at Craigholme School in 2005.

*Catherine Keddie took her degree from Napier University. She joined the Economics and Business Studies Department in 1998 and is now Head of Department.

*Alistair Kerr took his degree of BSc from Edinburgh University and joined the School as Head of Biology in 2014.

Martha L.M. Kerr DA became PT (Art) in HGGS in 1971 and took on the same post in HBGS in 1974.

*(Kathleen) Kate M. Keter took a BSc at Strathclyde and became the School Archivist in 2013.

Hugh Kilpatrick, groundsman for twenty-six years, retired in 1975. His wife, Jessie, provided regular catering.

John Kirk joined the HET in April 1951 and became Secretary and Treasurer in 1971. He retired in December 1982.

Thomson Kirkwood was appointed Drawing Master in HBGS in 1874 and resigned because of ill-health in July 1894.

David Hepburn Knox ('Johnny') (1893–1961) joined the staff in 1919 and became PT (English including History and Geography) in HBGS in 1929. He left for promotion in 1950.

(Rev. Dr) Andrew Laidlaw was the eleventh Chair of the HET, from 1919 until 1921.

*Stuart Lang took his degree from Jordanhill and joined the School in 1986. He became a Senior Teacher, then Director of PE in 1993, a role renamed Director of Sport in 2005.

Leslie L. Langley BSC won an All-Indian Scholarship to Glasgow University in 1909, graduating in Science in 1912. He was a science teacher in HBGS, 1936–55.

Esther M. Legge (b. 1886) took a FCH in English at Aberdeen University and was appointed PT of English (and History) in the HGGS in 1916. She resuscitated the School Magazine and wrote the Girls' School Song.[5] She retired in September 1945.

Alfie Leitch was Janitor in Crown Street from 1934 until his early death in 1958.

James Livingstone was on the staff of the HBGS as a teacher of Phonetics (from 1886 to 1889).

Mary Lochhead was the daughter of the first Rector of the HGGS. She was appointed an assistant to Miss Ewing, Head of Sewing, in 1886. She herself was promoted to be Head of the Needlework Department in January 1905 and retired from that post in September 1927.

*(Dr) Sandra Lonie graduated from Aberdeen University and joined the School as Head of Physics in 2008.

Robertson Lorimer joined the HET in May 1971 as Administrative Assistant. He was Secretary and Treasurer of the HET from 1983 until his early death aged 50 in February 1989.

Alice M.M. Lunan DA (1883–1981) joined HGGS in September 1912 and was PT (Art) 1932 until August 1946 (when she retired). She was Secretary of the Glasgow Society of Lady Artists, 1949–55.

(Dr) James McCallum was employed by the Trust to oversee the financial and legal business of HET as Treasurer and Law Agent for over forty years. He died in April 1948, leaving £4,500 to the Trust in his Will provided the Governors started building a new School within five years of the end of World War 2.

William A.C. McConnell joined the Classics staff of HBGS after war service. He remained until 1935 when he left to become Head of Foyle College, Londonderry, until 1961. He played an important part in establishing School rugby.

*Colin McCormick graduated from Glasgow University and joined the Technology Department in 2006. He became Head of Department in 2013.

Jeanie G. McCulloch ('Wee Jeanie') MA taught Classics in HGGS from 1919. She left to become PT in 1945 in the Girls' High before promotion to Deputy Head, retiring in 1962.

Archibald Gray Macdonald was the Preceptor of the Hospital from November 1874 until November 1877. He laid the memorial stone for the Girls' School in Crown Street in 1876.

Eric A. M. Macdonald joined the Mathematics staff at HBGS in 1910 and was promoted to PT (Mathematics) in 1929. He retired in June 1943.

Lillian McDonald MA BA left the staff of HGGS in 1938 to become Lady Superintendent at Stirling High School and from 1944–1962 was Headmistress of Park School.

Margaret M. MacDonald CM was appointed to the position of Mistress at Hutchesons' Grammar School in 1876. She held this position for thirty-seven years teaching the young Primary boys (mainly English and Arithmetic). She retired owing to ill-health in 1913.

Susan MacDonald joined the English Department in 1995. She became Director of Studies in 1996 and later Senior Depute Rector. She was

ABOVE. Menzies and an early staff photo c.1900.

LEFT. Robert Philp was Principal Teacher (Mathematics) at the Grammar School from 1876 until 1902 and was Head of the Boys' School between 1903 and 1913.

Photograph of Philp and his staff at the beginning of his Headship.

The new Girls' Grammar School in Kingarth Street was opened in 1912 to solve accommodation problems. Increased capacity ensured that Hutchesons' did not become a 'class school' open only to the rich.

William 'Pa' McVicar (with staff) was Headmaster of the Girls' School from 1914 to 1927. He adhered to the doctrine of 'social usefulness'.

The new Gymnasium in Kingarth Street in 1912, located on the top floor of a separate building especially designed for Physical Education, 'Housewifery' and Domestic Science.

RIGHT. W. King Gillies was Rector of the Boys' School for the comparatively short period of six years, between 1913 and 1919. [Bulletin 24 October 1919]

BELOW. The Soccer First Eleven, 1915–16. Rector W. King Gillies (in this picture) was not a soccer fan and quickly introduced rugby, if not to universal acclaim.

Girls' Hockey 1920s. The girls were not allowed to use the Boys' Playing Field in the 1920s.

The Cadet Corps being inspected in the Kingarth Street playground by Lord Strathclyde in April 1914.

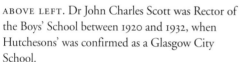

ABOVE LEFT. Dr John Charles Scott was Rector of the Boys' School between 1920 and 1932, when Hutchesons' was confirmed as a Glasgow City School.

ABOVE RIGHT. Margaret Kennedy was Principal of the Girls' School between 1927 and 1948.

RIGHT. W. Tod Ritchie was Rector of the Boys' School between 1932 and 1945. He was a scholar and athlete whose leadership left the School oversubscribed.

The Garden School was created by Miss Kennedy for infant education. [From a print of an original pen and ink (1993) by Christine J. Thomson – The Papercut Artist]

James Watson was Rector of the Boys' School from 1945 to 1955. He was the first Head since Philp to be appointed from within the School.

Isabella McIver was Principal of the Girls' School from 1948 until 1973. She became a legend in her own lifetime.

John M. Hutchison was Rector of the Boys' School from 1955 until 1966 and oversaw the building of the new Boys' School at Crossmyloof.

Peter Whyte was Rector of the Boys' School from 1966 until 1976 and of the amalgamated Hutchesons' Grammar School until 1978.

The Memorial Stone, brought from Crown Street, was sited at the entrance of the Beaton Road building.

The first mixed Prizegiving Day of the amalgamated School in 1977. Separate classes for boys and girls continued until the end of the 1980s.

ABOVE LEFT. Dr Gilmour D. Isaac was Rector of the School from 1978 until 1984 but ill-health led to an early retirement.

ABOVE RIGHT. Paul V. Brian was Rector for only a year, in 1984–5. He was the first Rector since Hutchison to come from a local authority school.

RIGHT. Miss J. C. Murray was Interim Rector for one year, 1985–6.

David Ward was Rector from 1986 until 1999 and was the first Hutchesons' Head never to have taught in Scotland before appointment.

John Knowles was Rector from 1999 to 2005. Like his predecessor he also had no experience of teaching in Scotland. He left to become an Episcopalian churchman in England.

Graham MacAllister taught History at Hutchesons' for almost all his career. He was Interim Rector during 2005.

Dr Kenneth Greig was appointed Rector in 2005.

Principal Examiner for Higher English. In 2003 she was appointed to the Governing Body of the Advisory Council of Learning and Teaching Scotland. She retired in 2005.

William H. Macdonald was appointed to the HET in 1885 and became Secretary to the Governors from 1892 until his death in September 1923.

*James McDougall took a degree of MA from Glasgow University. He worked at the School from April 1989 teaching Geography, before moving to St Columba's, Kilmacolm in June 1997. There he became PT and Deputy Rector. In 2007 he returned to HGS as Depute Rector (Ethos) with a wide-ranging remit.

Thomas Macdougall MA (1905–87) took a FCH in French and German before teaching at Hyndland. Then from January 1934 until 1964 he taught at the Boys' School, becoming PT Modern Languages in December 1946 and then, from 1956, Depute Rector. In January 1964 he became Head of St George's Road Secondary.

James McFarlane was the fourth Chair of the HET, from 1894 until 1897.

(Bailie) (Col.) John McFarlane (b. 1846) was a grain merchant who served twenty-three years on the Town Council from 1884. He was a Preceptor elected by the Patrons of the Hospital and became the eighth Chair of the HET, from 1905 until 1906. He joined the Board in 1894 and died in December 1910.

James H. McGregor MA BSc joined the School as PT (Science) in September 1959 and was promoted to PT Physics and Assistant Rector (Curriculum and Guidance). He died in 1977.

Thomas ('Pat') MacInnes CM reached retirement age in May 1919 after forty-three years on the English staff of HBGS, 1876–1919. He also taught Drawing and Primary classes. He turned down the headship of Keppochhill to remain at Hutchesons'.

Linda McIntosh joined Laurel Park as a Mathematics teacher in 1986 and was appointed Head of Mathematics in 1995 after the merger with Park. After a second merger with the School she was promoted to a Depute Head post in 1999 and was in charge of Lilybank Terrace. In 2005 she became Depute Rector in charge of Pastoral Care. She retired in 2012.

Ethel E.L. Mackay MA (b. 1896) was appointed in 1939 to teach English and History in HGGS. She was for a short period PT English at Jordanhill School but returned to the School in 1945 as PT English. She retired in June 1960.

R. McKechnie took a post in the Science Department of HGGS in 1949, retiring from there in 1964. He was a distinguished biologist who received the highest honour in his subject when he was made a Fellow of the Linnean Society.

Agnes McKendrick MA (b. 1890) joined the Classics staff of HGGS in September 1916. She became PT in 1919 and after World War 2 she served on the Secretary of State's Advisory Council on Education, the only classroom teacher in Scotland to do so. She was promoted to Deputy Head of the School and retired in November 1955.

Lorna McKie was appointed in August 1977 to a permanent post in the Infant Department. In 1987 she became Assistant Rector in charge of Infants, and in 2001 she was made Depute Rector and Head of Primary. She retired in 2010.

David McKinlay was Preceptor of the Hospital from November 1848 until November 1864. He was in office when Menzies became Head in 1861, but he did not support him. His wise investments led to the massively increased prosperity of the Hospital in the 1870s.

Malcolm A. Mackinnon ('Gymmy') qualified as a PE teacher at Dunfermline College in 1919. He taught PE (including Swimming) to boys in HBGS. In 1943 he was promoted to be Supervisor of PT Training with Glasgow Corporation.

Ian McLauchlan was a member of the PE Department in 1972. His record as Scottish Captain and British Lion complemented his skill as a rugby coach.

Donald MacLennan ('Puggy') was appointed to the Science staff of HBGS in September 1931. After a short break in 1950–1 at Lambhill Street Secondary he returned to become PT Science. He coached 1st XV rugby from 1934–50. He left for promotion in 1959 and became Head of Shawlands Academy.

John McLintock MA LLB joined the staff of HGGS in 1935. He left in November 1939 to take up duties in the RNVR. On his return he was promoted (in 1946) to become Depute Director of Education for Ross-shire.

George McMillan was appointed as an Assistant (or Second) Teacher just before the opening of the new school in 1841. His title suggests the greater autonomy accorded to the teacher when separate schoolrooms operate. His reputation was that of a very severe master.

May Madden, a native Aberdonian, began teaching at HGGS in 1970. Leaving to bring up her children in 1974 she returned to the combined School at Beaton Road in 1982 and was a member of the Classics Department from 1983, eventually becoming S1 Year Tutor. She retired in 2010.

James Mair (b. 1858) graduated with a Science degree from Glasgow University in 1886. He became a teacher at HBGS in 1887. He ended his career as Head Teacher in Tollcross Public School from September 1892.

Andrew Martin MA BSc became PT (Mathematics) at the HBGS in 1925. He left in November 1929 to become Rector of Cumnock Academy.

Jean P. Martin Dip Comm (1902–58) joined the staff in 1928 when Secretarial Studies were introduced. She was Business Manager for the School Magazine. She became PT (Commercial Subjects) in 1945.

*Michael Martin took a BSc degree from Heriot-Watt University. He taught Mathematics at George Heriot's, then moved to Abington School, Oxford for eighteen years, where he became Head of Middle Years. He was also a very successful rowing master and became coach of the GB Junior Rowing Squad. He joined HGS in 2008 as Senior Depute Rector.

Derek Mason CBE JP joined the Board of Governors in 1973 and became Chair in June 1997. When Mason retired from the Board in October 2003, he had served thirty years, including six years as Chairman and the previous ten as Vice-Chairman.

Thomas Adam Mathieson was a Town Councillor and Patron from 1886 until 1884 and was Preceptor of Hutchesons' Hospital, 1878–83. He was the second Chairman of the HET, from 1888 until 1891.

Jean Matthews joined the Mathematics Department in 1994 and became Head of Learning Support before retiring in 2012.

Thomas James Menzies was appointed to teach Science in 1874 in the School before becoming Headmaster of Stonelaw Public School in Rutherglen and then Rector of Stranraer Academy. He died in 1898, aged 39.

David Millar took up his Classics post at the School in September 1915. He served in the Highland Light Infantry in World War 1 and was killed in France in early 1917.

(Rev.) D. Millar was the third Chairman of the HET, from 1891 until 1894.

Janet W. Millar LL.A. (b. 1858) taught English in HGGS from 1885 until 1923, when she retired. She had a deep interest in the struggler and backward girl.

Janet G. Miller was appointed Head of Science in HGGS in 1961. She developed the Physics curriculum to help girls choose Medicine as a career option. She retired in June 1975.

William M. Miller was the Singing master at HGGS in Elgin Street when it opened in 1876. He promoted the Tonic Sol-fa system. He died in February 1894.

David B.C. Milne MA joined the English Department of the School in 1926 and left in 1946 to be PT (English) at Kelvinside Academy. He returned to be PT (English) at the School from October 1950 until August 1956, when he became Head at Bernard Street Junior Secondary.

(Rev. Archibald H. Minto was twentieth Chair of the Governors of HET, 1962–4. He died in 1998.

Douglas Mitchell joined the staff in 1979 as a Mathematics/Physics teacher. He was promoted to Senior Teacher in 1990. He retired after thirty-three years at the school.

Francis Mitchell joined the staff in 1982 and became PT of Economics, Accounting and Business Management in 1993. She completed twenty-three years' service.

Robert Macfarlane Mitchell (b. 1845) was a coal-master who joined the Town Council in 1884. He was Preceptor of the Hospital, 1902–5.

Thomas Moore (d. 1792), who taught in the Hospital School from 1756, attempted improvements in psalm singing and published the psalm tune 'Glasgow'.

William R. Morris was a Glasgow organist and choirmaster who joined the staff of HBGS in 1906 as Singing Master.

Alexander Muir was appointed in February 1892 to a teaching post at HGGS. He resigned in September 1893 and became Rector of Linlithgow Academy. He continued his career as Headmaster of Buckie Public School.

(Lt) Andrew Muir taught for two years before becoming a teacher for a year in the English and Primary Departments of the School. He was also a Church organist. He was killed in action In Gallipoli in November 1915.

(Sgt) John M. Muirhead (b. 1837) was popularly supposed to have been at the Charge of the Light Brigade. He was Drill Instructor in HBGS for forty-three years from 1870. His work was based on squad drill, the usual form of physical training, and was regularly praised by HMI. He extended the curriculum with physical exercises, sword-sticks, foils and rifle drills. From 1878 till 1889 he taught Callisthenics and Drill at Elgin Street.

Irene Munro arrived at the School in 1989, joining the Modern Languages Department. She became a Year Tutor and was Senior Year Tutor on her retirement in 2013.

Helen C. Murdoch retired in 1978 having been PT (Mathematics) in HGGS, 1958–77 and in the combined schools from 1975.

Margaret Murray taught Mathematics in the HGGS from 1905 until retirement in August 1934. She was PT of Mathematics in her senior years.

Thomas C. Neil, brother of Robert, joined the staff of the Boys' Junior School when the 'new' Primary building was opened at Beaton Road in 1957. He was the first Headmaster of the new Nether Robertland Primary School in Stewarton, Ayrshire.

Walter Nelson represented the City on HET from 1909–37. He became the fourteenth Chair of the Trust from 1935 until 1937, and then represented Merchants' House from 1937 until his death in 1946.

Alison Nisbet taught Modern Languages at the School 1958–60 and 1963–78. Her husband, Professor Stanley Nisbet was a School Governor from 1957 until 1979. He served as Convener of the Education Committee and, for a shorter period, Convener of the Foundationer and Scholarship Committee.

Margaret Norman joined the School Office in November 1985, was Rector's Secretary for many years and retired from her post as Admissions Registrar in January 2014.

Alfred Oswald joined the HGGS as teacher of German in 1899 and taught there until 1905.

Raymond C.J. Paterson (d. 2008) was PT (History), 1965–71, and AHT (Curriculum and Guidance), 1971–82. He retired in 1983.

Jean D. Paul joined the School in 1990 and taught Modern Languages, becoming a Senior Teacher with responsibility for European links. She later became a Year Tutor and retired in 2007.

Alec W. Percy DPE joined the PE Department in October 1970. He left in February 1972 to become PT in Smithycroft Secondary. He returned to HBGS as PT (PE) in January 1974.

Andrew Pringle CM taught at his old school in Dalry, Ayrshire; was Headmaster at Kersland Barony School and between 1877 and 1912 taught English, Latin, Book-keeping and Mathematics at HBGS.

George Taylor Pringle (1890–1955) was educated at Peebles HS, University of Edinburgh and Oxford. He was PT (Classics) HBGS (replacing Caddell) between 1920 and 1923; HMI of Schools, 1923–45; HMI Chief (Northern), 1945–8; HMI Senior Chief (SED), 1948–55. His father was General Secretary of the EIS.

(Dr) Andrew Ralston took degrees at Glasgow and Oxford Universities. He joined the English staff in 1980. He was a Year Tutor and retired in 2014.

(Very Rev.) Dean Watson Read was the seventh Chair of the HET, from 1903 until 1905.

Alistair H.J. Reid qualified from Jordanhill in 1971 and within three years had become a PT Physics. He was appointed to Hutchesons' in 1989 and retired in 2008 after nineteen years as Head of Physics.

James M. Reid joined HGGS in 1944 and was promoted to Head of Music in 1949. He retired in 1964.

Alex Rennie graduated in Modern Languages at Glasgow. He joined the staff in 1969 and took on the role of careers adviser in 1990. He was a founder member of the Staff-Governors' Joint Consultative Committee. He retired in 2001.

(Sir) David Richmond served on the Governing Body from 1885 until his death in February 1908.

(Bailie) Violet Mary Craig Roberton was the first woman Governor of HET, 1921–37, and first woman Preceptor of Hutchesons' Hospital in 1947. She was a member of the Royal Commission on Marriage and Divorce, 1951.

Forbes M.M. Robertson (b. 1887) was appointed PT (English) at HBGS in 1915. He died in November 1929.

*Kirsteen Robertson took her degree from Manchester Metropolitan University and joined the School as Head of Girls' PE in 2005.

(Rev. Dr) Lockhart Robertson was the first Secretary of the HET between December 1885 and his death in December 1892.

James Robson retired from the post of Singing Master at HBGS in April 1906 at the age of ninety-six. He had taken up the appointment in Crown Street in 1870. He was an early advocate of the Tonic Sol-fa method.

*Claire Rooney graduated from Stirling University, joined the Modern Languages Department in 2003 and later became Head of PSE.

George A. Roser joined the Board of Governors in 1968. He was twenty-second Chair of the Governors of HET between 1975–80.

Hope Ross served as PT (Modern Languages) in Hillhead HS and Hillpark Secondary until teaching at HGS from 1981 until September 1993. While here she produced a succession of successful School shows and gave many memorable performances in leading amateur roles.

James Ross ('Jimmy') (d. 2011) joined the staff of HBGS in 1980 and became Head of Geography in 1985 until retirement in June 1993.

(Miss) M. Lilian I. Ross took over the Qualifying Class at HBGS in January 1925. She retired in April 1955.

Linda Russell (1953–2010) was Office Manager in the Trust Office from 1991 until her untimely death.

*Peter Russell took his degree from Jordanhill and joined the PE Department in 1990. He is currently a Year Tutor.

Herr Heinrich Schroeder taught Oral German in the HGGS in the 1880s and 1890s. He was appointed German teacher in the HBGS in 1878 and died in May 1899.

Ivy Scott joined the Primary staff in November 1949 from Govan Secondary School. She retired in June 1977 after almost thirty years on the staff, in Infants, then the Girls' School in Kingarth Street and finally as APT in English (and History) at Beaton Road.

Saibal K. Sen BSc joined the Mathematics Department and spent thirty-four years at the School. He retired in 2010.

The Sharp sisters, Flora and Helen, joined the staff of HGGS in 1876 and

1879 respectively. Flora ('The Duchess') was a disciple of the old school and retired aged 65 in April 1915. Her quieter younger sister was associated with the Infants and retired in 1921.

William (Bill) D. Shaw taught at Heriot's and at Strathallan before arriving at Hutchesons' in 1971 as PT (Chemistry). He became PT for the combined Schools in 1976, a post he retained until early retirement in August 1996.

Norman F. Shead was PT History at Eastwood Secondary before joining the School staff in November 1979 as PT History, and after a number of years overcame the accommodation problems of his Department. He retired in June 1998 to further his research in medieval history and continued his role as Principal Assessor for Sixth Year Studies History.

Agnes Shearer (d. 2010) joined the English staff of HGGS in 1963, becoming PT in 1973. She became PT for the combined Schools in 1975, retiring in 1981.

Elsie M. Shedden joined the HGGS as PT (Home Economics) in 1956 in a Department which taught Home Management and Dress and Design. Following a School Inspection she resigned in June 1979.

Christina D. Sheridan (b. 1909) joined the HGGS staff in May 1935 as an additional Art teacher and succeeded Miss Lunan as Head of Art in 1946. She was forced to retire due to ill-health in 1971.

Amelia Simpson CM retired from the Junior School in December 1915 under the age regulations of the time. She had joined the Primary staff of the HBGS in 1876, teaching mainly English and Arithmetic.

Rhona Simpson joined the PE staff in September 1994 and produced a succession of successful hockey teams. A double Olympian, she also represented Scotland in the Commonwealth Games. She left in 2012 to become Director of Sport at Glasgow Academy.

Sir William Sinclair (1895–1976) became Director and CEO of Dunlop Rubber Co. Ltd. He was a Patron of the Hospital from 1968.

John V. Skinner taught at HBGS in 1946–7. He became Principal Lecturer in Classics and Methods at Jordanhill College and then Rector of Alloa Academy and Aberdeen Grammar School. He retired in 1973.

*Clare Smith graduated from Glasgow University and joined the Modern Studies Department in 2003. She is currently a Year Tutor.

*Pauline Smith graduated from Edinburgh University in Mathematics and Computing. She taught at Marlborough College in Wiltshire and joined the Mathematics Department of Hutchesons' in 2008. She is currently a Year Tutor.

Carl Otto Sonntag joined the Modern Language Department of the HBGS in 1888. Sonntag resigned in September 1892 due to ill-health and was replaced by Professor Paul Hirsch (who had been part-time since 1888).

*Craig Sorbie graduated from Edinburgh University and joined the PE Department in 2011, becoming Head of Rugby in 2005.

James Steele was the twelfth Chair of the HET, from 1921 until 1928.

Carol G. Stevenson taught at Jordanhill College School and was a pioneering Head of Biology in HGGS from 1974. She was Senior Mistress (from 1987) and became Depute Rector in 2003. She was co-author of over thirty textbooks, many of which were standard texts throughout Scottish schools. She retired in 2008.

John Stewart represented the City on the HET Board from 1935–45. He went on to become seventeenth Chair of the HET, from 1945 until 1956.

Rona P. Stratton (née McAdam) was appointed teacher of Mathematics and Science at HGGS in 1916. She became Head of the Science Department in 1939 and retired in 1948.

(Rev.) John A. Swan BD was Minister of Ramshorn Church and was elected to the HET in 1923, serving until 1958.

*Catherine Swanson took her degree from St Andrews University and joined the School as Head of Learning Support in 2012.

George Symington was sixteenth Chair of the HET, from 1943 until 1945.

*Michael J. Symington graduated from Glasgow University. He joined the English Department in 1986 and became Head of Department in 2011.

Ian B. Tainsh (b. 1943) attended Kelvinside Academy and trained as a CA. He was Secretary and Clerk to the HET Governors, from 1989 until 2003. He was involved in a radical development programme at Beaton Road and Kingarth Street.

William Tannock (b. 1877) was appointed PT (Science) at HBGS in 1906. He left to become Headmaster of Temple School in 1931.

(Rev.) Harry H. Tennent (1914–96) held the Chair of the Scottish Methodist Synod – the highest post in the Methodist Church – for three years. He was a Governor of HET, 1975–85.

Alexander Terries joined HBGS Primary in 1953 after service with the Royal Navy. He was appointed Assistant Rector of the Primary in August 1976. He retired in September 1982.

Agnes C.P. Thomson joined the Primary staff in 1913. She taught Latin at the Senior School during World War 1 but returned to the Junior School after the War. In 1929, as senior lady on the staff, she presented Rector Scott with his Glasgow University LLD robes. She retired in June 1946.

James McKelvie Thomson became an Art teacher in HBGS, 1919–53, being promoted to the post of PT in 1934. He submitted designs for a new uniform after World War 1 and on his prompting new colours were introduced in September 1938: light blue and white on a navy blue background.

James Thomson, the Mathematical Master in HGGS, was appointed Professor of Natural Philosophy in St Andrew's University in October 1899.

*Jane Thomson graduated in French and Spanish at Glasgow University. She joined the Modern Languages Department in 2001 and is currently a Year Tutor.

Jean P. Thomson (née Newlands) MA joined the Primary staff of HGGS in September 1949 and then moved to French, 1954 until June 1988, after which she retired.

Scott Thomson joined the Physics Department in 1975. He became an S4–S6 Year Tutor in 1978. He was Administrative Officer for Examinations from 2003 until his retirement in 2010,

L.E.R. Tissot MA taught French in HBGS from 1897 until 1905.

*Akiko Tomitaka graduated from Newcastle University and joined the Geography Department in 2006. She was appointed Head of International Education in 2014.

*(Dr) Philip Tonner took degrees from Glasgow and Warwick and joined the School in 2011, becoming Head of Philosophy and Religion in 2014.

*Edgar Trotter graduated from Belfast and joined the Music Department in 1988. He is now Head of Music (Curriculum).

*Peter Uprichard graduated from Glasgow and joined the Chemistry Department in 1989. He became Head of Department in 1997.

John M. Urquhart joined the English Department of Crown Street in December 1939. In 1945 he went into educational administration in Banffshire, Glasgow and Selkirkshire. In 1964 he was appointed the first Director of the Scottish Certificate of Education Examination Board (SCEEB) and remained in that post until retirement in 1975.

Seonid M. Vickerman worked as AHT with responsibility for the Upper Primary. In her final year, 1997–8, before retirement, she acted as Acting Depute for Primary.

*Kenneth D. Walton graduated from Glasgow and Manchester. He taught at the School from 1986–88 and returned in 2002, later becoming Head of Music (Performance).

Frederic A. Weston taught Art part-time at the School between 1904 and 1918. He was promoted to full-time and Head of the Department, a post he held from 1918 until retirement in January 1933. He designed the War Memorial with the names of the 135 FPs who served in World War 1 (including the four who died).

Elizabeth S.E. (Betha) Wheatley took a degree from Glasgow in 1920. She taught at the Primary from 1923 until 1951.

James Whyte became PT History at HBGS in 1947 and Deputy Rector of the School. He ended his career as Head at Eastbank Senior Secondary.

William Whyte was Preceptor of the Hospital from November 1864 until November 1867. He was instrumental in extending the benefits of the foundation to girls by means of a separate School for them.

*(Prof.) Brian Williams is a geriatrician and former President of the Royal College of Physicians and Surgeons of Glasgow. In late 2013 he became Chairman of HET Governors, the first non-FP to achieve this in recent times.

Liz Williamson (1956–2008) taught for twenty-seven years in the PE Department at the School, 1981–2008. She established the Primary Running Club.

*Amanda Wilson took her degree from Edinburgh Napier University and joined the School as Depute Rector (Lower Primary) in 2015 from George Heriot's School.

William Wilson was the first Chairman of the HET from 1885 until 1888.

William (Willie) D. Wilson joined HBGS Modern Language Department as Special Assistant in January 1948 following a distinguished Army career. He was coach of the 1st rugby XV in the 1950s and 1960s. He was appointed PT (Modern Languages) for the combined School in August 1973 and retired in June 1977.

*Marie Windows graduated from Sheffield University and joined the History Department in 2003. She became Head of History in 2012.

Harry Wiseman was appointed to take charge of Science, Geography and Nature Study in the HGGS in 1906. He was commandeered by the War Office after 1914 to make poison gases. He retired in August 1939.

Andrew William Wood (1952–2002) taught Classics at the School from 1975 until his sudden death in 2002. He will be remembered as a top cricket umpire and enthusiastic rugby and soccer referee.

Daniel Wyatt took his degree from Exeter University and joined the PE department in 2003. He became a Year Tutor and left to become Deputy Head at Kelvinside Academy in 2015.

William Wylie took an MA at Glasgow in 1868 and then a BD in 1871. Originally a 'stickit minister' he taught English and Classics at HBGS between 1876 and 1889. He moved on to a headmastership in Orkney.

Andre Yacoubian BSc was appointed to the Mathematics Department in 1970 and promoted to APT (Guidance) in 1973. He took on the post of AHT (Guidance) in 1982, retiring in 1988.

Allan C. Young was the nineteenth Chair of the HET, from 1959 until 1962.

A.M. Young was appointed Woman Adviser at HGGS in February 1956. This was the first post of this type since Ingleton had been Lady Superintendent.

Jean G. Young (b. 1890) joined the School staff in 1912. She was PT (Domestic Science), retiring in June 1953 after over forty years in post. Her advice was important in deciding on the School uniform.

Jessie M. Younger (b. 1893) took a FCH in Mathematics and Natural Philosophy at Glasgow University, winning the Breadalbane Scholarship in Mathematics. She joined the Mathematics staff of HGGS in 1919 and was promoted to PT (Mathematics) in 1934, a post she retained until retirement in April 1955.

THIRTEEN Biographies of
Prominent FPs

'In the West of Scotland, Hutchesons' is a byword for academic excellence
. . . At the pinnacle of the academic pecking order within the School sit
the Dux Medallists. Their position is unique – not only in terms of their
academic prowess (a fairly awe-inspiring level of achievement) – but because
their achievement is celebrated so briefly at the time of their award (medallists' names are announced shortly before Prize-Giving, itself held on the
last day of session and before a fairly exclusive audience of prize-winners,
parents and invited guests). Although their names are preserved on the dux
boards in School and engraved on the original medals (replicas of which are
retained by the duces), not for the medallists the adulation of fellow pupils
enjoyed by the Captains of the first XI or XV or Head Boy or Head Girl.
They do not perform publicly – on field or platform – during the course
of the session, nor do their photographs grace the pages of the School
Magazines on a regular basis.' (*Veritas* no. 5, November 1996.)

Readers will therefore forgive the author if this chapter on 'Prominent
Former Pupils' is somewhat dominated by past and present duces and
the academic professions, which many of them will fill in their successful
careers.

In a survey in 1996, one-third of Dux Medallists (35%) were pursuing
careers in education; 17% medical work; 8% finance and accounting, and 8%
in the civil service. Then followed, in descending order of popularity, careers
in engineering, law, clergy, computing, home management, administration
management, social work and commerce.

Graeme Adam left HBGS in 1971. He became a GP and Police Surgeon in
Carlisle. He won the Scottish Curling Men's Championship in 1989 and the
Scottish Curling Senior Men's Championship in 2008.

Eileen Adams (née Murray) (1953–2010) left HGGS in 1971 and was a
successful swimming coach in Aberdeen and Glasgow. Robert Renwick, a
swimming Gold medallist, dedicated his Men's 200-metre Freestyle win to
Mrs Adams after her death in April 2010.

(Dr) Rita Ahmad (née Poddar) left HGS in 1994. She was chosen as Entrepreneur of the Year at the 2010 Asian Business Awards for her business, Bath Street Dental. She also received an award for her Scottish Asian Woman's Business in March 2014.

(Prof.) James A. Aitchison (1899–1968) was Professor of Dental Surgery at the University of Glasgow, 1951–64.[1] He was the prime mover behind the Glasgow Diploma in Orthodontics.

William Sinclair Aitken (1925–2010) attended the HBGS 1930–1943, and taught Classics at King's College, London and George Watson's College, Edinburgh. He became BBC Head of Educational Broadcasting in Scotland, 1963–82, contributing significantly to cultural education.

(Dr) Anne Cunningham Aitkenhead (1907–79) left HGGS as Dux in 1924 and was one of the first women consultants in Medicine, specialising in Haematology/Diabetes.

(Rev.) Douglas Niven Alexander (b. 1935) left the HBGS in 1953. He became Minister, Erskine Parish Church, Bishopton, 1970–99, and was an advocate for social justice.[2] He is the father of Wendy and Douglas Alexander, prominent Scottish politicians. He conducted the funeral of Donald Dewar in Glasgow Cathedral in 2000. He was awarded a DUniv from Glasgow University in 2007.

Maev Alexander (or Dunmore) (née McConnell) (b. 1948) left HGGS in 1965 and became a successful Scottish television and stage actress.

(Dr) Spence Alexander left School in 1977. He became a specialist surgeon in Cardiff and a Fellow of the Royal Society of Surgeons in Edinburgh. He practised medicine in South Africa's Zulu province but was killed there in July 1997. He was awarded a G and THA posthumously.

(Dr) George Allison Allan (1876–1950) was in business before studying Medicine. He was awarded the Brunton Memorial Prize at Glasgow University for being the most distinguished graduate of the year in 1925. He gained FRCP (1932), being an expert on rheumatic heart disease.

John Allan left HBGS in 1843 as Dux.

(Professor) Norman J.W. Allan left HBGS in 1939 and became Professor of Obstetrics and Gynaecology at Ottawa University.

Richard Allan joined HBGS in 1948 and left in 1957. He became the

School's first FP rugby internationalist (against Ireland in 1969). Following the awarding of his cap he visited the School and a half-day was declared. He also swam for Scotland.

Tom Allan (b. 1946) attended HBGS, 1949–65. He graduated with an Honours degree in English from Glasgow University in 1969. He became a full-time sculptor in 2000, working predominately in stone and marble.

(Rear Admiral Sir) David Allen KCVO CBE (1933–1995) left HBGS to join the RN in 1949. He was Secretary of the First Sea Lord in 1982. He was the Founders' Day Speaker in 1986. He became Defence Services Secretary from 1988 until 1991, when he retired.

(Dr) Aileen B. Alston was Girls' Dux of HGS in 1988. She graduated MBChB from Glasgow University in 1993 and became a consultant paediatrician at Epsom and St Helier Hospitals.

Andrew Anderson left HBGS in 1862 as Dux.

(Prof.) Anne Harper Anderson (née Thomson) OBE was born in 1954 and left HGGS in 1972. She became Professor of Psychology, Glasgow University, 1997; Vice-Principal, Dundee University, 2006–10; and Vice-Principal and Head of the College of Social Sciences in Glasgow University in 2010.[3] She was awarded a G and THA in 2012.

(Dr) David A.R. Anderson (1915–2005) left HBGS in 1934. He was Senior MO at Barlinnie Prison for over twenty years.

Dorothy (Dot) Allison Anderson (née Bell) (1953–2009) left HGGS in 1970 and became a pioneering chemist. She worked at a national level and was an honorary lecturer at Strathclyde University.

Janette Anderson (née Fitzpatrick) left School in 1981. She became a successful businesswoman: a Director of Network Rail and Chief Executive of First Engineering from 2003 until 2007.

Jean I. Anderson left HGGS as joint-Dux in 1947.

Madge Easton Anderson (1896–1982) attended HGGS between 1904 and 1913. She matriculated at Glasgow University in 1913 and graduated MA (1916), BL (1919) and LLB (1920). She was Glasgow University's first female Law graduate and the first woman solicitor in Scotland in 1920. She was also the first woman entitled to practise law in both Scotland and England in 1937.

Peter David Anderson (b. 1947) (class of 1965) was Deputy Keeper, National Archives of Scotland (NAS), formerly the Scottish Record Office (SRO), 1993–2009.[4]

Thomas A. Anderson (b. 1940) was a Scottish skier.

Dorothea L. Antzoulatos left School in 2003 as Girls' Dux.

(Dr) Thomas D. Arbuckle left HGS in 1981 as Dux. He took FCH in Chemical Physics and PhDs in Electrical Engineering and Biochemistry He became Visiting Research Engineer at Mitsubishi Electric Corporation. He was a post-doctoral researcher at the Universities of Bonn and Limerick.

Susan Ashwell (née Montgomery) left School as Dux in 1977. She became a newsreader/continuity announcer with the BBC World Service in London in 1997.

Harley Atkinson left the HBGS as Dux in 1957. He became IT Director (UK) of APACS.[5]

Hilary K. Atkinson BSc (Hons) (class of 1997) delivered sports services for world-leading events including the London 2012 Olympic and Paralympic Games and the Glasgow 2014 Commonwealth Games. She has become a member of the Sports Committee of the Commonwealth Games Federation. She gave the Address at Founders' Day in 2015.

(Dr) Alison Auguste (née Boyle) left HGS in 1983 having achieved a hockey 'Blue'. She is a medical practitioner In Marseilles, France.

Douglas Auld (b. 1942) left HBGS aged sixteen, retiring ultimately as Det. Supt Metropolitan Police. He was a Councillor in Orpington, Kent, from 2006 and Mayor of Bromley in 2009–2010.

Janet (Jenny) Auld (b. 1921) was educated at HGGS between 1929 and 1939 and Glasgow University. She served in the ATS from 1942–46. She was unsuccessful as Labour candidate for Ayr in the elections of 1951 and 1955 but was elected as a Councillor in East Kilbride in 1963. She was appointed Dean of Guild in East Kilbride in 1966. She taught English at Duncanrig School. She was the Honorary Freeman of East Kilbride in 1993.

Ann J.V. Austin left HGS as Dux Girl in 1991 and took her degree at Cambridge University. She became Publications Manager with Zenith Optimedia.

(Dr) Robert Austin left HBGS in 1905. He spent his working life as the local doctor in Armidale, Australia, and retired in 1963.

Ian David Hunter Baillie CBE was born in 1940 (Class of 1959). He became a minister in the United Reform Church, after working eight years in life assurance and thirty-five years in social work.[6] His CBE was awarded in 1997 as Director of Social Work for the Church of Scotland.

John Graham Baird (1936–2007) left HBGS in 1954 as Dux. He worked for Sotheby's.

Nellie Baird (b. 1893) left the HGGS as Dux in 1910. She graduated MA from Glasgow University in 1913.

John Gibb Ballingall (1900–64) attended HBGS, 1913–17, and took a BSc degree in Applied Chemistry from Glasgow University. He became FRIC and gained an OBE in the Coronation Honours List in 1953. He retired in 1960 as Senior Principal Scientific Officer at the Underwater Weapons Establishment, Portland, but for most of his career he was at the Royal Naval Torpedo Factory at Greenock in Admiralty Service.

(Dr) Archibald Morton Ballantyne TD attended HBGS, 1918–26, and took a BSc and PhD from Glasgow University. He was with the RA in World War 2. He was senior lecturer in Civil Engineering at University College London. He was Secretary of the Aeronautical Society, 1951. He was awarded the OBE in 1966.

(Prof.) Colin Kerr Ballantyne was born in 1951 and left HBGS in 1969. He was Professor of Physical Geography, St Andrews University, from 1994.[7] He was elected FRSE and FRSA in 1996.

Samuel Westwood Ballardie was born in 1867 and left the HBGS as Dux in 1884. He took an MA in 1890 and taught at Inverness, Dundee and Garnethill School (the Girls' High).

Elizabeth Smellie Barr (b. 1888) left HGGS in 1905 as Dux. She won the Franco-Scottish Society Bursary – open to all Scottish universities – for the best student in French in 1909 and graduated MA from Glasgow University in 1910.

(Prof.) Ronald Barr left HBGS in 1960 and became Professor of Paediatrics, Pathology and Medicine at McMaster University, Ontario. He was elected a Fellow of the Royal College of Paediatrics and Child Health, 2003.

Agnes (Nancy) M.K. Barron (née Culver) (1920–2014) left the HGGS as Dux in 1937. She was Consultant Ophthalmologist at Greenock Eye Infirmary and Inverclyde Royal Hospital for eighteen years.

Allan Robertson Barrowman (1880–1903) left HBGS in 1896 as Dux. He died of tuberculosis while a medical student.

(Dr) J. Henry B. Baxter became Superintendent of Ruchill and, later, Bridge of Weir Hospitals.

(Prof.) Murdoch S. Baxter left HBGS in 1962 and was engaged by the UN as Director of the Marine Environment Laboratory in Monaco. He was elected FRSE. He was awarded the Chevalier of the Order of St Charles for services to the principality of Monaco in 1997.

Gareth Bayley (b. 1972) attended the School from 1981 until 1990 and Princeton and Oxford universities. He joined the Diplomatic Service and his first post was Second Secretary at the British Embassy in Cairo, 1998–2002. He became Deputy Head of the Conflict Department of the Foreign and Commonwealth Office, then Additional Director for Eastern Europe and Central Asia.

Donald Beaton (1905–95) joined the School in 1917 and left as Dux in 1923. He took his MA degree in Classics in 1927 and taught at North Kelvinside School.

William Beaton left HBGS in 1859 as Dux.

Moira Beaty (née Munro) (1922–2015) attended HGGS from 1932 until 1939. She was a cryptographer at Bletchley Park, 1942–45. She then completed her course at Glasgow School of Art. She taught in the Gorbals and Hawick before becoming an accomplished painter who exhibited nationwide from her base in Galloway.

Nicola L. Begg left School in 2004 as Girls' Dux.

(Dr) Thomas Ballantyne Begg TD (1926–2005) joined the HBGS in 1938 and left as Dux in 1945. After graduating he was awarded the Brunton Medal for being the most distinguished student of the year. He became Senior Registrar in Medicine at the Royal Victoria Infirmary, Glasgow. He was awarded FRCP and was an athletics internationalist.

Alexander G. Bell (b. 1933) left the HBGS in 1951. He became Chief Reporter for Public Inquiries, Scottish Office.

Millicent H.S. Bell (née Leslie) (1916–2011) left the HGGS in 1934 and studied Medicine at Glasgow. She became a pioneering cytologist, establishing a laboratory in 1965 at the Victoria Infirmary to screen cervical smears.

William Bell (1915–2002) left School in 1932. He became Assistant Clerk of Senate to the University of Glasgow.

Colin N. Berkley left School in 2003 as Boys' Dux. He studied Natural Sciences at Queens' College, Cambridge.

(Dr) Thomas Arthur Berry (1917–71) joined the HBGS in 1925 and left as Dux in 1935. He became a surgeon in Durham.

Marion King Binnie left HGGS in 1896. She was the first student of Glasgow University to graduate with FCH in Modern Languages.

Gillian Birrell (née Glover) (b. 1952) attended HGGS from 1968 to 1970. She is a successful journalist.

Wendy A. Bishop left School in 1993 as Girls' Dux.

Colin Black left HBGS in 1961 and became Headmaster of Camberwell Grammar School in Melbourne, Victoria. He retired in 2005.

Janet Henderson Blackwood left HGGS as Dux in 1925. She became a Carnegie Scholar researching into Biochemistry. She became a teacher.

Agnes Blair attended HGGS between 1881 and 1886, leaving the School as joint-Dux.

Anna Dempster Blair (née Law) was born in 1927 and, after Giffnock Primary, attended HGGS between 1936 and 1944. She graduated from Dunfermline College of Physical Education in 1947. She was the Founders' Day Speaker in 1992. She is a writer of novels and lecturer.[8]

(Rev.) Ronald Stanton Blakey (b. 1938) attended the School, 1947–56. He was Editor, *Church of Scotland Year Book*, 2000–2011.[9]

Thomas Y. Bonar left HBGS in 1871 as Dux. He took his MA in 1880 and intended to study further but died early in March 1883.

David T. Bone took second place in the Civil Service Examination (Clerical Class) open to candidates in the British Isles aged between sixteen and seventeen years.

(Rev.) Robert Bone (1919–98) was a Foundationer but left HBGS from S2 in 1933 to help support his family. Later he worked as an engineer in a Christian mission in Malawi. He was minister of Ibrox Church for fifteen years.

Hilary Booth (née Wood) left HGGS in 1956. She became Registrar in Orthodontics in the Manchester Dental School in 1965. As a second career she became a London Blue Badge Tour Guide in Parliament.

Margaret E. Boswell left School in 1980 as Girls' Dux and is now a partner in a firm of London solicitors.

Douglas T. Boyd OBE FRSAMD was born in 1939 and left HBGS in 1956. He qualified as a CA. He became Managing Partner of KPMG in Glasgow and Chair of the Finance Committee and Vice-Chair of the Governors of RSAMD, achieving its Fellowship Award in 2006. He was Chair of Hanover (Scotland) Housing association until 2010. He was Lord Dean of Guild at Merchants' House, 2011–13, and elected Preceptor of Hutchesons' Hospital in June 2014.

Mary Russell Boyd (1880–1965) left HGGS as Dux in 1896. She graduated MA from Glasgow University in 1901. She became a school teacher.

Margaret M. Boyes (née Peat) left HGGS as Dux in 1961. She became a teacher.

Donna Marie Boyle left School in 2001 and ended her competitive dancing career in 2007 after coming third in the World Irish Dance Championships. She went on to win the coveted lead role in *Riverdance*.

Muriel Clara Bradbrook (1909–93) attended HGGS in 1918–19. She gained a double First in English at Cambridge in the 1930s and became Professor of English at Girton College in 1965 – the English faculty's first woman professor. She became Mistress of Girton in 1968 and wrote seventeen books.[10] She was a leading British authority on Shakespeare.

Crawford Brankin (b. 1949) attended School, 1957–65. He became Deputy Editor of the Glasgow *Evening Times* and Editor of the *Scottish Daily Mirror*.

Emma Brankin left School in 2006 and has carved out a media career with the *Sun*.

Micheline H. Brannan (née Moss) was Dux of HGGS in 1972. She served the Scottish Government as Head of the Executive's Social Justice Group.

She retrained as a nurse. She was vice-chair of the Scottish Council of Jewish Communities.

(Dr Col) (Archibald) Douglas Bremner TD DL (1939–2011) left School in 1957. He studied Medicine and specialised in Pathology. He practised in Rutherglen. He was honorary surgeon to HM the Queen and Deputy Lord Lieutenant of Renfrewshire. He was the Founders' Day Speaker in 1983. He was first President of the 1641 Society. He was awarded a G and THA in 2006. He was Commandant-in-Chief of St Andrew's First Aid.

Agnes W. Broderick (née McDiarmid) (1906–99) came to HGGS in 1920 and left as Dux in 1923. She graduated from Glasgow University with FCH in an MA in 1927 and with FCH in a BA from Girton College, Cambridge, in Mathematics in 1930.

Andrew Broom left the School in 1951 and became Deputy Keeper at General Register House in Edinburgh. He was replaced by Peter Anderson, who left HBGS in 1965.

David Broom left HBGS in 1869 as Dux.

Robert Broom (1866–1951) entered HBGS in 1879. He became a palaeontologist and Professor of Zoology and Geology at Victoria College, South Africa (1903–10). He was elected FRS in 1920 and won its Gold Medal in 1928; he was elected FRSE in 1947. He made a major contribution to the study of hominid fossils and human origins.[11]

Tom Broom left HBGS in 1946. He trained at the Vet College in Glasgow and took over a practice in Stamford in 1963. He was the official vet for the Burghley International Horse Trials. He died in 1992.

Lesley Brough was born in 1964 and left School in 1981. She joined the Diplomatic Service stationed at Oslo, then Madrid. She has been working for the UN in New York.

Alexander Brown (1920–99) attended HBGS from 1930 until 1938. He became Chief Veterinary Officer to the Ministry of Agriculture, Fisheries and Food in England in 1973.

(Rev.) Alexander D. Brown came to HBGS in 1913 and left as Dux in 1918. He graduated with FCH in Classics and won the Clark Scholarship. He gained a BD with distinction in 1928 and was ordained at Mossgalen Parish Church, Fife. He died in 1979.

Alistair Brown left School in 2003 and became a PGA Professional.

Antony (Tony) P. Brown was born in 1947 and attended HBGS between 1959 and 1964. He qualified as a CA and became Director of Corporate Finance, British Linen Bank, and Standard Charter Merchant Bank. He is a partner for Nexus Corporate Finance LLP.

Catherine G. Brown (née Braithwaite) was born in 1941 and attended HGGS between 1946 and 1959. She became a freelance food writer, whose book *Scottish Cookery* was widely acclaimed.

Downie Brown was born in 1943 and left HGBS in 1960. He became a CA. He represented Scotland at Swimming in the Commonwealth Games of 1966 and 1970.

(Sir) John Brown BSc LLD (1901–2000) was a Foundationer at Crown Street in 1912. His grandfather, James Hanbridge, taught Art in the old Girls' School in Elgin Street. He left HBGS in 1918 and graduated with Distinction in Naval Architecture and Natural Philosophy. He became a naval architect and MD and Deputy Chairman of John Brown's Shipyard. He was the seventh Founders' Day Speaker in 1967. He was awarded a Knighthood and a G and THA in 1999.

(Major) John W. Brown MC (1910–2003) left the HBGS in 1927. He was President of the FP Club, 1939–40.

(Brig.) John Brown OBE MM TD DL (1923–2008) left HBGS in 1941 and volunteered for the Royal Engineers. He became a decorated war veteran and was one of the first of the British forces to hit the Normandy beaches on D-Day. As a businessman he joined the confectioners Bassett's, and rose to be their Scottish/Irish area manager.

John M. L. Brown left the School in 1972. He was the Secretary and President of the English Curling Association between 2001 and 2006. He has represented England at five European and two World Championships.

Leslie Armour Brown was born in 1963 and attended HGGS until 1980. He was Procurator Fiscal, Kilmarnock, 2005–2011 and has been Procurator Fiscal of Falkirk, Stirling and Alloa since 2011.[12]

Charlotte U. Browning left School in 2011 as Girls' Dux. She studied Law at Cambridge University.

Clare Bruce (née Capanni) left School in 1990. She became Head of Infants and Junior School at Nottingham High School in 2013.

Keith Bruce attended HGS, 1970–75. He has worked for the *Herald* in Glasgow for over twenty-five years. He was appointed the newspaper's Arts Editor in 1994.

Ken Bruce left School in 1969 and has been a Radio 2 Presenter since 1984. He has hosted the mid-morning slot since 1992. In December 2008 he was inducted into the Radio Academy Hall of Fame.[13]

Margaret (Maggie) Bruce left HGGS as Dux in 1891.

Robert Bryson left HBGS in 1851 as joint-Dux.

Anna Masterton Buchan (pseudonym O. Douglas) (1877–1948) attended HGGS but found the School 'somewhat overwhelming' and 'that hive of industry'[14] and completed her secondary education privately in Edinburgh. Her best-known novel *Penny Plain* appeared in 1920 but she enjoyed considerable success in the 1920s and 1930s. At the end of her life she published a reflective family biography which is an important source on her brother, John.[15]

Finlay D. Buchan left the HGS as Dux Boy in 1979.

(James) Walter Buchan MA LLB (1882–1953) became Town Clerk of Peebles and edited *The History of Peeblesshire* in three volumes in 1925. He was also Head of the Commercial Bank (and brother of John and Anna).

John Buchan (1875–1940) attended HBGS between 1888 and 1892, but for him the School was 'only a minor episode'. In 1890 he took the Classical course with James Caddell, finding it 'liberating'. Caddell had a lasting influence on Buchan, who developed a real enthusiasm for Classical Literature and Latin.[16] He won a bursary to Glasgow University and then attended Oxford University. He unveiled the original War Memorial in 1921 and presented the prizes with his sister Anna in 1932. He was the first Honorary President of the Grammar School Club (the forerunner to the FP Association). He held a University seat in the House of Commons for the Conservatives (1927–35). He was created First Baron Tweedsmuir of Elsfield in 1935, and appointed Chancellor of the University of Edinburgh in 1937.[17] He was Governor-General of Canada, 1935–37.[18] He was a major writer, novelist and historian. *The Thirty-Nine Steps*, 'the absolute essence of a page-turner', was published in 1915 and has never been out of print.[19]

W.G. Buchan (1916–2004) was Director of the Scottish Chamber of Commerce. He was Founders' Day Speaker in 1981.

Stephen Bull attended HBGS from 1951, leaving as Dux in 1958. He took first place in the Glasgow University Bursary Competition.

Alan Bulloch (b. 1977) attended School in 1989–95 and brother Gordon Bulloch (b. 1975) attended HBGS in 1987–93. Both won national caps for Scotland at rugby and Gordon, who left School in 1993, captained his country and achieved a Young Achiever Hutcheson Award in 1999. Gordon retired from the sport in 2010 after gaining 75 caps for Scotland and for the British Lions. Both were sons of FP, James Bulloch, born 1943.

John Burgess left HBGS in 1861 as Dux.

Robert Burgess left HBGS in 1866 as Dux.

John Barclay Burke (1924–83) left HBGS to begin his banking career in 1941. He became General Manager of the National Commercial Bank of Scotland and Managing Director of the Royal Bank of Scotland (1970–82) and The Royal Bank of Scotland Group (1976–82). He was chair of Loganair Ltd. He was the (ninth) Founders' Day Speaker in 1969. He was killed in a climbing accident.

Joan Bryson Burnie (b. 1941) attended the School between 1947 and 1959. She has been a columnist in the *Daily Record* since 1979. She was formerly Associate Editor.[20] She was given a lifetime achievement award at the Scottish Press Awards in 2008.

(Prof.) Alistair Stanyer Burns was born in 1958 and left HBGS in 1975. He has been Professor of Old Age Psychiatry and Hon. Consultant Psychiatrist at Manchester University since 1992. He became National Clinical Director for Dementia in 2010. He has published a significant number of medical papers.

(Prof.) John William Cairns (b. 1955) has been Professor of Legal History, University of Edinburgh, 2000–12 and Professor of Civil Law since 2012.[21]

Janette Calder (née Ritchie) attended the HGGS from 1942 until 1955. She was a Badminton internationalist and a coach in Canada.

Jessie S.N. Calder (née Alexander) (1872–1918) attended the HGGS from 1876 until leaving as Dux in 1889. She emigrated to USA in 1899 but was killed in a railway accident in Lexington, New York, in 1918.

Geoffrey M. Cameron (1941–95) left HBGS in 1959. After five years in journalism he spent thirty years in public service broadcasting and is remembered best for 'Good Morning, Scotland'. He was Editor for Current Affairs, Radio Scotland.

John Cameron (1883–1950) was born on Mull, the son of a carpenter. He took an MA (1904) and LLB (1908) at Glasgow University and became a solicitor. He became a member of the Faculty of Procurators of Glasgow in 1921 and took a PhD in Celtic Law in 1935. He was President of An Comunn Gaidhealach, Glasgow Highland Society and Clan Cameron Society.

Katrina Cameron left School in 1999 and was a member of Team Scotland Hockey which competed in the Commonwealth Games in Melbourne in 2006 and Delhi in 2010.

Stella Cameron (1909–90) left the HGGS as Dux in 1927. She worked as an Art Teacher.

(Dr) William Ross Cameron (b. 1957) has been Medical Director, NHS Borders, since 2003.[22]

(Prof. Sir) Donald Campbell CBE (1930–2004) left School in 1947. He was Professor of Anaesthetics, University of Glasgow, 1976–92; then Emeritus, Dean of Faculty of Medicine, 1987–91, and President of the Royal College of Physicians and Surgeons of Glasgow, 1992–4. He was awarded a G and THA in 2003.

James L. Campbell left School in 1989 as Boys' Dux. He studied Chemical Engineering at Cambridge University.

Neil L.A. Campbell left HBGS as Dux in 1911. He became a Church of Scotland minister. In 1925 he took over the charge of Chapel of Garioch.

(Dr) Thomas Simpson Campbell (b. 1887) left School as Dux in 1905. He took BSc (1909) and MB ChB (1910) at Glasgow University and practised Medicine in Melbourne.

(Dr) Isaac Camrass MBE (1909–2007) left School in 1926 and went into Medicine. He became Head of the Hadassah-Hebrew University's Medical Centre's Department of Occupational Health in 1971.

Innis R. Carmichael (1925–84) was Dux Medallist in Mathematics at HBGS and became General Manager (Administration) and Secretary of Scottish Amicable Life Assurance Society.

(Prof.) Katherine Carr left HGGS in 1958. She became Professor of Anatomy at Queen's University, Belfast, 1985. She became Emeritus Professor at Queen's in 2006.

Ronald Carr left School in 1958. He became Professor with the Open University in Hong Kong.

Catherine (Kate) Carson (née Nisbet) (1933–2001) left the HGGS in 1952. She became a speech therapist and a founder member of Scottish Opera.

William Steven Carswell was born in 1929. He was Chairman, General Trustees of the Church of Scotland, 1999–2003.[23]

Ben Carter was born in 1970. He became Sales and Marketing Director at Johnston and Johnston.[24]

Gordon (Fred) Casely (b. 1943) is a journalist and heraldist; Baron-Baillie of Miltonhaven; personal herald to the Chief of Irvine. He was Press Officer for the Commonwealth Games Council for Scotland and member of the Scotland team at the Commonwealth Games in Auckland, 1990.[25] He gave the Founders' Day Address in 2005.

Marjory Cassells (née Macsween) left School in 1974. She became a translator at the Ministry of Defence in London.

Daniel Cattrell left HBGS in 1858 as Dux. He died early in 1861.

George Buchanan Chalmers CMG (1929–90) left School in 1947 and joined the Diplomatic Service, serving in Russia, Indonesia, Thailand, South Korea, Israel and USA. He was Consul General in Chicago. He retired in 1982.

(William) Stewart Chalmers (b. 1907) trained as a CA and played football for five seasons with Queen's Park, before playing as a professional with Hearts, Manchester United and Dunfermline, retiring in 1938. He played once for Scotland (against Ireland in 1929). He was one of the last players to be capped while still an amateur.

(Prof.) Helen Elizabeth Chambers (b. 1947) left HGGS in 1965 as Dux. She became Emeritus Professor of German, St Andrews University and was previously Senior Lecturer in German at Leeds University. She has written and edited a number of publications.[26]

Douglas Cheah left as Boys' Dux in 2008. He scored 100% in all his A-Level papers. He continued his studies at Christ Church College, Oxford University.

Grace E.M. Cheah left School in 2013 as Girls' Dux. She is studying Business Management and Psychology at Glasgow University.

James Robertson Christie OBE (1866–1932) was a pupil at HBGS from 1878 until 1882. He was an Advocate at the Scottish Bar, 1891, made KC in 1913 and became Clerk of Justiciary in Scotland in 1918. He was elected FRSE in 1932.

David Charles Clapham was born in 1958. He became a solicitor. He has been a part-time Immigration Judge since 2001 and part-time Sheriff since 2007.[27]

Alex(ander) S. Clark (b. 1943) left HBGS in 1960 and became a gynaecologist.

(Robert) Brodie Clark (b. 1951) CBE became a consultant on security, risk and border operations.

C. Robert Clark (1970–94) was Boys' Dux and First in the Glasgow University Competition in 1988. He took a First at Oxford and became a solicitor but tragically drowned at the age of twenty-four.

Sally R. Clark left School in 1996 as Girls' Dux. She studied French and German at Glasgow University.

(Dr) J. Graham Clarkson (1924–2012) left School in 1942. His pioneering work with Medicare in Canada transformed the health care of the country. As a result he became special adviser to the Canadian Government. He achieved a G and THA in 2007.

(Prof.) Douglas Clelland left School in 1963. He became Emeritus Professor of Architecture and Urban Design at John Moore's University, Liverpool.

Stuart Clumpas left School in 1976. He became Britain's largest music promoter and created T in the Park. He was awarded a G and THA in 2001. He moved to New Zealand in 2001 where he is a Director and Shareholder of the Vector Arena in Auckland.

Thomas Cockburn held the post of Glasgow Corporation Chemist and City Analyst, 1935–45. He was the author of scientific papers. He died in 1961.

(Dr) William F. Cockburn (1923–2011) attended School from 1934 to 1941. He gained FCH in Organic Chemistry. He later took charge of senior policy development at the Ministry of State for Science and Technology in

Ottawa. He was Science Counsellor at Canadian embassies in Bonn and Washington DC.

Ben(zion) Cohen (b. 1915) left HBGS in 1932. He became a Harley Street ENT surgeon. He was awarded FRCS.

Brenda G. Cohen left School in 1994 as Girls' Dux. She studied Physics at Oxford University.

Lisa Cohen (née Tuck) left School in 1978. She became a businesswoman who developed high-profile innovative communication approaches in health. She set up XL Communications in 2006. She was awarded a G and THA in 2008.

Anni Cole-Hamilton (née Watt) was born in 1949. She was the Founder (in 1999) of the Moray Firth School, and Principal, from 2002–2010, of the Moray Firth Tutorial College.[28]

(Rev.) John M. Condie MA BD (1907–83) was Dux of the School and Classics and School Captain in 1925. He was President of the School Council, Captain of Bruce House and War Memorial scholar. He was a journalist and teacher. He died in Otago, New Zealand.

David W. Connell left School in 1998 as Boys' Dux and took FCH in Physiology from Cambridge; he qualified in Medicine from Oxford in 2004.

Brian Conway took a Bachelor of Education at Calgary University (1980–84) and a Bachelor of Law at Dalhousie University, Halifax (1984–87). He has practised as a barrister and solicitor in Calgary. He has refereed, coached and administered rugby in Canada. In 2005 he was appointed by World Rugby as a Judicial Appeal Officer for the World Series Sevens event in Las Vegas.

Alistair Cook left School in 1977 and practised as a CA for nineteen years. He then took up the ministry and is Minister of Lylesland Parish Church in Paisley.

Davida Cook (née McGeachy) left School in 1968. She became Headmistress of the Junior School of St Columba's Kilmacolm, retiring in 2012.

Gordon Bower Cosh was born in 1939 and left School in 1957. He was a Scottish golf international (1964–9) and played in the 1965 European Team Championships and the Walker Cup the same year, when he twice defeated an American in singles play and helped Britain to achieve a tie. He won the Scottish Amateur at Muirfield in 1968 and was runner-up in 1965.

James Cowan (1867–1963) attended HBGS, 1876–81. He fought with the RA during World War 1. He worked for Templeton and Co., carpet manufacturers. He became an authority on old Glasgow.[29]

William Christie Cowan CBE (1878–1950) took a BL from Glasgow University in 1902. He became a solicitor and senior partner in the firm of Honeyman, Henderson and Christie Cowan.

(Dr) Derek Cox was born in 1945. He became Director of Public Health, Dumfries and Galloway Health Board, in 1999.[30]

Ethel Craig left the HGGS in 1923. She became a painter of still life, topographical subjects and landscapes. She exhibited regularly at the RSA between 1932 and 1944. She died in 1991.

Lillian Craig (née McNab) left HGGS in 1943. She became Vice-Principal, Department of Education, Northern Ireland.

Mary A.B. Craig left the School as Dux in 1974. She worked for British Gas.

(Prof.) Robert C. Crawford was born in 1959 and left School as Dux in 1977 and achieved a G and THA in 1997. He won the Logan Prize for the most distinguished Arts graduate at Glasgow University and received a Snell Exhibition to Oxford University. He has been Professor of Modern Scottish Literature, since 1995, and Bishop Wardlaw Professor of Poetry, at the School of English, University of St Andrews.[31] He has produced a number of publications.

Robert (Bert) Cromar (1931–2007) began a career with Queen's Park Football Club which lasted over ten years and took him to its captaincy and presidency. His versatility led to being capped for five Scottish amateur international matches where he played in five different positions. He epitomised the Queen's Park motto – Laudere causa ludendi.[32] He was General Manager of the Bank of Scotland and was appointed Depute Chair of the School Board of Governors in 2000.

(Dr) Harry Crone (1918–2002) left HBGS in 1935. He was badly wounded in World War 2. He returned to complete a BSc in Chemistry at Glasgow University. He became Chief Chemist at Templeton Carpets and a FRSC. He was Director of the Glasgow City Mission for twenty-five years. He served almost twenty years on Court of Strathclyde University.

William D. Crouch left School in 2005 as Boys' Dux and went on to Cambridge University.

Adrian Cruden left School in 1981 and was employed by the Joseph Rowntree Foundation as Joint-Head of Human Resources. He unsuccessfully contested Bury South for the Liberal Democrats in 1992 and Dewsbury for the Green Party in 2010.

William Cullen (1867–1948) left School in 1883 and became a chemist and metallurgist. He managed the largest explosives works in the world in South Africa until 1924. He was President of the Institute of Chemical Engineers (1937–9) and of the Chemical Industry Society (1941–3).

Robert Currie Cumming was born in 1921. He was formerly Executive Director, Royal Bank of Scotland Group PLC and Chairman, English Speaking Union.[33]

Ian W. Cunningham (1912–91) left the HBGS as joint Dux in 1930. He took MA (Hons) BL from Glasgow University and became Depute Director of Education.

(Sheriff) Douglas James Cusine (b. 1946) has been Sheriff, Grampian, Highland and Islands at Aberdeen, 2001–2011.[34]

(Dr) John Lamont Cameron Dall OBE attended School in Sixth Year (1947–48) He was a Consultant Geriatrician and chaired the Glasgow Division of the BMA, 1985–86.

Alexander Davidson (1832–1904) left HBGS in 1845 as joint-Dux. He was minister of the United Free Church of West Kilbirnie for thirty-two years.

Euan Davidson left School in 1975. He began his career as a corporate lawyer. Between 2000 and 2006 he was Director and Chief Executive of the Prince's Trust Scotland

Jane Moyes Davidson (1881–1969) left HGGS as Dux in 1898. She became Headteacher of Eastmuir (Special) School, Glasgow.

(Dr) Margaret Davidson (1902–80) left the HGGS as Dux in 1920. She took a degree in Medicine from Glasgow University and became a GP.

Deidre Davies (née Gardiner) (1949–2001) left HGGS in 1967. She became a partner in PricewaterhouseCoopers. She founded the Daisy Foundation in memory of her sister, Elizabeth Taylor, School Captain 1967/8, who died of breast cancer in 1988. She was awarded a G and THA in 2000.

(Prof.) Phyllis Mary Deane (1918–2012) left School in 1936 and was first in Economics at Glasgow University. She worked in the Colonial Office before joining the Department of Applied Economics at Cambridge University in 1950. She became Professor of Economic History at Cambridge University, Editor of *The Economic Journal* and President of the Royal Economic Society. She was awarded a G and THA in 2003.

(James) Allan Denholm CBE (b. 1936) left School in 1953 and trained as a CA and was Secretary of William Grant & Sons Ltd, 1968 to 1996. He became a Director of Abbey National plc and President of the Institute of CAs in Scotland.[35]

(Rev.) David William Denniston (b. 1956) has been Minister, St Cuthberts, Edinburgh, since 2008. He was formerly Minister of Ruchazie, Glasgow, 1981–86; Kennoway, Fife, 1986–96, and North Church, Perth, 1996–2008.[36]

Anish P. Deshpande left School in 2008 as joint-Boys' Dux having scored 100% in all his A-Level Physics papers. He continued his English studies at Trinity College, Cambridge.

(Dr) Alison M. Deveson MA PhD (née Richards) left the HGGS as Dux in 1959. She became a local historian and author in Hampshire.

Robert Scott Dewar (1880–1939) left HBGS in 1897 as Dux. He graduated MA from Glasgow University in 1901 and then In Medicine in 1905 and went into practice in Govan. He was mentioned in dispatches twice for special and distinguished war service in the Salonica campaign. He was commissioned Captain in the RAMC in 1916.

Andrew Dick left HBGS in 1959 and emigrated to New Zealand in 1960. He took up a computer programming career which included work for Air New Zealand, Eastern Airlines, British Airways and JetBlue (Miami)

(Rev.) Charles Hill Dick (1875–1952) attended the HBGS, 1888–92. He took MA in 1898 and BD in 1901, both from Glasgow University. He was chosen by John Buchan to be his Chaplain when Buchan was Lord High Commissioner to the Church of Scotland Assembly. He wrote a number of publications. He was minister of St Mary's UF Church in Moffat.

(Dr) John Carson Dick (1911–67) became Senior Lecturer in Pathology at Glasgow University and was in charge of the Pathology Department at Stobhill Hospital, Glasgow.

(Dr) William Carson Dick (1941–95) graduated from Glasgow University in 1965 and became a distinguished Rheumatologist. He was awarded the MRCP in 1968. He became Reader in Rheumatology at Newcastle, 1979.

Murray Dickie OBE (1924–95) left School in 1940. He was a Scottish tenor opera singer and director, who established a career in Britain, Austria and Italy in the 1960s. He was a permanent member of the Vienna State Opera. In addition to his extensive stage work he was also a prolific recording artist. He was one of the most admired lyric and character tenors of his day. His older brother, William, was also an opera singer.

Robert Dickie (1919–2014) graduated MBChB from Glasgow University in 1942. He became Medical Officer in Nigeria and British Cameroons, 1943–55. He was Director of Medical Services in Sarawak, 1964–67 and Director of Hospital Services for New Zealand from 1967 until retirement in 1980.

(Rev.) (Matthew) Scott Dickson (b. 1866) took his MA in 1890 and became minister at Old Monkland.

Ailsa Jane Di Emidio (née Carmichael) left School in 1986. She took LLB (Hons) from Glasgow University and was admitted to the Faculty of Advocates in 1993. She became a QC in 2008.

Jean McInnes Dixon left the HGGS as Dux in 1919.

Rachel Dodds left School in 2009 as Girls' Dux.

Cherrie D. Donald (1913–2005) left HGGS as Dux in 1931 and took an MA in English Language and Literature from Glasgow University in 1935. She was Treasurer of the FP Club from 1952 until 1963.

Ian M. Donaldson left School in 1983 and joined the Diplomatic Service, serving in Indonesia. He was Head of the Foreign Office's Environment Section but promoted to become Deputy UK Permanent Representative to the UN Conference on Disarmament in Geneva, 1999–2004.

Agnes M. Dougans (née Martin) left HGGS as Dux in 1944. Her brother, James D. Martin, was Dux in HBGS in 1942. She taught Mathematics.

William Douglas left HBGS in 1842 as Dux.

(Dr) Eileen D. Downie (née Flynn) left HGGS as joint-Dux in 1951. She became a biochemist.

William Beatson Drummond was born in 1890 and left HBGS as Dux in 1907. He qualified in Medicine at Glasgow University in 1912 and served in the RAMC during World War I. He changed his name to Douglas-Drummond in 1920. He became a GP in Manchester before emigrating to South Africa in 1926.

Lorna Drummond (b. 1967) graduated from Glasgow University and Sidney Sussex College, Cambridge. She became a QC (Scotland) in 2011.

Oliver Dryer (1881–1949) attended HBGS, 1896–98, and took an MA from Glasgow University in 1902. He was General Secretary of the International Fellowship of Reconciliation, 1921–28.

(2nd Lieut.) William M. Duff HLI left Kilmarnock Academy and joined HBGS in the Fourth Year. He was School Captain in his final year. He enrolled for Medicine at Glasgow University but was killed on service in France in November 1916.

(Prof.) William Duguid (1927–2000) left HBGS in 1945. He became Pathologist in Chief, Montreal General Hospital.

William N. Duguid left School in 1978 as Boys' Dux. He graduated BA from Oxford University in Classics and Philosophy. After a career in banking, IT and Shell he has become a creative writer.

Nan Dunbar left the HGGS as joint-Dux in 1946.

Jessie Galloway Duncan (née Cameron) attended the HGGS from 1911 until 1914, leaving as Dux.

Margaret Dundas (née Hood) left School in 1968 and became Assistant Principal of Borders' College in Galashiels.

(Prof.) Jack David Dunitz (b. 1923) left School in 1940. He became Professor of Chemical Crystallography at the Swiss Federal Institute of Technology, Zurich, 1957–90. He was awarded FRS in 1974.

J. Alan Dunlop left HBGS in 1975. He became the Director of the Center for American and International Law.

(Prof.) Ernest McMurchie Dunlop (1893–1969) left HBGS in 1910 to study Medicine at Glasgow. He was awarded the Brunton Memorial Prize for being the most distinguished graduate in Medicine in his year in 1916. He had a distinguished war, too, being awarded the MC. He was Professor of Bacteriology, University of Durham, 1932–59. He was elected FRSE, 1944.

(Prof. Dr) James Douglas Graham Dunn (b. 1939) left the School in 1957. He was Lightfoot Professor of Divinity, University of Durham, 1990–2003; now Emeritus. He was the Founders' Day Speaker in 1987. He was elected a Fellow of the British Academy in 2006. He produced a number of publications.

Fiona A.I. Duthie left School in 2000 as joint-Girls' Dux.

Marguerite Morton Dyer (b. 1885) took her MA at Glasgow University in 1906. She became a pioneering missionary, holding office at the Tabeetha Mission in Jaffa.

Robert M. Easson left HBGS in 1960 as Dux. He became an electrical engineer.

John Edgar (b. 1876) attended HBGS, 1884–93. He took FCH at Glasgow University and a BA from Oxford in 1915. He lectured in History at Cairo University and became Professor of History at Cape Town, 1903–11. He was Editor of the *Transvaal Leader,* 1911–14. He was Senior Inspector of English in the Egyptian Educational Department, 1914–32. He was awarded Order of the Nile, Third Class, in 1931. (He was a friend of John Buchan, the author.)

Eileen Edmondson (née King) left HGGS as Dux in 1952. She was awarded a FCH in Classics at St Andrews University. She taught at Bradford Girls' Grammar and became a Bible translator.

William A. Edward (1916–2005) became an all-round cricketer playing for Clydesdale. He scored 3,284 runs and took 343 wickets in his first-class cricket career. He represented Scotland from 1947 until 1955 and made a best score of 90 against Ireland in 1950.

(Dr) Janet H. Edwards (née Blackwood) left the HGGS as Dux in 1925.

Harold S.M. Elborn (1915–93) left the HBGS as Dux in 1933. He was a Classics scholar who attained a senior position with the Inland Revenue.

(Rev.) (Lance-Corp.) Gilbert Wilkie Elliott (1884–1918) left HBGS in 1901 as Dux. He graduated with an MA at Glasgow University in 1905 and became Free Church minister of St Margaret's, Forfar. He joined the Royal Scots and was killed in action in France in March 1918.

Richard Emanuel MBE left School in 1984 and gained a G and THA in 1997. He proved to be a dynamic and ubiquitous entrepreneur, known for his mobile telephone company DX Communications. He became a millionaire when he sold out.

(Dr) John Emslie (1936–2000) left School in 1953. He became Deputy Director at the Scottish Centre for Infection and Environmental Health at Ruchill Hospital in Glasgow. He retired in 1995.

(Prof.) Colin Espie left the School in 1974. He became Emeritus Professor of Clinical Psychology at Glasgow University. He works in the Nuffield Department of Clinical Neuroscience at Oxford University (Professor of Sleep Medicine).

Graham Everett was born in 1934 and left HBGS in 1951. He won the Scottish Mile Championships eight times (seven of these consecutively) between 1955 and 1963. He set Scottish records for the Mile and Two Miles, and competed for Scotland in the 1958 Empire and Commonwealth Games in Cardiff.

J. Douglas Fairley QC left School in 1985. He won the Theodore David-Lowe Prize for Public Law and the MacCormick Prize for the most distinguished graduate in Law in Glasgow University, 1988–89. He was called to the Bar in 1999. He has been a full time Advocate Depute since 2011 and Queen's Counsel since 2012.[37]

(Rev.) Ian C.M. Fairweather MA BD (1920–2003) left HBGS in 1938 as Dux. He became Honorary Associate Minister at Glasgow Cathedral and served on the Scottish Joint Committee on Religious Education.

David S. Ferguson left School in 1990 as Boys' Dux. He took FCH In Mathematics and Computation from Oxford University.

Alexander Watt Donald Ferguson (1911–70) left HBGS as Dux in 1928. He became Secretary/Director of the Central News Agency in South Africa.

(Dr) Margaret Ferguson was born in 1962 and left HGGS in 1973. She became Director of a pioneering 'Languages for All' scheme at the University of York. Her parents were both Staff members.

James Ferrie left HBGS in 1845 as joint-Dux.

Eileen Fidelo (née McCallum) MBE (b. 1936) left School in 1953 and is now regarded as one of the finest actresses produced by Scotland. She was chosen as Scotswoman of the Year in 2010 for her work in raising awareness of Duchenne Muscular Dystrophy.

James Wilkie Findlay, Professor of Theology (b. 1885), took his MA at Glasgow University in 1907. He became Principal of Mukden Theological College,[38] Manchuria, in 1935.

Jane (Sheena) Finlay became Deputy Chair of the Equal Opportunities Commission in 1980 and represented the UK at UNESCO and the UN.

(Dr) Alastair Alexander Finlayson (1917–2009) left School in 1936 and qualified in Medicine. He spent his career of some forty years working in Psychiatry. He was involved in founding the Canadian FP Association.

(Dr) Isabel D.B. Finlayson (née Simpson) (1916–2006) was Dux of HGGS in 1933. She became a senior educational psychologist in the Glasgow Education Department.

John Fisher left HBGS in 1847 as Dux.

Adam Fleming MA (b. 1980) attended the School between 1989 and 1998. He took FCH in Geography at Oxford University. He has worked in journalism for the *Herald* newspaper in Glasgow, the *Daily Record* and STV. He became political correspondent for the BBC. He gave the Address at Founders' Day in 2007.

(Dr) John Fleming (1921–2010) was Vice-Captain, and Captain of rugby at the School, leaving in 1940. As a GP he set up the Clydebank Health Centre and looked after the workforce of Singer sewing machines, Turner's asbestos factory and John Brown's shipyards.

(2nd Lieutenant) Joseph Fleming left HBGS as Dux and First Bursar in 1912. He won the John Clark bursary at Glasgow University and was a student of the Theological College of the Baptist Church. He was killed in action in France in September 1916.

(Dr) Rachel L. Fleurence (née Shroot) left School as Girls' Dux in 1989. She became Programme Director, Science, at the Patient-Centred Outcomes Research Institute (PCORI).

Eileen D. Flynn left HGGS as joint-Dux in 1951.

Michael E. Ford left School in 2004 as Boys' Dux and took FCH in Materials Science at Oxford University.

Jean R. Forrest OBE left HGGS in 1921. She was Senior Dentistry Officer in the Ministry of Health, researching into fluoride. She died in December 1982.

Samuel Forrest (1913–79) left the HBGS as Dux in 1931.

Calum Forrester left HGS in 2004. He played professional rugby with

Glasgow Warriors, 2006–08. He played for Scotland at Under-18, Under-19 and Under-21. He is the Head Coach at Ayr Rugby Club. He was awarded a G and THA (Young Achiever) in 2009.

Lynn S. Fotheringham left School in 1986 as Dux. She gained FCH in Classics from Edinburgh University in 1991 and completed her PhD in Philadelphia. She became a Classics lecturer at Nottingham University.

(Dr) Jesme Fox MBChB MBA (née Baird) left School in 1984 and achieved a G and THA in 2009. She became a cancer specialist and is Medical Director of the Roy Castle Cancer Foundation. She gave the Address at Founders' Day in 2011.

Wilma Ann Frame left HGGS in 1971 as Dux.

(Dr) Jonathan Frank left HBGS in 1970. He was appointed Associate Professor of Computer Information Systems at Suffolk University, Boston.

Alexander Fraser left HBGS in 1892 as Dux.

Daniel Fraser left HBGS in 1831 as Dux. He took his MA (1839) and LLD (1858) from Glasgow University and became a Classical Tutor in Airedale College, Bradford.

Harry Fraser (1924–99) left HBGS in 1940. He was a member of the FP Rugby XV for eleven years from 1947–58, captaining the side in season 1955/6, and acting as Match Secretary for the Club from 1947–52.

(Rev.) Kenneth M. Fraser left the HBGS as joint-Dux in 1959.

(Lady) Marion Anne Fraser (née Forbes) (b. 1932) left School in 1950. She was Chair of the Board of Christian Aid, 1990–7; Chair of the Scottish Association of Mental Health; Lord High Commissioner, then HM High Commissioner, General Assembly of the Church of Scotland, 1994–5. She was awarded the Order of the Thistle, 1996. She was the Founders' Day Speaker in 1994 and awarded a G and THA in 1997 for her major contribution to the School.[39]

Air Vice Marshal Sir Matthew Brown Frew (1895–1974) was a senior officer in the RAF and a World War 1 flying ace credited with twenty-three aerial victories. His awards included a KBE (1948), CB, DSO and Bar and MC and Bar.

Wilma Frew (née Arthur) left HGGS in 1957. She was installed as Moderator of the General Assembly of the United Reform Church (generally regarded as the Church of Scotland's sister Church south of the Border) in 1998.

Bernard Derek Frutin (b. 1944) MBE attended HBGS Primary 5 and 6 in 1953–54 before going on to Kelvinside Academy. He became famous for his inventions.

Kate Fulton (née Audrey Matheson Craig Brown) (1936–2005) left HGGS in 1950. She became an actress and author and the wife of Rikki Fulton, a well-known Scottish actor.

Alexander William Galbraith won Dux prize at HBGS in 1909 and took his MA from Glasgow University in 1914.

(Baron) Myer Galpern (1903–93) was educated at HBGS in 1917–18) and Glasgow University before working as a house-furnisher. He was a Labour councillor for Shettleston from 1932 and became Lord Provost of Glasgow in 1958–59. He became Labour MP for Shettleston, 1959–79 and Deputy Speaker of the House of Commons, 1974–79. He was knighted in 1960 and made a life peer in 1979. He was a member of the Court of Glasgow University and a Governor of the Royal College of Science.

Iain Derek Gardiner was born in 1933 and left School in 1950. He has been a Chartered Surveyor, since 1957 and Senior Partner, Souter & Jaffrey, Chartered Surveyors, 1986–95.[40]

Craig L. Gardner left HBGS in 1975 as Dux. He became an accountant.

Olivia Garrett (née Giles) OBE left School in 1982 and until 2002 was a commercial property partner. Meningitis led to the amputation of her lower legs and arms. She is now a prominent fundraiser, having founded the charity '500 Miles'. She was awarded an honorary degree from Glasgow University for her achievements. She gave the Founders' Day Address in 2004 and was awarded a G and THA in the same year.

Kathleen Mary Evelyn Garscadden (1897–1991) worked for the BBC for nearly forty years between 1923 and 1960 as presenter, broadcaster, programme organiser and producer. She was a legendary character in Scottish broadcasting.[41]

Anne Garside left the HGGS as Dux in 1958 and took an MA in Russian Studies. She became a PR/Publications Director at Peabody Institute in Baltimore. She has written books and articles (especially on the Kennedys).

Recently she has been a history tutor at Fishguard Community Learning Centre.

(Dr) Douglas G. Garvie OBE left HBGS in 1950 as Dux. He became an occupational physician. He received his OBE for 'services to the employment of disabled people'.

Douglas de R. Gentleman was born in 1954 and left HBGS in 1971. He was awarded the Brunton Medal for the most distinguished graduate in Medicine, 1977–78. He was Head of Surgical Neurology, University of Dundee, 1995–97, and Consultant in charge of the Centre for Brain Injury Rehabilitation since 1997.

Sheila L.M. Gibson (née Browning) of the class of 1954 won the Brunton Memorial Prize for the most distinguished graduate in Medicine in 1962 at Glasgow University.

Thomas Gibson, a pupil at HBGS from 1886–88, became a stockbroker in Johannesburg in South Africa.

Alexander Gilbert left HBGS in 1848 as Dux.

Duncan Gilbert left HBGS in 1839 as Dux.

(Prof.) Fiona Jane Gilbert (née Davidson) MBChB DMRB FRCP FRCR (b. 1956) left School in 1973 and achieved a G and THA in 2006. She gave the Address at Founders' Day in 2009. She was Professor of Radiology and Head of Department, Aberdeen University, 1996–2006; Head, Imaging Resolution Programme, 2006–11; and Professor of Radiology, University of Cambridge since 2011.[42]

Jean M. Gilchrist left the HGGS in 1916 as Dux. She studied Medicine.

(Dr) Thomas Gilfillan (1922–2011) left School in 1940 having won a scholarship to HBGS. He qualified in Medicine in 1945 and was consultant at Hull Royal Infirmary, 1953–87.

(Dr) Robert Dick Gillespie (1897–1945) was Dux in the School in 1915 and won many prizes at Glasgow University when graduating in Medicine in 1920. He also won a Gold Medal for his doctorate in Medicine in 1924. He was physician for Psychological Medicine and Lecturer in the subject at Guy's, London, taking over from Sir Maurice Baring. He published widely and gained an international reputation. He was an Air Commodore, RAFVR.

(Prof.) Donald J.M. Gillies left School in 1977 and worked for twenty years in secondary schools before moving into Higher Education in 2005. In 2014 he was appointed Head of Education at the UWS.

Gillian Gillman (née Guzzan) (1961–2013) left the School in 1979 and set up the very successful After-School Club in 1995.

Lara M. R. Gilmour left the School in 2012 as Girls' Dux.

Paul Gilroy (b. 1962) became a QC (barrister) in 2006.

Allan Girdwood left the School in 1987 and gained a FCH in Classics at Glasgow and, as Snell Exhibitioner, a DPhil at Balliol, Oxford. He is now Head of the Classics Department at Albyn School, Aberdeen.

(Dr) Michael Golombok left the School in 1976. He became a principal scientist with Shell Exploration and Production.

(Prof.) Susan Golombok left HGGS in 1972 and became the Professor of Family Research at Cambridge University.

Paul Scott Goodman left School in 1974 (class of 1975). He has become a composer and songwriter based in New York. He has written several musicals and won a number of awards.

Adam J.H. Gordon left School in 2006 as Boys' Dux.

Andrew E.J. Gordon left School in 1986 as Dux Boy.

Laura Gordon (née Groden) left the HGGS in 1983 and became a leading corporate lawyer. She was the first Director of the Edinburgh-Glasgow Collaboration Initiative. Now she is CEO of Corporate Connections International.

(Dr) Robert McIntyre Gordon (1899–1983) attended HBGS, 1911–16. He was a flying ace in World War 1, awarded the DFC. After the war he became a doctor, and served in the RAMC in World War 2, when he was awarded the DSO and George Medal.

(Prof) Robert (Rab) Barclay Goudie (1928–2004) left School in 1946 as Dux and came First in the Glasgow University Bursary Competition. He won the Brunton Award for the most distinguished student in his medical class of 220. As Professor of Pathology at the Glasgow Royal Infirmary he proved a talented physician and medical researcher. He was awarded an FRSE.

Alan Gouk (b. 1939) attended HBGS from 1948 to 1956 before studying architecture in Glasgow and London and psychology and philosophy at Edinburgh University. His paintings are in numerous collections including the Tate Gallery, the Arts Council, the Scottish Arts Council and the Calouste Gulbenkian. He is widely admired and respected as a pre-eminent abstract painter and has written widely on art.

(Dr) June I. Gow MA left the School in 1950. She became Professor of American History in the University of British Columbia. She has been a significant benefactor in upgrading and modernising the Library, opening the Kingarth Street Library on 10 March 2008.

Alison Graham left School in 1977 and since 1980 has been a member of the Foreign and Commonwealth Office of HM Diplomatic Service.

W. Gordon Graham MC (1920–2015) left School in 1937, graduated from Glasgow University in 1940 and became a newspaper correspondent. He was awarded an MC and Bar in World War 2. He was International Sales Manager of McGraw Hill Book Company in New York, then ran the company's business in the UK, Europe, Middle East and Africa. From 1975 until retirement in 1990 he was Chair and CE of Butterworths, legal and scientific publishers.

(Dr) Kerr Graham attended the HBGS from 1961 until 1969. He was a Curling internationalist. He took up Medicine and became a GP in Canada.

Mary C. Graham (née Biggar) attended HGGS between 1896 and 1900, when she left as Dux. She took her MA in 1903 and in the following year became the first woman (and fourth person) to be awarded a Diploma in Education (with distinction in French and German) by Glasgow University. She became a teacher in Polmont.

Fiona E. Grant left School in 1999 as Girls' Dux.

(Dr) James Grant left School in 2006 and studied at Glasgow and Cambridge Universities. In 2014 he completed a DPhil in Law at Oxford University. He was appointed as a Lecturer in Law at Sheffield University and is the School of Law's Director of International Affairs.

(Dr) Ethel Marian Gray CBE (née Rennie) (1923–2008) left School in 1939 and became a pioneering educationist. She was founding Principal of Craigie College of Education, Ayr, from 1963 until 1975. She was the first woman on the Court of Heriot-Watt University, 1974, and Vice-Chair of Queen's College, Glasgow, 1980.

Winifred H. B. Greenwood (née McBride) (1929–97) left HGGS as joint-Dux in 1947. She took charge of the Department of Russian in the University of Dublin in 1965. Her mother, Nellie Baird, was Dux of HGGS in 1910.

Kristina Greig left HGS in 2008. She became a martial arts expert and the first British female Tukido Champion.

Matilda L. Greig, daughter of the Rector, Ken Greig, left School in 2010 as Girls' Dux. She completed a BA in History from Cambridge University in 2013.

Iain William Grimmond was born in 1955. He became a CA, and General Treasurer, Church of Scotland, since 2005. He was formerly Director of Finance at Erskine Hospital, 1981–2004.[43]

(Dr) Fiona H. Groom (née Danskin) was the most distinguished Medicine graduate in Glasgow University in 1984–5. She became a GP in Surrey.

David I. Guthrie left School as Dux in 1980. He became a freelance writer/editor specialising in economics and current affairs.

(Dr) Sydney Haase (1912–93) left the HBGS as joint Dux in 1930. He was a physician who lived in Newton Mearns. (His nephew, Matthew L. Levine, was Dux in 1987).

(Prof.) W. Allan Hamilton left HBGS in 1954. He became Chair of Molecular and Cell Biology at Aberdeen University. He was awarded FRSE in 1980. He is now Emeritus Professor of Microbiology at Aberdeen. He is a noted piper.

(Dr) Kenneth Hamilton left School in 1981 and took degrees from Glasgow University and Balliol College, Oxford. He became Reader of Music at Birmingham University. In 2012 he became Professor of Music at Cardiff University. He is an internationally acclaimed pianist.

Loudon Pearson Hamilton CB (1932–2005) left HBGS in 1949. He became a senior civil servant. He was Head of the Department of Agriculture and Fisheries for Scotland, and Chair of the Hanover Housing Association.

(Dr) William M. Hamilton attended the HBGS between 1951 and 1958 and became Director of Public Health in Orkney.

Rachel Hanretty attended HGS, 2002–07, and graduated from the University of St Andrews in 2012 with an honours degree in English and

French. She is now Director of Mademoiselle Macaron, a Parisian cafe in the centre of Edinburgh which brings French macarons to Scotland. She was awarded a G and THA Young Achiever in 2014.

John L. Hardie MA BEd became a Lecturer in Psychology in the University of Glasgow and later Director of Studies at Aberdeen Training Centre. From 1939 until 1961 he was Principal of Aberdeen College of Education.

Sallie Harkness (née Moodie) left HGGS in 1955 (class of 1956). She became one of the Jordanhill College of Education Staff Tutor Team which developed *Storyline* in the Scottish Primary curriculum from the 1960s onwards.

(Prof.) A. Murray Harper (1933–2005) left School in 1951 and became Professor of Surgical Physiology at Glasgow University. He was a world leader in medical research in cerebral blood flow. He was a prolific author.

(Prof.) (John) Ross Harper CBE MA LLB was born in 1935 and left HBGS in 1952. He was Consultant and Founder of Ross Harper and Murphy and Harper MacLeod, Solicitors. He was Emeritus Professor of Law at Strathclyde University.[44] He was Founders' Day Speaker in 1978. He played Bridge for England and now lives in Australia.

David Harrower left HBGS in 1883 as Dux.

Catherine B. Hart (née Reid) left School in 1984 and was joint winner of the MacCormick Prize for the most distinguished graduate in Law at Glasgow University in 1987/88.

(Prof.) Alan L. Harvey was born in 1950 and left HBGS in 1967. He was Director, Strathclyde Innovations in Drug Research, 1988–2010. He has been Vice-Dean (Research) Faculty of Science at Strathclyde University, since 2010; and Professor in Pharmacology since 1986.[45]

Jonathan Hay left HBGS in 1874 as Dux.

(The Hon.) Margaret Hay (née McColl), sister of Lord McColl, left the HGGS in 1948, after the First Year. She became a Superior Court Judge in the state of California. She retired in 2004. She was the Founders' Day Speaker in 2000.

Alan Hazeldine (1948–2008) left School in 1965 and became a successful pianist and conductor. He graduated from the RSAMD in 1969, working extensively in Bulgaria and teaching at the Guildhall. He founded the Corinthian Chamber Orchestra in 1995.

Timothy J. Heelis left School in 2011 as Boys' Dux. He went on to study Natural Sciences at Cambridge University.

(Miss) Agnes Boyd Henderson (b. 1889) left School in 1907 as Dux. She took her MA at Glasgow University in 1910.

Eliza Bella Henderson (b. 1885) attended HGGS from 1900 until 1904, when she left as Dux. She took her MA from Glasgow University in 1908.

Maggie H. Henderson (1869–1951) left HGGS in 1886 as joint-Dux. She became a teacher of Languages and Mathematics.

Jeff Henry left School in 1978. In August 2014 he became new Chief Executive of Archant, a media business owning a number of regional newspapers in the UK.

John W. (Jack) Hepburn (1938–2014) was School Captain and Dux in 1955 and took First Place in the 1956 Glasgow University Bursary Competition: some fifteen boys – a record for any school – were placed in the top 100. He took FCH in Classics at Glasgow University. After a further degree from Brasenose College, Oxford, he spent his career in the Ministry of Agriculture and Fisheries and became its Under-Secretary.

Vic Hepburn left HBGS in 1961. He qualified in Glasgow as a CA in 1966 and the following year emigrated to Canada. Before retirement in 2000 he was President and CEO of the largest brick manufacturer in North America. He is a Trustee of the Canadian Bursary Fund.

Scott Herald left School in 2003 and attended university in Nashville, Tennessee, on a golf scholarship. He turned professional in 2008.

(Dr) Murdoch A. Herbert TD QSO (1924–2014) was Deputy Head Boy and School rugby captain in 1940 and went into Medicine. He became President of the New Zealand Medical Association in 2005.

Robert F. Herbert (1920–99) left HBGS as Dux in 1939 and became a Law graduate and CA. He became a President of the FP Club.

Isa(bella) L. Herriot attended HGGS from 1877 until leaving as Dux in 1887. She became a teacher.

(Dr) James Arthur Hewitt (1889–1953) attended HBGS from 1904 until 1908. He became Senior Lecturer in Physiology, King's College, London. He was elected FRSE, 1947.

Susan J. Hide was joint Girls' Dux in 1983.

Pamela Hill left HGGS in 1937. She became a well-known writer (in America) and novelist.

(Sir) (Robert) Russell Hillhouse KCB FRSE FRSA (b. 1938) left the School in 1956 as Dux and gained First Place in the University of Glasgow Bursary Competition.[46] He entered the Home Civil Service and through promotion became the Permanent Under-Secretary of State, Scottish Office, between 1988 and 1998.[47] He was the Founders' Day Speaker in 1988. He was made FRSE in 1995. He was awarded a G and THA in 2004.

George Hillian (1921–2013) left HBGS in 1939. He served in Italy with the Intelligence Corps in World War 2. After the War he graduated with Honours from Glasgow University. He emigrated to British Columbia and became Head of the English Department at Kelowna Secondary until his retirement in 1987.

Jane Hislop attended HGGS from 1882 until leaving as Dux in 1888. Before women were able to graduate she was First in the Senior Certificate in the Glasgow University Local Examinations and awarded the Elder Scholarship in 1889. She was also First in the Higher Certificate for women. She went on to teach French and German.

John Hodge (1855–1937) left school at thirteen years of age to become a solicitor's clerk. He then worked in a grocer's shop before joining an ironworks as a puddler – the same job as his father. He became a trade unionist and politician. He was Secretary of the Steel Smelters' Association and his union was the first to affiliate with the Labour Party. He was President of the TUC, 1892. He was Labour MP for Gorton, east of Manchester, from 1903 until 1923. He supported involvement in World War I and joined Lloyd George's Government as Minister of Labour.[48] His autobiography *Workman's Cottage to Windsor Castle* was published in London in 1931.

(Dr) Diana Hoff (née Young) FRCS left HGGS in 1962. She became an ophthalmologist. She and her family circumnavigated the world in their partly home-made yacht, 1977–82. She rowed 3,000 miles across the Atlantic solo in 2001. She was the recipient of a G and THA in 2001.

Jean Hood (née Watson) left the HGGS in 1939 as Dux and gained First Place in the Glasgow University Bursary Competition. She won the Herkless Prize for the most distinguished woman graduate at Glasgow University.

John M.S. Horsburgh (b. 1938) became a QC (Scotland) in 1980. He was Sheriff of Lothian and the Borders, 1990–2011.

James C. Howie was Dux in 1941 and First Bursar in the Glasgow University Bursary Competition. He joined the RAF and eventually flew with Quantas.

(Dr) John Howie left School in 1972. He became Associate Professor of Civil Engineering at the University of British Columbia in 1997.

John R. Hume OBE was born in 1939 and left HBGS in 1957. He was Principal Inspector of Historic Buildings for Historic Scotland, 1993–9. He was Honorary Professor, Faculty of Arts, Glasgow University, since 1998; School of History, University of St Andrews, since 1999.[49]

Ailene Hunter (née Cunningham) left School in 1965 and is a former scientist in the NHS. She is Convener of Voluntary Guides of the Society of Friends of Glasgow Cathedral.

(Rev. Prof.) Archibald MacBride Hunter PhD DPhil DD (1906–91) left HBGS in 1924. He became Professor of New Testament Exegesis (formerly Biblical Criticism) in the University of Aberdeen, 1945–71, and Master of Christ's College, Aberdeen, 1957–71. He was the fifth Founders' Day Speaker in 1965. He produced numerous publications.

(Prof.) Margaret J. Hunter (1922–95) left School in 1939. She became Professor of Biological Chemistry at the University of Michigan, 1979–88.

(Dr) Isobel H. Hunter-Brown (1918–2009) left School in 1935 as Dux. She took a FCH in English Literature at Glasgow University. She then turned to Medicine and Psychology and became a psychoanalyst.

William Huntly left HBGS in 1873 as Dux. He took his MA (1880), BSc (1885), MB CM (1885), and MD (1889), before becoming a United Presbyterian Missionary to Rajpootana, India.

(Dr) Robert Thomson Hutcheson OBE JP MA PhD (1903–2003) left HBGS in 1920. He was Registrar of the University of Glasgow, 1942–74, and added the role of Secretary of the University Court, 1944–74. He was the (fourth) Founders' Day Speaker in 1964.

John Hutchison (1842–1924) left HBGS in 1855 as Dux. He became Rector of the High School of Glasgow.

Douglas Hutton left HBGS in 1945. He became MD of Unilever

Corporation in South America. After retirement he trained as a priest in Rome. He wrote his autobiography, *A Roving Scot*.

Robert Imrie left HBGS in 1849 as Dux.

Irvine of Lairg, Baron (Alexander Andrew Mackay Irvine called Derry) PC QC (b. 1940) was the son of an Inverness slater. He left the School in 1957 (class of 1958) and attended Glasgow and Cambridge Universities, coming top (of 220 students) in the Law Tripos and graduating with FCH in his BA and LLB. He was called to the Bar in 1967. He was the Founders' Day Speaker and the recipient of a G and THA, both in 1998. He became Lord High Chancellor of Great Britain, 1997 until 2003, and a member of the Privy Council.[50]

Chris Irvine left School in 2003 and joined the *Daily Telegraph* in 2007 as a member of the graduate training scheme. He was Assistant Foreign Editor of the newspaper until December 2013. He has since become Deputy Foreign Editor at *Mail Online*.

Carol S. Jack (née Ellison) left HGGS as Dux in 1973. She worked for Standard Life.

Gavin Jack secured the highest academic distinction obtainable in British banking by taking first place and Beckett Memorial Prize in the final examination of the Institute of Bankers in England.

Robert T.B. Jack left the School as Dux in 1979. He became a solicitor in Edinburgh. His father was Chair of Governors.

Alison Jackson (née Henderson) was of the class of 1964. She won the Herkless Prize for the most distinguished woman graduate of 1968 at Glasgow University.

(Prof.) Ivor M. Jackson left School in 1954 and is Professor Emeritus at Alpert Medical School, Brown University, Rhode Island. He specialised in Endocrinology and Otolaryngologism and has contributed to two hundred publications.

David James (b. 1862) left HBGS in 1875 as Dux. He took his MA (1882) and BD (1885) at Glasgow University before becoming a United Presbtyerian minister in Galston and then Kirkcaldy.

Gavin James left School in 1948. He graduated in Dentistry from Glasgow University and took specialist training in orthodontics at London University.

He became Senior Lecturer in Orthodontics in Glasgow before emigrating with his wife, Joyce (née Paterson) who attended HGGS. He was in private practice for twenty years: she retrained as a cranial therapist.

(Dr) Alex Jamieson attended HBGS, 1958–67. He became a GP and medical educationist in London. His father –

(Dr) Arthur Jamieson of Barnach (1918–2007) left the School in 1935 and qualified in Medicine from Glasgow University in 1944. He followed a career of general medical practitioner, first in Rutherglen and then from 1960 in Beith. A keen genealogist, he contributed significantly to Glasgow Archives by his meticulous transcribing of records dating back to the seventeenth century. He was also a noted heraldist.

Charles Reginald Wingate Jamieson (b. 1952) left School in 1969 and has acted in many TV and film productions. He has also exhibited paintings widely with solo shows.[51] He produced *Glasgow*, a stunning collection of images and words which portray Glasgow.

(Dr) Lewis Johnman CBE TD OStJ (1932–2011) attended HGS, 1944–50. He became a GP. In 1989 he was appointed Brigadier of the Territorial Army Medical Service, the TA's most senior medical officer. He was one of the Queen's Honorary Physicians, 1986–98. He was Director of the Earl Haig Fund and Deacon of the Incorporation of Tailors, Glasgow.

Alexander (Alistair) D.K. Johnston became a CA and Global Vice-Chairman of KPMG, 2007–10. He was awarded the CMG in 2011.

Frances E. Johnston left HGGS as Dux in 1954.

(Dr) Elizabeth L. Jones (née Ellis) left School in 1979. She qualified in Medicine in 1984 and was awarded FRCOG in 1990.

Nan Vance Jones (1929–2005) (née Dunbar) left HGGS in 1946 as co-Dux. She became a Classical scholar and an Oxford don, ornithologist and author. She was appointed Tutor in Classics, Somerville College, Oxford, in 1965 and retired as a Fellow in 1995. She was Founders' Day Speaker in 1980.

(Prof. Dr) Jack Joseph (1913–98) attended the School between 1926 and 1931. He studied Medicine at Glasgow University. He became Professor of Anatomy at Gray's, London University, 1965–81, and was Professor Emeritus in 1993.

Samantha Judge (b. 1978) left the School in 1996 and was a member of Team Scotland Hockey which represented Scotland in the Commonwealth

Games in Manchester (2002), Melbourne (2006) and Delhi (2010). She teaches PE at St George's School for Girls in Edinburgh.

Rachel F. Kane (née Arthur) left School in 1984 as Dux Girl. She became an accountant.

Euan R. Kay left the School in 1997 as joint-Boys' Dux. He became a Research Fellow at St Andrews University School of Chemistry.

P. A. Joyce Kay (née Freeman) left HGGS in 1952 and became Assistant Professor of Clinical Psychiatry in the University of Medicine, New Jersey.

Alison Keen MBE (1912–94) left HGGS in 1931 and took an MA from Glasgow University in 1934 and a Diploma in Social Studies in 1935. She was Head of Social Work at Glasgow Royal Infirmary between 1942 and 1972. She was awarded an MBE in the New Year Honours List of 1971.

Graham A. Keith left HBGS in 1968 as Dux. He became a teacher of Latin and Religious Education at Kyle Academy.

Alison C. Kennedy left School in 1979 and joined the Diplomatic Service, serving as Third Secretary in Khartoum.

Alastair Kennedy (1925–2008) left School in 1944. He was a Christian missionary among the Jola people of Senegal from 1953 to 1965. He spent much of his lifetime working in Africa.

(Dr) David Kennedy (1931–2003) left the HBGS as Dux in 1949. He became a consultant psychiatrist.

(Dr) Hugh B. Kennedy (1927–2010) (brother of Alastair) left School in 1945 and qualified in Medicine from Glasgow University. He worked for the Baptist Missionary Society and was President of the Baptist Union of Scotland. He specialised in ophthalmology in Scotland and Zaire.

Lyle Kennedy was born in 1965 and left School in 1981. He became a Chartered Engineer. He was awarded the Gold Medal in the Royal National Mod solo singing competition in 2008.

(Prof.) Malcolm William Kennedy left HBGS in 1970 (class of 1971). He has been Professor of Natural History at the University of Glasgow since 1996.[52]

David C.A. Ker (1906–99) was a Foundationer who attended HBGS from c.1914, leaving after third year in 1921. He became Principal of Chiswick Polytechnic in London.

Mary (Maisie) B. Kermack (née Farquharson) (1910–2014) was the second oldest Hutchesons' FP, living to the age of 104.

(Dr) James Kerr (1924–2004) left the School in 1942. He became a leading figure in Respiratory Medicine in the country.

Margaret Louise Kerr left HGGS in 1942 as Dux and became a senior educational psychologist with the Glasgow Education Department. She was a Scottish hockey internationalist.

William Caird Kerr (b. 1864) left HBGS in 1876 as Dux. He took his MA (1886), BL (1892), and LLB (1892) before becoming a Writer in Glasgow.

Elizabeth Kidd (née McCulloch) left School in 1968 and became HMI of schools in Cardiff.

Margaret Montgomery Killin (1880–1907) left HGGS as Dux in 1899. She graduated MA from Glasgow University in 1903. She became a school teacher and died young.

Simon Kinder (1962–2010) left School in 1979. He was Director of Marketing for Europe for Black and Decker until 1999. He became MD for catering equipment company Magimix UK Ltd and a major figure in the food industry.

Stephen Kinder left School in 1977 and joined Shell Chemicals in London in 1984. He was Strategy Manager for the Company, 2006–12, and in September 2012 took on the post of New Business Development.

W. J. Ean King Gillies (1903–93) was the son of the legendary Rector of the School. He attended HGBS, 1917–20. He was founder member and Chair of the Edinburgh Section of the FP Club.

Eileen King left HGGS as Dux in 1952.

Zoe L. King (née Russell) (1922–2014) left HGGS as Dux in 1941. She took an Honours MA at Glasgow University and became a University Lecturer.

Manuel Abraham Kissen (orig. Kissenisky) (Lord Kissen) QC (1912–81) moved from Lithuania to Scotland and attended HBGS from 1923 until 1928. He qualified in Law from Glasgow University in 1931. He became an advocate in 1946 and a QC in 1955. He was appointed a Senator of the College of Justice in 1963, becoming Scotland's first Jewish High Court judge. He was chair of the Law Reform Committee for Scotland, 1964–70.

Carol Knight (née Smillie) left School in 1979 and had a successful TV career. She was awarded a G and THA in 1999. She does a great deal of charity work.

Christina A.A. Knox left School in 2005 as Girls' Dux. She gained FCH in Music at Manchester University. She is now a violinist and teacher in Manchester.

Karen Kurtis (née Edwards) left HGS in 1978. She became the lawyer for the Discovery Channel, Blockbuster Video, Palm Computing and Specsavers. She has been a member of the New York Bar since 1985.

Grace H. Laidlaw left the School in 1911 as Dux.

(Dr) Ronald David Laing (1927–89) attended HBGS between 1936 and 1945 as a foundationer, an experience he looked back upon with affection. While at School he joined the debating society and became involved with Christian activities.[53] He became a psychiatrist and psychoanalyst who worked at the Tavistock Clinic and Institute in London, 1956–67, and produced data showing that schizophrenia was not an illness. He became a leading cult figure in the counterculture of the 1960s.[54]

(Dr) David Lamb (b. 1870) left the HBGS in 1887 as Dux. He graduated MB CM in 1891 from Glasgow University and became a ship-surgeon. He became Chairman of the Old Boys Club in 1930. He became FRFPS (G) in 1934.

(Rev.) John Lamb CVO DD (1886–1974) was minister in Fyvie Church, Aberdeenshire; Hyndland, Glasgow, and between 1937 and 1963 Crathie Church, where he was Domestic Chaplain to HM The Queen.

(Dr) Frederic Lamond (1868–1948) was a pupil in the 1870s. He was taught to play the piano and organ by his brother, David. He attended the Conservatory of Frankfurt-am-Main. He was a pupil of Liszt (1885–6) and Brahms and an exponent of Beethoven. Among his pupils was Victor Borge, who became an international entertainer. He gained an honorary degree from Glasgow University in 1937.

(Very Rev. Prof.) Daniel Lamont (1869–1950) BD was Minister at Kilmarnock, Edinburgh, Glasgow, Park Church, Helensburgh and Moderator of the General Assembly of the Church of Scotland, 1936–7. He was also Professor of Apologetics, Christian Ethics and Practical Training at New College, Edinburgh, 1927–45.[55]

Mary M. Lamont left School in 1987 as Dux.

Rebecca J. Lane left School in 1992 as Girls' Dux. She continued her studies at Girton College, Cambridge.

Helen C.R. Laurie (1915–93) left the HGGS as Dux in 1934. She took an MA from Glasgow University.

Edward Laverock (1919–2007) left School in 1938. He moved to Peebles in 1945 and became a solicitor in the family firm of J. & W. Buchan, the practice founded by Walter Buchan, brother of John Buchan, Hutchie former pupil and First Lord Tweedsmuir. He was the last Town Clerk of the Royal burgh of Peebles, 1948–75. He was made an Honorary Sheriff, 1983. He was also Procurator Fiscal and jointly managed the Peebles Building Society. His lifetime passion was the Riding of the Marches in Beltane Week each June, and Peebles Beltane elected him a life member in 1985.

Alan B. Lawson (1910–92) left HBGS in 1928. He became Depute Director of Education for Inverness, retiring in 1975.

Ronald Lean taught Classics and English in the Collegiate School, Queen's Park. He became Principal of Education in Sierra Leone. He and his wife were drowned following a torpedo attack by a German U-boat on their way back from West Africa in 1917. His extensive papers can be found in the Special Collections of Glasgow University.

Stuart Leckie OBE left School in 1963. He became Chair of Stirling Finance Ltd., and a Hong-Kong based pensions and investments expert dedicated to forging links between the UK and China, since 1998. He was a Scottish International Swimmer, 1960–67.

Moira P. Ledingham (née Wright) left HGGS as Dux in 1967.

Euan A.M. Lees left School in 1991 as Dux. He was awarded a 'Blue' at Oxford University. He represented Great Britain at the World Triathlon Championships.

Ebenezer Lehtern left HBGS in 1837 as Dux.

Archibald Leitch (1865–1939) attended HBGS between 1876 and 1880 and became an engineer and architect. He produced ambitious plans which led to the construction of the new Ibrox Park of 1900 for Glasgow Rangers. He was the world's first specialist designer of football grounds. By 1939 his company had created over thirty grounds – for football, rugby, greyhound racing and speedway.[56]

(Prof.) David Leith left HBGS in 1955. He became Director of Research at the Stanford University Linear Accumulator Centre in California, 1991–2000. He is now Emeritus Director.

(Rev.) William Larnack Tennison Levack (1874–1935) was minister of Leuchars St Athernase, Fife, 1907–23 then Belmont Church, Glasgow. He was chaplain in Malta during World War 1. He was awarded an Honorary Degree of DD from Glasgow University in 1929.

Matthew L. Levine left the School as Dux in 1987. He achieved a FCH BSc in Mathematics at Glasgow University in 1991.

Mary Lewis (née Jack) left HGGS in the 1920s from Class III (a pupil of Mr Harrower's Elocution class held in HGGS). She became Head of Drama at the Italia Conti Stage School in London, and became Chair of its Board of Trustees. She died in 1994.

John E. Liddell (1908–91) attended the School, 1919–25, and was responsible for the care of the School Archives. The 350th Anniversary Exhibition was largely the result of his work. He died in September 1991.

Robert Liddell left HBGS as Dux in 1840.

(Prof.) Andrew Liddle left School in 1982 (class of 1983). He became the Professor of Astrophysics at the University of Sussex. Since 2013 he has been Professor of Theoretical Astrophysics at the Institute of Astronomy, Edinburgh University.

Alison J. Lindsay left School in 1983. She won the Herkless Award for the most outstanding female Arts graduate at Glasgow University in 1987. She also won the Honeyman Award.

Elspeth Lindsay left School in 1969. She was Head Teacher in three primaries before taking on Ayrshire's largest primary school, Onthank in Kilmarnock.

(Dr) Susan E. Lindsay left School in 1995 as Girls' Dux and took Science and Medicine degrees at Glasgow University. She was awarded RCPS by Glasgow.

(Dr) Jacob (Jack) Lipsey (Lipshitz) (1895–1978) attended HBGS from 1907, leaving as Dux in 1913. He qualified in Medicine at Glasgow University, winning the William Hunter Medal.

Gilbert Lithgow (1921–84) left HBGS in 1939 and served with the RA. He won a Snell Exhibition to Balliol College, Oxford. He became a Lecturer at the University of Tasmania.

(Rev.) Fergus G. Little (1898–1978) became a minister in the Baptist Church and held ministries in Helensburgh (1922), Huddersfield, Newcastle (1939–54), Sheffield and Biggar, Lanarkshire.

Aaron J. Livingston left HBGS in 1992 as Dux. He took a degree at Cambridge University and became a CA. He has a managerial post in Planning and Strategy with Easyjet.

Jonathan L. Livingstone left HBGS in 1995 as Dux. He became a CA. He was recently appointed Vice-President at Moody's Investor Services.

Rona (Robina) Livingston (née Scholes) left School in 1957 and became Assistant Head at Robert Gordon's College in 1989 in charge of the first girls to enter that School. She organised the fifty-year reunion of the HGGS Class of 1958.

Isaac Losowsky (1894–1972) attended HBGS as a Foundationer, 1908–11. He was appointed leader of the Scottish Orchestra in 1922. He received his musical education at the Athenaeum School of Music and at the RCM, London.

Felicity M.M. Loudon left School in 2007 as Girls' Dux.

(Julius) Lewis Lyons ('Louie') (1905–99) attended HBGS, 1916–21. He left to join his father's jewellery business in St Enoch's Square. The business gained an international reputation, especially when he took over its running. He left a considerable private collection of paintings and silver to Glasgow Museums. The School also benefited from a legacy and an annual lecture is held in his name.

Dave Lyons left School in 1984 and became sub-Principal Percussion with the BBC Scottish Symphony Orchestra.

(Dr) Irene McAlpine BSc PhD left HGGS in 1921. She was appointed to the Chemistry staff of Glasgow University in 1931. She died in 1993.

Robert McAulay left HBGS in 1868 as Dux.

Kennneth George McBain (1946–89) attended HBGS from 1958 until 1963, before going on to Harvard University. He became a leading independent TV producer.

(Prof.) Alexander MacBeath (1888–1964) attended HBGS 1905–09 and graduated MA in 1915 at Glasgow University. He was Professor of Logic and Metaphysics, Queen's University, Belfast, from 1925 until retirement in 1954.

Brian MacBride left School in 1976. He became the Managing Partner of MacBride Munro & Company and the Honorary Secretary of the FP Club.

Florence MacBride gave a recital to FPs in February 1928. She was praised for her musicianship in an article on the HGGS in the *Glasgow Herald* on 22 February 1938.

Nellie MacBride (née Baird) left the HGGS as Dux in 1910. (Her daughter, Winifred Greenwood, was joint-Dux in 1947.)

(Prof.) Charles Hugh Alexander MacCallum (1935–2013) left School in 1952. He became Professor of Architecture, Glasgow University, and Head, Mackintosh School of Architecture, Glasgow School of Art, 1994–2000. He was particularly proud of his work on the new building of the Scots Kirk in Paris, opened in 2002.

John McCallum left HBGS in 1882 as Dux.

(Prof.) Kenneth MacCallum left School in 1961 and took FCH at Glasgow University. He became Principal of Bell College of Technology in Hamilton, Lanarkshire.

Moira MacCallum left School in 1985 and rowed for Scotland, 1984, 1987 and 1988.

McColl of Dulwich, Baron (Ian McColl) CBE FRCS FACS FRCSE (b. 1933) left School in 1948 and was the Founders' Day Speaker in 1991. He achieved a G and THA in 2000. He became Professor of Surgery, University of London, at Guys', King's and St Thomas' School of Medicine of King's College, London, 1971–98. He was created a life peer in 1989.[57] He became UK Chair of Mercy Ships, a Christian charity.

Jane McCormick attended the HGS, 1990–98. She swam the Channel in 2005 for Headway and again in 2013 as part of a team to raise money for the British Heart Foundation. She has also swum the Hudson River in New York. She was awarded a G and T Young Achiever Award, 2006. She was one of the 'Flying Scot' UNICEF ambassadors at the 2014 Glasgow Commonwealth Games.

Calum C. Macdonald left School in 2008 as joint-Boys' Dux. He took BA (Hons) in Law at Downing College, Cambridge University.

(Prof.) James Hogg MacDonald (1877–1956) left the School in 1894 and graduated in 1899 in Medicine at Glasgow University. He became Medical Superintendent of Hawkhead Asylum, 1913, and Professor of Psychological Medicine at Glasgow University. In 1932 he was appointed by the King of Italy as a Caviliere della Corona d'Italia 'for valuable services rendered to Italy, for helping to spread among Scotsman the knowledge of Italy, and for arousing interest in Italian history, art and literature'.[58]

(Prof.) Jan B.I. McDonald (née Caldwell) MA FRSE FRSAMD FRSA (b. 1941) left HGGS in 1959. She was the Founders' Day Speaker in 1989 and achieved a G and THA in 2005. She is the Emerita Professor of Drama, Glasgow University in the Department of Theatre, Film and Television Studies, 2001–4.[59] Latterly she was Dean of Faculties at Glasgow University from 2007.

Jesse Oliver MacDonald (née Ramsay) (1910–2004) left HGGS as Dux in 1928. She was Headmistress of St Denis School, Edinburgh, between 1950 until 1964, by which time the School roll, and breadth of curriculum, had expanded.

(Sir) Kenneth (Carmichael) Macdonald (b. 1930) left School as Dux in 1948 and gained a KCB in 1990 and a G and THA in 2005. He was Private Secretary to the Permanent Secretary, 1958–61, Counsellor (Defence) UK Delegation to NATO, 1973–5, and Second Permanent Under-Secretary of State, 1988–90. He was Chairman, Raytheon Systems Ltd., 1991–2000.

Sharman Macdonald (b. 1951) became a playwright, screen-writer and novelist. She attended HGGS, Watson's College and Edinburgh University.

(Dr) Jean McDougall (née Roberts) left the School in 1940 as Dux of the HGGS. She is aunt of Jim McDougall, Depute Rector.

Tom Duncan McEwan (1881–1924) was the son of the well-known Scottish artist, Tom McEwan. He left HBGS in 1899 as Dux and graduated MB from Glasgow University in 1904, having won various prizes throughout his university studies. He served in RNVR as a surgeon during World War I.

Donald James Dobbie Macfadyen, Lord Macfadyen (1945–2008), left School in 1963. He was admitted to the Scottish Bar in 1969 and took silk in 1983. He was appointed a Senator of the College of Justice in Scotland in 1995 and a Privy Counsellor in 2002.[60]

John Edgar McFadyen (1870–1933) left HBGS in 1886 as Dux and became a Biblical scholar at Glasgow and Oxford. After a professorship in Toronto he was Professor at Trinity College, Glasgow, from 1910 until 1933. He left a large body of writing.[61]

(Rev. Dr) Joseph F. Mcfadyen (1873–1949) was Principal of Hislop Educational Society of the University of Nagpur in India, 1918–20. He was awarded the Kaisar-i-Hind Medal First Class for Public Service in India by George V in the 1932 New Year's Honours List when he was Vice-Chancellor of Nagpur University, India.

William K. McFadyean left the HBGS as Dux in 1916. He became Procurator-Fiscal of Moray and Nairn.

Bill McFarlan left School in 1975 and married Caroline (née Brown) who left in 1976. He has been a BBC and STV Presenter and has his own business. They have raised much money for children's charities.

James Waddell Macfarlane (1877–1952) was Treasurer (General Manager), Bank of Scotland, and Chairman, Committee of Scottish Bank General Managers, 1938–42.

Esme R.E. Macfarlane left School in 2002 as Girls' Dux.

(Rev.) John Macfarlane (b. 1881) took his MA (1904) and BD (1907) from Glasgow University. He was minister at Pollokshaws Parish Church before taking the post of minister in the Scottish Church in Brussels in 1927.

Sheena Macfarlane (née Sutherland) left School in 1972. She was the most distinguished Glasgow Dentistry graduate of 1979. She is an orthodontics specialist.

(Dr) Duncan J. McGeoch (b. 1944) became Director, Medical Research Virology Unit, Glasgow, 1995–2009.

Craig McGinlay attended HGS, 1991–2004. He played for Scotland Under-18s Rugby. He became a Sports Scientist and Strength and Conditioning Coach for St Mirren FC, 2010–12. He is also an actor and presenter.

Alastair H. McGlashan was Dux of HBGS in 1961 and took an MA from Glasgow University.

Professor 1st Baron McGowan (created 1937) of Ardeer (Harry Duncan McGowan) OBE (1874–1961) attended the School 1882–87 and was made a KBE in 1928. He became Hon. President of Imperial Chemical Ltd. (Chairman, 1930–50) and President, Society of Chemical Industry, 1931. He was a Director of the Midland Bank Ltd. He gained an honorary LLD from Glasgow University in 1934. He was awarded G and THA in 2000.

(Dr) Stuart W. McGowan (1929–2010) joined the School on a scholarship and left as Dux in 1947. He qualified in Medicine, specialising in anaesthetics. He was a consultant in Neurosurgery in Dundee.

(Sir) Alexander Stuart Murray MacGregor OBE (1881–1967) attended HBGS, 1896–99. He became Medical Officer of Health, Glasgow, 1925–46. He was appointed one of the King's physicians in Scotland, 1938. He was created a Knight in 1941 and KBE in 1955.

Colin McGregor (1945–2013) left School in 1964 and became a CA in Scotland before emigrating to Canada. He was Vice-President and Chief Accountant of the Bank of Montreal.

(Rt Rev.) Gregor Macgregor (1933–2003) left School in 1951. He was the Founders' Day Speaker in 1996. He became the Episcopal Bishop of Moray, Ross and Caithness in 1994.

(Prof) Kenneth J. MacGregor left the School in 1963 and became Professor of Computing Science at the University of Cape Town. He has built his Department into one of the best on the continent.

Mary B. MacGregor (née Souter) left HGGS as Dux in 1945. She was Principal Teacher of History at Westbourne School for Girls.

(Prof.) Richard McGregor left HBGS in 1971. He became Professor of Music in St Martin's College, Lancaster. He is now Emeritus Professor at the University of Cumbria.

Sandra McGruther (née Lang) left School in 1968 and, under the pseudonym Alex Gray, became the award-winning author of crime novels set in Glasgow. She was awarded a G and THA in 2011.

Frances McGuckin (née Johnston) left the HGGS as Dux in 1954.

George McIlwham (b. 1926) left School in the early 1940s and had a distinguished career as principal Piccolo and Flute with the BBC Symphony

Orchestra. (He is also a piper.) His sons, the late Cameron and Stewart, also became talented musicians.

(Prof.) Iain B. McInnes (b. 1964) became Muirhead Professor of Medicine at Glasgow University in 2012.

David McIntosh (1938–98) left the School in 1956. He was a talented musician and became HM Inspector of Schools in Music in England, 1984–97.

Jeanie (Jane) R.S. McJannett (1875–1901) attended HGGS between 1885 and 1892 when she left as Dux. She was the only woman graduate at Glasgow University in 1896 and won the first prize in Logic. She studied further at the Maria Gray Training College for Teachers in London.

(Dr) Alison Mack (née Mitchell) MBE left HGGS 1954. She graduated in Medicine from Glasgow University in 1960 with distinction in Anatomy and Surgery. She was Acting Clinical Director of the Family Planning Association, 1966–94, and GP, 1972–88.

(Prof.) Heather McKay (née Ayre) left School in 1958. Since then she has achieved distinction as an internationally recognised scholar in the field of Religious Studies.

(Prof.) John L. MacKay left School as Dux in 1966. He was Professor of Old Testament Language, Exegesis and Theology for over thirty years. He was appointed Principal of the Free Church College, 2010–13. Since retirement in 2013 he has been Emeritus Professor.

(Dr) Thomas (Tommy) A.W.N. MacKay (of Ardoch) (b. 1946) left the School in 1964 and became an educational psychologist. He has been Visiting Professor of Autism Studies, University of Strathclyde, since 2008. He was described as 'visionary and inspirational' by former Prime Minister Gordon Brown in his book *Britain's Everyday Heroes* (2007). He was awarded a G and THA in 2008.

Graham Hamilton McKee (b. 1951) left School in 1969 (class of 1970) and was Projects' Director, University of Dundee.[62]

Paul McKellar left School in 1974 and became an international golfer. He was a Walker Cup player.

Alexander Graham Mackenzie (1928–2005) attended the School from 1939 until 1946. He became the founding Librarian of Lancaster University and led the modernisation of the ancient library at St Andrews University in 1976.

Eliza Jane McKenzie (née Miller) (1879–1977) left HGGS as Dux in 1897. She graduated MBChB from Glasgow University in 1903, having gained a total of fifteen prizes. She became a medical missionary in Manchuria, 1910–20 and 1934–40, and Shenking, China, 1920–34.

Thomas H. Mackenzie (1914–92) left the HBGS as Dux in 1932. He was an engineer.

Agnes S. Mackie (née Paterson) left the HGGS as Dux in 1948. She was a teacher.

Andrew McKie MA (Hons) left the School in 1986 and is now a journalist, writer and broadcaster. For some years he was Obituaries' Editor of the *Daily Telegraph*. He is the son of John, former Head of Classics at the School, and Lorna, Depute Rector of the Junior School, who retired in 2010. He gave the Address at Founders' Day in 2010.

Daniel McKinlay left the School in 1890. He became Provost of Alloa.

(Dr) Neil C. McKinlay left School in 1986 and became Spanish Tutor at New College, Oxford.

(Captain) Alasdair MacKinnon (1941–88) left School in 1958. He was tragically murdered while at sea.

Craig McKnight left School in 1987 and became a cricket internationalist.

Peter McLachlan left School in 2004 and became a PGA Professional in 2011.

Christine M. Maclaren (née Nicolson) left the HGGS as Dux in 1964. She became a Modern Languages Teacher.

William Boyd McLauchlan (1908–74) left School as Dux in 1926. He gained the Gold Medal for Engineering Mathematics and took FCH in Civil Engineering. He was the civil engineer who constructed the West Highland Hydro Electric Scheme.

Aileen McLaughlin (née Falconer) left the HGGS as Dux in 1956. She was a teacher of Guidance and Mathematics at St Aloysius College.

Annie Wallace McLay (born c. 1898) left the HGGS as Dux in 1915.

Wendy McLean (née Johnstone) joined the School in P4 in 1945 and left the

HGGS in 1953. She went on to gain ten Scottish hockey caps. She chaired the GB Olympic Hockey Committee and became Vice-Chairperson of the GB Olympic Hockey Board. She was the recipient of a G and THA in 2002.

James A. S. McLeish left the HBGS as Dux in 1917. He went on to win the Cowan Gold Medal for Latin and the Jeffrey Gold Medal for Greek at Glasgow University. He completed a FCH in Classics in 1920 and took an LLB with distinction in 1923. He became a CA and actuary.

John Crawford McLellan (b. 1962) attended Glasgow High School primary but moved when its future was in doubt. He left HBGS in 1979 (class of 1980). He was Editor of the *Scotsman* from 2009–11, and was formerly Editor of *Scotland on Sunday* and Edinburgh's *Evening News*.[63] He was Scottish Conservative Party media chief, 2012–13. Now he is Director of the Scottish Newspaper Society.

Kirsty E. McLellan left School in 2006 as Girls' Dux.

Morag A. McLellan left the School in 2008 as Head Girl, Dux and Captain of the First Hockey XI. She became a hockey internationalist and played for Scotland in the 2010 Commonwealth Games in Delhi and the 2014 Games in Glasgow. She was the G and THA Young Achiever for 2013.

(Rev.) J.M. MacLennan became Moderator of the Free Church of Scotland in 1938.

(Prof.) William J. MacLennan left School in 1958 and became Professor of Geriatric Medicine at Edinburgh University, 1986–98.

Angus MacLeod CBE (1906–91) was Procurator Fiscal of Dumfries, Aberdeen, 1952–5, and then Edinburgh and Midlothian, 1955–71. He was Honorary Sheriff of Lothian and Peebles from 1972.

(Dr) Jessie M. McMahon (née Steele) left the HGGS as Dux in 1951. She qualified in Medicine and specialised in Obstetrics and Gynaecology.

Christopher R. McMillan left School in 1996 as Boys' Dux. He took an outstanding FCH in Chemistry at Oxford University. He became a management consultant with Oliver Wyman, a leading global company.

Peter R. McNaught left HBGS as Dux in 1903. He completed degrees of MB and BSc and the higher degree of DSc in Public Health.

James T. McNeil (1920–2003) left HBGS in 1935 (class of 1938) and entered his father's joinery business. He was the first Hutchesonian elected to the position of President of the Scottish Rugby Union, at the beginning of season 1989/90.

(Dr) Evelyn McNicol (née Camrass) left HGGS in 1945 and was the Medical Adviser on the 1964 Scottish Andean Expedition. She was one of the three members of the first all-female expedition to the Himalayas.

(Col.) George McNish (c.1866–1943) CBE TD JP attended HBGS 1876–81. He was created Deputy Lieutenant of the County of the City of Glasgow in 1926.

Alan A. MacPherson left the School as Boys' Dux in 1994. He became an actuary.

(Rev.) Allan S. Macpherson (1939–2012) left the School in 1959 and became the Assistant Minister at Paisley Abbey. He joined the staff of George Heriot's in Edinburgh, taking charge of Personal Guidance. Although he took over the parish at Huntly, Aberdeenshire, he returned to schooling at Merchiston Castle.

Major General Duncan L. Macphie left School in 1949 and served in the RAMC. He was Honorary Surgeon to HM The Queen.

(Prof. Emeritus) Jack (John) MacQueen (b. 1929) left School in 1946. He was given a university chair aged only 34 and has been Professor Emeritus, Medieval and Renaissance English Literature, Edinburgh University, since 1988.[64] He was Founders' Day Speaker in 1974.

Jack McQueen (b. 1943) became Assistant General Manager of the Clydesdale Bank.

James McQueen left School in 1952. He was elected by the people of Renfrew as their Citizen of the Year for 2009–10, for a lifetime of voluntary work in the community.

Winifred W. MacQueen (née McWalter) left HGGS as co-Dux in 1946. She was awarded a major scholarship in Classics at Girton, Cambridge, and became a distinguished Classicist. She published many academic texts in collaboration with her husband, Jack.

(Prof.) David John McRae left School in 1967. He became Special Professor of Language in Literature Studies at Nottingham University.

(Rev.) Doug McRoberts left School in 1967. Although he was ordained in 1975 he has spent most of his life in broadcast news and communications.

He returned full-time to the ministry in 2002 and is Minister at St Andrew's Scots Church in Valletta, Malta He is an expert in World War 2 Fighter Command.

Archibald MacWhirter (c.1889–1968) joined the Sheriff Court service in 1926 and served in Glasgow, Perth and Orkney. He became principal sheriff-clerk depute of Fife.

(Prof.) Nigel Mace left HBGS in 1962. He was elected to the Vernon Chair of Biography at Dartmouth College, New Hampshire, in 1984.

Sharon Mail (b. 1953) graduated from Strathclyde University in 1986 with a degree in Business Studies. She became a full-time writer and has worked for the Jewish Telegraph group of newspapers. She has written a biography of Ian Richardson, the actor.

James A. Malcolm left HBGS as Dux in 1970. He took a BA from Cambridge University and became a Senior Lecturer in Computer Science at the University of Hertfordshire.

Peter A.R. Malcolm left School in 2009 as Boys' Dux.

Laura Mallick (née Donachie) left HGGS in 1945. She attended Glasgow University before emigrating as a teacher to Canada in 1956.

(Dr) Matthew L. Manson left HGS in 1983. He graduated from Edinburgh University in Geophysics in 1987 and won a Commonwealth Scholarship to Canada. He took an MSc (1989) and PhD (1996) in Geology at Toronto and stayed there to work in mineral exploration. Most recently he has been involved in diamond-mine working in Quebec. He is CEO of Stornoway Diamond Corporation. He is Hon. Chairman of the Canadian Bursary Fund Trust.

Pranav B. Manoharan left School in 2013 as Boys' Dux. He continued his studies of Economics at Jesus College, Cambridge.

(Dr) Yanlan Mao left School in 2001 as joint-Girls' Dux. She gained FCH in Natural Sciences and won a Downing College Scholarship. She took her PhD in 2008 and works in Molecular Cell Biology.

John Marco (1979–2007) left School in 1995. He became a federal judge in New York and legal adviser to Austria in the UN. He was killed in a motorcycle accident in South Africa.

Colin Marr (b. 1966) was Theatre and Commercial Manager, Traverse

Theatre, Edinburgh, 1992–97; Theatre Director, Eden Court Theatre, since 1997.[65] He became a Board Member of Regional Screen Scotland in 2009.

William Marshall left HBGS in 1893 as Dux.

Andrew D.M. Martin left the School as Boys' Dux in 1983. He took a degree in Pharmacy and is now a Senior Strategic Pharmacist with the NHS in Manchester.

James D. Martin left the HBGS as Dux in 1942. He became a Telecommunications Engineer with Plessey Telecoms Ltd.

(Dr) William Barr Martin (1924–2004) left HBGS in 1942. He graduated from Glasgow Vet College with an MRCVS in 1947. He became a pioneering veterinary surgeon, involved in ground-breaking research into infectious diseases including BSE. He was Director of the Moredun Research Institute in Edinburgh, 1977–85. He was elected FRSE, 1983.

Pat Marwick left School in 1965 and became Deputy Chief Commissioner for Girlguiding Scotland. She was awarded the Laurel Award, its highest award, in March 2014.

(Dr) Margaret Wylie Martin (née Thomas) (1903–2002) left the HGGS as Dux in 1922. She won the RAMC Memorial Prize in 1927 on her way to her MB (Hons). She became resident doctor at Mearnskirk TB Hospital in 1931 under Glasgow Corporation. She was the first woman to hold such a post.

John Fingland Mason (b. 1957) left School in 1974 and qualified as a CA in 1980. He was Leader of the SNP Opposition in Glasgow Town Council, 1999–2008; MP for Glasgow East, 2008–10 and SNP MSP for Glasgow Shettleston since 2011.

Mary Renfrew Mather (b. 1889) left HGGS in 1906 as Dux. She graduated from Glasgow University in 1910 with Honours in French and German.

(Dr) Farquhar A. Matheson of Glen Urquhart (1889–1962) was Dux of HBGS in 1906. He took his medical degree in 1911. He went to Tonga in 1946 as Chief Medical Officer.

(Dr) John C.M. Matheson (1893–1972) CBE DSO was Dux of HBGS in 1910. He was a final year Medical student when World War 1 broke out. He was mentioned in dispatches four times on the Italian front and had his left leg amputated below the knee-joint. He served as Governor of Holloway Prison and was in charge of the Medical Unit of Brixton Prison.

William M. Matheson (1885–1977, the brother of Farquhar and John) was Dux of HBGS in 1904. He worked in Samoa and New Zealand before returning to Scotland.

James (Jimmy) Maxton (1885–1946) was taught by his teacher parents and won a Renfrew County scholarship to HBGS in 1897, remaining there until 1900. He left in keeping with his father's wishes. Maxton wanted to become a teacher and his father believed that teachers should start young, in the pupil-teacher role then widely accepted as legitimate teacher training.[66] 'At Hutchesons' he joined a great educational tradition, famous in Glasgow and the West of Scotland.'[67] He served as Secretary of the Independent Labour Party (ILP), 1913–9. His opposition to the Great War led to conviction for sedition and a jail sentence. His decisive victory at Bridgeton in the 1922 General Election resulted in his chairmanship of the ILP. He opposed Ramsay MacDonald's 1929 Government and remained a charismatic radical.[68]

(Dr) Peter Watts Mayhew (b. 1959) left School in 1976 (class of 1977). He was Senior Conservation Manager, RSPB, from 1990; and a member of the Scottish Natural Heritage Deer Panel.[69]

Scott Meek (b. 1950) left HBGS in 1968. He joined the British Film Institute in 1972 as Deputy Manager of the National Film Theatre, then as Feature Films Officer of the National Film Archive. CEO of Zenith Productions and Joint CEO of Deep Indigo Productions, he was also a creative consultant in Australia until 2012.

Scott Meenan left School in 2012 as Boys' Dux.

(Dr) (Madeline) Ruth Megaw (née Miller) (1938–2013) left the School in 1955 as Dux of HGGS, gaining a FCH in History from Glasgow University in 1959. She was second in the UK Civil Service Exam and became the youngest Third Secretary in the Foreign Office. In 1972 she became Head of American Studies at Nene College, Northampton, and wrote on aspects of Aboriginal Art.

James Menzies attended HBGS between 1877 and 1881, leaving in the latter year as Dux.

Joseph Hume Menzies (1875–1954) left HBGS in 1890 as Dux and gained a MA at Glasgow University in 1895. He was admitted to the Middle Temple in 1898. He served as a Captain in the Royal Scots in World War 1. He stood unsuccessfully as Coalition Conservative candidate for the Fife West constituency in the General Election of 1918.

(Prof.) Alistair Millar left HBGS in 1967 and became professor of Clinical Pharmacology, University of Western Australia.

Archibald Millar left the HBGS in 1947. He became Honorary Sheriff of South Strathclyde, Dumfries and Galloway at Kirkcudbright.

John Norman Miller MVO left the School in 1922 and became a metallurgist. He was Secretary of the Braemar Royal Highland Society, 1964–78.

(Dr) William Miller (b. 1883) left HBGS in 1900 as Dux. He took his MA (1903), BSc (1904) and DSc (1909) at Glasgow University.

(Dr) John Desmond Milligan (1893–1920) left School in 1910 and qualified with Honours in Medicine in 1915. He saw active service in the RN. A School Prize in his name is awarded annually to a pupil going forward to study Medicine.

Alexander Mitchell left HBGS as Dux in 1872. He took his MA in 1879 and became the Free Church minister at Linlithgow.

(Rev.) Robert Aitken Montgomery (1927–2009) left the HBGS in 1944. He was appointed a member of the Working Party which led to the creation of the Children's Hearings system. He was the Church of Scotland minister for Portsoy in Banffshire from 1955–78. He then took on the Chaplaincy of Quarrier's Homes in Bridge of Weir, from which he retired in 1992.

Susan Montgomery left the School as Girls' Dux in 1977 and continued Hispanic Studies at St Andrew's University. She became a newsreader/continuity announcer with the BBC World Service.

(Dr) M.E. Imogen Morgan left School in 1970 as Dux and was First in the Glasgow University Bursary Competition that year. She became a consultant neonatologist.

Linda E. Morpurgo (née Benzie) left HGGS as Dux in 1966. After a successful career at St Andrews University she gained FCH in Classics in 1970. She took her PhD from Birmingham University and joined the English Department of Christ's Hospital School. She was a Financial Consultant in Glasgow in 1995.

Jeremiah (Jerry) Noah Morris CBE (1910–2009) – physician and epidemiologist. He won a scholarship to HBGS, leaving in 1926, and later qualified in

Medicine in 1934. In 1967 he became a Professor of Public Health and was seen as 'the man who invented exercise'.[70]

Max Morris (1913–2008), the younger brother of Jerry, became a headteacher and trade unionist. He too attended the School (1924–20). He later joined the Communist Party (and stayed a member until 1976). He was Head of Willesden High School from 1967 until 1978. He proved a strong supporter of comprehensive education and was influential in the National Union of Teachers.[71]

Marion Armstrong Morton (1934–2013) (née Chadwin) left HGGS in 1952 and became an English teacher. She was Deputy Provost, City of Edinburgh, between 1999 and 2003 and a member (Labour) of Edinburgh City Council from 1995 until 2003.[72]

Robert S. Morton MBE (1917–2002) left School in 1934 and went into Medicine.

(Sir) (William) Wilfred Morton (1906–81) entered the Inland Revenue in 1927. He was appointed Third Secretary at HM Treasury, 1958–65, and Chair, Board of Customs and Excise, 1965–9. He was made KCB in 1966.

James Moyes (1881–1958) left HBGS in 1898 as Dux. He took an MA (1901) and BSc (1905) from Glasgow University. He emigrated to Australia in 1912 and became a teacher and orchardist in Sydney.

Jeanie S. Muir (1875–1964) attended HGGS from 1890 to 1893 when she left as Dux. She became a teacher of Music and Languages.

(Dr) Kenneth W. Muir left the HBGS as joint-Dux in 1959. He spent his career in the Department of Chemistry at Glasgow University. He is now a Honorary Research Fellow at Glasgow.

David Munro left HBGS as joint-Dux in 1870.

Kenneth Munro (1936–2008) left School in 1954. He was a Trades Union official, Deputy Head of the European Commission Office in London, 1982–88, and Head of the European Commission Office in Edinburgh, 1988–98. He was the Founders' Day Speaker in 1995.

(Prof.) Jim L. Murdoch (b. 1955) left School in 1973. He was awarded the McCormick Prize for the most distinguished graduate in Law in 1977. He has been Professor of Public Law, Glasgow University, since 1998. He gained the Pro Merito Medal of the Council of Europe for his work in human rights education.[73]

Thomas Murdoch (with wife, Isobel) was the founder of the Hansel Village for the mentally handicapped, set up in Symington, Ayrshire. He died in 1985.

Ian Murray MBE left School in 1949 at the end of S2. He and his wife went to Murree in the foothills of the Himalayas in Pakistan as Assistant Principal and Christian school-teacher in 1962, returning to Edinburgh in 2000.

Ray Nelson attended Kelvinside Primary but moved to Hutchesons' Secondary. He was part of the School's winning Scottish Schools' Relay Squad. He left School in 1979. He attended university in California. He went on to win twenty-five caps for the USA in rugby (scoring a try against England at Twickenham in the 1991 World Cup).

Judith Nemtanu (née Shapiro) left School in 1975. She became a violinist in the Bordeaux Symphony Orchestra.

Fraser E. Newham left HGS in 1993 as Boys' Dux. Following a History degree from Worcester College, Oxford University, he became Director of Inbox Education, and as a journalist publishes regularly.

William Niblo left HBGS in 1838 as Dux.

John M. Nicolson left School in 1979. He became Scottish, British and World Debating Champion. He won scholarships including one to Harvard University. He became a reporter and presenter of BBC TV programmes. He was awarded a G and THA in 2000.

(Prof.) James Wilkie Nisbet MA LLB (1903–74) attended HBGS 1915–21. He graduated with FCH in Economic Science and Philosophy in 1925 at Glasgow University and completed an outstanding academic career by winning the Thomas Logan Memorial Prize, awarded to the most distinguished graduate of the year. He kept the spirit of Adam Smith alive mainly through his work of 1929, *A Case for Laissez Faire*. He was appointed Professor of Economics at St Andrew's University in 1947, retiring in 1970. He was the sixth Founders' Day Speaker in 1966.

Frederick John Niven (1878–1944) was educated in the School from a young age. He lived most of his life in Vancouver and became a respected Canadian author, following production of his 'Prairie Trilogy', 1935–44. He is better known in Britain for his novels of Scottish urban life. He wrote over forty books.[74]

Janet G. Niven (d. 1954) was a talented and outstanding FP. She began her own school with five pupils and by 1917 she took a large number of pupils to Cranley School in Edinburgh, which she made famous for sound education of a high moral standard.

(Prof.) Thomas A. Noble left School in 1964. He became Professor of Theology at the Nazarene Theological Seminary, Kansas City, Missouri, and Senior Research Fellow in Theology at the Nazarine Theological College, Didsbury, Manchester.

Edith M.E. Oelrichs (née Laycock) (1897–1966) attended HGGS, 1913–17, leaving as Dux in her final year. She became a teacher.

Cordelia Oliver (née Patrick) (1923–2009) left the HGGS in 1941 and attended Glasgow School of Art. She became a writer and artist. She was one of the first female art critics in the UK, becoming Drama critic for the *Guardian*.

Jean H. Oliver (née MacArthur) left HGGS as Dux in 1957.

William Morton Ogilvy (b. 1885) left HBGS in 1902 as Dux. He graduated from Glasgow University with an MA in 1907.

Alexander Old left HBGS in 1832 as Dux.

Daniel O'May (1878–1935) left HBGS in 1895 as Dux. He became a Tax Inspector. He endowed a Prize in Mathematics in his Will.

Thomas Ormiston (1878–1937) CBE (1929) was a lawyer, Chairman of Motherwell F.C. and a Governor of the British Film Institute. He became Scottish Unionist MP for Motherwell, 1931–35.

Alistair Orr left School in 1981 and took FCH in Law and MLitt at Oxford. He became Legal Director and Company Secretary of Scottish Power.

Russell L. Park left School in 2010 as Boys' Dux. He took a BA and MSc from Durham University and now is an audit assistant at KPMG (UK).

John Parkhill left School in 2001 as Boys' Dux and gained FCH in Mathematics from Oxford University in 2006.

Dorothy Elder (née Parsons) (1908–77) became a pianist and piano teacher.

John Parsell (d. 1885) left HBGS in 1834 as Dux. He matriculated in Arts in 1838. He became a theatre actor, manager and playwright from 1847.

(Dr) Andrew Cecil Paterson (1876–1942) took his MA in 1898 and added a PhD before he became Headmaster of Clydebank Secondary School, 1921–41.

Alan Sinclair Paterson (1928–99) stood just under six foot seven inches and created School and national records for the High Jump, breaking a British record that had stood for twenty-five years. He left School in 1945. He won silver at the European Championships in Oslo in 1946 and gold in Brussels four years later; he won a silver medal at the Empire Games in 1950; and despite his disappointing seventh place at London in the Olympics of 1948 he remains the School's only Olympic finalist. The 'Alan S. Paterson' Cup is awarded annually to the School Third Year Sports' Champion.

Amelia Paterson (b. 1890) left HGGS in 1908 as Dux. She took her MA in 1911.

George Paterson left HBGS in 1830 as Dux.

(Prof.) Joy (Johanna) Paterson (aka Peters), was a sister of Alan Paterson, and left School in 1950. She became an international opera singer and Head of Vocal Studies at the Guildhall of Music. She died in 2000.

George Weir Patterson (1909–81) attended HBGS 1917–25. He was capped in amateur football against Wales, Ireland and Belgium in 1935 and in 1936 he gained more caps against Wales and England.

Robert Pattison (1872–1917) left HBGS in 1888 as Dux and took an MA in Arts at Glasgow University in 1894. He became a lawyer. He was promoted to the rank of Captain during World War 1 but was killed in action on 27 December 1917. He had been recommended for the MC but died before it could be awarded. He is the oldest known FP to die in World War 1.

Alexander R. Peters left School in 2014 as Boys' Dux. He is studying Law at Selwyn College, Cambridge University.

Thomas Pettigrew left HBGS in 1841 as Dux.

John Phillips left HBGS in 1850 as Dux.

(Prof.) Louise Phillips left School in 1984 and became Professor in the Department of Communication at the University of Roskilde in Denmark.

John Philp left HBGS in 1878 as Dux.

John Cassels Pinkerton MC CBE (b. 1895) attended HBGS, 1908–11, and was the City Assessor of Glasgow, 1935–60. He was President of the Institute of Chartered Surveyors, 1952.

Robert M. Pinkerton left HBGS in 1963 as Dux. He taught at HBGS for five weeks and became a Lecturer in Classics at Edinburgh University.

Agnes L.J. Pirie took charge of Mile End Nursery in 1931, the first institution of its kind in Glasgow.

(Dame) Joyce Evelyn Plotnikoff, class of 1967, was made DBE (Dame Commander of the Order of the British Empire) in the 2015 New Year Honours List for services to justice, particularly to vulnerable and child witnesses. She worked with her husband, Richard Woolfson and their company conducting justice system research. In 2013 she received an Administration of Justice Award from the US Supreme Court Fellows Alumni Association.

Arti Poddar left HGS in 1999. He manages and owns several businesses, including care homes and kindergartens. He was awarded a G and THA (Young Achiever) in 2008.

Thelma Pollock (née MacIntyre) (1922–2002) left HGGS in 1941. She became PT (English) at Westbourne Girls' School.

(Rev. Prof.) A(rthur) Morton Price MA, BD, PhD (1930–1983) was called to E.U. Congregational Church, Pathhead, Kirkcaldy in 1936. He was also minister at Perth Congregational Church, 1944–64. He was Founders' Day Speaker in 1975.

Clare Proudfoot (née Bone) left HGS in 1991 and became Strathclyde University 'Student of the Year' in 1996. She was Depute Procurator Fiscal in Dumbarton until 2001.

Dorothy Radwanski (née Warnock) (1928–2012) left School in 1943 (class of 1946) and became a pioneer in the training of occupational nurses. She was a former advisor to the Health and Safety Executive, the Department of Employment and HM's Prison Service.

Gavin D.L. Ralston left HBGS as Dux in 1976. He joined Schroders in 1980 and became their Head of Official Institutions in 2012. He serves St Paul's Cathedral as Lay Canon (Finance).

Alison L. Ram (née Smith) left the School as Dux in 1981. She became a GP in Helensburgh.

(Baroness) Meta (Margaret Mildred) Ramsay of Cartvale was born in 1936 and left School in 1955. She was with the Diplomatic Service, 1969–91; was an MI6 operative (a spy); was Foreign Policy adviser to the Leader of the Opposition, 1992–4; and was created a life peer in 2006, achieving a G and THA in 1998. She was the Founders' Day Speaker in 2002. She is an international affairs consultant and was Deputy Speaker of the House of Lords, 2006–10.[75]

(Dr) Scott Ramsay left School in 1984 and rowed for Scotland from 1987 until 1989. He became a Consultant Physician and Geriatrician.

Elspeth B. Randall (née McAllister) was a Foundationer. She left HGGS as Dux in 1969.

Forrest Thomas Randell (1923–2008) left School in 1938. He was Managing Director of the Weir Group.

Gordon Rankin left School in 1972. He became a self-employed consultant experienced in marketing, product management and advertising. He worked closely with the Department of International Development on 1GOAL.

John James Rankin (b. 1957) left School in 1975 and became a solicitor. He joined HM Diplomatic Service and was High Commissioner to Sri Lanka and the Maldives from 2011–15. He was the recipient of a G and THA in 2014. He was appointed Chargé d'Affaires to Nepal in April 2015.

Paul Rankin (b. 1959) was trained by the Roux brothers and became a celebrity TV chef, author and restauranteur. He helped to develop Irish cuisine. He attended for only one session (1976–77).

William R. Ravie (1911–43) left the HBGS as Dux in 1929. He gained a FCH in Classics from Glasgow and a First in Moderns from Oxford whilst a Snell Exhibitioner. He was killed as a result of enemy action in New Guinea during World War 2 in 1943.

Peter J. Reader-Harris left School in 2007 as Boys' Dux and took an Open Scholarship to Brasenose College, Oxford. He gained FCH in Natural Philosophy at Oxford and is completing a PhD at St Andrews University.

(Dr) Kyla J. Reardon (née Brown) left School in 2000 as joint-Girls' Dux. She had a distinguished university career in Medical Science.

George Smith Reid (1904–85) left HBGS as Dux in 1922, and was Captain of the Swimming Club, 1919–22. He was called to the Scottish Bar in 1935. He was Sheriff of Ayr and Bute, later South Strathclyde, Dumfries and Galloway, at Ayr, 1948–76. He was a water-polo internationalist.

Richard ('Dick') Gavin Reid (1879–1980) attended the School, 1892–4, and arrived in Canada in 1903. He served as a Cabinet Minister for thirteen years before becoming Premier of Alberta, 1934–5. He provided debt relief to farmers and access to telephone service for all Albertans. His party (United Farmers of Alberta) was swept from office in the general election of 1935 by the Great Depression.

Fiona R. Reiderman (née Burt) left School as Girls' Dux in 1978. She won the Harkness Residential Scholarship in the St Andrews Bursary Competition.

Austin Reilly left the HBGS in 1964 as Vice-Captain. He played for Queen's Park FC and was the Stadium Director of Hampden Park.

Grace Fenton Rennick (née Hill) (1903–2010) joined the HGGS in the original building in Elgin Street in 1908 and left in 1921. At various times in her life she taught in Scottish schools. When she had to retire from the state system she became the Head of the Junior School in the private school of Craigholme.

Kenneth Revie attended HBGS, 1965–74. In 1974 he became the first ever Scot to win the coveted British Under-18 Junior Tennis Title. He then went on to win the British Under-21 title in 1977. He became the most capped Scottish Internationalist with 44 caps. He became an Advocate and was called to the Bar in 2008.

Derick Riddell (b. 1967) attended HGS, 1976–84. He took a degree in Business from Strathclyde University. He attended the London Academy of Music and Drama, graduating in 1990. He has become a successful Scottish television actor.

Anne Ritchie left the School in 1963. She was Senior Mistress at Giggleswick in Yorkshire and Head of Runton and Sutherland School in Norfolk, before being appointed as Head of St Margaret's School for Girls in Aberdeen. She organised the 45th Anniversary Reunion.

David Ritchie left HBGS in 1829 as Dux.

(Sir) James Martin Ritchie (1874–1951) CBE (1926) was Chairman and Managing Director of Andrew Ritchie & Son Ltd. (the manufacturing company of Bridgeton); General Commissioner of Income Tax for the Lower Ward of Lanarkshire from 1941; Town Councillor for Kelvinside Ward, 1927–32, and Governor of Hutchesons' Educational Trust, 1928–38. He was created a Knight in 1939.

Mabel Ritchie was a talented musician and in the *Glasgow Herald* of 22 February 1938 it was stated that she was an FP of HGGS.

Kenneth Roberton (1913–2003), known as the *Red Knight of Clydeside*, was a son of Sir Hugh, founder of the Orpheus Choir. He left the HBGS in 1931. He became a music publisher and peace activist and campaigner.

(Dr) (James) Graeme Roberts (b. 1942) attended the School from 1951 until 1960, when he was School Captain. He became Professor Emeritus, Aberdeen University, formerly Vice Principal (Teaching and Learning), 2001–05.[76] He was Chair of the Board of Aberdeen Performing Arts until 2014.

Andrew M. Robertson left the HBGS as Dux in 1914. He graduated in Medicine from Glasgow University in 1921 with Distinction in Midwifery. He practised medicine in Wales with his brother, Alexander.

Annie Stewart Robertson (b. 1885) attended HGGS between 1895 and 1902, when she left as Dux. She took her MA from Glasgow University in 1906. She died in 1955.

(Prof.) Donald James Robertson MA (1926–70) attended HBGS, 1935–44. He was Professor of Applied Economics at Glasgow University, 1961–9; and Professor of Industrial Relations, 1969–70. He was the eighth Founders' Day Speaker in 1968. He produced a significant number of publications.

H. Eileen Robertson (1957–2013) left HGGS as Dux in 1975. She took a BA from Oxford University.

Hamish Robertson left HBGS in 1965 as Captain of Athletics. He represented Scotland for twelve years at long- and triple-jump. In the 1970 Commonwealth Games he was placed eighth in the long-jump and thirteenth in the triple-jump. He was a Human Resources Director for Menzies retail.

(Sir) James Jackson Robertson FRSE (1893–1970) was educated at

Kilmarnock Academy, HBGS and Glasgow High School, before becoming First Bursar in the Glasgow Competition. He was headmaster in four schools: between 1926–31 of Fort William Secondary; between 1931–40 of Falkirk HS; between 1940–2 of the Royal High; and between 1942–59 of Aberdeen GS. He was the second Founders' Day Speaker in 1962. He made a vital contribution to Scottish education, particularly for primary children.

John A. Robertson left HBGS as Dux in 1962. He took a MA from Glasgow University.

Robert R. Robertson, OBE, brother of Andrew M., left HBGS in 1912. He served in World War 1 and awarded the Croix de Guerre. His OBE was for his services to the volunteer movement in the Straits Colony.

(Prof.) Gordon Robin (1928–99) left School in 1946 as Dux of Science. He became an authority on disorders of the spine and, in 1974, he was appointed Professor of Orthopaedic Surgery at Hadassah University Hospital in Jerusalem.

Gary T. Robinson left School in 1999 as Boys' Dux. He became an Investment Manager at Baillie Gifford.

Elizabeth Roddick (née Ure) left school in 1967. She was awarded a Fellowship by the Royal Pharmaceutical Society of Great Britain for distinction in her profession. She was runner-up in the 2009 Scots Businesswoman of the Year.

T. Iain Ronald (b. 1933) attended HBGS between 1946 and 1950. He qualified in Law, became a CA and took an MBA from Harvard Business School. He was Director and Vice Chairman of the Canadian Imperial Bank of Commerce. He was awarded a G and THA in 2006.

Michael Rosenberg left School in 1971 and became an international Bridge player. He was World Tournament Team Championship Gold medallist and Pairs Silver medallist.

Colin S. Rosenthal left School as Dux in 1982. He became a research astronomer.

Andrew Ross (1965–2013) left HBGS in 1983. He graduated with FCH in Electronic Engineering and was Engineering Student of the Year. He worked in telecommunications.

A. David Ross left HBGS as Dux in 1952. He became an International Tax Partner at Neville Russell. He later worked with Mazar Tax Services.

Douglas B. Ross left School in 1980 and was a Glasgow and Cambridge Law graduate. He worked for UNRWA (United Nations Relief and Works' Agency) in the Gaza Strip, 1988, and was seconded to UNPROFOR (United Nations Protection Force), serving in Bosnia, 1994–95. He was called to the Bar in 1998. He was appointed Standing Junior Counsel to the Scottish Government in 2000 and has been First Standing Junior Counsel since 2012.

Kenneth Alexander Ross (b. 1949) left School in 1966 and became Sheriff of South Strathclyde, Dumfries and Galloway at Dumfries, 2000–14. He was President of the Law Society, 1994–5.[77]

(Sir) T(homas) Mackenzie Ross (d. 1927) was Chairman of Madras Chamber of Commerce. He was knighted in 1927.

Walter Milne Ross BL Ca CPA attended the HBGS between 1940 and 1946. He became a successful CA and lawyer, reaching the top echelons of Shell and Occidental oil companies before running his own real estate business in Houston, Texas. He and his wife (Cathleen McFarlane Ross (1926–2010) were significant benefactors to the School. He was awarded the first G and THA in 1997. He gave the Address at Founders' Day in 2008. With the support of his wife, Helen, the Assembly Hall was refurbished and is now known as the Helen and Walter Ross Assembly Hall.

Elizabeth A. Roy left School in 1998 as Girls' Dux. She took a BA In Modern History and English at Oxford University.

Alexander (Sandy) B. Russell OBE (1910–96) left the HBGS in 1928 and gained a FCH in English from Glasgow University. He taught at Hamilton Academy, Aberdeen Grammar School and Kelso HS, where he remained in his post as Head for twenty-two years until retirement.

David A. Russell left School in 1984 as Dux. He became a Consultant with PWC in London.

Eleanor J. Russell (née Russell) left School in 1983 and was joint winner of the MacCormick Prize for the most distinguished graduate in Law at Glasgow University in 1988/9. She became Lecturer in Law at Glasgow Caledonian University.

(Dr) James Russell CBE (died 1960) developed an extensive surgical practice in Glasgow and the south-west. Largely as a result of his efforts, the first orthopaedic department in Scotland was opened at the Victoria Infirmary in the early 1930s, and a hospital built at Philipshill to deal with convalescents and long-term patients.

(Prof.) Leonard James Russell (1884–1971) gained a Research Exhibition for Emmanuel College, Cambridge in 1909. He was Professor of Philosophy at Bristol University, 1923–5, before taking the post of Professor of Philosophy at Birmingham University, a position he held from 1925 until 1950.

(Dr) Alasdair K.B. Ruthven MBChB (Hons) BSC (Hons) (class of 2002) became a Special Trainee in Anaesthesia, Edinburgh Royal Infirmary. He gave the Address at Founders' Day in 2014.

David Samson left the HBGS in 1969. He became Registrar at the Nottingham Trent University, retiring in August 2014.

Anas Sarwar (b. 1983) left School in 2001 and practised as an NHS dentist, 2005–10. At the General Election of 2010 he became the Labour MP for Glasgow Central. He became Deputy Leader of the Scottish Labour Party in 2011.[78] In November 2014 he became Shadow Minister of State for International Development.

Derek Saville left School in 1960. He became Head of Treasury, UK and Europe, at the Standard Chartered Bank in London, retiring in 1998.

Carol Schmulian (née Cohen) (1944–84) attended HGGS 1957–62. She won the Marion Gilchrist Prize for the most distinguished Medical student in first year in 1968 at Glasgow University (joint).

Jane Schopflin (née Morton) (1936–2007) won a scholarship to HGGS and left School in 1954. She became a journalist and radio producer, specialising in housing. She was Lib. Dem. Councillor for Fortune Green Ward, Camden.

Alistair Scott (b. 1950) left School in 1969 and played football for Queen's Park before making seventy appearances and scoring twenty-four goals as a striker for Glasgow Rangers in seasons 1973–4 and 1974–5.

(Ian) Bruce Scott left HBGS in 1959. He was awarded a G and THA in 2012 for his business ventures. He has been Chairman of the CBI in England and sat on the CBI Grand Council in London.

Elizabeth S. Scrimgeour (1912–2002) left HGGS as Dux in 1930 and became

Principal of a Church of Scotland Teacher Training College in Kalimpong, India.

Tracey Severne (née Stuart-Smith) left HGGS as Dux in 1982.

(Dr) David Shapiro left HBGS as Dux in 1971. He became the Principal Biochemist and now Honorary Lecturer in Biochemistry at Glasgow Royal Infirmary.

John Sharp left HBGS in 1836 as Dux.

William Sharp left HBGS in 1844 as Dux.

Christopher Shead attended the HGS, 1977–83. He took LLB (Hons) at Edinburgh University. He became an Advocate and was called to the Bar in 1996. He was appointed Sheriff in Grampian, Highlands and Islands in 2012.

(Prof.) Alan Shenkin (b. 1943) attended HBGS, 1952–61. He qualified in Medicine and obtained his PhD in Biochemistry. In 1990 he was appointed Professor of Clinical Medicine at Liverpool University. He is Clinical Director of Chemical Biochemistry and Metabolic Medicine. He is European editor of the magazine *Nutrition*.

Arthur Manfred Shenkin (1915–2002) left HBGS in 1931. He was the son of a carpet importer. He qualified in Medicine from Glasgow University in 1942. He became a psychiatrist at the Southern General Hospital and was President of the Royal Philosophical Society of Glasgow, 1996–98.

Barnet Shenkin left School in 1967 and became an international Bridge player.

(Dr) Lilian Links Shenkin (1918–2012) left School in 1936 and qualified in Medicine in 1942. She worked from a surgery in Pollokshaws Road between 1947 and 1990.

Mabel A. Shepherd (née Stevenson) left the HGGS as Dux in 1953. She took a BSc (Hons) at Glasgow University and is a research chemist at BP Chemicals.

Keith Sheridan left School in 1988 and became an international cricketer at a very young age. He was awarded a G. and T. Young Achievers' Award in 2004.

(Sir) (Maurice) Adrian Shinwell (b. 1951) became a solicitor, and has been senior partner, Kerr Barrie, Glasgow, since 1991; and Deputy Lieutenant, Renfrewshire, 1999–2011. He was former President of the Scottish Conservative and Unionist Party.

(Prof.) Keith Sillar left the School in 1976 and became the Professor of Neuroscience and Head of the School of Psychology and Neuroscience at St Andrews University.

(Dr) Malcolm A.B. Sim left School in 1992. He was awarded FRCP and FICM. He is organist at Glasgow Cathedral.

J. David Simons (b. 1953) left School in 1970 and gave up his legal partnership in 1978. He has become a Scottish novelist and short-story writer.

(Dr) Grant G. Simpson left School in 1948 and became President of the Scottish History Society. He was Assistant Keeper of the Scottish Records Office. When he retired he was Senior Lecturer in History at Aberdeen University.

James Reid Simpson left HBGS in 1835 as Dux.

Jennifer Singerman left School in 2001 as joint-Girls' Dux. She graduated with FCH in Social and Political Science, 2005.

Paul Slater left School in 1976 and joined the family firm. He is now Managing Director of the largest privately-owned menswear retailer in UK, with twenty-three retail stores and a Head Office in Glasgow.

(Dr) Arthur Slight left School in 1961 and his career has included academic, directorial and management appointments with Glasgow University, Pilkington Optronics and Barr & Stroud Ltd.

Joseph Sluglett OBE (1910–95) left School in 1927 and went into G.P. Medicine in Bristol. He was an early advocate of Health Centres.

Gillean (Sam) Petrie Small (b. 1936) left HBGS in 1954. He practised as an architect in public and private sectors including the East Kilbride Development Corporation. Since retirement in 1991 he has been involved in estate buildings research and cataloguing drawings' collections (RIAS). He published an architectural guide to Greater Glasgow in 2008.

James Smart left HBGS in 1846 as Dux.

Smith of Gilmorehill, Baroness (Elizabeth Margaret Smith) (née Bennett) (b. 1940) was a pupil at the HGGS between 1948 and 1958 and was created a life peer in 1995. She is Deputy Lieutenant, City of Edinburgh. She was awarded a G and THA in 2013.[79]

Agnes (Nancy) Houston Smith (née Boyd) (b. 1933) attended HGGS, 1944–50. She was a solicitor in Paisley, Edinburgh and Dundee between 1955 and 1992. She has been an Honorary Sheriff in Dundee since 1990.[80]

J. Clark Smith left HBGS as Dux in 1951.

Deborah Smith left the School in 1990 and gained a FCH (Russian/Politics) at Durham University and a Master's Degree from Bradford. She joined the Scottish Office in 1997.

(Dr) (Elizabeth) Dorothea Chalmers Smith (née Lyness) (1871–1944) attended HGGS from 1883 to 1889 and was among the first four women to graduate in Medicine from Glasgow University in 1894. She was a militant suffragette and was imprisoned for fire-raising. She went on hunger-strike while in jail.

Graeme N. Smith (1968–2013) left School in 1986 and developed into a gifted journalist. He wrote for the *Alloa Advertiser*, *Falkirk Herald*, *Scotsman* and *Herald*. When diagnosed with an incurable brain tumour he started a blog in the *Herald* which charted his journey through his illness.

Helen S. Smith (née Bryden) attended HGGS between 1963 and 1976. Following qualification in Medicine she became a GP in Hong Kong.

(Prof.) Ian K. Smith (b. 1953) is Professor of Education, University of the West of Scotland (formerly Paisley University).[81]

(Miss) Jean Taylor Smith (1900–90) was a well-known Scottish actress who made her name in Drama on BBC Radio and Television. She had a lengthy career from the 1920s until the 1970s, and the *Glasgow Herald* held she was one of the best known FPs of HGGS (22 February 1938).

Kenneth Smith left School in 1957 and trained as a teacher in Toronto. In 1962 he began teaching with East York. He was promoted to Vice-Principal (1970) and Principal (1978) and completed both BA (Psychology) and an MEd (Applied Psychology). He played rugby till age 47 and was Chairman of Selection of the Rugby Canada XV. He has been inducted into the Rugby Ontario Hall of Fame.

Leon Smith (b. 1976) left School in 1993 and went on to become a leading tennis coach. He coached Andy Murray when the latter was eleven to fifteen years old. He was appointed captain of the British Davis Cup Team in 2010 and simultaneously he became the Lawn Tennis Association's Head of Men's Tennis. He became Head of Ladies' Tennis in 2011.

Toby Smith, brother of Leon, attended HGS, 1985–91. He became Tennis Coach of the Year at Tennis Scotland, 2011.

(Prof.) William Ewen Smith FRSE (b. 1941) attended the HBGS, He is Emeritus Professor of Inorganic Chemistry (Professor since 1987) in Strathclyde University.[82]

Kevin D. Sneader LLB MBA left School in 1986 and was World Champion debater. He graduated with FCH in Law at Glasgow University. He qualified with an MBA with highest distinction at Harvard Business School. He is McKinsey and Company Chair in Asia. He gave the address at Founders' Day in 2012.

(Rev) Alan Kenneth Sorensen (b. 1957) attended HBGS, 1969–74. He has been Minister, Wellpark Mid Church, Greenock, since 2000; and a broadcaster since 1979.

Barbara Speakman (née Walker) (class of 1964) graduated from Strathclyde University in 1967. She emigrated to Toronto in 1968. She spent her working career in the civil service, becoming Executive Director of Assembly Services at the Ontario Legislature, where she was in charge of the restoration of the Parliament building. She is a Trustee of the Canadian Bursary Fund.

Charles A. Spencer left HBGS as Dux in 1973.

John E. Spiers left HBGS in 1852 as Dux.

(Dr) Walter Gerson Spence Spilg (b. 1937) left HBGS in 1956. He was Consultant Pathologist, Victoria Infirmary, Glasgow, 1972–99.[83]

Rebecca Stäheli (née Evans) was Dux in 1985 and studied Law at St John's, Cambridge. She was called to the Bar, 1989. She is Head of Fair Trade and Competition Law at the BBC.

(Dr) Alan Stanfield left School in 1971. He became an international curling umpire. He was Chief Umpire at the Olympic Winter Games in Sochi, 2014.

Ian Stanger left School in 1988 and became an international cricketer.

(Dr) Alexander (Sandy) Steel attended HGS, 1999–2005. He took a BA and PhD in Law at Corpus Christi College, Cambridge. From 2010 to 2014 he was a Lecturer at King's College, London. He joined Wadham College, Oxford, as Professor of Law in 2014.

Jane Graham Stephen attended HGGS between 1900 and 1903, when she left as Dux. She graduated MA from Glasgow University in 1908.

Alix Stevenson (née Jamieson) left the School in 1960 and represented Great Britain as a long jumper in the 1964 Olympic Games in Tokyo. She graciously agreed to give her maiden name to Hutchesons' sports stadium which she formally opened in November 2009.

(Dr) Alex G. Stewart attended the School (1962–68) and was Geography Dux in his final year. He went on to become a medical missionary in Baltistan, a remote area in northern Pakistan, 1976–96. He became a Consultant in Communicable Disease Control in Cheshire and Merseyside.

David Macfarlane Stewart CBE (1878–1950) took a Glasgow Law degree and then studied at Oxford. He made a distinguished career in the Indian Civil Service, retiring in 1927. He was Secretary of the Glasgow University Extra-Mural Committee and the West of Scotland Committee on Adult Education, 1928–46.

Iain Stewart (b. 1972) left School in 1990 and trained as a CA. He was Director, Scottish Conservative Party, 2001–6. At the General Election of 2010 he was elected as Conservative MP for Milton Keynes South. In a Government reshuffle in 2013 he was appointed PPS to the Minister of Transport.

(Dr) Janet McLeod Stewart (1900–93) was Dux of HGGS in 1918 and after a brilliant career in Medicine devoted herself in 1925 to the service of the United Free Church Medical Mission in China.

(Sir) Robert Sproul Stewart CBE (1874–1969) became a solicitor in 1898; Chairman, Glasgow Unionist Association, 1934–7; Chairman, Scottish Unionist Association, 1946–7; Chair, RSAM, 1951–4.

(Dr) Catherine Stirling left School in 1985 and became a hockey internationalist.

(Prof.) Gordon Stirrat left School in 1958 and became (now Emeritus) Professor of Obstetrics and Gynaecology at Bristol University; Dean of the Faculty of Medicine and Pro-Vice Chancellor. He was the Founders' Day Speaker in 1985.

(Dr) Sir Alexander Stone (1907–98) was born soon after his family arrived penniless from Russia in 1903. He attended the School between 1912 and 1923, qualified in law and went into banking. He was knighted in 1994. He supported the School by generous philanthrophic deeds. In his lifetime he had been an auctioneer, lawyer, banker, entrepreneur and philanthropist.

(Dr) Muriel Easton Stowe of Bhopal was admitted a member of the British College of Obstetricians and Gynaecologists in 1936, in recognition of her work in India.

(Capt.) Robert Strang (1850–1917) won the Dux medal at School in 1865. He became a master mariner and cabinet-maker and emigrated to New Zealand, dying in Dunedin and being buried in Wellington.

Ancell Stronach (1901–81) attended HBGS, 1914–18. He was a painter who exhibited at Paris Salon, RA, WAG, RSA, Canada, New Zealand and North America. He was Professor of Mural Painting in the Glasgow School of Art until 1939.

(Prof.) Allan David Struthers (b. 1952) left School in 1969 and has been Professor of Cardiovascular Medicine, Dundee University, since 2000 and heads the Heart Failure Service at Ninewells Hospital. He gained FRSE in 2010. He has written numerous publications.[84]

(Prof.) Richard Eric Susskind OBE DPhil FRSE (b. 1961) left School in 1978 and became a Tutor and Professor of Law at Strathclyde University and Professor of Internet Studies at Oxford. He has been an author and independent consultant since 1997 and Information Technology adviser to the Lord Chief Justice of England since 1998. He was the Founders' Day Speaker and achieved a G and THA, both in 2001.

(Dr) Alastair M. Sutherland left the HBGS as Dux in 1953. According to classmates he was top in every class examination since the age of nine. He was also top Bursar at Glasgow University. He became a GP and a Genealogist.

Catherine Sutherland left School in 2014 as Girls' Dux.

John Sutherland (1925–2004), brother of Alastair, left the HBGS as Dux in 1943.

(Dr) Margaret B. Sutherland (1920–2011) left the HGGS as Dux in 1938, taking a FCH at Glasgow in French and German in 1942 and the Herkless Prize for the most distinguished Arts student. She became Professor of

Education at Leeds University and later Dean of the Faculty and was honoured by the French Government.

(Sir) Alexander Brown Swan (1869–1941) was Head of the manufacturing firm of Munro & Co. (Glasgow) Ltd. He was elected to the Glasgow Town Council in 1923 and was the Lord Provost of the City between 1932 and 1935. He was created a Knight in 1935.

Alexander Swan left HBGS in 1864 as Dux.

Charles Coverly Swan left HBGS in 1860 as Dux.

(Dr) Beth (Elizabeth) Taylor (née Slimming) left School as Dux in 1968 and worked for the UK Department of Energy, the University of New Mexico, the Los Alamos Laboratory and the UK Atomic Energy Authority. Most recently, since 2007, she was Director of Communications and External Relations for the Institute of Physics until 2014. She was awarded a HA in 2010. She is now Deputy Chair, UK National Commission for UNESCO. She was awarded a G and THA in 2010.

Joyce Taylor left HGGS in 1965. She was declared by the television industry 'Television Businesswoman of the Year' in 1997. She was the Founders' Day Speaker in 1999.

(Dr) (Kenneth) Kenny Taylor left School in 1972 and has become an award-winning wildlife film-maker and author. He has appeared frequently on national television and radio programmes. He was awarded a G and THA in 2011.

(Prof.) Milton W. Taylor left the School in 1947 and became an accomplished microbiologist, working at Bloomington University, Indiana, since 1967. Now Emeritus, he is writing on the influence of viruses and a history of virology.

(The Rev. Prof.) J. Patton Taylor TD MBE left School in 1968. He became Professor of Old Testament Literature, Language and Theology at the Union Theological College/Queen's University, Belfast. He is now Principal Emeritus.

Elizabeth A. Templeton (née MacLaren) MA BD (1945–2015) was Dux of HGGS in 1963. She gained the Logan Prize at Glasgow University for the most distinguished Arts graduate of 1967 and the Herkless Prize for the most distinguished woman graduate in the same year. She was the first woman to give the Founders' Day Service Address in Glasgow Cathedral in March 1971. More recently she has been lecturing in Divinity at Edinburgh University.

William L. Thompson joined S1 in 1890 and left HBGS as Dux in 1894. At Glasgow University he took MA, BSc and the Logan Memorial Prize for being the most distinguished graduate of his year. He followed his father, David, who was by then an HMI, into teaching. He taught in Allan Glen's and became Headmaster of Hawick GS.

(Miss) Annie Thomson (b. 1884) attended HGGS between 1895 and 1901, when she left as Dux. She took her MA from Glasgow University in 1905.

Christine J. Thomson left HGGS in 1974. She attended Glasgow School of Art and worked in a commercial agency, but now is freelance producing papercuts. She was commissioned to produce papercuts and prints for the Glasgow 2014 Commonwealth Games. She has produced a papercut for the School that can be customised as required.

Ian Douglas Thomson CBE (1921–2008) attended HBGS from 1931, and in his final year (1940) was Classical Dux and Gold Medallist. He joined the Civil Service and retired as Comptroller, Inland Revenue (Scotland).

Martina Thomson (née Hyslop) (1927–2014) attended the HGGS, 1938–43. She became a significant benefactor to the Bursary fund.

Thomas D. Thomson left School in 1966 and became News Editor for Reuters for the Americas (based in New York).

William Thomson (b. 1926) attended the HBGS between 1937 and 1944. He was former Director of Shell and of Coats Viyella.

Winnie Thomson (1914–2007) left School in 1932 and was founding member of the Children's Panel. She served on the Board of Glasgow's Citizen's Advice Bureau and was a member of the Marriage Guidance Council, and was actively involved with Girl-guiding.

(Prof.) John Aiton Todd (1875–1954) was a solicitor in Glasgow until 1907. He lectured in Economics in Cairo and Lahore before being professor at Nottingham, 1912–9. He was also a lecturer at Balliol, Oxford, until 1923, and was Principal of the City School of Commerce, Liverpool, 1923–40. He wrote a number of publications.

(Dr) Philip H. Todd left HBGS in 1974 as Dux. He took further degrees in Mathematics and became Founder and President of Saltire Software, a company developing Mathematics based software.

Alan Tomkins attended HBGS, 1964–73. His first business venture opened in Glasgow in 1982. His current interests include Vroni's Wine Bar in West Nile Street. He is former chairman of Glasgow Restaurateurs Association, 2001–05.

Isabel Traill (née Davidson) left HGGS in 1924 and graduated in Law. She was awarded an OBE for services to the Arts in Scotland.

Tracy Traynor was joint Girls' Dux in 1983 and has a career in journalism and as an author.

John Tubman left the school in 1977 and was the most distinguished graduate in Engineering at Glasgow University, 1980–1. He is now Group Director at the URS Corporation, a global engineering and environmental services agency.

(Rev. Dr) Julian S. Turnbull left the HBGS as Dux in 1972. He became a senior Network Engineer and ordained minister.

Turner of Ecchinswell, Baron (Jonathan) Adair Turner (b. 1955) left School in 1968. He was elected President of Cambridge University Union, 1977–8, and was awarded a G and THA in 2000. He was Director-General of the CBI. He was created a life peer, 2005, and was Chairman, Financial Services Authority, 2008–13.[85] He is now Senior Fellow in the London office of George Soros' Think Tank.

(Prof.) Kenneth John Turner (b. 1949) left HBGS in 1966. He has been Professor Emeritus of Computing Science, Stirling University, from 1987.[86]

John Tweed (1869–1933) attended HBGS until the death of his father in 1885 necessitated his leaving to run the family business of publishing. He developed into a prolific and successful sculptor of public monuments. His reputation was enhanced in 1912 by the completion of the equestrian group surmounting the Wellington Monument in St Paul's Cathedral. He is best remembered for his long and close friendship with Rodin.[87]

(Prof.) Alistair Ulph left HBGS in 1964. He took degrees at Glasgow and Oxford and became Professor of Economics at Southampton University. He was then appointed Vice-Principal of the University of Manchester and Dean of the Humanities Faculty.

(Prof.) David Tregar Ulph FRSE FRSA (b. 1946) left School as Dux in 1964, gaining a Snell Exhibition. He has been Professor of Economics, University of St Andrews, since 2006; and Head of School of Economics and Finance, since 2006.[88] In 2010 he was appointed Director of the Scottish Institute for Research in Economics.

(Elizabeth) Betty Ure (née McMillan) attended HGGS between 1928 and 1933. She was past Convener of the '57 Group, which raised money for the School. She was awarded a G and THA in 2001.

Barbara C.M. Uttamchandani (née MacPherson) left the School as Girls' Dux in 1979. She became a radiologist.

(Dr) Heather M. Valencia (née Ritchie) left HGGS as Dux in 1960. She lectured at Stirling University. She has taught on Yiddish summer programmes across Europe.

Ian Valentine MBE left HBGS in 1958. He was awarded an MBE in the Queen's Birthday Honours List in 2013. He was the former Chair of the Board of Management of Ayr College.

(Dr) James Valentine (1906–2007) won a scholarship to HBGS where he proved an outstanding pupil. In his final year at school in 1924 he was Dux, School Captain and Captain of cricket. He followed a career in medicine and proved an outstanding clinical psychiatrist with the University of Leeds Health Service.

Alex Verth (1938–98) left School in 1954 as Dux of Modern Languages. He took a CA qualification and became an established member of the Spanish business community. He was a partner with KPMG in Madrid.

A. Maurice Volti (1878–1971) attended the HBGS from 1883 until 1886. He was a musician and composer.

R. Russell Waddell (1919–44) left the HBGS as joint-Dux in 1937. He qualified in Medicine in 1942, but was killed in World War 2.

(Dr) Agnes Walker (née McDonald) (1930–2011) left HGGS as Dux in 1948. She became Keeper of Natural History at Glasgow Museum, Kelvingrove. (Her sister, Dr Rachel I. Douglas, née McDonald, was Dux in 1950.)

Catherine Mary Walker (b. 1891) left HGGS in 1909 as Dux. She took her MA in 1914 from Glasgow University.

(Dr) Catriona Walker (née Boyle) left School in 1982 and became Doctor for Scotland's Commonwealth Games Team in Malaysia in 1998.

(Prof.) Graham Walker (b. 1956) was educated at Glasgow, McMaster and Manchester Universities. Following several publications he became Professor of Political History at Queen's, Belfast.

(Prof.) (William) Bill Villiers Wallace (1926–2011) gained a scholarship to HBGS and left as Dux in 1944. He also was First in the Glasgow University Bursary Competition. He became influential globally, particularly when Director of the Institute of Soviet and Eastern European Studies at Glasgow University.

(Elizabeth) Betty Anne Cameron Walls (1914–2013) left HGGS in 1931. She became General Secretary of the Overseas Council of the Church of Scotland (jointly in 1955) in 1972 and was the first woman to hold this appointment. She was responsible for organising two hundred missionaries.

Morag Walls (née Kennedy) played for Scotland at hockey against Wales, England and Ireland in 1934–35 and 1935–36.

Isidore Aaron Walton CBE died in 1979, aged 66. He was one of Scotland's 'best known, best liked and most successful financial magnates'.[89] He left HGS aged fifteen to join his father in the property business. He became Chairman and MD of the Scottish Metropolitan Property Company. His charitable associations were legion and he gained honorary doctorates from Glasgow and Strathclyde Universities.

(Prof.) David Ward left HBGS in 1965 and became professor of Clinical Medicine at the University of California, San Diego.

Sue Ward left School in 1971 and was recently awarded the MBE in the Queen's Birthday Honours for her services to Further Education and to young people with mental health conditions.

Alistair Warnock left School in 1993 and won a bronze rowing medal at the Commonwealth Games in 1994.

Pat Warwick (née Begg) left School in 1965. She was presented with the highest award possible from the organisation for outstanding service to Guiding. Her Laurel Award celebrated her forty-four years as a leader with Guiding UK.

Russell Waters (1908–82) was educated at HBGS and Glasgow University. He appeared in repertory theatre and, until 1974, in feature films.

Ann Watkin (née Sibbald) left HGGS in 1967 as Head Girl. She became Director of the Scottish Consumer Council until 2005 and Chair, Financial Services Consumer Panel.

Gillian A.M. Watson (b. 1964) became MD of E.S. Noble and Co. Ltd since 2013.

Douglas J. Watson left School in 2000 as Boys' Dux. He studied Law at Oxford and works for an American Law firm in London.

Iain P. Watts left School in 2002 as Boys' Dux. He has been studying for a PhD in History and the History of Science at Princeton University.

The Hon. David Maclaren Webster QC (b. 1937) left School in 1956 and went on to become a judge. He was Honorary Recorder for the City of Salisbury Law Courts in 2001.

David Weitzman (1898–1987) attended HBGS, 1905–11, leaving School to go to England. He was called to the Bar (Gray's Inn), 1922; Labour MP for Stoke Newington, 1945–50; QC, 1951; Labour MP for Hackney North and Stoke Newington, 1950–79.[90]

George White left HBGS in 1833 as Dux.

Kenneth White (1894–1969) became Consul General to HM Foreign Service. He retired in 1954.

(Dr) Peter L. White left the School as Dux in 1985. He completed his PhD in Mathematics at Imperial College, London.

(Dr) Rehema White left the School in 1982 and graduated with FCH in Agriculture from Aberdeen University. After further study in Canada, Australia and South Africa she joined the Geography Department of St Andrews University.

(Prof.) Dorothy A. Whittington (b. 1941) attended HGGS and became professor of Health Psychology at Ulster University, 1999–2003.

William Whyte left HBGS in 1877 as Dux.

Hon. Sir Alan (Fraser) Wilkie (b. 1947) became a Judge at the Crown Court in 2004.

James Wilkie left HBGS in 1851 as joint-Dux.

(Miss) Jill C. Williamson left the School as Girls' Dux in 1990. Following a degree in Mathematics at Edinburgh University, she became an actuary at PWC.

Morven Williamson left School in 1989 and joined the Diplomatic Service. She served in the British Embassy in Hanoi, Vietnam, and became Vice-Consul at the British Consulate in Jeddah.

Rachel M. Williamson left School in 1997 as Girls' Dux and Head Girl.

Thomas F. Williamson (1922–2012) attended HBGS from 1935 until 1940. He was appointed HM Chief Inspector of Schools in Scotland in 1975.

(Dr) James Willocks (1928–2004) left School in 1946 and became an obstetrician, gynaecologist and a pioneer of ultra-sound. His particular contribution was in the scanning of the foetal head to assess the size and growth of the foetus.

(Judge) David Alec Wilson (1864–1933) was Dux of HBGS in 1879 and in 1880. He took his MA from Glasgow University in 1884. He was a member of the Indian Civil Service, 1883–1912; became a barrister in 1890, and worked as a judge in Burma. He was the biographer of Thomas Carlyle.

James Wilson (b. 1841) left HBGS in 1856 as Dux. He became minister at Lumsden, Aberdeenshire, 1869–73; Inspector of Schools in the West Indies, 1873–77; and minister at Gardenstoun, Banffshire.

James Cameron Wilson (1943–86) was Deputy Editor of the *Scottish Daily Record*.

(Prof) Arlene D. Wilson-Gordon (née Wilson) left School in 1964 and studied at Glasgow and Oxford. Since 2000 she has been Professor of Chemistry at Bar-Llan University, Israel working at the atomic and molecular level.

Walter Wingate (1865–1918) was the son of David Wingate, 'The Collier Poet'. He attended HBGS from 1876 and left aged fifteen in 1880. He gained Honours in Mathematics at Glasgow University. He taught at St John's GS in Hamilton until his untimely early death. He was the author of 'The Sair Finger'.

(Dr) John Wishart (1879–1970) was Organising Secretary of the Educational Institute of Scotland, 1941–6; and President of the EIS, 1946–7.

Ronald B. Woods left HBGS as Dux in 1967. He became Principal Teacher of History at Glasgow Academy.

William F. Woods left the HBGS as Dux in 1965.

Winnie Wooldridge (née Shaw) (1947–92) reached the ranking of no. 3 tennis player in Britain and the quarter-finals of Wimbledon in 1970 and 1971.

Daniel Wright (d. 1885) left HBGS in 1853 as Dux. He took his MA from Glasgow University in 1867 and became minister of Bellahouston.

Moira P. Wright left HGGS as Dux in 1967.

Rosemary Muir Wright (1943–2006) left HGGS in 1961. She became Senior Lecturer in Art History at St Andrew's University in 1997.

(Very Rev. Dr) Hugh Rutherford Wyllie MA MCIBS (b. 1934) attended HBGS from 1945 until 1951. He was Minister, Old Parish Church of Hamilton, 1981–2000; and Moderator of the General Assembly of the Church of Scotland, 1992–3.[91] He was the Founders' Day Speaker in 1993 and achieved a G and THA in 2002

Elizabeth (Elspeth) M. Yearling (née McConnell) (1944–1983) was Dux of HGGS in 1962 and attended Glasgow and Oxford Universities. She became a university lecturer.

Annie E. Young was joint winner of the Herkless Prize in 1928, awarded to the best woman graduate in the Faculty of Arts

Archibald Young left HBGS in 1857 as Dux.

(Dr) Gavin Young (1892–1977) was a pupil at HBGS, 1903–9, and qualified in Medicine. He gained an MC in World War 1 and later became Head of the Department of Otolaryngology at the Western infirmary, Glasgow.

John Young (b. 1875) left HBGS in 1891 as Dux. He took an MA (1896) and became a student of theology in the United Presbyterian College in Edinburgh.

Walter Young left HBGS in 1854 as Dux.

Humza Yousaf (b. 1985) left the School in 2003. He became the SNP MSP (Glasgow List) since 2011 and Minister for External Affairs and International Development since 2012.

Daniel Yuill left HBGS in 1867 as Dux.

John L. Yuill (b. 1868) left HBGS in 1885 as Dux. He graduated with a MB CM in 1891.

William Yuill left HBGS in 1863 as Dux.

Armin Zanner left the School in 1997 as joint-Boys' Dux. In 2014 he became Head of Vocal Studies at Guildhall School of Music and Drama.

(Dr) Avivah Zornberg (née Gottlieb) attended Langside Primary and left HGGS in 1961 (class of 1962). She gained a BA with FCH and her PhD in English Literature from Cambridge University in 1965. Originally an academic, but more recently has concentrated on teaching the Torah and Biblical scholarship.

FOURTEEN   Hutchesons' Today

Given the leadership problems faced by the School in the 1980s and in the first decade of this century, the appointment of the new Rector of the School in 2005 was the most important of decisions. The Governors of that time appreciated this and care was taken to choose someone who had considerable empathy with Hutchesons' and its particular Scottish history and traditions.

The news that Ken Greig had been appointed, and this by a unanimous decision, was greeted with enthusiasm by those with a Hutchie connection. A clear message had been sent out that the School was back on track, confirmed by Greig's assuring of staff and parents that his aim was to deliver the best of Scottish education.

The new Rector also spelled out that time would be spent in his early meetings 'binding the community together' and doing all that could be done to improve the ethos and 'make the School more at ease with itself'. The development of his management team to include a Depute Rector (Ethos) underlined his commitment to a theme which was further strengthened by his regular sitting in on lessons and giving feedback to staff. Such actions proved an excellent and effective way of getting to know a significant number of people, in as short a time as possible.

Greig inherited a school which had become in recent years one of the largest in the independent sector in Scotland, and since taking office he has been clearly aware of the need to ensure that separate departments do not become isolated and that senior staff do not concentrate exclusively on their own remits because of the size of the School and the geography of the buildings.

Mention of the size of the School highlights one of issues for the future. A comparison with its major rivals, St Aloysius' College, Glasgow Academy and the High School of Glasgow, suggests that, despite economies of scale, a school of about 1,000 pupils has distinct advantages over one with around

1,500 pupils. Indeed, it is likely that a number of prospective parents may well have been put off by the increasing numbers of Hutchie, preferring somewhat smaller schools. In the case of a larger school one would expect children to be more independent, while in the case of a smaller school one would expect its whole community to be far closer. Those with experience of more than one independent Glasgow school generally comment that while the larger school can offer a wider curriculum, in the smaller school it is much easier for staff to know more pupils and to know them better.

Rector Greig soon appreciated the need to develop the pastoral care side of his school and he made an important change to his Senior Management Team by appointing a Depute Rector to have overall responsibility for pastoral care of all secondary year groups. Her responsibility also extended to pastoral care of teaching staff as well.

Another apparent difference between schools relates to expectations. Historically at Hutchie, pupils have generally committed themselves to one area or another of school life – music, rugby, hockey, drama or whatever. At a smaller establishment, the pupils are usually expected to be involved in everything on offer. This produces tensions as pupils are pulled in different directions, but participation in diverse activities means pupils have a marked breadth of interests.

Not only does this look good on UCAS (University) applications but it also goes some way to explaining why progress in one area of school life in smaller schools is often accompanied by progress in another. Once a breakthrough comes in one activity, then self-belief leads to more success. In rugby, hockey, tennis, swimming, skiing and badminton, success comes to be expected at local, then district, then national level. Perhaps this is a possible explanation of why a small school can do surprisingly well in competition with a larger neighbour.

Despite some differences, however, most independent schools have much in common. This seems to be particularly the case with the ethos of such schools in Scotland. While this appears to remain constant, parents appear more demanding as paying customers, and treat the teaching staff with less reverence and respect. The success of Rector David Ward in the 1990s had much to do with his partnership with his Depute, Sandy Strang, who was adept in dealing with difficult pupils and parents.

The School worked hard and played hard. There were no airs or graces about Hutchie pupils. They were not arrogant in the slightest, but very down to earth, unassuming and straightforward. This was ideal given the variety of intake in terms of ethnic diversity and social class.

Traditionally school assemblies of the whole School were held at the start of each day and were significant in establishing community spirit and in fostering shared values. This was not an avenue open to Hutchie, but nonetheless Rector Greig and the School appear comfortable with the tradition of catering for a very wide spread of religious belief and non-belief.

By the 1970s about 10 per cent of pupils were Jewish. The effect of this could be seen in daily life in the School. When it was belatedly (in 1961) decided to hold an annual Founders' Day, it did not take very long for a Jewish Service to be introduced on the same day and this included a separate Jewish Address. This became the norm between 1974 and 1983.

A similar percentage were Muslim, and they expected the School to accord them at least some of the privileges available to Jewish pupils. It was also surprising how many Hindus and Sikhs attended. The dozen or so Japanese and a larger number of Koreans and Australians all added to its diversity.

Certainly, being a more ethnically diverse school, it has been perceived by a number of primary Head Teachers as different from other 'private schools' in Glasgow, and therefore acceptable to approach for a pupil from a very disadvantaged parental background.

Taking a longer view, the School has found itself being frequented by the less wealthy Glasgow bourgeoisie, and many poorer than this, in the twentieth century. Both Boys' and Girls' Schools offered a demanding but successful academic training to their pupils which facilitated their social progress and, if they returned to Glasgow, would often lead them to choose a different school for their children: the High School or the Academy; Laurel Bank or Park.

This was partly the result of the move toward ending Grant-Aided status, which was also significant in the decision to merge the two Schools. Although Miss McIver feared that the Governors might abandon the education of girls, this was unlikely to happen, given that the Governors' commitment to girls' education went back a century.

Hutchie had a reputation for being very old-fashioned. Even after amalgamation of the Schools, pupils were taught in single-sex classes for English – very much against the modern educational thinking of the time. This, however, did not worry the School, as it was felt that it worked.

Educational decisions elsewhere – in particular the closure of the Boys' High School in 1976 and the growth of a new High School at Anniesland – seemed to play into Hutchie's hands, until the setback to its reputation in 1985–6. It took a while for Hutchie to regain its awesome reputation.

It remains fiercely academic, but its pupils achieve their impressive results from a fairly unselective background. The Hutchie experience is traditional teaching at its very best, nowadays using the most up-to-date tools available and with a significant degree of Scottish emphasis on breadth.

Another part of the reputation of the School involves fee levels. Hutchie placed great emphasis on value for money, and seemed always determined to keep fees to a minimum. For a number of years – continuing on into the 1990s – Hutchesons' fees were among the lowest in Scotland. The School was run on a shoestring: it had no Bursar until Ian Tainsh took office, and only in the last few decades have Finance Conveners of the Governors moved away from the belief that their main role was to keep Hutchie's fees at the bottom of all fee tables. This led to the School falling behind its rivals, a fact that only changed when complete amalgamation was finally introduced.

The SQA results of the School have edged upwards in recent years, enabling the School to retain its position in the top four of all league tables in the country. In 2008 twelve Hutchie pupils sat six Highers, and of these six attained six As. Of the pupils nationally who gained six A-Grade Highers at band 1, four came from Hutchie. In 2010 some 58% of pupils achieved five (or more) Highers at A Grade, allowing the School to aim for a target of 60%. In December 2011 the *Sunday Times* named Hutchie as the 'Scottish Independent School of the Year' based on the criteria of the volume of presentations coupled with the quality of grades achieved. At the same diet of examinations, Hutchie pupils had the highest marks in Scotland in Higher Technology, Higher Modern Studies and Advanced Higher Physics. In 2012, some 42 pupils in S5 sat six Highers rather than the customary five. Such results say much about pupils' commitment to academic study.

The same week as the *Sunday Times* announced its award, the School had more welcome news – the OSCR judgment confirming the School's charitable status. Just as the impressive menu of extra-curricular activities on offer gave the lie to the myth that the School was no more than an 'examination factory', so the increased number of bursaries on offer in the School, 9.9%, and the income spent on them, 4.9%,[1] confirmed that the ethos of the school through the centuries has been the same: if you are clever enough and prepared to work hard, you can go to Hutchie, As a former Rector said, 'It's cool to be clever here', and this remains the ethos of this remarkable school.

The future for Hutchie looks healthy. The School is stable at the moment despite a very marked change-over in staffing in the last decade or so, largely as a result of the retirement of a large number of experienced, older staff. It is the biggest change since Rector John Hutchison's time. Yet the numbers applying to join the staff are larger than ever before. The expectation is for this to continue during the tenure of the current Rector, with a further raising of the quality of teaching in the School.

Provided the Governing Board produces a succession plan and a vision for the future, the School can expect to advance on the firm foundations of its proud history.

APPENDIX ONE
Genealogy of the Founders

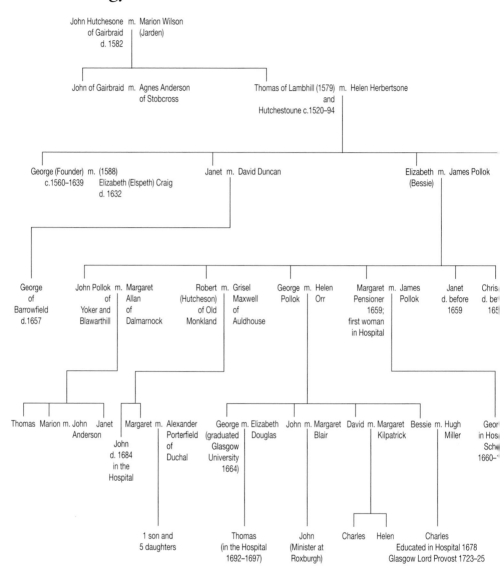

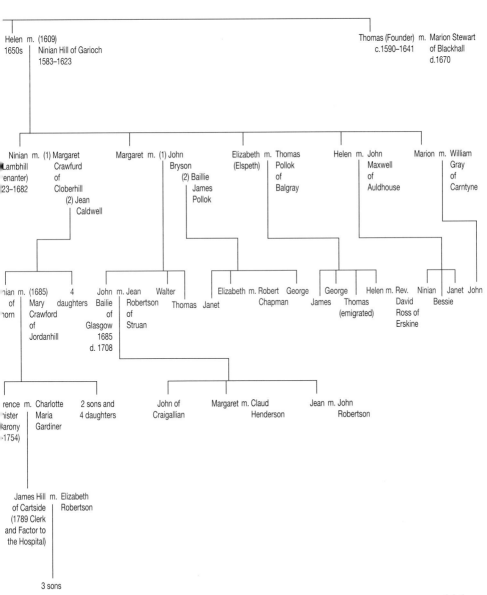

Helen m. (1609)
1650s   Ninian Hill of Garioch
         1583–1623

Thomas (Founder) m. Marion Stewart
c.1590–1641   of Blackhall
                    d.1670

Ninian m. (1) Margaret   Margaret m. (1) John   Elizabeth m. Thomas   Helen m. John   Marion m. William
Lambhill   Crawfurd   Bryson   (Elspeth)   Pollok   Maxwell   Gray
enanter)   of   (2) Baillie   of   of   of
23–1682   Cloberhill   James   Balgray   Auldhouse   Carntyne
            (2) Jean   Pollok
            Caldwell

nian m. (1685)   4   John m. Jean   Walter   Elizabeth m. Robert George   George   Helen m. Rev.   Ninian Janet John
of   Mary   daughters Bailie Robertson   Thomas Janet   Chapman   James   Thomas   David   Bessie
horn   Crawford   of   of Struan   (emigrated)   Ross of
       of   Glasgow   Erskine
       Jordanhill   1685
                            d. 1708

rence m. Charlotte   2 sons and   John of   Margaret m. Claud   Jean m. John
hister   Maria   4 daughters   Craigallian   Henderson   Robertson
arony   Gardiner
–1754)

James Hill m. Elizabeth
of Cartside   Robertson
(1789 Clerk
and Factor to
the Hospital)

3 sons

335

APPENDIX TWO

Hutchie Heraldry

The coat of arms of the School dates from relatively recent times, though it bears an ancient connection. The so-called 'badge' dates from 4 February 1929, when the Lord Lyon George Swinton granted arms to the Governors of Hutchesons' Educational Trust.[1] Legally, the Trust arms were for use by the Trust alone, not the School, but through use and wont, habit and repute, very gradually they became assumed as those of the School.

Seven decades passed, and in 1997, moves were made to regularise the position. On 13 February that year, the Governors of the Trust in a petition to Lord Lyon Sir Malcolm Innes of Edingight,[2] resigned their arms, and petitioned for a new grant of arms for the Trust. At the same time, the Governors petitioned that the arms previously used by them be matriculated for sole use of the School; and so from 1 May 1997, the 'badge' so long used by the School was finally given legal status. Meanwhile, four months later, on 5 September 1997, the new arms[3] for the Trust were matriculated.

How has the School heraldry been used? The Prospectus of the Boys' School of 1952 (when Rector Watson was in office) stated that boys were expected to wear uniform of at least tie plus cap-with-badge. Blazer with 'badge' was recommended, but not compulsory. At this time a very few older boys in the Boys' School in Crown Street wore plain navy-blue caps bearing a metal badge of the arms, rather than the woven badge forming part of the cap. This fashion was not unusual: St Aloysius boys used metal cap badges into the early 1960s.

How did the arms of the School originate? Popular belief is that the arms are based on those borne by the Hutcheson founders, but evidence is merely circumstantial. The historical background is that Thomas Hutcheson of Lambhill held position in Glasgow as a prosperous merchant and laird, and when he died in 1594, his arms would have been inherited by his elder son George, and on his death in 1639 they would have passed to Thomas as next heir. There is, however, no actual documentary evidence for arms having been held by any of the family.

Any confirmation possibly perished in a fire in Lyon Office in 1670. Clues remain. Sir George Mackenzie of Rosehaugh, writing in 1680, described arms for an unnamed Hutcheson as 'Argent, a fesse azur surmounted of three Arrows; the middlemost in pale, and the other two in bend with the points downward, and meeting in the base counterchanged of the first and second, in chief a Boars head erased sable'. In other words, these are the arms of the School today, all except the book in base.

The Forman/Workman Roll, a catalogue of various arms extant in Scotland, lists a shield for Hutcheson, exactly akin to that described by Mackenzie of Rosehaugh. The Forman/Workman Roll dates from c.1565, exactly the period when Thomas Hutcheson of Lambhill flourished. Arms like this, or closely akin, are also to be found in Sir James Balfour of Denmylne's *Scottish Surnames* of c. 1630; Pont's *Armorial*, 1624; a mention by Sir David Linday of Rathillet, c. 1570, and the Dunvegan *Armorial* of 1560. While there is clear Hutcheson generality of heraldic design, there is nowhere any reference to a specific Hutcheson family or person.

Hutchesons' Hospital in Ingram Street yields what may be the strongest pointer. On the elevation facing Hutcheson Street stand the statues of George and Thomas, either side of the frontage. Between them and high on the pediment supported by two Corinthian columns are Hutcheson arms, just as described by Mackenzie of Rosehaugh in 1680 and exactly as illustrated in the Forman/Workman Roll. The present Hutchesons' Hospital (since the early 1980s renamed Hutchesons' Hall) was built from 1802 onwards by the architect David Hamilton to replace the original hospital of 1641 in nearby Trongate. Hamilton however built into his new structure several features from the old Hospital, notably the statues of George and Thomas carved in 1649 by James Colquhoun. Other unnamed stone features from the original Hospital were incorporated by Hamilton into his building, and it seems likely that the Hutcheson arms on today's frontage were removed from the Trongate. If so, then the Hutchesons' Hall-Trongate heraldry could well illustrate the arms used by George Hutcheson of Lambhill. They were inherited by Thomas in 1639, and when he died without heirs of his name, his arms reverted to the Crown.

Hutcheson heraldry decorates the family monument standing on the east side of the main south door of Glasgow Cathedral. The marital arms of Thomas Hutcheson and his wife, Marion Stewart of Blackhall, crown the pinnacle of what is one of the larger memorials in the old graveyard. It is undeniably Hutcheson in style and meaning. No date exists for its creation. However, in 1731, an order was made for the repair of the tomb and thus suggests the antiquity of the monument.[4]

It is from these presumed arms of Hutcheson of Lambhill that the School's 'badge' of today is taken, with the addition of the book in base to represent learning. The School shield is white, crossed by a wide blue bar. The colours white and blue are held to represent purity and idealism respectively. The arrows are 'instruments of war'. As for the boar's head above the arrows, in Celtic times the boar was venerated as a sacred beast, so powerful that representations of it appear in heraldry across Scotland from Berwick to Caithness, and from Sutherland to Stranraer. Above the shield is the crest of the Sun, source of all energy, a motivating force. So taken together, Hutchie heraldry contains the six elements of the sacred, the warlike, the pure, the idealistic, the educational and the motivating, as well as being surmounted by a seventh, the motto (*Veritas*) Truth.

The School 'badge' appears in different forms for boys' and girls' uniforms, the former displaying simply shield, crest and motto, while the latter exhibits the full heraldic achievement of shield, helmet, crest, motto and mantling. The so-called 'FP badge' used by both sexes is exactly similar to that of the girls. Heraldically, all are the same.

The School can be justifiably proud of its use of heraldry. The arms are maximised to the full – on buildings, badges, banners, books, bookplates, business cards, signage, stationery, flags, uniforms and even litter bins. In the wider world of merchandise, the arms appear on china, coasters, bottle-labels, mugs, glassware, ties, scarves, caps, T-shirts, cufflinks and pens.

The arms serve as more than just as decoration: they are the overall identity of the School. Whatever its origin, Hutchie heraldry represents a living memorial to the founding Hutcheson brothers.

Hutchesons' Grammar School: The Tartan

Hutchesons' was by no means the first school to gain its own tartan, but it bears more of a story than most, and comes with a pedigree that can be traced to the early eighteenth century.

The tartan has its genesis in the work of Colin Hutcheson, businessman, textile designer and one-time managing director of Kinloch Anderson Ltd, the internationally known manufacturers and retailers of tartans in Edinburgh, and who had designed and recorded a family tartan for his surname. Gordon Casely was a fellow director with him of the Scottish Tartans Authority and, intrigued by the Hutcheson family tartan, determined that a tartan be suggested to the School with Colin Hutcheson as designer. It was, however, the Interim Rector of the time, Graham MacAllister, who took forward the project.

The School tartan was based on that of the Hutcheson family, itself a classically simple sett[1] in red and green, designed and registered in 2000. Colin Hutcheson used his own tartan as a template on which he brought together the livery colours of the School, those of the boys' and girls' uniforms. The outcome was a School tartan that joins the range of the more unusual setts of Scotland in having not one but two shades of blue. White and black also appear, while in an artistic move red was introduced as a counterpoint.

The Hutchie tartan carries antiquity of lineage; Colin Hutcheson based the pattern of his family tartan on an old form of Douglas of the early eighteenth century, then based the School tartan on that. Thus Hutchie's modern sett follows exactly Hutcheson's family design, yet maintains a classic style that bears within it three centuries of history.

When the first suggestion for a School tartan was made in July 2004, there was a muted reaction, and nothing much happened until November of that year. Then came the request from Interim Rector, Graham MacAllister, and director of development, Catherine Gillen: would it be possible to have the tartan designed, approved, woven and made into a kilt for the Head Boy and Head Girl to wear in Glasgow Cathedral on Founders' Day, 2005? Given that the normal timescale from initial concept to finished product is around two years, this was going to be a major task. The race commenced.

Inside a week, Colin Hutcheson produced four draft designs and a flurry of email exchanges took place between the School in Glasgow, Hutcheson in Edinburgh, Johnstons the weavers in Elgin and Casely in Aberdeen. There was immediate unanimity over the design – what is now the School tartan – and a decision was made in early February 2005 to have a four-metre trial length woven. Eight days later the informal focus group in the School, composed of Governors, staff, Former Pupils, tartan experts and kiltmaker, unanimously accepted, as stunning, the pilot length. Tailor John Howie arrived at the School and wasted no time in measuring the Head Boy, Ian Miller, and the Head Girl, Emma Lindsay, before returning to his Coupar Angus workroom to await the tartan to make a kilt and skirt.

It proved a race that went to the wire. The finished cloth went direct from weaver to John Howie with no time for fittings, so when Ian and Emma arrived at Glasgow Cathedral on Wednesday 16 March, an hour before the 2005 Founders' Day service, they met John carrying the precious garments plus his emergency workbox, in case of last-minute alterations. It says much for his skill that all that was needed was removal of the basting that kept the garments in shape for the journey from Coupar Angus to Glasgow. Everything fitted. So when Ian and Emma stepped up to read the lessons in the Cathedral, they effectively inaugurated the tartan. The Interim Rector and members of the Hutchesons' Pipe Band sported brand-new Hutchie tartan ties. To Gordon Casely fell the honour of delivering the Founders' Day Oration, and due mention of the tartan was made. For designer Colin Hutcheson, the event was another high point in a career spanning some fifty years in the textile industry.

Technical details:

The tartan, designed by Colin Hutcheson, was recorded by the Scottish Tartans Authority on 1 February 2005, and is online at the Scottish Register of Tartans: *www.tartanregister.gov.uk/tartanDetails.aspx?ref=1799.*

The ITI (International Tartan Index) number is 6518; the category of the tartan is corporate.

Legacies and Donations to Which No Special Condition Was Attached

1648	John Wilson, a pensioner in the Hospital	£19 8s 11d
1706	John Bryson[1], merchant, grand-nephew of the Hutchesons: Three acres at Garngadhill	£100
1709	Andrew Morison,[2] mariner	£12 19s 7d
1715	The town of Glasgow towards purchase of a new clock	£16 13s 4d
1718	The town of Glasgow to straighten land of Ramshorn	£55 11s 2d
1736 *and*		
1737	The Glasgow Assembly	£18 17s 9d
1740	Magistrates of Glasgow (fines levied)	£23 15s
1745	Aitkenhead	£5
1745	Provost Culter	£5
1748	Mrs Luke, widow of Robert Luke, a goldsmith	£5 11s 1d
1754	Provost Peter Murdoch	£20
1759	Andrew Buchanan	£10
1759	George Buchanan, his son	£10
1761	Archibald Buchanan	£10
1739–67	Anonymous (various)	£240
1768	Sir Michael Stewart of Blackhall, on account of his sister, Margaret Stewart, widow of John Pedie of Ruchhill	£5 11s 1d
1775	Mrs Lilias Grahame, daughter of James Grahame of Kilmannan	£20
1776	Jean Murdoch, daughter of Zacharias Murdoch, Merchant in Glasgow	£5

1776	John Murdoch, Merchant and late Provost of Glasgow, paid by Mr William Miller, his grandson and heir	£15
1777	James Brown, Merchant in Glasgow, heir of Provost Andrew Cochrane out of respect to him, and knowledge of his attention to make a bequest to the Hospital	£100
1781	Agnes Murdoch	£5
1786	Thomas Nicolson	£50
1788	James Coulter, Merchant	£25
1798	Christian Dunlop, a Pensioner of the Hospital	£74 13s 6d
1802	Peter Reid, Merchant, Glasgow	£47
1804	John Campbell of Clathic, late Preceptor	£46
1811	William Telfer, a pensioner in the Hospital	£7 10s
1814	James Henderson, Merchant in Virginia	£400
1814	John Snow, Barber in Glasgow: half his means	£485 7s 6d
1814	James Forrester, Merchant, Glasgow	£35
1815	Margaret and Janet Telfour, daughters of John Telfour, watchmaker	£20
1821	David Carrick Buchanan	£50
1828	Charles Hutcheson	£15
1829	Miss Margaret Johnston	£180
1833	Captain Robert Tennant, Ayr	£594 3s 3d
1863	Miss Barbara Aitcheson, erstwhile Pensioner	£100
1868	Miss Margaret Alexander	£225 10s
1875	George Thomson, Watchmaker, Glasgow (p.a.)	£25

NOTES

ACKNOWLEDGEMENTS

1 Gordon Brown: *Maxton* (Edinburgh 1986) p. 23.

CHAPTER I

1 James Grant: *The History of the Burgh Schools of Scotland* (London 1876) p. 2.
2 A step in woollen cloth-making involving the cleansing of cloth to eliminate impurities.
3 E. Patricia Dennison in Michael Lynch (ed.): *Oxford Companion to Scottish History* (Oxford 2007) pp. 267–8.
4 Weavers.
5 Burgesses of merchant-rank numbered 214 at this time.
6 Bakers.
7 Susan Milligan: *The Merchants' House of Glasgow, 1605–2005* (Glasgow 2004) p. 7.
8 A five-storey stone Tolbooth was built on the site of the old one.
9 Then meaning a hostel for the old and destitute and a boarding school for orphans.
10 It had nine pedimented (with the triangular upper part of the front of a classical building) windows ranged above and on either side of a pend (a Scottish architectural term for a passageway that passes through a building, often from a street through to a courtyard) where classical columns supported a fully detailed entablature, all of which was reproduced above in miniature to house a coat of arms.
11 Frank Arneil Walker: 'Origins and First Growths' in Peter Reed (ed.): *Glasgow: The Forming of the City* (Edinburgh 1999) p. 21.
12 Tenure of land in a town held in return for service or annual rent.
13 Or 'ridges' referring to parallel strips of ploughed cultivated land.
14 Of a bishop or bishops.
15 £1 sterling equalled eighteen merks which equalled twelve pounds Scots.
16 William H. Hill: *History of the Hospital and School in Glasgow Founded by George and Thomas Hutcheson* (Glasgow 1881) p. 1.
17 George Eyre-Todd: *History of Glasgow* vol. 2 (Glasgow 1931) p. 232 ff.
18 A large manor or estate.
19 J.O. Mitchell: *Old Glasgow Essays* (Glasgow 1905) p. 278.

20 Hill: *History of the Hospital* p.4.

21 These included Nicolhouse and Broomward in what came to be known as the parish of Calton.

22 A maker or repairer of casks and barrels.

23 Acquired by George from Matthew Stuart for 13,000 merks in October 1625.

24 *Hospital Records* vol. 1 (17 August 1641 to 27 December 1764): 3 May 1678.

25 *Ibid.* 31 July 1685 and 12 June 1691.

26 Leather worker.

27 Six other children – four boys and two girls – died in infancy.

28 In Scots Law, a gift disposing of lands for charitable purposes.

29 See Appendix 1, Genealogy of the Founders.

30 Thomas Somerville: *Two Great Glasgow Men: George and Thomas Huchesone. A Lecture* (Glasgow 1901).

31 High.

32 Chest. It is still in existence and can be seen in the Library of the Procurators in the now renamed Nelson Mandela Place (formerly St George's Place). It was gifted to the Library in 1912 as part of the Hill collection for the people of Glasgow. James Whyte (PT History in HBGS): *A Lecture in the School Assembly Hall on 11 January, 1963 to the Members and Friends of the '1650' Club* (Glasgow 1963) p. 5.

33 William Greenhorne: *History of Partick, 550–1912* (Glasgow 1928) pp. 12–13. The property was eventually demolished in the 1830s.

34 Hill: *History of the Hospital* p. 27.

35 *Burgh Records* 5 June 1637 and 14 January 1638.

36 And second only in the country to George Heriot, the jeweller and banker of Queen Anne of Scotland from 1599.

37 *Burgh Records* 24 July 1680.

38 In ecclesiastic law, secular persons commended to be trustees of Church benefices.

39 The Court of a bishop.

40 In Scots Law, delivery or granting of legal possession of feudal land.

41 Maintenance.

42 Cathedral.

43 Eyre-Todd: *History of Glasgow* p.234.

44 The Lord Provost, three Bailies (two Merchant and one Trades), Dean of Guild, Deacon Convener, fifteen Councillors of the burgh and three Ministers (of Cathedral, Tron and Blackfriars Churches).

45 In Scots Law, a supplement to a Testament, added some time later: it being necessary to extend confirmation of an executor to cover property not originally included.

46 Treasurer.

47 The Tomb was restored by the architect, T.L. Watson, and sculptor, William Vickers, in 1902.

48 About £4 million in purchasing power today.

49 Heriot originally had wanted his Hospital to be for orphans, but Balqanquall dropped this provision because he believed there would not be sufficient demand for this. Heriot would have approved, for he was more interested in locality – Edinburgh – and class – burgesses (middle class) fallen on hard times.

50 The Heriot Governors bought their first land, the Broughton estate, in July 1625.
51 Hill: *History of the Hospital* p. 23.

CHAPTER 2

1 Blair died in 1723 aged sixty-one. He also left a considerable amount to Merchants' House.
2 Hill: *History of the Hospital* p. 156.
3 Brian R.W. Lockhart: *Jinglin' Geordie's Legacy* (East Linton, 2003) p. 21.
4 Hill: *History of the Hospital* p. 74.
5 £408 14s Scots.
6 £591 14s Scots.
7 *Hospital Minutes*: 1 November 1651; 3 June 1654 and 31 December 1655.
8 1626–83.
9 *Council Minutes*: 24 November 1655 and 16 August 1656.
10 Former or late.
11 *Hospital Minutes vol. 1*: 13 September 1659.
12 Crumbled and decayed parts of the stone.
13 *Hospital Minutes* vol. 1: 13 September 1659; 17 August 1699; 6 December 1715; 23 September 1718 and 5 July 1787.
14 This section of the book relies heavily on Ray McKenzie: *Public Sculpture of Glasgow* (Liverpool, 2002) pp. 205–8.
15 Rev. W. Wade: *The History of Glasgow, Ancient and Modern* (Glasgow 1822) p. 126.
16 Glasgow *Directory* for 1787, p. 21, and for 1789, p. 80.
17 Known as the closs.
18 J. McUre: *Glasghu Facies: A View of the City of Glasgow* (Glasgow 1736) 1830 edition p. 68
19 Hewn or dressed masonry.
20 James Bell: *Glasgow, Its Municipal Organisation and Administration* (Glasgow 1896).
21 John Tweed: *Glasgow Ancient and Modern* (Glasgow 1872) p. 907.
22 Hill: *History of the Hospital* p. 87.
23 In Scots Law, a perpetual lease at a fixed rent.
24 *Hospital Minutes* vol. 2: 18 February and 1 March 1791.
25 *Constitution, Rules and History* p. 91. By 1820 charitable provision was being made for 213 old people and 102 boys.
26 Hill: *History of the Hospital* p. 89.
27 A.D. Dunlop: *Hutchesons' Grammar: the History of a Glasgow School* (Glasgow 1992) p. 8.
28 The Town Council dominating membership of the Patrons.
29 *Hospital Minutes* vol. 1: 9 December 1695.
30 He had acquired the lands from Sir George Elphinstone in 1634.
31 The early history of the lands south of the river, in the barony of Gorbals, is recounted in John Ord: *The Story of the Barony of Gorbals* (Paisley 1919) pp. 17–60 and Hill: *History of the Hospital* pp. 99–134.

32 *Hospital Minutes*, vol. 2;1 December 1788

33 *Hospital Minutes* vol. 2; 10 February 1790 and also 1794.

34 Hill: *History of the Hospital* p. 131.

35 Report of the Committee of the Lands, February 1802 in *Constitution, Rules and History of Hutchesons' Hospital* (Glasgow 1850) p. 150.

36 John R. Kellett: *Glasgow* (Glasgow 1961) pp. 214–15.

37 5 July 1787; 18 February and 1 March 1791; Hill: *History of the Hospital* pp 86–8.

38 Kellett: *Glasgow* pp. 215–17.

39 A fund formed by periodically setting aside money for the gradual repayment of a debt or replacement of a wasting asset.

40 *Annals* vol. 1: p. 84.

41 Wade's *History of Glasgow* p. 171 gives a more critical assessment of the building.

42 Account paid in February 1796.

43 *Hospital Minutes* vol. 3: 29 November 1804.

CHAPTER 3

1 £26 12s 4d Scots.

2 Hill: *History of the Hospital* p. 205.

3 13 May 1648 and 20 May 1648.

4 Glasgow Cathedral.

5 Robert Alison: *The Anecdotage of Glasgow* (Glasgow 1892) p. 68.

6 *Hospital Minutes* vol. 1: 25 December 1649.

7 June Steeds: 'It Began with Two Brothers', *Scottish Field*, May 1962 pp. 65–9.

8 Cabbage.

9 Reducing costs or expenditure in response to economic difficulty.

10 From the Account Books it appears that even before this resolution was passed it had become the practice to board at least some of the boys out of the Hospital, as an entry occurs of the payment of £28 8s Scots 'for two boys' entertainment with Simon Pickersgill, preceding Candlemas 1652'. (1 January 1653).

11 *Burgh Records* 27 October 1655. Neither James Clerk nor James King were dignified with the title of Schoolmaster.

12 Dunlop: *Hutchesons' Grammar* p. 22.

13 Son of the deceased James Pollock, cordiner, and Margaret Pollock, sister's daughter to the Founders.

14 7 March 1667.

15 Dunlop: *Hutchesons' Grammar* pp. 23–4.

16 An educated man, Forrest went on to become a Writer.

17 The Darien Scheme was the unsuccessful attempt by Scotland to become a world trading nation by establishing a colony on the isthmus of Panama in the later 1690s.

18 Douglas Watt: *The Price of Scotland: Darien, Union and the Wealth of Nations* (King's Lynn 2007) p. 69.

19 See Chapter 2 p. 23.

20 Dunlop: *Hutchesons' Grammar* p. 27.

21 Hill: *History of the Hospital* p. 223.
22 Or 'College' as it was known.
23 From February 1815 until February 1822.
24 A series of successive stages.
25 A second saviour following the events of 1652.
26 The Grammar School moved to George Street in 1788.

CHAPTER 4

1 Written by Robert Dodsley, its third edition dated from 1751. All told, it went through 142 editions.
2 William Perry was a Lecturer in English at an Academy in Edinburgh and wrote a number of textbooks and reference works, which were popular as guides to pronunciation. The 22nd Improved Edition of his *Spelling Book* was published in 1817.
3 Women had been admitted in 1737 following the urgings of Thomas's widow.
4 Dunlop: *Hutchesons' Grammar* p. 35.
5 There was little significance in this, as paper qualifications were less important at this time.
6 *Hospital Minutes* vol. 2: 19 February 1801.
7 Not conforming with accepted or orthodox standards or belief.
8 Dunlop: *Hutchesons' Grammar* pp 44–45.
9 The roll in 1839 and 1840 was 120 boys.
10 Separate classrooms had been introduced in 1824 to the newly-built Edinburgh Academy.
11 Knox obtained an MA in 1812.
12 The bounds of the medieval burgh of Glasgow north of the River Clyde.
13 Hill: *History of the Hospital* p. 229.
14 The roll in 1875 was 286 boys.
15 The rolls in 1876 were 1,002 boys (and at the new Girls' School some 728 joined).
16 University Bursaries had been introduced in the 1860s. These went further than Thomas in his Will. He had merely hoped that such bursaries would be provided by the Town Council.
17 1830–1902. See Norman Graves: *School Textbook Research: The Case of Geography, 1800–2000* (London 2001).
18 John D. Meiklejohn: *Secondary Education in Glasgow* (Glasgow 1875).
19 Without adjoining corridors, classrooms could only be reached through other classrooms.
20 The Gorbals' Youths' School had been built in 1835–6 at a cost of nearly £900, its site in Greenside Street being gifted by Hutchesons' Hospital. It was bought over compulsorily by the Union Railway Company in 1864 for £4,000, and the Hospital and School determined to create a permanent site for the school on the south side of Elgin Street. In 1868 the foundations were laid and the new school opened in 1869.
21 With universities still closed to women there were no University bursaries.

22 The Educational Endowments Commission (1882–89) was chaired by Lord Balfour of Burleigh, whose abiding interest was Scottish education. He introduced the term 'primary', which is still in use over a hundred years later and clarifies each child's entitlement to a two-stage education. David Torrance: *The Scottish Secretaries* (Edinburgh 2006) pp. 42–50.

23 And one-half of Scott's mortification.

24 Measurement. The part of Geometry concerned with ascertaining lengths, areas and volumes.

CHAPTER 5

1 Assistant or Second Teacher.

2 A favourite game where players in one team seek to tag and imprison players of the other team.

3 Trick, hoax or practical joke.

4 Small bonnets.

5 This new uniform was agreed in 1836, but the bonnets were unpopular and changed to plain Glengarries in 1842. The trousers were also changed – to breeks of blue army cloth in 1846. The cut of the new uniform, an Eton suit, or 'monkey jaiket', led to the name-calling of 'Hutchy Bug'!

6 The day of Glasgow's annual procession of charity schools had begun in 1775.

7 A combined spear and battleaxe.

8 In 1816 Hutchesons' had led the procession as the oldest and largest charity, but by the 1840s Wilson's School had precedence (the parade was their founder's idea and his anniversary).

9 They marched from the Hospital along Hutcheson Street, Trongate, Saltmarket and St Andrew's Square to the Church.

10 The first Dux Medal was presented in 1824, but we know the names of Medallists only from 1829, perhaps suggesting the School was slow to take to competitive education.

11 The success of its summer outing led Heriot's Hospital in Edinburgh to begin annual excursions in 1848.

12 The marriage took place on 10 February 1840 at the Chapel Royal, St James's Palace.

13 There seems to be no protest at this time about such drinking. By 1858–62 the Temperance Movement had taken hold and the use of alcoholic beverages in Hospitals became a major issue.

14 (1780–1847). Held to be Scotland's greatest nineteenth-century churchman.

15 Before 1834 the High School had been called the Grammar School.

16 In Edinburgh the same arrangements applied. 'Hopeful scholars' left Heriot's Hospital for the High School there. However, given improvements in teaching in the Hospital, the Heriot Governors decided in 1809 no longer to send its pupils to the Royal High.

17 Likely to have been Thomas Harrower.

18 The popularity of these had much to do with Charles Dickens, who travelled the country reading from the 1840s on.

19 Dynamics was a branch of Mechanics concerned with the motion of bodies under the action of forces. It was first introduced into the Scottish school curriculum as part of Natural Philosophy (Physics) in Perth Academy in 1761.

20 Euclid was a Greek Mathematician fl. 300BC who laid the basis of Geometry.

21 John Casey FRS (1820–91) was a respected Irish geometer. His 'Sequel' to Euclid was published in Dublin in 1881.

22 Isaac Todhunter FRS (1820–84) was an English mathematician who became Senior Wrangler (first in Mathematics in the final year at Cambridge) in 1848. He is best remembered for his books, e.g. *Plane Trigonometry* (1859, 4th edn 1869).

23 'Stickit minister' was a term of shame in Scotland for a candidate for the ministry who failed to pass the necessary examinations.

24 He was born in 1810.

25 General Gordon was killed and Khartoum was taken by the Khedive.

26 The Crimean War between Britain and her allies against Russia took place from 1854 until 1856.

CHAPTER 6

1 Adherents of the National Covenant (1638) or of the Solemn League and Covenant (1643), upholding the organisation of the Scottish Presbyterian Church.

2 Campbell had been chosen by Thomas Hutcheson on 17 August 1641 to be the first Preceptor, and this was confirmed by the Patrons.

3 Figures before 1736 are in pounds Scots.

4 Simple reading was called English at this time. It was the most fundamental of the three Rs.

5 Agreed by the General Assembly of the Church of Scotland in July 1648.

6 In line with the restriction mentioned only in Thomas Hutchesons' Mortification.

7 After 1736 figures are in sterling. A merk equals thirteen and a half old pence sterling, whilst a pound, or 20s Scots, may be equated with twenty pence sterling. One pound sterling was thus equivalent to eighteen merks, or twelve pounds Scots.

8 It was demolished in the 1790s.

9 Maggie Craig: *Bare-Arsed Banditti: The Men of the '45* (Edinburgh 2010) pp. 135–9.

10 Psalms.

11 This represented the payment of apprentice fees as laid down by the Mortification.

12 Hill: *History of the Hospital* p. 153, of which the lands of Gorbals dominated and were valued at £21,785 5s 7d.

13 Thomas had wanted his School within those boundaries.

14 26 April 1841.

15 No distinction was made in the Hood provision between male and female except it was confined to unmarried females.

16 Details of Foundations, Scholarships and School and University Bursaries can be found in Hill: *History of the Hospital* pp. 216–7, 225–9, 230, 233 and 289–91.

CHAPTER 7

1 Although he was a kindly man particularly in his later years.
2 The Grammar School of Glasgow had changed its name in 1834 to High School to denote the introduction of a broader curriculum than the purely Classical, and it seems that after these changes the High School was only coming up to a standard already provided by Hutchesons', which was as yet not formally recognised as a provider of Secondary Education.
3 There was also a visiting Music teacher.
4 Correct Spelling taught through Etymology (the origin of words).
5 Stimulated by the Paris Exhibition of 1867.
6 p. 90. Greig and Harvey were Assistant Commissioners for the Royal Commission.
7 See Chapter 4 for details of this development.
8 Professor of the Theory, History and Practice of Education in the University of St Andrews.
9 Grant: *History of the Burgh Schools*.
10 This was the highest rank of the EIS founded by Royal Charter in 1847.
11 Although Menzies himself opposed fee-paying.
12 And then tried to avoid paying the builders.
13 This was a system of mutual instruction, introduced by Andrew Bell (1753–1832), into the institution at Madras for the education of orphan children of the European military. It was later known as the monitorial system: a teacher would teach a small group of brighter/older pupils basic lessons, and each of them would then relate the lesson to another group of children.
14 A handicraft in which yarn is made up into a textured fabric by means of a hooked needle.
15 Gymnastic exercises to achieve bodily fitness and grace of movement.
16 The branch of biology that deals with the normal functions of living organisms and their parts.
17 *Glasgow Herald*, 28 March 1885.
18 Church of Scotland Session schools for the poor.
19 *Glasgow Herald*, 16 May 1925.
20 Hutchesons' Girls' Grammar School.
21 Dunlop: *Hutchesons' Grammar* p. 68.
22 First Class Honours.
23 Succeeding Patrons after the 1885 Endowments Act.
24 (Rt Hon. Sir) Henry Craik (1846–1927) was Secretary of the SED, 1885–1904. He was responsible for the abolition of fees in Elementary schools. He raised standards by creating a Leaving Certificate linked to university entrance (1888) and extending state grants to Secondary schools in 1892.
25 Named after Sir John Vanbrugh (1664–1726), English architect.

26 Elizabeth Williamson, Anne Riches and Malcolm Higgs: *Glasgow* (London 1990) p. 550.
27 It became a listed building in 1992.
28 Maria Montessori (1870–1952) was an Italian educationist. In her book *The Montessori Method* (1909) she advocated a child-centred approach to education, developed from her success with children with learning difficulties.
29 Hutchesons' Boys Grammar School.
30 The twentieth Head and second Rector.
31 The Trust lacked positive leadership at this time and the Governors were unwilling to take control until the threat of a School Board takeover had diminished.
32 Which generally was seen by HMI as too much.
33 HMI Report 1907–8.
34 Dunlop: *Hutchesons' Grammar* p. 87.
35 *HET* Minutes; 11 April 1913.
36 Such debt securities were issued by the Government to finance military operations and other expenditure in time of war.
37 The first bouts of which took place on Clydeside.
38 *Glasgow Herald*, 29 October 1927.
39 Barr, Craig and Tannock were the other internal candidates and there were twenty-five external candidates.
40 Dunlop: *Hutchesons' Grammar* p. 90.
41 For appointments the Corporation supplied a list of suitable candidates for Hutchesons' Board to choose from.
42 Although an Officer Training Corps like the High School would have been preferred.
43 Currently these can be found in the School Library at Beaton Road..
44 Dr John Murray: *A History of the RHS* (Edinburgh 1997) p. 72.
45 Iain MacLeod: *The Glasgow Academy. 150 Years* (Glasgow 1997) pp. 91–2.
46 There were nine boys and four girls in the 'distinguished list'.
47 Dunlop: *Hutchesons' Grammar* p. 100. *Trust Minutes* 30 June 1921.
48 These evolved in the 1960s and 70s to Blair, Biggar, Marshall and Scott, and in more modern times to Argyll, Stuart, Montrose and Lochiel.
49 Lord Provost Paxton joined the Governing Body in June 1922.
50 Her title was Principal because the original documentation in the 1872 Hospital Act permitted only a 'head master'.
51 Wartime evacuation gave her the idea that every school should have its own country house, where every junior would spend a term in the course of their time, and every senior a week every year, the purpose being to build a different conception of education, one built on sharing and co-operation.
52 Sir Hector Hetherington of Glasgow University.
53 The Girls' *Magazine* 1976 p. 15.
54 Dunlop: *Hutchesons' Grammar* p.111.
55 A person who represented Oxford (or Cambridge) at a particular sport in a match between the two universities.
56 Dunlop: *Hutchesons' Grammar* p. 109.
57 *Glasgow Herald*, 9 February 1939.

58 From 1920 onwards, both schools were included in the City's scheme of Secondary Education and they were part-funded both by Council ratepayers and by block grant.

59 *Trust Minutes*: 22 June 1945.

60 He retained the post of PT Classics throughout his Headship.

61 *The Hutchesonian*, 1955.

62 *Trust Minutes*: 14 September 1949.

63 *Trust Minutes*: 26 June 1953.

64 Brian Lockhart: *The Town School: A History of the High School of Glasgow* (Edinburgh 2010) p. 185.

65 In 1963 the thirteen Headmaster Conference Schools in Scotland were: Robert Gordon's College, Aberdeen; Stewart's Melville College, Edinburgh; Edinburgh Academy; Fettes College, Edinburgh; George Heriot's School, Edinburgh; George Watson's College; Glasgow Academy; Gordonstoun School; Kelvinside Academy, Glasgow; Loretto School, Musselburgh; Merchiston Castle School, Edinburgh; Strathallan School and Glenalmond College.

66 He reached the rank of Squadron Leader.

67 The short leet of two were interviewed in March 1966; Whyte and the PT (English) at King's Park Secondary, James B. Glen.

68 The first purpose-built comprehensive school, Crookston Castle School, in the south-west of the city, was built in 1954.

69 Only the High Schools went independent.

70 Whyte being in Malaysia.

71 Dunlop: *Hutchesons' Grammar* p. 139. The fate of Glasgow High – closure – was avoided.

72 Alasdair Gray: *Ten Tall and True* (Glasgow 1993).

73 Her MBE was for work in education, especially Classics.

74 These were: Harry A. Ashmall, Kenneth W. Dron and John G. Forsyth.

75 He drove every day from Troon to School and back.

76 His competition on the short-leet was Gordon G. Stewart; Mrs Joan C. Clanchy; Frank B. Gerstenberg (the runner-up) and John G. Forsyth.

77 *Glasgow Herald*, 21 September 1985.

78 Brian had been an Assistant Rector at Marr College when Isaac was Rector. He gave full support to his former colleague: 'as my Depute he was a very fine administrator and hard worker, and he was full of ideas for the future'.

79 Young Report (December 1985) pp. 5–6.

80 *The Hutchesonian* 2002.

81 His competition on the short-leet was C.C. Bayne-Jardine, David Christie and Brian Lockhart.

CHAPTER 8

1 Margaret Black (1830–1903) founded the West End (of Glasgow) School of Cookery in 1878 and remained its Principal until her death.

2 David Murray: *Miss Janet Ann Galloway and the Higher Education of Women in Glasgow* (Glasgow 1914).

3 Elizabeth Dorothea Lyness was born in 1872 and qualified MB CM at Glasgow University in 1894. She married Rev. Robert Chalmers Smith in 1899. She died in May 1944.

4 Professor G.G. Ramsay, Professor of Latin at the University of Glasgow, was a leading figure in the movement for secondary education and in the reform of endowments in Glasgow.

5 The celebration of the relief of Mafeking during the Boer War with boisterous public demonstrations.

6 Stall-bars or rings are gymnastic equipment.

7 Joan Rix Tebbutt (1910–2005) was an artist, calligrapher and inspirational teacher.

8 Joan Eardley (1921–63) was a British artist who after an early death was recognised as an artist of international importance.

9 Copeland and Lye moved their drapery, clothing and dressmaking shop from Cowcaddens to Sauchiehall Street (Caledonian House) in 1878. It expanded to include premises at the Bath Street corner in 1901.

10 A lever worked by the foot and imparting motion to a machine.

CHAPTER 9

1 Hampden Terrace.

2 The name given to the belt which was manufactured in Lochgelly in Fife.

3 Left 1964.

4 Thomas Macdougall, Modern Languages/Depute Rector, 1934–64.

5 Mr Howard Howie arrived at the same time as Professor Pontecorvo famously disappeared, hence 'Ponty'.

CHAPTER 10

1 Dunlop: *Hutchesons' Grammar* p. 67.

2 *Glasgow Herald*, 23 January 1934.

3 The Hutchesons' Educational Board was made up of twenty representatives: eight from the Town Council; three educationists elected by the Town Council; two representing the Church of Scotland Presbyteries; two representing the Patrons; two representing Glasgow Educational Trust and one each from the University of Glasgow, the Merchants' House and the Trades' House.

4 *Glasgow Herald*, 16 January 1951.

5 Dunlop: *Hutchesons' Grammar* p. 132.

6 Using the following terms for the social classes: A, upper; B1, upper-middle; B2, middle-middle; B3, lower-middle; C1, upper-working; C2, middle-working, C3, lower-working; D, poor.

7 He also managed a nursery of some forty children and four nursery staff.

8 Hutchie's roll at the beginning of session 2001–02 increased by 151 (to 2,079).

9 The Kelvinside roll increased by 80 (to 649); Craigholme by 49 (to 547); Belmont by 40 (to 335) and St Columba's Kilmacolm by 29 more. Even the 'full' Glasgow Academy took 24 more (to 1,129) and the High School some 16 more (to 1,064).

10 *The Good Schools Guide 2011* p. 433.

CHAPTER 11

1 A School Song existed as early as 1894, but it was not popular.

2 *WWS* (2014).

3 *WW* (2014).

4 She was first PT (Modern Languages) at Westbourne from 1950–1, after which she returned to the School as PT (Modern Languages). She gave up her PT (Modern Languages) post in 1973 to spend more time as Depute Principal.

5 *WWS* (2014).

6 He was Depute Head (Primary) from 1965.

7 She was promoted to APT in 1976.

8 He was only 5 feet 4 inches tall.

CHAPTER 12

1 Until 1892 women were not admitted to Scottish universities, and the LLA (Lady Literate in Arts) was the nearest qualification to a degree which was open to women in Scotland.

2 Dunlop: *Hutchesons' Grammar* p. 40.

3 PT (Music) was a new post in 1965.

4 The nickname refers to his habit of keeping two belts – one in each sleeve of his gown – and his ability to throw them at pupils with unerring accuracy.

5 There had been a previous School Song in Latin, written about 1916.

CHAPTER 13

1 *WWS* (2011).

2 *WWS* (2014).

3 *WW* (2013).

4 *WWS* (2014).

5 Association for Payment Clearing Services.

6 *WWS* (2014).

7 *WWS* (2011).

8 *WWS* (2014).

9 *WWS* (2014).

10 *ODNB*: Eric Salmon (2009).
11 *ODNB*: Peter J. Bowler (2009).
12 *WWS* (2014).
13 See his autobiography *The Tracks of My Years* (London 2009).
14 *Unforgettable, Unforgiven* (London 1945).
15 *ODNB*: Louis Stott (2009).
16 Michael and Isobel Haslett: *Buchan and the Classics: School and University.*
17 *ODNB*: H.G.C. Matthew (2011).
18 John Buchan: *Memory Hold-the-Door* (London 1940).
19 Paul Donovan: 'The Buchan Tradition' *Sunday Times Culture*, 16 April 2015.
20 *WWS* (2014).
21 *WWS* (2014).
22 *WWS* (2011).
23 *WWS* (2014).
24 *WWW* (2014).
25 *WWS* (2014).
26 *WWS* (2014).
27 *WWS* (2014).
28 *WWS* (2014).
29 James Cowan: *From Glasgow's Treasure Chest* (Glasgow 1949).
30 *WWS* (2014).
31 *WW* (2014).
32 Translates as 'The game for the game's sake'.
33 *WWS* (2014).
34 *WWS* (2014).
35 *WWS* (2014).
36 *WWS* (2014).
37 *WWS* (2014).
38 Now known as Shenyang.
39 *WW* (2014).
40 *WWS* (2014).
41 *ODNB*: W.H. McDowell (2009).
42 *WW* (2013).
43 *WWS* (2014).
44 *WW* (2013).
45 *WWS* (2014).
46 In 1955 the School took five places of the top seven in the Competition.
47 *WW* (2013).
48 *ODNB*: David Howell (2013).
49 *WWS* (2014).
50 *WW* (2013).
51 *WWS* (2014).
52 *WWS* (2014).
53 Allan Beveridge: *Portrait of the Psychiatrist as a Young Man: The Early Writing and Work of R.D. Laing, 1927–60* (Oxford 2011).
54 *ODNB*: Rev. Charles Rycroft (2009).
55 *WWS* (2011).

56 *ODNB*: Simon Inglis (2009).
57 *WW* (2013).
58 *Glasgow Herald*, 5 February 1932.
59 *WWS* (2014).
60 *ODNB*: A.C. Hamilton (2012).
61 *ODNB*: John Mauchline, Rev. Gerald Law (2009).
62 *WWS* (2014).
63 *WWS* (2011).
64 *WWS* (2014).
65 *WWS* (2014).
66 Maxton collected his teacher's certificate in March 1904.
67 Gordon Brown: *Maxton* (Edinburgh 1986) p. 23.
68 *ODNB*: Graham Walker (2011).
69 *WWS* (2014).
70 *ODNB*: Tom Arie (2013).
71 *ODNB*: Richard Pring (2013). According to the *Guardian* in 2008 he was 'the most influential President the NUT ever had'.
72 *WWS* (2011).
73 *WWS* (2014).
74 *ODNB*: Moira Burgess (2009).
75 *WW* (2013).
76 *WWS* (2014).
77 *WWS* (2014).
78 *WWS* (2014).
79 *WWS* (2014).
80 *WWS* (2014).
81 *WWS* (2014).
82 *WWS* (2014).
83 *WWS* (2004).
84 *WWS* (2014).
85 *WW* (2013).
86 *WWS* (2014).
87 *ODNB*: Mark Stocker (2009).
88 *WWS* (2014).
89 *Glasgow Herald*, 12 June 1979.
90 *WW* (2013).
91 *WWS* (2014).

CHAPTER 14

1 The 4.6% target was £566,000.

APPENDIX 2

1 These were arms granted to the Governors as a corporate body: *Argent, three arrows points downwards, the middlemost in pale, the other two in bend dexter- and*

sinister-wise proper, surmounted of a fess Azure, in chief a boar's head erased proper, and in base an open book of the second leaved Gules. Above the shield is placed a helmet befitting their degree *mantling Azure doubled Argent* and on a wreath of their liveries is set for Crest *the sun in his splendour Or*, and in an Escrol over the same this motto, *Veritas*.

2 By happy coincidence, Sir Malcolm is in direct descent of Helen Hutcheson, sister of the founding brothers George and Thomas.

3 *Argent, three arrows points downwards, the middlemost in pale, the other two in bend dexter and sinister wise Proper, surmounted of a fess embattled Azure, in chief a boar's head erased Proper, and in base an opened book of the Second, leaved Gules.* Above the Shield on a Wreath of the Liveries is set for Crest *the sun in his splendour Or*, and in an Escrol over the same this Motto *'Luceo Non Uro'*.

4 Hill: *History of the Hospital* p.52.

APPENDIX 3

1 The particular pattern of stripes in a tartan.

APPENDIX 4

1 He died in October 1706 (aged seventy-six).
2 He died in 1705 and left £283 sterling to Merchants' House.

BIBLIOGRAPHY

PRIMARY SOURCES

Hutchesons' Hospital Minute books (Mitchell Library, T-HH1/1/1-4)

Volume 1: 17 August 1641–27 December 1764.

Volume 2: 10 December 1772–12 November 1801.

Volume 3: 18 February 1802–11 February 1831.

Volume 4: 22 February 1831–26 January 1839.

Volume 5: 28 January 1839–27 March 1848.

Volume 6: 31 March 1848–30 March 1860.

Volume 7: 3 May 1860–29 January 1870.

Volume 8: 3 February 1870–11 June 1877.

Volume 9: 14 June 1877–8 June 1883 (with index in vols.9–15).

Volume 10: 26 June 1883–16 November 1888.

Volume 11: 26 November 1888–29 January 1895.

Volume 12: 29 January 1895–1 November 1898.

Volume 13: 14 November 1898–10 October 1904.

Volume 14: 9 November 1904–28 October 1910.

Volume 15: 18 November 1910–16 June 1920.

Volume 16: 21 November 1890–26 June 1924.

Hutchesons' Educational Trust Minute Books (School Archives)

1/1: 1885–1901, no 1.
1/2: 1901–18, no 2.
1/3: 1918–73, no 3.
1/4: 1973–79.
1/5: 1980–87.

Teachers' Salary Ledgers

4/1: 1885–1910, no 1.
4/2: 1910–23, no 2.
4/3: 1924–38, no 3.
4/4: 1939–62, no 4.

Log Books

6/1: 1913–17.
6/2: 1915–56.

Letter Books

8/1: 1878–83, no 3, Lists of teachers' salaries.
8/2: 1883–1902, no 4, Lists of teachers' salaries.
8/3: 1902–49, no 5, Staff and teachers' salaries.

Inspection of Schools

14/1/1: 1880–86, Various reports of inspectors of schools.
14/1/2: 1887–1910, Various inspection visits.

Job Applications and Testimonials
20/6: 1914–27.

School Magazines

22/1: *Hutchesonian.*
22/1/1: 1894–99 Monthly Magazine.
22/1/2: 1908–09 Monthly Magazine.
22/1/3: 1915–19 *Hutchesonian* vol. I–II.
22/1/4: 1919–26 *Hutchesonian* vol. III–IV.
22/1/5: 1920 *Hutchesonian* (June).
22/1/6: 1920 *Hutchesonian* (December).
22/1/7: 1921 *Hutchesonian* (June).
22/1/8: 1921 *Hutchesonian* (December).
22/1/9: 1922 *Hutchesonian* (June).
22/1/10: 1922 *Hutchesonian* (December).
22/1/11: 1923 *Hutchesonian* (June).
22/1/12: 1923 *Hutchesonian* (December).
22/1/13: 1924 *Hutchesonian* (June).
22/1/14: 1924 Hutchesoanian (December).
22/1/15: 1925 *Hutchesonian* (June).
22/1/16: 1925 *Hutchesonian* (December).
22/1/17: 1926 *Hutchesonian* (June).
22/1/18: 1926 *Hutchesonian* (December).
22/1/19: 1927 *Hutchesonian* (June).
22/1/20: 1927 *Hutchesonian* (December).
22/1/21: 1928 *Hutchesonian* (June).
22/1/22: 1928 *Hutchesonian* (December).
22/1/23: 1929 *Hutchesonian* (June).
22/1/24: 1929 *Hutchesonian* (December).
22/1/25: 1930 *Hutchesonian* (June).
22/1/26: 1930 *Hutchesonian* (December).
22/1/27: 1931 *Hutchesonian* (June).
22/1/28: 1931 *Hutchesonian* (December).
22/1/29: 1932 *Hutchesonian* (June).
22/1/30: 1932 *Hutchesonian* (December).
22/1/31: 1932 *Hutchesonian* vol. XVIII.
22/1/32: 1933 *Hutchesonian* (June).
22/1/33: 1933 *Hutchesonian* (December).
21/1/34: 1934 *Hutchesonian* (June).
21/1/35: 1934 *Hutchesonian* (December).
22/1/36: 1935 *Hutchesonian* (June).
22/1/37: 1935 *Hutchesonian* (December).
22/1/38: 1936 *Hutchesonian* (June).
22/1/39: 1936 *Hutchesonian* (December).
22/1/40: 1937 *Hutchesonian* Vol. XXIII.
22/1/41: 1938 *Hutchesonian* (June).
22/1/42: 1938 *Hutchesonian* (December).
22/1/43: 1939 *Hutchesonian* (June).
22/1/44: 1939 *Hutchesonian* (December).
22/1/45: 1940 *Hutchesonian* (June).
22/1/46: 1941 *Hutchesonian* (June).
22/1/47: 1942 *Hutchesonian* (June).
22/1/48: 1944 *Hutchesonian* (June).
22/1/49: 1949 *Hutchesonian* (June).
22/1/51: 1943 *Hutchesonian* (June).
22/1/55: 1945 *Hutchesonian* (June).
22/1/57: 1946 *Hutchesonian* (June).
22/1/59: 1947 *Hutchesonian* (June).
22/1/61: 1948 *Hutchesonian* (June).
22/1/62: 1949 *Hutchesonian* (June).
22/1/64: 1950 *Hutchesonian* (Tri-centennial issue).
22/1/65: 1950 *Hutchesonian* (Celebration supplement).
22/1/66: 1951 *Hutchesonian* (June).
22/1/67: 1952 *Hutchesonian* (June).
22/1/70: 1953–54 *Hutchesonian* vol. XXXI.
22/1/71: 1955 *Hutchesonian* (June).
22/1/72: 1956 *Hutchesonian* (June).
22/1/73: 1957 *Hutchesonian* (June).
22/1/74: 1958 *Hutchesonian* (June).
22/1/75: 1959 *Hutchesonian* (June).
22/1/76: 1960 *Hutchesonian* (June).

22/1/77: 1961 *Hutchesonian* (June).
22/1/78: 1962 *Hutchesonian* (June).
22/1/80: 1963 *Hutchesonian*.
22/1/81: 1964 *Hutchesonian*.
22/1/82: 1965 *Hutchesonian*.
22/1/83: 1966 *Hutchesonian*.
22/1/84: 1967 *Hutchesonian*.
22/1/85: 1968 *Hutchesonian*.
22/1/86: 1969 *Hutchesonian*.
22/1/87: 1970 *Hutchesonian*.
22/1/88: 1971 *Hutchesonian*.
22/1/89: 1972 *Hutchesonian*.
22/1/90: 1973 *Hutchesonian*.
22/1/91: 1974 *Hutchesonian*.
22/1/92: 1975 *Hutchesonian*.
22/1/93: 1976 *Hutchesonian*.
22/1/94: 1977 *Hutchesonian*.
22/1/95: 1978 *Hutchesonian*.
22/1/96: 1979 *Hutchesonian*.
22/1/97: 1980 *Hutchesonian*.
22/1/98: 1981 *Hutchesonian*.
22/1/99: 1982 *Hutchesonian*.
22/1/100: 1983 *Hutchesonian*.

22/1/101: 1984 *Hutchesonian*.
22/1/102: 1985 *Hutchesonian*.
22/1/103: 1986 *Hutchesonian*.
22/1/104: 1987 *Hutchesonian*.
22/1/105: 1988 *Hutchesonian*.
22/1/106: 1989 *Hutchesonian*.
22/1/107: 1990 *Hutchesonian*.
22/1/108: 1991 *Hutchesonian*.
22/1/109: 1992 *Hutchesonian*.

Hutchesons' Girls' Grammar School Magazine

22/2/1: 1924-31 *HGGS* vol. I.
22/2/2: 1932-39 *HGGS* vol. II.
22/2/3: 1948-55 *HGGS* vol. III.
22/2/4: 1956-63 *HGGS* vol. IV.
22/2/5: 1964-72 *HGGS* vol. V.
22/2/9: 1946 *HGGS Magazine* (70th Anniversary Edition).
22/2/11: 1976 HGGS Magazine (100th Anniversary Edition).

Reports

James Greig and Thomas Harvey: *Report on the State of Education in Glasgow* (Edinburgh 1866).
Education Commission (Scotland): *Second Report of Argyll Commission on Elementary Schools* (Edinburgh 1867), vol. 14: Scotland Part II.
Educational Commission (Scotland): *Third Report on Burgh and Middle-Class Schools* (Edinburgh 1868), vols I and II: Special Reports.
Colebrooke Commission (Scotland): *Appendix into Endowed Schools and Hospitals* (1875), vol. I: pp. 327–361.

Newspapers

Glasgow Herald
1860, 1861, 1870–79, 1880–89, 1890–99, 1900–09, 1964, 1970–76, 1982–87.

SECONDARY SOURCES

Early Printed Sources (before 1900, in alphabetical order)

Abstract of the Rules and Regulations by which Hutchesons' Hospital is Governed, and the History of said Hospital (Glasgow 1800).

Robert Alison: *The Anecdotage of Glasgow* (Glasgow 1892).

James Bell: *Glasgow: Its municipal organisation and administration* (Glasgow 1896).

J. Clelland: *Annals of Glasgow* vols I and II (Glasgow 1819).

The Constitution, Rules and History of the Royal Incorporation of Hutchesons' Hospital (Glasgow 1850).

John Edgar: *History of Early Scottish Education* (Edinburgh 1893).

J. Gibson: *History of Glasgow* (Glasgow 1777).

James Grant: *The History of the Burgh Schools of Scotland* (London 1876).

W.H. Hill: *History of the Hospital and School in Glasgow Founded by George and Thomas Hutcheson of Lambhill in AD 1639–41* (Glasgow 1881).

Hutchesons' Educational Trust Scheme, 1885.

Andrew MacGeorge: *Old Glasgow* (Glasgow 1888).

James MacLehose: *Memoirs and Portraits of One Hundred Glasgow Men* (Glasgow 1886).

John McUre: *Glasghu Facies: A View of the City of Glasgow* (Glasgow 1736).

John M.D. Meiklejohn: *Secondary Education in Glasgow* (Glasgow 1875).

Senex: *Glasgow Past and Present* (Glasgow 1884).

John Tweed: *Glasgow Ancient and Modern* (Glasgow 1872).

(Rev) W.M. Wade: *The History of Glasgow: Ancient and Modern* (Glasgow 1822).

Modern Printed Sources (after 1900, in alphabetical order)

R.D. Anderson: *Education and Opportunity in Victorian Scotland: Schools and Universities* (Oxford 1983).

R.D. Anderson: *Education and the Scottish People, 1750–1918* (Oxford 1995).

Harry A. Ashmall: *The High School of Glasgow* (Edinburgh 1976).

Neil Baxter (Ed): *A Tale of Two Towns: A History of Medieval Glasgow* (Glasgow 2008).

Allan Beveridge: *Portrait of a Psychiatrist as a Young Man, R.D. Laing 1927–60* (Oxford 2011).

Gordon Brown: *Maxton* (Edinburgh 1986).

Ken Bruce: The Tracks of My Life (London 2009).

Anna Buchan: *Unforgettable, Unforgotten* (London 1945).

John Buchan: *Memory Hold-the-Door* (London 1940).

James Cowan: *From Glasgow's Treasure Chest* (Glasgow 1949 and 1951).

Maggie Craig: *Bare-arsed Banditti. The Men of the 'Forty-Five* (Edinburgh 2010).

T.M. Devine and Gordon Jackson (Eds): *Glasgow, vol. I: Beginnings to 1830* (Manchester 1995).

A.D. Dunlop: *Hutchesons' Grammar. The History of a Glasgow School* (Glasgow 1992).

George Eyre-Todd: *History of Glasgow from Reformation to Reform Acts* vol. II (Glasgow 1931).

George Eyre-Todd: *Who's Who in Glasgow* (Glasgow 1909 and 1929).

W. Hamish Fraser and Irene Maver (eds): *Glasgow, vol. II: 1830–1912* (Manchester 1996).

Norman Graves: *Social Textbook Research. The Case of Geography, 1800–2000* (London 2001).

William Greenhorne: *History of Partick, 550–1912* (Glasgow 1928).

John Highet: *A School of One's Choice. A Sociological Study of the Fee-Paying Schools of Scotland* (London 1969).

Les Howie et al.: *George Watson's College: An Illustrated History* (Edinburgh 2006).

Walter M. Humes and Hamish M. Paterson: *Scottish Culture and Scottish Education 1800–1980* (Edinburgh 1983).

John Pratt Insh: *School Life in Old Scotland* (Edinburgh 1925).

John R. Kellett: *Glasgow* (Glasgow 1961).

John Kerr: *Scottish Education. Schools and Universities from Early Times to 1908* (Cambridge 1913).

H.M. Knox: *Two Hundred and Fifty Years of Scottish Education, 1696–1946* (Edinburgh 1953).

Alexander Law: *Education in Edinburgh in the Eighteenth Century* (Edinburgh 1965).

Brian R.W. Lockhart: *Jinglin' Geordie's Legacy* (East Linton 2003).

Brian R.W. Lockhart: *The Town School. A History of the High School of Glasgow* (Edinburgh 2010).

M. Lynch (Ed): *The Oxford Companion to Scottish History* (Oxford 2007).

Jane McDermid: *The Schooling of Working-Class Girls in Victorian Scotland. Gender, Education and Identity* (Abingdon 2005).

James Macfarlane: *History of the Hospital and School 1881–1914* (Glasgow 1914).

James Macfarlane: *Hutchesons' Hospital and Its Founders. A Chapter in the Life of Glasgow* (Glasgow 1914).

Colin H. Mackay: *Kelvinside Academy 1878–1978* (Glasgow 1978).

Ray McKenzie: *Public Sculpture of Glasgow* (Liverpool 2002).

Iain MacLeod: *The Glasgow Academy* (Glasgow 1997).

Andrew McPherson and Charles D. Rabb: *Governing Education. A Sociology of Policy since 1945* (Edinburgh 1988).

Susan Milligan: *The Merchants' House of Glasgow, 1605–2005* (Glasgow 2004).

J.O. Mitchell: *Old Glasgow Essays* (Glasgow 1905).

J.B. Monteith: *Reminiscences of My Schooldays in Hutchesons' Hospital in Ingram Street 1837–41* (Glasgow 1901).

Alexander Morgan: *Rise and Progress of Scottish Education* (Edinburgh 1927).

Alexander Morgan: *The Makers of Scottish Education* (London 1929).

James Murray: *The History of Allan Glen's School and School Club 1853–2003* (Glasgow 2003).

John Murray: *A History of the Royal High School* (Edinburgh 1997).

John Ord: *The Story of the Barony of Gorbals* (Paisley 1919).

Lindsay Paterson: *Scottish Education in the Twentieth Century* (Edinburgh 2003).

Henry Philip: *The Higher Tradition. A History of the Public Examinations in Scottish Schools and How They Influenced the Development of Secondary Education* (Dalkeith 1992).

Peter Reed (ed.): *Glasgow: The Forming of a City* (Edinburgh 1999).

Robert Renwick (ed.): *[Sir James D. Marwick's] Early Glasgow. A History of Glasgow from Earliest Times to 1611* (Glasgow 1911).

James M. Roxburgh: *The School Board of Glasgow 1873–1919* (London 1971).

James Scotland: *The History of Scottish Education*, vol. I *From the Beginning to 1872* (London 1969).

James Scotland: *The History of Scottish Education*, vol. II. *From 1872 to the Present Day* (London 1969).

Thomas Somerville: *Two Great Glasgow Men – George and Thomas Huchesone* (Glasgow 1901).

June Steeds: *Scottish Field*, May 1962, pp. 65–69.

John Strong: *A History of Secondary Education in Scotland: An Account of Scottish Secondary Education from Early Times to the Education Act of 1908* (Oxford 1909).

Ted Tapper: *Fee-Paying Schools and Educational Change in Britain between the State and the Market-Place* (London 1997).

Stephen Terry: *A Glasgow Almanac* (Glasgow 2005).

William Thomson: *The Basis of English Rhythm* (Glasgow 1904).

William Thomson: *The Rhythm of Speech* (Glasgow 1923).

Douglas Watt: *The Price of Scotland: Darien, Union and the Wealth of Nations* (King's Lynn 2007).

James Whyte: *Hutchesons': The Origin and Development of One of Glasgow's Greatest Institutions* (Glasgow 1963).

Elizabeth Williamson, Anne Riches and Malcolm Higgs: *Glasgow* (London 1991).

INDEX OF FORMER PUPILS

Chapter 13 includes listings of over 800 FPs in alphabetical order, most of which are not included in this index. This index includes all FPs mentioned elsewhere in the text, and selected FPs from Chapter 13 (Duces from1945 onwards and those given a G and THA Award).

INDEX OF STAFF AND GOVERNORS

Pinkerton, Robert (Roy) (Classics HBGS 1967) 219

Pringle, Andrew (English/Maths HBGS 1877–1912) 73, 242

Pringle, George Taylor (Classics HBGS 1920–3) 242

Pritchard, Dr Thomas (Music HBGS 1925–36) 171, 219

Queen, Lisa (Drama 2012–) 219

Rae, Janet (née Stewart) (Music HGS 1990s) 219

Ralston, Dr Andrew (English HGS 1980–2014) 242

Reid, Alistair (Physics HGS 1989–2008) 242

Reid, James (Music HGGS 1944–64) 116, 157, 159, 242

Reid, Mr (Music HGGS 1890s–1910s) 138, 149

Reid, Peter (Master, 1691–1705) 39

Rennie, Alex (Languages/careers advisor 1969–2001) 242

Ritchie, W. Tod (Rector HBGS 1932–45) 111–13, 124, 169–71, 194

Robertson, Forbes (English HBGS 1915–29) 242

Robertson, Kirsteen (PE HGS 2005–) 243

Robertson, Rev Dr Lockhart (first Secretary of HET, 1885–92) 59, 95, 138, 188, 189, 243

Robson, James (Singing HBGS 1870–1906) 74, 243

Rooney, Claire (Languages HGS 2003–) 243

Rose, Elspeth (née Crosbie) (Geography HGS 1985–2001) 219, 220

Ross, Hope (Languages HGS 1981–91) 243

Ross, James 'Jimmy' (Geography HBGS/HGS 1980–93) 243

Ross, Lilian (HBGS 1925–55) 243

Ross, Miss (Science HGGS 1950s) 158, 179

Russell, Judith (née Brown) (primary 1999–2000s) 220

Russell, Linda (Office Manager 1991–2010) 243

Russell, Peter (PE HGS 1990–) 243

Schroeder, Heinrich (German, HGGS/HBGS 1878–99) 73, 137, 243

Scott, Alexandrina (Spanish HGGS/Head of Infants 1916–59) 220

Scott, Ivy (Primary/HGGS 1949–77) 157, 243

Scott, Dr John Charles (Rector, HBGS 1919–32) 104–8, 193

Sen, Saibal (Maths HBGS/HGS 1976–2010) 243

Shanks, Islay (English HBGS 1950s) 176

Sharp, Elizabeth (Art HGGS 1972–85) 220

Sharp, Flora 'the Duchess' (HGGS 1876–1915) 137, 144, 243, 244

Sharp, Helen (HGGS 1879–1921) 137, 243, 244

Shaw, William (Chemistry HBGS/HGS 1971–96) 244

Shead, Norman (History HGS 1979–98) 244

Shearer, Agnes (English HGGS 1963–81) 160, 244

Shedden, Elsie (Home Economics HGGS 1956–79) 244

Sheridan, Christina D. (Art HGGS 1935–71) 152, 156, 244

Simpson, Amelia (Primary 1876–1915) 244

Simpson, Rhona (PE HGS 1994–2012) 244

Skinner, John V. (Classics HBGS 1946–7) 244

Sloss, James (Preceptor, 1700–10) 77

Smith, Clare (Modern Studies HGS 2003–) 244

Smith, Mary (HGGS 1910s–20s) 148

Smith, Pauline (Maths HGS 2008–) 245

GENERAL INDEX